Books by A T Mann

The Phenomenon Book of Calendars
The Round Art: The Astrology of Time and Space
Life Time Astrology
The Divine Plot: Astrology & Reincarnation
Astrology and the Art of Healing
The Mandala Astrological Tarot
The Future of Astrology
Millennium Prophecies
Sacred Architecture
Secrets of the Tarot (previously *Elements of the Tarot*)
Sacred Sexuality (with Jane Lyle)
Elements of Reincarnation
A New Vision of Astrology

The Divine Life:

Astrology and Reincarnation

By A T Mann

2002

vega

London

© A T Mann 2002

This book is a compilation and revision of two books:
Life Time Astrology
© A T Mann 1984
First published in Great Britain in 1984 by Allen & Unwin
First published in paperback in Great Britain in 1991 by
Element Books Limited
Published in the USA in 1986 by Harper & Row, San Francisco

The Divine Plot
© A T Mann 1986
First published in Great Britain in 1986 by Allen & Unwin
First published in paperback in Great Britain in 1991 by
Element Books Limited
Published in the USA in 1991 by Element Books, Inc

Published in Great Britain in 2002 by Vega

A member of **Chrysalis** Books plc

ISBN 1-84333-463-1

Cover design by
Design and layout by A T Mann
© Text, Images & Tables, A T Mann 2002

Printed and bound in Great Britain by CPD, Wales.

British Library Cataloguing in Publication Data

A catalogue record for this book is
available from the British Library

Library of Congress Catalog Card Number available

Author's Preface to the Revised Edition

I wrote *Life Time Astrology* (1984) and *The Divine Plot* (1986) in sequence, and they are a natural pair of books. *Life Time Astrology* describes a unique logarithmic time scale for interpreting the astrological horoscope from conception to old age, incorporating a transcendent octave of higher consciousness, outside of time. I wrote the book following the *The Round Art* so astrologers could utilize these powerful ideas in their counselling, predictive and therapeutic work.

In working with clients, I discovered two important principles. By reconstructing events at conception, I realized that the horoscope often showed events that happened before conception: a previous miscarriage or abortion, a family tragedy, a separation, or other traumatic influences. This fascinated me and led to much deep study and meditation. I realized the truth of the Freudian axiom that we recapitulate the life of our species in our own life, which he called 'ontogeny recapitulates phylogeny'. In many ways, this evokes both the idea of reincarnation and foreshadows potential higher functions of the DNA molecule as a repository of all history within us – the legendary Akashic Record of esoteric mysticism.

These ideas led me to write *The Divine Plot*, which places our individual life in the context of a logarithmically graded panorama of history and cyclical time: reincarnation is how we mirror history in ourselves. Indeed the system proved so accurate that one could determine the exact times in history of previous reincarnations. Positive validations happened in cases when people 'knew' previous incarnations or did creative work that reconstructed history. It worked with historical individuals who remembered their past lives, incarnate lamas, authors, musicians, historians, archaeologists, and those with an interest in the past. The accuracy of *The Divine Plot* has helped many of my clients and has proven to be a valuable and testable guide to our inner history.

These books have been in print for almost two decades and I realized that it would be timely to combine them in this unique edition so that we can see them as the intended whole. I discovered in the process the uncanny relevance of many of my early intuitions about history, genetics, time, physics and other developments.

The Divine Life is a model of reality rather than a literal truth. It is an attempt to map the territory, rather than claiming to be the territory itself. This is especially the case when I applied the reincarnation time scale to history. I initially used the millennial date 2000 as the end of a world age as a working hypothesis, although I would now modify that to 2012 as a logical date indicated by the Mayan calendar and other sources. However, the ideas and timings remain just as valid and the reader should consider them seriously.

I would especially like to acknowledge Margo Russell (1938-2001) for her perceptive and penetrating editing of both of my original books. My literary agents Sandra Martin and Lisa Hagan of Paraview have supported me in bringing this new edition into being. I would also like to thank Judith Taylor Wheelock for her friendship and philosophical support, her wise counsel, and her astute and helpful reading of the book. Laurence Henderson of Vega has been a supportive publisher.

A T Mann   Hudson, NY

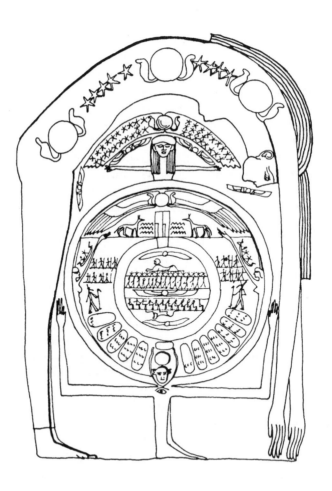

Table of Contents

Papyrus Anana

Behold it is written in this roll. Read ye who shall find in the days unborn, if your gods have given you the skill.

Read, O children, of the future and learn the secrets of the past, which to you is so far away and yet truth is so near.

Men do not live once only to depart hence forever, they live many times in many places, though not only in this world.

That between each life is a Veil of Darkness. The doors will open at last and show us all the chambers through which our feet wandered from the beginning.

Our religion teaches us that we live on eternally... now eternity, having no end, can have no beginning: it is a circle. Therefore, if one were true, namely that we live on forever, it would seem that the other must be true also... namely, that we have always lived.

To men's eyes, God has many faces. Each swears that the one he sees is the only true God, yet they are all wrong, for all are true.

Our Kas, which are our spiritual selves, show themselves to us in various ways. Drawing from the infinite veil of wisdom, hidden in the being of every man, they give us who are instructed glimpses of truth and the power to work miracles.

Among the Egyptians, the scarabaeus beetle is no god, but a symbol of the Creator, because it rolls a ball of mud between its feet, and gets therein its eggs to hatch; just as the Creator rolls the world around, which seems to be causing it to produce Life.

All gods send their gift of love upon this earth, without which it would cease to be. My faith teaches me more clearly, perhaps, than yours, that life does not end with death, and therefore that love being life's soul, must endure for all eternity.

The strength of the invisible time will bind souls together long after the world is dead. In the end, however, all the various pasts will reveal themselves.

Anana, Chief Scribe and companion to Pharaoh Jentle Leti II; about 1320BC

Prologue

The apocalyptic fury of the 'Last World War' was the culmination of a social and ecological breakdown that accompanied the end of the world age. Collective physical and psychological shocks devastated humanity. The final years of chaos and anxiety negated thousands of years of civilization.

Humanity, in its ultimate arrogance, had challenged nature and reaped a self-imposed ejection from Eden. The population had exploded into emaciated billions fanatically ravaging the land in search of anything to eat, eliminating all life in the process. The biosphere barely admitted the Sun's light, creating a hostile Ice Age. The depletion of fossil fuels and poisoning by nuclear reactor leakages accompanied the collapse of technology and completed the irreversible. The momentous end-time everyone feared had come.

The civilized world had consumed itself. Total panic fanned across every continent. The most civilized were the first to die – shrieking with terror, barricaded within concrete deserts, surrounded by their powerless instruments of leisure and destruction. Domesticated pets and servants devoured obese bodies. The masses settled scores grossly uneven since the dawn of time. Humanity had finally manifested its greatest fear: a return to the unconscious, to the source, and found nightmarish brutality, both unnatural and inorganic.

Survivors wandered through lost Eden, the fantasy of humanity's evolutionary position as apex of some quaint cosmic pyramid of ordained, scientific development having lapsed ages ago. The return to a prehistoric survival state happened with absurd ease and great speed. Cultural, religious, ethnic and racial schisms accelerated the descent into an abyss that alienated father from mother, brother from brother, and parents from children until the confusion was absolute. The primary aim of the dying age was to quench its perpetual hunger to consume.

Such a fight for survival was natural for the least civilized as it was their lot throughout history, but there were few exempt from the few centuries of civilization. Most isolated primitives had been rooted out, featured in documentaries, had their homelands become the site of exotic package holidays, and then 'civilized'. World population plummeted rapidly from its peak of more than five billion to a few million. The survival rate was less than one in a thousand. It was like a science-fiction fantasy of widespread disease, malnutrition, multiple plagues of locusts, army ants, and man-eating jungle beasts translated into quasi-human form. The atrocities of previous wars, famines, and repressive governments seemed like child's play by comparison.

The survivors tried to get further and further away from the others. Psychotic behaviour was dominant – there was no relief from the nightmare. It was Hell on Earth. Kill or be killed was the name of the game.

The political and economic structure of the world before the fall mirrored its anthropology afterwards. The protagonists in the final battles were the industrialized one-tenth of humanity, including the USA, Russia, Japan and western Europe, against the agrarian nine-tenths of humanity, including South America, Africa, the Middle East and Asia. Four billion starving have-nots surged into and devastated civilization. When the dust cleared, the Caucasian races were virtually non-existent. The situation was reminiscent of anthropological descriptions of the millennia before the modern age when only the strongest and most brutal survived.

The poison of their own pollution finally destroyed the industrialized races, acid rains sterilizing lakes and rivers and baring trees, faulty diet, cruelly propagated animals, chemically corrupt foods, unnatural medical practices, sexual plagues, and uncontrolled genetic experiments – in the latter days, the only manner of conception was artificial. Humanity degenerated to proto-primate reality, as survivors wandered aimlessly over the earth like the Neanderthal seeking whatever growing things gradually began to appear after the radiation dispersed. Mutations caused by the cumulative effect of pollution and radiation upon genetic code produced wild deviations in those species that survived. Frightening extremes in climate assisted in generating a virtual *Planet of the Apes*.

Volcanoes and earthquakes, endless cycles of floods and droughts battered the earth and purified it by shifting tectonic plates, which devastated and yet cleansed its surface. Advancing and retreating walls of ice played with metamorphosing continental landmasses. Supposed permanent sprawling cities and their monuments were devastated, raided, pulverized, and blasted back into their component parts. Newly created seas submerged entire civilizations and sandwiched them between layers of thousand-foot high mountain chains. It happened at an unimaginable scale and speed. By the time equilibrium returned, climactic change eradicated almost all traces of the previous world age from the face of the earth, except in the minds of the survivors.

These conditions echoed the disappearance of great ancient civilizations during the earliest historic eras, but infinitely more rapidly and completely. The technological world before the Apocalypse, believing itself to be eternal and non-biodegradable, vanished without trace.

Geographical localities that escaped annihilation were rare, but there were islands of amnesty for the survival of the spirit of humanity, places distinguished by natural fortification or stability of position that allowed the few vestiges of existing life to carry on amid the chaos outside. These refuges, buffered from the madness of the outside world, were fabled 'lost continents' that existed in fantasy beyond humanity and time. Isolated valleys, thousands of feet up in great mountain chains, protected by sheer walls of stone; fertile valleys shifted upwards by congenial fluke upheavals of nature; islands arising from voracious seas. Benign ecology eventually cleared the air, purified the prime materia and began the re-establishment of life, but also prevented access, creating safe havens during the cosmic storm. References to places such as the Garden of Eden, Valhalla, Noah's Ark, Mount Meru, and Paradise permeate all mythologies.

These natural strongholds were what the previous age had recognized as spiritual centres. The indefinable qualities that made them revered lay in their unimagined purpose, and they possessed an attraction that truly was 'cosmic'. They radiated the finest levels of energy and thus adduced individuals of the most benign understanding to them. During the collapse of the world age they sent out their subtle call to all those refined enough to hear it. It was as though the guiding hand of destiny operated to preserve the world order through the end of an age.

Small enclaves of enlightened survivors of the obliterated world age lived with single-minded joy, yet with the preposterous limitations of Adam and Eve in Paradise. The restricted environment provided peace and happiness, yet the threat of instant destruction from any contact with the world beyond. Utopian survival rested on total containment. The taboo on the outside world depended on regulating sexuality and perpetuating insularity over many generations. The tree of good and evil – knowledge of world ages – grew just beyond their domain.

Although the surviving founders knew the fate of the rest of the world and of their mission – the survival of civilized humanity – succeeding generations could only speculate upon what seemed exaggerated myths of great wars and the wild primitive half-humans populating the world beyond Eden. The survivors had experienced the death and rebirth of a world age, but they were irrevocably changed. The extreme shock to their psychophysical organisms had eradicated conscious awareness. Although enlightened, they were as infants. They had no link back to their heritage in the last world age, or an inkling of their future. The sheer enormity of the demise of civilization had erased their memories, removed all elements of logic, and so affected their mental perspective that they reverted to pure spirit. It evoked the worshipping of epileptics as sacred channels in ancient times.

The cosmically lobotomized survivors emerged as illiterate adult-children in the Garden of Eden – incorruptible, naive and innocent to the point of simple-mindedness. They had achieved the state that had been the aim of ecstatic mystics throughout history: total union with nature.

The description of the end of a world age, as such an end approaches, is also a description of the end of the last world age 50,000 years ago, which is called 'The Destruction of Atlantis'. It has all happened before.

Chapter One — The Divine Plot

The world indeed is sacred; but paradoxically, one cannot see the sacredness of the world until one discovers that it is a divine play.

Mircea Eliade

The Divine Plot is the grand plan of the universe, carried through the mechanism of time. The Divine Plot requires a divine plotter – the divinity as god/dess. Higher consciousness manifests through the universe, which comes into being in time, and yet god/dess is beyond time. Without time, there is no space – without space-time, there is no universe. In all creation myths, space and time come into being simultaneously at the beginning. The Divine Plot is the 'great secret'. Definitions of 'plot' are as follows, all of which are relevant:[1]

plot, (subject):
– The site, situation, of a building, town, city, etc.
– A ground plan of a building, field, farm, etc; a map, a chart.
– A sketch or outline of a literary work.
– The plan or scheme of a play, poem, work of fiction, etc.
– A plan or project, secretly contrived; a conspiracy, a sly plan, a scheme.
plot, (verb):
– To make a plan, map or diagram; to lay down on a map; to represent by a plan or diagram (the course of any action or process).
– To make a plan of (something to be laid out, constructed, or made).
– To plan, contrive or devise (something to be carried out or accomplished).
– To scheme, lay plans, contrive, conspire.

The Divine Plot postulates that the organization of creation, from the smallest sub-atomic particles to the largest galaxies, lies in the exponential nature of time. In this scheme, every part relates to every other part; everything is alive, from apparently inert matter to the infinite electron; everything intercommunicates at all times and in all ways; and every component of the universe has echoes in us. We are quite literally 'the measure of all things', as Shakespeare said. Ideas that express this are: 'The microcosm is the macrocosm' and 'As above, so below'.

Cosmologists project the history of the universe backwards to denser compactions of energy, to shrinking volumes and into shorter durations. However, what does the universe come from in the first place? I believe that the universe comes into being with its entire history implicit, just as we are conceived with our history implicit in us. This universe cannot be anything other than what it is. Other dimensional universes almost certainly coexist with ours, but they are not ours. Modern cosmology has created a conundrum by postulating that this universe was created by the destruction of a previous universe in the Big Bang. Is the nucleus of the creation in the known universe, or is there a 'Special Creation', a divine action of god? In modern times, scientists and fundamentalist Christians align on opposite sides of this dispute.

We recapitulate the life of the universe in our own life from conception to death. The burst of pure energy at conception is the creation of the universe, which elongates time sense. The so-called white light of life is infinite and eternal, arising from the Big Bang of creation. It can only come into being at creation. Indeed, conception is creation.

Our intrauterine development recapitulates the evolution of all life from a single cell. As our body develops, our metabolism gradually slows down. However the soul perceives the process of gestation, taking the billions of years from creation until our birth. By the time of our birth, we experience the emergence of consciousness about 50,000 years ago. When we die, the universe ends. It can only be this way.

The stars are the key to the great secret. When a world age ends, as thousands have ended and thousands more will end, the only possible orientation is by the stars. Astrology is one of the oldest systems of knowledge, originally used as a way of organizing the psyche. Renaissance magicians practised celestial magic as an attempt to gain knowledge of time, which to them meant knowledge of God or the gods. God is in everything, moves everything, and creates everything. The only liberation is dis-identification from the components of reality and process of things, and concentration, over many lives, on a godlike meditative vision of the whole.

Circular Time

The Prologue relates, from some future time, the end of a World Age and its implications. The description is evocative of the cataclysm many believe we are heading toward, but it is also a description of our prehistory, 50,000 years ago. The end and beginning of world ages form the basis of all religions, mythologies, philosophies, mysticisms, cosmologies and sciences. Craving utopia, world revolution or a return to Eden are all reflections of a universal desire to recapture the purity of primal paradise.

Before the almost universal adoption of linear, mechanist Darwinian evolution, many cultures accepted the eternal repetition of time and history, and based their cosmologies and mythologies on circular, recurrent time. The Egyptians, Buddhists, Stoics, Zoroastrians, Hebrews, Gnostics and Ismailis believed that individual and world cycles repeat eternally. These recurrent great years range in duration from 7,000 years to an inconceivable 864,000,000,000 years long.

The Divine Plot is a creation theory that utilizes the principle of eternal recurrence; that time is circular and repetitive. Within the fabric of time itself are woven many diverse strands of history, mythology, mysticism, religion, science, psychology, mathematics, philosophy, art and medicine into a unified theory of life in the universe, organized according to the celestial science and art, astrology. By reconciling archetypal historical concepts with the biologically based LifeTime Astrology technique that describes an individual life from conception to death, a truly relative history emerges.

My basic postulate is that the spiralling pattern of the solar system as it hurtles through time and space is similar in form and resonant with the double-heliacal genetic code that encapsulates the patterns of growth of all species and individuals. Just as planetary movements carry past patterns, so our reincarnations are available within the genetic code. The geometric principles and mathematics of astrology is the key to deciphering this reincarnational genetic code, and all previous incarnations may be determined with elementary tables. The present moment is the culmination and sum of all past experience, yet one can discover one's significant historical layers.

Humanity faces the threat of extinction and it is essential to discover a model that explains reality more profoundly than destructive science or obscure and hierarchical philosophy. We assume the world situation to be unique and without prototype, but there is evidence that similar circumstances have occurred in previous world ages.

The schism in the human race even extends to projections of what will or should happen in the future. Some believe that with the dawning of the 'Age of Aquarius' all men and women will instantaneously life in peace together. Others believe that it is already too late to reverse the destruction of life on earth. What is clear in either view is that a dramatic transformation is immanent. We must be clear.

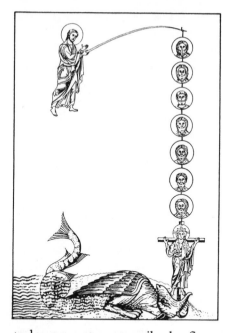

Figure 1: Sacred Christian Lineage
The lineage of David shown as fishing tackle for catching the Leviathan of time, with the crucifix as bait. There are seven images, also representing the planets as a hierarchy of transformational influences. *(Herrad, Hortus deliciarum, 12th century)*

Everyone alive on earth is the result of 100% successful experiment in evolution. Our parents reproduced successfully, as their parents did, and so on, back to the first humans, and before that to the first life, back to the origin of the universe. At no point could anyone have entered the system from outside, as there is no outside. Those of us alive today are not necessarily the fittest, the strongest, the most intelligent, or the most successful – but we are the survivors. We link back to the origin *(ab-origine)* through the genes directing the creation of our body, the structure of our brain, the fabric of the time and through our deeper spirit and soul reality. Some religions transmit their spiritual inheritance by successions of prophets or gurus. To track our common origin we must reconstruct the unfolding of all life in time. The most natural starting point is human embryological development. We embody the universal creative mechanisms that lie behind psychology, philosophy, mysticism and science. The ancient term for the process by which previous influences affect the world is reincarnation. Every person has specific prototypes in the biological, mythological and individual being that can be determined mathematically, dated and deciphered.

At conception, the universe begins and at death, the universe ends. While usually taken as a metaphor, it is quite literally true. The universality of human life makes everyone a participant in the cosmic drama from the beginning, just as we all participate at the end. The mysteries of life are available to everyone who has lived and who lives now. Mircea Eliade realized that an increasingly prominent characteristic of modern society is its obsession with history. Until the last century, history was a behavioural guide, albeit modified to suit the winners of historical movements, while now we worship, modify and dramatize history for its own sake. The passion for the past reflects a troubled world situation.

Folklore carries the belief that at death, we relive our entire past down to the smallest detail, and that we cannot pass from the body until our personal and collective history is re-experienced. This 'panoramic memory' is the Last Judgement described by Buddhism, Christianity, Hinduism, Egyptian and other religions. Considered from this point of view, the passion for history is a sign portending humanity's imminent death.[2] We see everywhere a collective anxiety, similar to the fears of the savage about to undergo an initiation that included ritual death, the extinction of the personality and ego, a descent into hell, and finally rebirth as a new being. Women's initiation dramatizes the process of gestation and birth, while men abstract the processes of life and death. The initiate is shocked into remembering and revaluing their whole life. When our individual life ends we experience this judgement, and when a world age ends the entire population does.

The great historian Arnold Toynbee estimated that as many people will live from 1950 to 2000 as have lived in the last 50,000 years, since our Cro-Magnon ancestors emerged from the mists of time and humanity, and we became conscious. Every individual from the world age is returning to experience the possibility of rebirth into the new world age. All ancient religions, cultures, artefacts and their behavioural surrogates are returning, as though we must make a choice about where (and when) we wish to find our centre of gravity in the next world age. It is not accidental that fundamentalist Christians battle fundamentalist Islamic warriors, who in turn fight fundamentalist Jews. Fundamentalism is everywhere.

Electrons exist in all matter in the universe by forming atomic structures that exist for seconds or millennia, until they decay into unbound form. When they decay, other electrons rush to replace them, reproducing other atoms in their place. Electrons create patterns in time into which their successors recur. Molecules die (break down into their component atoms) within us at a rate of five to six million per second and regenerate at the same rate. Cells recur so exactly that the cellular body only gradually reflects changes in appearance. Many millions of incarnations of such recurrences are required for there to be noticeable change in atoms or cells. The same is true of stars and galaxies. They recur in time as they reproduce virtually the same developmental stages. When we look out into space, we see the various stages from the conception to the death of galaxies.

There is a formal similarity between the nature of atoms and galaxies. Just as atoms continuously die and are recreated, so galaxies explode and re-form. All existence in the universe, from atoms to galaxies, is only concentrations of energy fields that recur in time. An eternal flux of energy enfolds all processes in universal space-time, at every scale from the sub-molecular to the galactic, so that there is a reflection of the whole in every fragment, at every time. The great paradox is that we accept recurrent processes everywhere in the universe except in ourselves. Yet this acceptance is the key to transcendence. We must understand the circular and cyclic nature of the universe within.

The worldview of physics has undergone a radical change in recent years. The objective Euclidian-Newtonian universe was rectilinear, time was absolute, and clocks would keep the same time wherever they were. In a relativistic universe, there are no preferential reference points, and time runs at variable rates, making the universe curved. Time becomes cyclical rather than linear, exponential rather than additive. There are no objective vantage points as everything is subjective, dependent upon an observer. The emphasis shifts from particles to patterns of events, including history in physics. Chaos theory replaces logic. No preferential reference points require an interaction between the observer and the observed. The powerful Hubble telescope peers out into the universe in every direction, making us the very centre of the universe, and everyone is the centre of their own universe, a state known in ancient models of reality thousands of years ago.

In biology, a revolution is in process. How can we find health by studying dead bodies in order to discover how they work? Pathology has replaced healing. Must we extinguish all life on earth to find out where life came from? The patterns governing life processes do not reside in particular parts of the brain, nor exclusively in our genes, but are inherent in the morphogenetic and other fields that affect all living beings and may well be the invisible medium by which heredity, body form and even ESP are transmitted from individual to individual, and from generation to generation. What if our body is a receiver? The keys to the organization of the universe exist within everyone.

There are formal structures inherent in the universe but the actual nature of such structures is still unknown to science. Circular, recurrent patterns are required to restructure our destructive views of the universe and to restore balance and wholeness to life on earth. Such a cosmological pattern has existed for thousands of years in the most ancient science and art – astrology. Astrology describes patterns in time that potentially integrate science, psychology, history and mythology: a map that humankind has used since the dawn of time and that provides the key to unlocking the secrets of the universe. The history of the universe structured along astrological lines allows us not only to identify the cycles of life at every level from electron to galaxy, but for the first time, the matrix of the universe may be glimpsed. That itself may be the purpose of the next stage in the development of intelligent life.

The Unity of History

But before the curtain falls, there is one more task for the historical Faustian spirit, a task not yet specified, hitherto not even imagined as possible. There has still to be written a morphology of the exact sciences, which shall discover how all laws, concept and theories inwardly hang together as forms and what they have meant as such in the life-course of the Faustian Culture. The re-treatment of theoretical physics, of chemistry, of mathematics as the sum of symbols – this will be the definitive conquest of the mechanical world-aspect by an intuitive, once more religious, world-outlook, a last master-effort of physiognomic to break down even systematic and absorb it, as expression and symbol, into its own domain.[3]

Oswald Spengler, *The Decline of the West*

In order to integrate history, it is essential to join many disparate belief systems with a mathematical methodology. The resulting synthesis is both a model for organizing time and for linking subjective, personal experience that animates our history transmitted through the generations. This is no less than linking the universe with its invisible mirror anti-universe, the left and right halves of the brain, the unconscious with consciousness, science and mythology, white and black, male and female, west and east. The unification of opposites integrates the entire range of qualities in the universe. Division and fragmentation is within us in the way that our mind's reality categorizes, qualifies and constructs. Dreams are a unitary timeless state, but to express the remembered dream it is necessary to apply sequence and temporal order to its timelessness. The same principle operates in our perception of history. We are beings in time, but we also exist beyond time in our transcendent and transpersonal reality.

The birth horoscope is a context for describing our life pattern and the transpersonal realm, as described in my books *The Round Art, Life Time Astrology* and *Astrology and the Art of Healing*.[4] The Life Time Astrology technique is a mechanism for unlocking our knowledge of time in our own life, the mysteries of the psyche and of the world. Instead of grading time additively, a logarithmic time scale reflects the relativity of our perception in time. Time sense changes as we age. Our earliest developments in life, within the womb, happen very rapidly. As we age, time seems to pass more and more quickly. Days in childhood take much longer to pass than days in maturity, a mechanism inherent in the way metabolism determines time perception – a biological time sense. Our lifetime graded logarithmically describes 12 developmental stages, from conception to death, through which we pass in life. The planets signify events, archetypal behavioural mechanisms and the cast of characters in life.

Schopenhauer and Freud believed that an individual life recapitulates the life process of the entire species. Our lives are microcosmic to the macrocosm of all humanity. We all carry a record of our collective past, and we can decode it with a symbolic language. The Divine Plot is a symbolic model that uses a logarithmic Universal Time Scale, a series of nested, repetitive cycles from the Big Bang to the lifetime of subatomic particles, the longest to the shortest cycles known. When we grade the intermediate cycles continuously, the ends join like the ouroburos snake eating its tail – an image of eternity. The result is a description of universal time.

We carry the history of creation and remain as an energetic pattern until the end of time. Every being is eternal and immortal. However, it is necessary for every sentient being to understand and accept the transcendent reality. At the transition shock-points that occur at the beginning and end of world ages, all individuals have a unique opportunity to pass beyond the mundane world to higher levels of reality. Approaching the year 2012, every person on earth has an opportunity, if only we can remain conscious. Everyone will experience the Last Judgement or Grand Resurrection to have the singular chance to pass through the ultimate vortex – TIME.

And I saw the dead, small and great, stand before God, and the books were opened: And another book was opened, which is the Book of Life, and the dead were judged out of those things which were written in the book, according to their works.
Book of Revelations, 20:12

The Book of Life is within you.

Chapter Two — Life History

A very important fact conditions all theories of the nature of time, humankind and the universe: they all happen within time and history. Every theory reflects the attitudes, belief systems, needs, language and levels of consciousness of those from whom they issue. We express ideas that come from archetypal levels or beyond reality, in a medium, a language, symbol system, or specific vocabulary in use at a particular time and place. Society rejects or ignores profound ideas ahead of their time or presented to cultures not yet ready for them, and they dismiss or persecute their originators. As civilizations gestate, are born, mature and die, their symbol systems, ideas, concepts and realities die with them. Only rarely do ideas really transcend their civilization of origin and affect others who follow.

The Buddhist prophet Nichiren described a human truth:

> The learning of just one word or phrase of the Right Law, if only it accords with the time and propensity of the learner, could lead to the attainment of the Way. The mastery of a thousand scriptures and ten thousand theories, if they should not accord with the time and the propensity of the one who masters them, would lead nowhere.[5]

Whatever the message, the time of its saying is critical. To understand history, all times must be compacted into the eternal present. There is no such thing as 'objective' history – history only exists within each of us. All time is contained in the present moment. In order to understand time, it is necessary to define its mechanism.

Throughout recorded history, humankind has measured time. Initially we measured time by the cycle of day and night, caused by the rotation of earth around its axis. The moon's cycle begins with the silver crescent (the beginning of Hebrew and Islamic lunar months), becomes fuller until it dominates the sky, and then shrinks until it disappears for three days, only to be reborn from the 'underworld'. The solar year is a cycle of four seasons of spring, summer, autumn and the death of nature in winter. The basic natural cycles are astronomical.

A second, minute, hour, day and year are absolute units of time agreed by convention. Worldwide time standards use the vibrations of caesium atoms, measured to thousandths of a second. Universal Time is the timekeeping standard for science. In spite of the apparent accuracy of timekeeping, in the context of Eastern mysticism, psychology and more recently physics, time is not absolute, but is subject to great variance and distortion, and may be an illusory perception.

In the pre-relativistic Cartesian model of perception, space was a rectilinear grid and time simply another dimension, but in Relativity Theory, the speed of light in a vacuum is the universal constant. Space and time are inseparable in a space-time continuum that curves. Time expands or contracts according to the velocity of the perceiver, and since everything in the universe moves at a great speed, everything has its own unique time sense and its own relative history. An oak tree exists just as much as we do, only for a vastly longer duration.

We teach history as though it is fact accepted by everyone, but history is also relative. The victors write history and pass it on as a *fait accompli*. Goethe said, 'History, that error of hodge-podge and brute force. Each of us who feels his worth starts from the beginning!'[6] Each successive civilization assimilates the history of its predecessors and extends its own influence into the future by teaching its successors. It is natural for each culture to see itself as the culmination of all previous ages – and they usually are because previous cultures are necessary roots. The same may be said about religions, scientific attitudes and individuals, all conditioned by inherited structures and beliefs inherited from earlier times. We believe that our reality is the only one, and that our beliefs are special in history.

The history of individual life changes with age. We know the earliest events in life primarily through stories told by our parents, who have told these stories for years and years, altering them from telling to telling to make them more interesting. We forget, exaggerate, or include bits until the past becomes a collage of stories. Our parents censor the stories, often without realizing it, which present them in an unfavourable light and delight in telling the stories that present them favourably. Our parents' reality determines the quality of our stories. By the time we are able to understand the implications of our life story, we assume their stories are fact without distortion.

We carry most of what we know about ourselves by stories. When meeting someone new, we introduce ourselves by selecting, editing and telling stories in particular sequences, with certain points made. We store and transmit our individual histories as stories.

We construct a worldview in the same way. Our world is informed by school and conditioned by our home and family system as though it is an objective reality. History is presented to us as absolute fact. By maturity, we accept the world and its values as fact. Our attitude to the world is dependent upon relationship or adaptation to other individuals and the collective values of the environment. If we are unwilling or unable to adapt, we are either rebellious or insane.

One of Freud's great insights was to interiorize time and history as phenomena that had previously been approached from without, rather in the way that a naturalist treats his subject.[7]

> *The lives of each of us comprise a history, whether that history be articulated in a full narrative account or array of accounts or remain fragmentary, incomplete or latent. No life is without its personal experiences of myth, epic, romance, and tragedy. These exemplary and recurrent themes of experience belong for Freud to the species as much as they do to each of us. Yet what helps in part to animate these processes as history is that each one of us actually sustains in his own person that which the species, our ancestors, or a character we will read about is said to have passed through. And what also helps to animate them as history is that each one of us can testify to goings-on in the past that appear to have the warrant of actuality; but the shape of that testimony is invariably a conjectural reconstruction, a fabrication, something we have made, a history.[8]*

We must understand the nature of the continuum in which our life is lived in the context of the collective reality of our entire race, the 'collective unconscious' of Jung. 'The world of archetypes of Jung is like the Platonic world of ideas, in that the archetypes are impersonal and do not participate in the historical time of the individual life, but in the time of the species – even of organic life itself.'[9] The collective unconscious is not a receptacle of repressed contents as for Freud, but rather a deeper layer of innate structural forms that exist in every individual beyond space and time. What is relevant for the entire species is the basis of individual psychology, and leads naturally to the study of history and individual life as integrated subjects.

History has ego and personality, and we must understand it as such, as a 'series of stages which must be traversed, and traversed moreover in an ordered and obligatory sequence. For everything organic the notions of birth, death, youth, age and lifetime are fundamentals – may not these notions possess a rigorous meaning which no one has as yet extracted?'[10]

Mythic Reality

We can understand the world in many ways. While they are not histories, all views of individual life imply a particular attitude to history.

Earliest humanity had no history. Our primitive ancestors lived one day at a time as though each day was all of time, much like children. The most basic fear was that when the sun set in the evening, it might not rise the following morning. Many cultures worshipped the sun because they associated the appearance of the sun with the power of creation. One of the earliest myths is that of the Egyptian goddess Nut (Night) – she swallowed the Sun at sunset and gave birth to him at dawn. Myth is a description of natural processes transmitted as a story.

With the advent of language, human perspective enlarged. The experiences of previous hunts were told as stories – stories that carried great power because they were not just hollow tales but formulae for survival. The efficient transmission of stories ensured survival. These stories passed from generation to generation, creating a fund of knowledge that became a legacy and inspiration for the whole tribe. The hunts occurred in time, however the myths associated with them were trans-historical; they happened outside of time, in a sacred world. The teller of the story was in a powerful and responsible position because of the implication of access to the divine world.

In Thomas Mann's *Joseph and His Brothers*, Joseph realized that his tutor Eliezer's ego was not clearly demarcated: '…it opened at the back, as it were, and overflowed into spheres external to his own individuality both in space and time; embodying in his own experience events which, remembered and related in the clear light of day, ought actually to have been put in the third person'.[11] Eliezer remembered stories of previous tutors of the same name (who were also his ancestors) and telescoped their histories into his own, just as he accumulated the exploits of all his and his predecessors' masters and attributed them to his master. An entire lineage finds its summation in the present, making flesh of the past. History is a stratified past embedded within us. Its deeper levels precede the earliest records and live beyond the fleshy confines of our ego as they feed and condition us.

The stories of the earliest tribes or cultures were transmitted in the form of myths, fairy tales, heroic sagas or religions, in which time was circular, repetitive and recurrent, an echo of the timeless days of the ancestors. Most of us ignore or repress the vast times back to the dawn of history, yet we all have a direct connection back to those times. A record of the developmental process of all life exists within the electrons, particles, physical bodies, and almost certainly the genetic

Figure 2: The Alchemical Womb
In alchemy the base for transformation is
the furnace, the womb of Mercurius, which
was round in imitation of the spherical
cosmos so that the stars might contribute
to the success of the operation.
(Barchausen, Elementa chemicae, 1718)

code of which everything living is made. The Chinese reverence for
ancestors is the basis of their culture, and reflects the importance of
such a linking back to the origin.

Central mythic themes are the creation and destruction of the
world, both of which exist in a mystical realm of the spirit always
connected to each other. Sacred moments of birth and death,
initiation, healing and sacrifice are 'rites of passage', echoing the two
primary events in time and essentially making mundane events
participate in the sacred.

The search for origins embodied by myth is evident in the world
today, but in different guises: theories of the Big Bang and the origin of
life; the genealogy of individuals and humanity; the inner search of
psychoanalysis into the mythology of early childhood; and the return
to nature. Disciplines investigating origins are everywhere, as though to
satisfy a deep instinctive desire to return to the paradise that existed
before the Fall. The primary impetus is the terror we face in the
degeneration of modern life.

The world is dying in preparation for the attainment of a different
mode of existence and only by knowing about creation can we know
the future. Psychotherapy encourages individual return and in society
there is a collective going back; in religion, in school and even in
fashion. The initiation ceremony was a symbolic death and rebirth, and
in order to find immortality and liberation from time and karma, the
womb of nature was re-entered.[12] The only way to become master of
one's destiny is to remember births, former lives and relive the origin of
the world. 'Being in the womb, I knew all the births of the gods.'[13]

Early humanity recorded history to transmit models of culture and
behaviour patterns, but since the 19th century the aim of history is to
reconstitute the entire past of the species and make us conscious of it.

In many religions, as well as the folklore of Europeans, is the belief that one remembers the entire past life down to the minutest details at death. The dying once more reviews the past on the screen of memory. Considered from this point of view, the passion for historiography in modern culture would be a sign portending its imminent death.[14]

The ancients believed that the further back to the origin individuals existed, the closer they were to the gods. The creator, triple goddess, divine king, great mother and hero are embodiments of a transcendent reality that the present world craves. We search within the atom, in outer space, in the depths of the oceans and on the highest mountains for the meaning of the origin of life, and neglect the origin within each of us.

The nature of time, particularly primordial time, is the most profound mystery of all. The historical approach works backwards until knowledge dissolves into myths, dreams, or fantasies, analogous to the seemingly irrational quantum world of particle physics or the realm of the psyche in psychology – in these realms intuition and pattern are the only stepping-stones. The meaning of the psyche is as elusive as finding elementary particles – as deep as we go there are new layers with which to contend. The complexity of creation mythology evokes a similar feeling to the Big Bang – both exist in seemingly familiar inner and outer worlds and yet are difficult to describe.

The repetitive nature of myth makes it impossible to know how far back the original event setting a pattern occurred. In this sense the origin or Moses, Jesus, Mohammed, or Shakespeare are truly myths. Subsequent tellings do not clarify the mystery, but renew its magic. In early times, 'what concerns us is not calculable time. Rather it is time's abrogation and dissolution in the alternation of tradition and prophecy, which lends to the phrase "once upon a time" its double sense of past and future and therewith its burden of the potential present'.[15] Myths inculcate strong feelings about the future, almost as though the earliest memories are simultaneously prophecies. Past events continually repeat until they become prototypes. Repetition reminds us that not only is the past as mysterious as the future, but they are firmly linked to each other.

Our human paradox is the coexistence of the desire for freedom from the constraint of time with the wish for an eternal individuality from life to life. Our understanding of time as an infinite straight line denies of the possibility of redemption. Salvation is an understanding of the circular and repetitive nature of time.

The Greeks believed that after death the soul is purified by passing over the River Lethe, the stream of forgetting. Death is the annihilation of consciousness and memory and an exit from time.

When we die, the soul leaves the individual world, as it re-enters wholeness, experiencing an initiation into the realm of the spirit. Death is not the end, but rather a joining of soul with boundless spirit. The ultimate primordial event has its surrogates in ordinary life; birth, death and healing.

The soul enters the underworld after death, a descent into ever darker and denser realms, devoid of movement, where life is absent and time sense slows down. The soul descends the scale of energy, consciousness, and organizational levels, from the pure light of god-consciousness to the mineral realm. In Dante's *Inferno* and the *Tibetan Book of the Dead*, souls of the dead experience eternal torture, chained to or trapped within rock-hewn caverns, subjected to enormous heat and restriction of movement, cut into pieces and inundated with molten metals – precisely like life in the mineral realm. The vast times of the mineral realm, the pressure, heat and crystallized forces in operation would be experienced in this way. The duration of life in the mineral realm dwarfs that of humanity so totally that it does not have what we define as consciousness.

The descent into hell traces evolution back through human life into the geological life of matter, back by definition to the origin of the universe. The human body contains all known elements; therefore, the link is not only theoretical, but also tangible. The body and psyche carry both the history of the universe and the solution to its origin.

Cyclic World Ages

All forms of time in their measurable cycles imitate eternity.
Plato[16]

In the current worldview, time, history and evolution are linear, one-directional and irreversible. Development always occurs from simple to complex, which implies that humanity is the apex of the development of life, its highest form. In this model, humankind can only evolve higher and become wiser, which is patently not the case.

In the study of the universe, however, cyclic behaviour is the rule in both macrocosm and the microcosm because molecules, small and large cells, simple organisms, planets, moons, suns, galaxies and even universes all recur in time. Does humanity not partake of circularity?

An early formulation of linear time was in St Augustine's AD427 work, *The City of God*, recanting his previously held views of cyclic Manichaean beliefs in favour of the prevailing Christian dogma that the world was less than 6,000 years old, history was not cyclic and

Christ died once for our sins. Augustine was highly respected well into the Renaissance, probably because he represented the watershed of the earlier cyclic theory of time and history.

The cosmologies of Heraclitus, Pythagoras and Plato were cyclic and astral and after Augustine were reinforced by Albertus Magnus, St Thomas Aquinas, Roger Bacon and Dante until the Renaissance philosophers Joachim of Floris, Galileo, Tycho Brahe, Kepler, Cardan, Bruno and Dee kept the tradition alive. These profound and spiritual men all believed that 'the cycles and periodicities of the world's history are governed by the influence of the stars, whether this influence obeys the will of God and is his instrument in history or whether – a hypothesis that gains increasing adherence – it is regarded as a force immanent in the cosmos'.[17] Even accepting heliocentricity did not lessen the interest of great thinkers.

Leibniz applied the final blow to cyclic theory and shifted opinion toward the linear view by proclaiming faith in infinite progress, later instituted by Darwinian materialist science and capitalist economics. At present, one rarely hears any mention of cyclic theories except from the McKenna brothers and this author. Nevertheless, the revival of recurrence by Nietzsche, Spengler, Toynbee, J B S Haldane, Gurdjieff, Rodney Collin, P D Ouspensky and Mircea Eliade shows that cyclic theory itself awaits resurrection.

The cycles of early cosmologies were periodic cataclysms – an extension of the eternal daily cycle of prehistoric ancestors. Cyclic life was natural and obvious for agrarian cultures governed by lunar months and solar seasons.

We are more concerned with understanding the circular mechanism transmitted by myths of cataclysms followed by burgeoning world ages than with exact chronologies. The literal study of the world is an illusory trap, but transcending the world of time and history is to enter a godlike realm of the spirit. The myth of the eternal return permeates all important early cultures and religions including Egyptian, Chinese, Hindu, Buddhist, Jain, Ismaili, Hebrew, Roman, Mexican, Hawaiian, Polynesian, Icelandic, Scandinavian, Greek, Incan, Aztec, American Indian, and especially the shamanistic cultures of North America and Russia.

The variable in a cyclic worldview is the duration of the cycle and the way in which one cycle transforms into another. The dating is more than a measurement of quantity; it is the mathematical relationship of man to god. Each culture defines its antiquity by the length of its world ages, from the 7,000-year Jubilee cycles of the Jews, to Hindu yugas of thousands of years, to Buddhist paras of hundreds of billions of years.

Figure 3: The Wheel of Samsara
The Tibetan Buddhists represent the course of human existence in various forms, centring around the cock or amorality, the serpent of hatred, and the pig of ignorance. Liberation is freedom from the bondage of the wheel of life.

Hindus and Buddhists grade creation with a variety of cycles, each with its own function. Each world age is the creation and then destruction of parts of the world. Successive world ages decrease in duration and quality, as the lifetime of beings living in the age shorten. World ages regress and deteriorate from an originally perfect state, opposite to modern evolutionary views but consistent with the concept of entropy. Primordial rhythms contract through time until a cataclysm ending an even greater series of cycles starts the process over again. There are endless series of cycles within cycles from the lifetime of the universe to a fragment of a single breath, within which human life span varies from 80,000 years to 10 years, and sizes from colossal giants to one foot high.[18]

The duration of the Hindu universe is the life of Brahma. After the void following a cataclysm, Brahma is the first to be reborn. He is lonely and wishes for company, so other beings arise spontaneously because of their karma, but Brahma falsely believes that he has created them just as he believes he created himself. Brahma rules the sphere of form as creator and originator of time, labouring from his delusion of grandeur.

The smallest Hindu time cycle is the blink of one fifth of a second, followed by the muhurta of 48 minutes. Thirty muhurtas make up one day, and the 30-day piturah is a day of the fathers. A year is a day of the gods, and it takes 360 earth years to make one divine year of the gods. The proportion amplifies the transitoriness of humanity. The major unit of time is the yuga. Four yugas make a mahayuga, or Great Yuga of 12,000 divine years, with a length in earth years of 4,320,000 years (12,000 × 360). Within a mahayuga, the four yugas diminish in length as they succeed each other. Krita Yuga is a golden age of 4,000 divine years during which men live very long lives in perfect peace and wisdom, preceded by a dawn of 400 years and followed by a twilight of 400 years. The destruction following Krita Yuga yields Treta Yuga of 3,000 divine years with its dawn and twilight of 300 years; then Dvarupa Yuga of 2,000 divine years and its dawn and twilight of 200 years; and finally the present Kali Yuga of 1,000 divine years (360,000 earth years) and its dawn and twilight of 100 years. We now live in the twilight of the Kali Yuga, called the 'Age of Misery' because lifetimes are shortest and reality is the most decadent of all the ages. The end of the Kali Yuga twilight is the dissolution of the universe – the 'praylaya'.

To illustrate the immensity of these concepts, when 1000 mahayugas have elapsed, they constitute a kalpa – one day and night in the life of Brahma. One kalpa is 8,640,000,000 earth years, and since Brahma lives 100 such days, his lifetime of one para is 100 kalpas or 864,000,000,000 earth years. According to the sacred Vishnu Purana, at the beginning of the present kalpa half the para had elapsed. Brahma therefore has just had his 50th birthday.

The Hindus, Buddhists, and Jains symbolize the dominion of time over humanity as the Wheel of Samsara with twelve spokes (see Figure 3). Salvation is escape from the karmic wheel – freedom from time. The immense lengths of time show that the gods live in exalted realms separated by immeasurable time.

Elaborate Eastern cosmologies come from civilizations and religions that recognized the necessity for transmitting a world view through many dissolutions of humanity. The action of diminishing cycles through time is very important and the changing nature of the ages foreshadows the concept of entropy – the binding of energy in information through time. In the East, these ideas are not metaphors but literal images of great spiritual forces within a system that replicate, albeit in inferior form, from world age to world age. The manifestation of the universe guides the universe itself, in the form of Brahma, who reflects the spirit of every being.

At the end of time, Brahma retreats into the void for immeasurable time, until:

> *When the world-night comes to an end, Brahma wakes up and has the world come out of him. There arises from him first the great being that still counts as the undifferentiated. From the great Being, springs thought (manas), which already belongs to the realm of the differentiated. Thought is then the origin of the elements. From it comes ether, from ether wind, from wind fire, from fire water and from water earth. This concludes the creation of the underlying essences of which all things are constituted, and the creation of living creatures and worlds begins. First, there arises the creator god Brahma, alias Prajapati. He creates the gods, father, and humankind; also, the worlds with all that fills them… finally he creates the Vedas and sacrifices, the orders of society and the stages of life.*[19]

Universal cycles never end: their organization of the world bears a striking resemblance to modern cosmological theory of the Big Bang.

> *Darkness was in the beginning hidden by darkness; indistinguishable, all this was water. That which, coming into being, was covered with the void, that One arose through the power of heat.*[20]

Mind stirs in the water, a symbol of time, and the act of creation is a golden germ of fire that springs up within the water.

The world egg is a metaphor for the universe. The proportions of the layers of the egg vary, but the overall concept is consistent. The outermost layer is undifferentiated matter; within it is a layer of intelligence; within that is a layer of egocentricity; and within that layers of ether, wind, fire and at the centre, water (time). Each layer is 10 times as thick as the next one in, and there are seven layers in all. It is significant that the structure is similar to that of atomic electron shells. In Hebrew mysticism, we call the layers of reality *qlipthoth*, literally translated as 'shells'.

The Hindu sacred Puranas describe two sets of seven layers that

Figure 4: The Snake of Time Encircling the World Egg
An alchemical image of the dominance of time.

define the universe from the realm of immortals at the top to the lowest hells of the nagas (snakes) below, with the realm of earth in the middle. Their distance above and below the surface of earth and their temporal periods define their level.[21] The snake is a universal symbol of time, often shown encircling the world egg (see Figure 4).

The Jain cosmos is composed of concentric circles around the eternal wheel of time. The lifetime of the world has 12 ages divided into two equal sets of ascending and descending series of developmental stages. The scheme is similar to those described in *Up From Eden* by Ken Wilber and *The Reflexive Universe* by Arthur M Young. We will learn more about these books later.

Most early cosmologies describe periodic contractions and evolutions of the universe, endless series of aeons punctuated by destructions of various sorts (by water, fire and wind), Brahmas who command each world, and structures that represent circular nested levels of reality, like the symbol of creation, the lotus. The lotus appears on the surface of the primordial waters, unfolds to become the universe, and when it has finished its cycle, enfolds all being back into itself. The unfolding of the universe happens within the domain of time.

The Babylonian and Sumerian *Epic of Creation* states that in the beginning, Alala (Earth) and Belili (Time) alone existed and Anu (Heaven) descended from them, an image evocative of the space-time continuum of modern physics. The world was a repetitive cosmic drama enacted periodically throughout the durations of many worlds.

Mandaean world ages telescope in a similar fashion to the Hindu-Buddhist and are additive. A great cycle is 480,000 years, with sub-cycles of 60,000, 240, and five years. They allotted 50 days each year to the worship and ceremonial repetition of the grand life of time.[22]

Early Eastern cyclical cosmologies contain obvious correlations to modern views of the unfolding of the universe, but science ridicules their concepts as meaningless and insignificant because the mathematics is absurd, with the notable exception of *The Tao of Physics* by Fritjof Capra and *The Dancing Wu Li Masters* by Gary Zukov. Within the context of such early cultures, the poetic description of universal processes is remarkably accurate and relevant, besides possessing a spiritual quality absent from the modern view of the world. The Shemitah, a Jewish theory of cosmic cycles, is based on a sequence of seven cycles, each composed of 7,000 years with a 1,000-year sabbath, similar to the organization of the week, and also related to the then known planets. Each 7,000-year cycle is the enactment of a variation of the torah (the law). Seven complete cycles culminate in 49,000 years with a Great Jubilee of 1,000 years. Every 50,000 years the whole cycle begins again and recurs almost identically.[23]

The Great Year

The ancients located themselves within cyclic theory by determining when world ages began and ended. Some believed that it all began when the seven known planets conjoined in a specific alignment, for example, in the equinoctial sign Aries. It required astronomical calculations beyond their skills to discover when such a constellation would occur, so even the most sophisticated cultures were only able to estimate the duration of the Great Year. The positions of the planets were believed to determine the appearance, behaviour, parents, fate, and events in the world, and it was thought that repetitive astronomical cycles would produce identical repetitive world ages.

The Greek Stoic philosophers Zeno, Chrysippus and Eudemus believed that world ages repeated themselves identically, down to the smallest detail. Plato also reasoned that identical world cycles were probable, originating as they do in the Idea, and that the cycles of men were shorter than the cycles of all nature. Plato's *Timaeus* describes a story told by the Egyptian priests at Sais to Solon: 'There have been and will be many different calamities to destroy humanity, the greatest of them by fire and water, lesser ones by countless means.' Plato then told the story of Atlantis, a tale that was 'real' but also a metaphor for a previous world age. 'We will transfer the imaginary citizens and city which you (Socrates) described yesterday to the real world and say that your city is the city of my story and your citizens those historical ancestors of ours whom the priests described. They will fit exactly, and there will be no disharmony if we speak as if they were the men who lived at that time.' Plato taught the idea of identically recurrent world ages, repetitive down to the character of individuals, even those present in the dialogue. He personified time as a living being, the nature of which is eternal: 'It was not possible to bestow this attribute of eternity fully on the created universe; but he (God) determined to make a moving image of eternity which remains for ever at one.' The eternal moving image is the soul of the universe contained within the bowl of the heavens, 'and when he had compounded the whole, he divided it up into as many souls as there are stars, and allotted each soul a star. And mounting them on their stars, as if on chariots, he showed them the nature of the universe and told them the laws of their destiny'.

Origen and Hipparchus believed in Great Years of 36,000 years of identical recurrence, as did Bartholomeus Anglicus (ca.1230), Siger of Brabant (ca.1277) and Pietro d'Albano (d.1316) – they all thought that even minute details of each age were duplicated exactly.[24] J Hsing of eighth century China proposed a cycle of 96,961,740 years and the philosopher Wu Lin-Chuaun (1249-1333) a cycle of 129,600 years.[25]

The Greek Lindos astronomer of Rhodes believed in a 290,000-year cycle. The Mandaeans followed cycles of 480,000 years, as well as minor cycles of 5,240 and 60,000 years.[26] Heraclitus assumed a cycle of 10,800 years and Aristarchus of Samos 2,484 years.

The Bible describes the creation and destruction of the world. The Old Testament begins with seven days of Creation and ends with Elijah's admonition that 'the day cometh that shall burn as an oven'.[27] The New Testament reiterates the theme by applying the life, death and resurrection of worlds to the life, death and resurrection of the cosmic man, Jesus Christ. The mystery of resurrection reflects the lifetime of the Universe, of humanity, the seven sacraments of life, the sacred round of yearly festivals and the daily cycle of prayers. The process of the universe is re-enacted by every Christian every day.

In the Christian church the length of world ages was derived from the Bible, and renowned churchmen such as Clement of Alexandria (c. 150-220), Minucius Felix (c. AD175) and Arnobius (c. 285-340) believed in an Annus Magnus (Great Year), the Biblical Creation dated in history. Scholars and churchmen worked out Biblical lineages and tried to date Creation itself, with considerable variation. Septuagint dated Creation at 5960BC, Josephus at 3952BC, the Venerable Bede at 3949BC, Abraham Judeus at 3761BC, and one creation time was even given as six o'clock in the evening on 22 October, 4004BC.

The Precession of the Equinoxes

The most natural astronomically-based cycle was the *Precession of the Equinoxes*, first identified by the Egyptians. The Earth rotates on its inclined axis imperfectly, wobbling like a pointer moving backwards through the zodiac, and this creates a precession of the equinoctial (spring) point. The polar axis moves backwards around the true north pole of the ecliptic in about 25,000 years, called the Platonic Year by the Greeks, subdivided into 12 Platonic Months of about 2,100 years each. Initially the Platonic Year was 36,000 years, before the true figure was determined. Over the ages, estimates of the duration of the Platonic Year have been as follows:

36,000 years	Original Platonic Year
28,800 years	Ptolemy (1st century AD)
26,000 years	Medieval[28]
25,920 years	Man and Time
25,725.6 years	Modern astronomical calculation[29]
25,411 years	Ancient[30]
24,120 years	Tycho Brahe

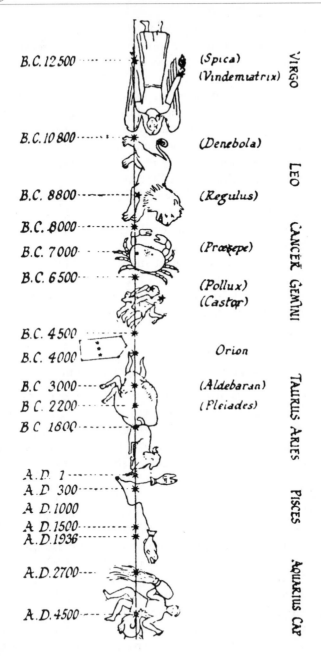

B.C. 12 500 ········ ···· — (Spica)
(Vindemiatrix) — VIRGO

B.C. 10 800 ······ · ··· — (Denebola)

LEO

B.C. 8800 ···—·········· — (Regulus)

B.C. 8000 ··· ········ —

B.C. 7000· ··· ········ — (Praesepe) — CANCER GEMINI

B.C. 6500·· ···· ········ —

(Pollux)
(Castor)

B.C. 4500 ···········

B.C. 4000 — Orion

B.C 3000 ····

(Aldebaran) — TAURUS ARIES

B C. 2200 ···

(Pleiades)

B C 1600 ·········

A.D 1 ·········

A.D 300 ·········· — PISCES

A D.1000

A D.1500 ·········

A.D.1936 ········· — AQUARIUS CAP

A.D.2700 ···

A.D.4500 ····

Figure 5: Precessional Zodiac Signs
Symbols of the zodiac signs superimposed on the ecliptic, showing at which time
the equinox point passes into and out of the each sign. It can be clearly seen
that although the signs are considered equal 30 divisions of the ecliptic, the
constellations are uneven and their equivalent precessional periods vary considerably.

The equinoctial pointer is the Sun's position at the Vernal (Spring) Equinox, when day is equal to night and the days are getting longer. If at sunrise on the day of the equinox a pointer projected into space, it would intersect the ecliptic in its sign of precession. In ancient times, major deities correlated with the then current precessional sign. During the precessional Age of Taurus the Bull, from approximately 4000BC to 2000BC, the primary gods were bull-gods, the prototypes of the later Egyptian Apis and Hathoor, the Hebrew Golden Calf or the bull-headed Minotaur of Crete. During the Age of Aries, from 2000BC to the time of Christ, the Ram cults of Ammon in Egypt and the sacrifice of the ram by the 'two-horn crowned' Moses replaced the Bull. The Piscean Age, from the birth of Christ to AD2000, saw the Christian motif of the Fishes: *Ictheos,* which means fishes in Greek, is also the word for Christos.

The 12 zodiac constellations in the night sky are not exact 30-degree segments of the ecliptic so the dates for the entrance and exit of the ages are unspecific. The coming precessional Age of Aquarius could begin anytime from the middle of the 19th century to the end of the 21st century.

Myths of the World Axis

Hamlet's Mill by Giorgio Santillana and Hertha von Dechand postulates that myth is the original form of science; and that the basis of myth is not terrestrial but celestial. Before writing, counting and measure provided the armature for the texture of myth. The most potent myths of creation – whirlpools, shamans and smiths, cosmic axes, world trees, the Garden of Eden, Mount Meru and others – were representations of the precessional movement of the equinoxes. The Pole Star pointer is the axis of the world and is analogous to the tent-pole. The Greek omphalos (navel) symbolizes the same idea, and decorations spiralling around the omphalos at the Temple of Apollo at Delphi clearly show that it is the 'centre of the world', even though there were many such centres.

Representations of drilling or churning in Hindu, Chinese, Egyptian, Babylonian, and Mayan mythologies, as well as the central Norse myth of Hamlet's Mill, reiterate the theme that the millstone symbolizes the precessional mechanism. In these myths, power over time resides in the centre of the mill, navel, or wheel. Mount Meru in Hindu religion is an image of the centre of the world and presents another common concept – enlightened souls ascend to heaven via the world axis.

To the Persian Ismailis, there never was a time when the world did

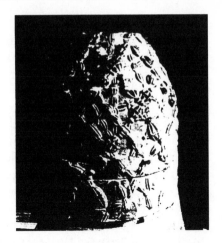

Figure 6: Omphalos at Delphi
The stone omphalos at Delphi is set on the site where the ark of Deucalion (the Greek Noak) landed. It shows the mesh symbolizing the latitude and longitude grid of the earth. The sun god Apollo was reputed to have slain Python, a serpent representing time, and bound time to earth at Delphi, which became the site of the oracular centre sacred to Apollo. (Photo by the author)

not exist. The present world is the most recent of 18,000 cycles of humanity. Adam is the last survivor of the Cycle of Epiphany preceding our cycle of occultation. As grave symptoms of the end of a world age appear, Koranic dignitaries are obliged to restore the discipline of the Arcanum of the 'Gnosis of Resurrection'. The doctrine does not refer to the outward forms of Islam but to the secret inner transformation of the last Imam (Adam) of each world – and by extension, every human is potentially last and first. The Eve of Adam is the spiritual, secret meaning of the esoteric law, which he craves in his nostalgia for paradise.[31]

Myths of the end of the world abound. Many cultures possess cataclysmic mythologies. Bertrand Russell believed that only a few of the 21 past civilizations are known, and then only the names, and that another 14 have disappeared without a trace.[32]

The following is a partial list of cultures that accept cyclical world ages, with an indication of the number of the present recurrent world age:

1. Hindu – Fifth Pralaya of an era of decline
2. Buddhist – Kali Yuga (began in 3102BC) of the First Descending interval period of an uncountable in an evolved state.
3. Mexican – IVth lxtilxochiti
4. Roman – Fifth World Age (according to Lucius Ampelius)
5. Hebrew – Eighth Jubilee Cycle (Era of Creation 3761BC)
6. Hawaiian – end of the Ninth
7. Icelandic – end of the Ninth leading to the Tenth
8. lsmaeli Iranian – more than the 18,000th cycle
9. Mayan – Third World Cycle (began 3375BC)
10. North Borneo – Eighth
11. Chinese – the neo-Confucians accept the idea
12. Norse

Myths of the end of the world also describe the rebirth of a renewed world. An example is the Norse myth, the Volpuspa, which tells about the end of the world embodied by the fate of the gods. Both are called *Ragnarok*, the 'twilight of the gods', simultaneously the end and the entire process of events, fate and destiny. The collapse affects and is affected by giants, gods and men and is fought on a battlefield 100 leagues each way. Morality is rejected, brothers slay each other, and kinship is profaned. All actions are criminal and bloody, and decay reigns. It indeed sounds like modern times. The primary cause is that the gods disregard their promises to men and to each other. The tempo of downfall increases, the sun darkens and storms rage over the earth. Myriad demons enchained within the earth break loose and arrive to persecute humanity. A yellow eagle shrieks at the prospect of carrion and the ship of death shatters its moorings. The world groans, mountains crash, the sky is rent and the demons demolish the gods with their fiery swords. The stars vanish, smoke and fire abound, and the earth falls back into the sea. It is the end of the world, and its termination sounds like a primitive description of now! Even though men and gods die, the world does not disappear forever. A terrible winter follows the great fire of Ragnarok, and when it passes, the remaining gods raise the earth from the sea. Two men survive, hiding in the forest Hoddmimisholt, eating only the morning dew, and from them a new race of men descends.

The history of the survivors of a World Age describes the fate of the deceased world age and a pattern for its renewal. All images that carry the exegesis are included. World ages are endless and repetitive, so the stories and myths of the end and every fragment of history are magnified, distorted and grafted onto personal stories and histories. Every battle becomes a battle with the gods.

After thousands of generations and tens of thousands of years, creation myths assume the character of a cosmic drama: The Divine Plot. In retelling the stories, the reality of the end of a previous highly developed world becomes foggy, misunderstood and seen as fantasy, much as few individuals on earth now could claim to 'understand' the state of the world at the present time, including the leaders of the major nations of the earth. Successive generations of elders appropriate tales told them during childhood and assume their burden and authority. The responsibility for the transmission becomes so great that the stories themselves assume godlike proportions. The transmission gradually becomes sacred.

The Norse creation bears a strong resemblance to the time scale in its metaphors. The creation of earth contrasts a dark, frozen world (the void) with a blazing, fiery world (creation). The rivers froze and sparks from the hot world melted them to form a giant called Ymir (an Aries celestial god) and the cow Audumbla (Taurus earth mother), who fed him with her milk. Audumbla licking salt into his form (Gemini) creates the first man. After a brief time, a set of giant brothers (Cancer) born of an evil thorn tree kill Ymir, and all but one are drowned in his blood. The surviving brother and his family are saved by climbing on a luor, variously described as a cradle, coffin, bier or ship (the flood). The brothers use Ymir's body to make the earth after carrying it to the centre of the world. The seas and lakes come from the blood, the earth from his flesh, the sky from his skull, supported at its corners by four dwarfs. The clouds come from his brains, and the stars and heavenly bodies from sparks from the hot world, and all are ordered by the gods, establishing days and years.

The anthropomorphic creation, with a cosmos created from the body of the divine one, is similar to Iranian and Indian sources. The metempsychosis of giant, first cow and then man is reminiscent of eastern and primitive creations. Jung quotes a Hindu creation myth:

> He (Atman) was as big as a man and woman joined together; he divided himself into two, and thus husband and wife were born... He joined himself to her, and thus men were born. She thought: 'How should he lie with me after having produced me? I will hide myself'. She became a cow, he became a bull; they joined and cattle were born. She became a mare, he a stallion; she became a she-ass, he an ass; they joined and the hoofed animals were born. Thus he created everything down to the ants, male and female... Then he knew: 'I am this creation, for I produced it all from myself'. Such was creation. He who possesses this knowledge creates his own being in that creation.[33]

The evolution of the myth is a transformative symbol of psychic processes in humanity. For Snorri (c. 1179-1241), the author of the *Edda*, creation was the first step towards Ragnarok.[34]

At the centre of the Norse world was the Yggdrasil tree, the tree of fate where the gods hold council every day to determine the welfare of the universe. Beneath it, the well of fate, Uroarbrunnr, conceives the female fates who lay down the courses of men and women's lives for all time. The tree rises to the sky; its branches cover the whole world. Its three roots reach down to the world of death, Hel, to the world of the frost-giants and to the world of men. Odin hangs himself on this tree, questing for wisdom, and upon it depends the very essence of the world. Nevertheless, by the time it reaches its full growth, it has already begun decaying. The fate of the Yggdrasil tree is the fate of the world.

Flood Legends

Flood legends exist in virtually every culture and are so pervasive that they have given rise to cults of universal destruction by water. The best known in the West is the biblical great flood of Noah and the ark in Genesis. Following is a list of many cultures that have a deluge legend:

1. Biblical Flood of Noah and his Ark
2. Greek legend of Deucalian and Phyrra
3. Babylonian and Sumerian Utnapishtim in the Gilgamesh Epic
4. Chaldean records
5. North Syrian Sisthes
6. Hindu Puranos of Satyavarata; Rig-Vedas; Satapatha Brahmana; four in the Upangas; three in the Matsya Purana
7. Icelandic Eddas of Bergelmir
8. Siberian shaman rituals
9. Norse epics
10. Welsh ballads of Dwyfan and Dwyfach
11. African Masai
12. American Indians, especially Minabozho of the Algonquins
13. Tarascan Indians of Central America
14. Guatemalan Nala and Nata
15. Toltec giant Shelua
16. Hottentots
17. Australian Aborigines
18. Fiji Islanders
19. Eskimos
20. Malays
21. Samoans
22. Burmese
23. Cambodians
24. Maori warriors
25. Dyaks of Borneo
26. Chinese
27. Arawakans of Guyana, Northern Brazil and Columbia
28. Phoenician cosmology of Sanchuniathon
29. Cushites
30. Iranian hero Yima in the Zend-Avesta
31. Thessalian Cerambos
32. Cos Island hero Merops
33. Aztec codex Chimalpopoca of Nata and Nena
34. Central American Popul Vuh
35. Chibchas of Bogota
36. Mandan Indians of North America
37. Iroquois, Chicksaws, Sioux and Okanagaus of America
38. Nicaraguans
39. Pima Indian tribe

Flood legends are similar in structure, and often contain the theme that a god collects and saves representative species from a worldwide catastrophe. Figure 7 shows the many places on earth where such legends have existed and affected virtually every culture before the present.

Memories of the world before a cataclysm emphasize a great, corrupt power of technology as a worldwide phenomenon. Legends describe gigantic shining metal cities reaching up to the sky, vast harvest lands stretching beyond the horizon. Blur-fast metal birds streaked overhead, spewing out flames, and men rode spaceships to the realm of the gods, the stars. Mass religious spectacles attended by millions of people vied with dissolute orgies involving whole cities. Humanity knew all there was to know, but it had fallen into devilish ways and ignorantly destroyed itself in a burst of fire and brimstone. The corruption of spiritual decline attended a proliferation of base and exploitative kings who shackled humanity in their greed. Propriety went to the winds, and populaces indulged in endless intoxicated revels of Dionysiac frenzy, everyone following the uninhibited pursuit of gross material wealth. The wealthy invented progressively more brutal ways to dispossess the masses and nations of underprivileged who created the wealth. There was continuous warfare between hopelessly decadent nations of rapists and developing nations with violent and corrupt leadership trying to regain their sovereignty.

The downfall of a world age saw aerial combat between warmongering silver birds and dragons breathing thunderbolts upon helpless populations. Hideous explosions created quasi-suns that burned all those within sight, followed by years of impenetrable darkness. Poisonous vapours filled the air, choking the life out of all vegetation and life. The carnage only terminated when the gods arose in fury and initiated a total conflagration that was so powerful that it altered the course of the earth and the planets in the sky. The evil ended only when the entire world consumed itself.

The rites of elders, as they huddled in fear and horror in their places of relative safety, transmit visions of the end of the world. The survivors of the holocaust gathered in remote Edens, protected by impenetrable mountain ranges or impassable deserts, and survival of the enlightened few implied isolation.

Atlantis

Myths depicting floods, cataclysms or the destruction by water or fire of a highly advanced civilization that has conquered the entire known world all point to Atlantis. Atlantis, so-called because European legends place its capital to the west while American legends place it to the east, was thought to be the acme of civilization of a previous world age that existed in the middle of the Atlantic Ocean.

Atlantis was the home of the gods, the Garden of Eden, Mount Meru, Paradise and the site of the 'golden age' of humanity before the present era. The scientific or historical establishment does not accept the existence of Atlantis, but an estimated 20,000 books have been written about it. Proof is circumstantial because Atlantis is a decimated former world age civilization. The sheer number of books proves that the principle of a previous golden age is inherent in human nature.

One of the earliest references to Atlantis is also the most persuasive. Plato described the physical design, history, laws, agricultural practices, shortcomings and virtues of Atlantis in *Timaeus*. Critias describes the destruction of Atlantis, but the manuscript ends in mid-sentence.

According to Plato, the revered sage of Athens, Solon (640-558BC) told the story to the grandfather of Critias. Solon heard it from Egyptian priests at the sacred centre of Sais, and dated the fall of Atlantis approximately 9,000 years previously, in the 10th millennium BC. Many attempts have since been made to locate the exact site of Atlantis and to trace its effects on the mainstream of human mythologies, customs, art and architecture. Rudolf Steiner and the Theosophists believed that Atlantis is the spiritual predecessor of our present world age.

There are various theories that seek to explain why Atlantis was destroyed:

- By comets bombarding the earth and great floods (Donnelly);
- By a volcano erupting on the Cycladic island of Thera in 1600BC (Galanopoulos and Professor Marinatos);
- For no apparent physical reason, but because of its decay (Spence);
- By the earth capturing a satellite Luna (Hoerbiger's Cosmogonic Theory and H S Bellamy);
- Through axis shifts (Velikovsky).

Figure 7: Map of Cataclysm and Flood Legends
The world map shows those cultures and their locations that have flood legends (o symbol) or legends of cyclic cataclysms (● symbol) . Such legends are common to the entire world. The A symbol shows suggested locations for the legendary Atlantis.

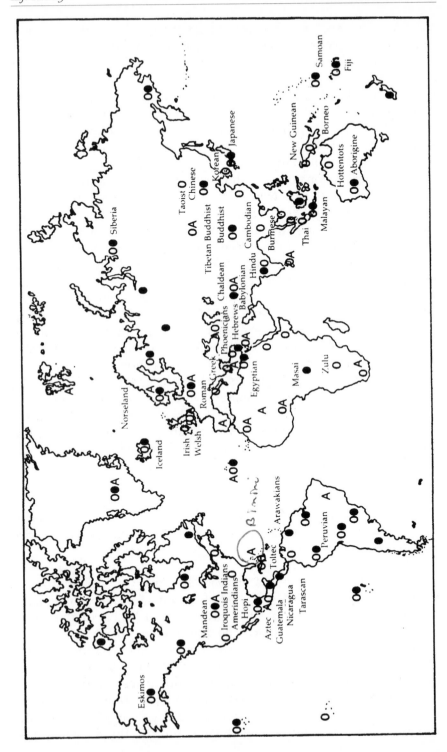

All traces of such an ancient civilization have been either covered up by later humanity or, what is more likely, integrated into the art and culture of early cultures, but no theory is conclusive. Proof of the existence of Atlantis, as well as the even earlier legendary civilizations of Lemuria and Mu in art, architecture and language, are compelling and fantastic. Desmond Lee, translator of Timaeus, avoids the issue by considering Plato the inventor of science fiction – and presents Atlantis as a construction typical of the imagination of all advanced civilizations.

Atlantis lore is consonant with eternal recurrence, as described in *The Secret Doctrine* and *Isis Unveiled* by Madame Blavatsky, the founder of the Theosophical Society. Believers in great cycles of history accept the myth of Atlantis as proof of their hypotheses. An important assumption follows from the circularity of world ages: the destruction of Atlantis was not just the end of a former world age but also a collective memory of the last recurrent world cycle. The doctrine of eternal recurrence implies an exact repetition of all events within each cycle and an Atlantean cataclysm caused by unrighteous avarice and power correlates with the present state of the world cycle, as we approach the end of a world age. The Atlantis myths of many ancient civilizations corroborate the idea of recurrent history, including traces such as the ceremonial ball courts of the Mayans that evoke the major stadiums of modern societies.

Plato's description of the capital of Atlantis corresponds in many details to the organization and geography of New York City, although the terms used in 4th century BC are obviously antique. In *Timaeus*, one of the priests of Saïs told Solon:

> *There is a story which even you have preserved, that once upon a time Phaethon, the son of Helios, having yoked the steeds in his father's chariot, because he was not able to drive them in the path of his father, burnt up all that was upon the earth, and was himself destroyed by a thunder-bolt.*[35]

The story is a prologue to a detailed description of Atlantis, but is symbolically the attempt by the child of the sun god Helios (humanity) to yoke his father's steeds (nuclear energy similar to that of the sun?), but being unable to control them, he destroys the earth.

Most commentators have seen this episode as a metaphor for the deviation of planets from their courses in the heavens during a periodic conflagration of earth. The priest differentiates conflagrations caused and related to cosmic phenomena, for which it is disastrous to be upon mountains and dry, lofty places but safe to be near sea-level and low-lying land, and the floods, when it is best to be high and not to below. He implies that because of the location and special features of Egypt, both types of cataclysm have spared the sacred land. The elderly priest chastised the young Solon by telling him that history as kept by other civilizations records only letters of State, while Egyptians recorded previous great ages in their temples.

> *...when the stream from heaven descends like a pestilence, and leaves only those of you who are destitute of letters and education; and thus you have to begin all over again as children, and know nothing of what happened in ancient times, either among us or yourselves. As for those genealogies of yours which you have recounted to us, Solon, they are no better than the tales of children; for, in the first place, you remember one deluge only, whereas there were many before that; and, in the next place, you do not know that there dwelt in your land the fairest and noblest race of men which ever lived, of whom you and your whole city are but a seed or remnant.*[36]

If a catastrophe occurred in modern civilization tomorrow, the primary record of extensive information of previous ages transmitted by books and in computers would both be fragile and likely to disappear in time. There are few monuments to carry modern knowledge, and even the most rudimentary attempts seem failures. An example is the plaque designed for the Mariner spacecraft, which is incomprehensible to the average person. A prototype presented to a seminar of top scientists was completely misunderstood. To modern society, history is vague, and the ability to transmit knowledge beyond a breakdown of civilization is virtually non-existent.

The following parallels between Atlantis and the modern world are interesting and striking. Phrases in brackets denote modern parallels.

'He himself, as he was a god, found no difficulty in making special arrangements for the centre island, bringing two streams of water under the earth, which he caused to ascend as springs, one of warm water and the other of cold.' *(The ancient Greeks could not have known of hot and cold running water.)*

'...they dug out of the earth whatever was to be found there, mineral as well as metal, and that which is now only a name, and was then something more than a name – orichalcum – was dug out of the earth in many parts of the island.' *(The word orichalcum confuses scholars, but the temples were all made of this wonderful and valuable substance, which could be aluminium!)*

A long segment describes the multitude of animals, plants, flowers and fruits that grew on Atlantis: 'First of all they bridged over the zones of the sea which surrounded the ancient metropolis, and made a passage into and out of the royal palace; and then they began to build the palace in the habitation of the god and their ancestors. This they continued to ornament in successive generations, every king surpassing the one who came before him to the utmost of his power, until they made the building a marvel to behold for size and beauty.' *(An apt description of a modern city.)*

'...constructing bridges of such a width as would leave a passage for a single trireme to pass out of one into another, and roofed them over; and there was a way underneath for the ships.' *(Bridges link Manhattan Island to the mainland New Jersey, New York State and Long Island.)*

'Here, too, was Poseidon's own temple, of a stadium in length and half a stadium in width, and of a proportionate height, having a sort of barbaric splendour.' *(One of many large sports stadia in New York.)*

'In the interior of the temple... adorned everywhere with gold and silver and orichalcum; all the other parts of the walls and pillars and floor they lined with orichalcum.' *(Aluminum is everywhere in the modern city, anodized to look like silver or gold.)*

'In both of the two islands formed by the zones; and in the centre of the larger of the two there was a racecourse of a stadium in width, and in length allowed to extend all round the island, for horses to race in. Also there were guard-houses at intervals for the body-guards.' *(The horses race at the racetracks on Long Island, larger than Manhattan, and the horses pulling chariots are automobiles travelling around Long Island and Manhattan on expressways, with the toll gates being guard-houses.)*

The farmlands of the Great Plains are in rectangular grids like the Midwest, and the surrounding mountains, celebrated for their number, size, and beauty, are like the Rocky Mountains in the western United States.

Plato described the structure of government, where areas of the country are proportionally represented and have required military service. The leaders of the country give a portion of their earnings to furnish war-chariots, to make up a total of 10,000 of them, and thousands of ships to sail the seas. The rulers meet every five years to consult about the laws. The general structure of Atlantis sounds very like modern democratic government, down to elections held at regular times. The traditions of the country are very noble and aspirations high, but the vast power carried b the citizenry led them to overvalue the material world. Their divinity began to fade.

...then, they being unable to bear their fortune, became unseemly, and to him who had an eye to see, they began to appear base, and had lost the fairest of their

precious gifts; but to those who had no eye to see the true happiness, they still appeared glorious and blessed at the very time when they were filled with unrighteous avarice and power. Zeus, the god of gods, who rules with law, and is able to see into such things, perceiving that an honourable race was in a most wretched state, and wanting to inflict punishment on them that they might be chastened and improved, collected all the gods into his most holy habitation, which, being placed in the centre of the world, could see all things that partake of generation. And when he had called them together he spoke as follows...

Plato's story ends abruptly. There are no goblins, no tales of giants – it is a reasonable tale of people who built cities and ships and farmed the land, like inhabitants of the modern world do. Atlantis describes the end of the last world age.

Ignatius Donnelly presented an extensive historical and scientific theory of the existence of Atlantis, calling it an 'antediluvian' world, meaning a world before the flood. He made parallels between Atlantis and the Garden of Eden, the Garden of the Hesperides, the Elysian Fields, the Navel of the Earth, the Asgard of the Eddas and the Mount Olympus of the Greeks – a symbol of the universal memory of a great land where early humanity dwelt in peace and happiness. Donnelly divided the early history of the world into a stage before and after the deluge, but did not recognize that the world of Atlantis was his world.

In his life readings, the American psychic prophet Edgar Cayce described Atlantis as a great civilization destroyed by a worldwide catastrophe. He located the lowland plains of Atlantis on the eastern seaboard of the United States and predicted that evidence of Atlantis would be found in 1968-1969 off the coast of America. Charles Berlitz and others did discover fabricated structures in the sea near Bimini, off the Bahamas coast, at the time predicted by Cayce – the remains of huge stone buildings, gigantic steps, a causeway, and even a circular formation of 44 marble columns. Although photographed, the finds were not recovered.[37]

Evidence for Atlantis

Traces of ancient Atlantis are encoded in ancient and modern alphabets and languages, the cultivation of vegetables and the domestication and raising of animals unknown to the Greeks. Domestication is a mysterious process that we do not understand today. Plato's story describes a proliferation of technological achievements unknown in Greek times and unheard of until recent history, such as the mariner's compass, the magnet, gunpowder, navigation skills and devices, paper and silk.

Donnelly said that the Greeks associated the origin of astronomy with Atlas and Hercules, who were Atlantean kings or heroes. The Egyptians regarded Taut, Thoth, or At-hotes as the originator of astronomy and the alphabet.[38] Many books have been written to validate the existence of Atlantis on iconographic grounds, especially through the similarities of artefacts from the Mayan, Aztec, Toltec, North American Indian, and many other civilizations.

There have been numerous volcanoes in the past 50,000 years that could have been the source of the Atlantis myth, enough of them to justify the idea of periodic destructions.

The Greek island of Thera (Santorini) was the site of a volcanic explosion sometime between 1600BC and 1400BC. Professor Marinatos of the Greek Department of Antiquities proposed Thera as the site of Atlantis, but evidence for a civilization as grand and technologically proficient as the myth is inconclusive, resting as it does on magnificent wall paintings and frescos and little more.[39] More recently, Jacques Cousteau explored Santorini in 1976, finding traces of two volcanic explosions, one of them occurring in about 2500BC.

Otto Muck's *The Secret of Atlantis* (1976) presented scientific evidence for Atlantis. He stated that the Thera volcano happened after Plato's story, and that it and the traces found in the Bahamas and Caribbean waters must have been outposts of the Atlantean empire. He includes a testimony from the Soviet scientist N F Zhirov that a large landmass dropped out of the mid-Atlantic ridge in recent geological times. He concluded that Asteroid A plunged into the area of the Bermuda Triangle in 8498BC and destroyed an ancient civilization and a majority of the world's population in one day. He adduced evidence from anthropology, calendar systems, climatic phenomena, astronomy, architecture, archaeology and many other fields. His book is extremely convincing.

Another way to look at the Atlantis phenomenon is Lewis Spence's *Will Europe Follow Atlantis?*, which compares the social and moral conditions in the modern world with that of Atlantis. He draws on a wide variety of mythological material and makes parallels between Atlantis and our present day logical.

H S Bellamy's *The Atlantis Myth* correlates the destruction of Babylon in the Book of Revelations with references from the books of Ezekiel, Isaiah, Jeremiah about Babylon, and concludes that they refer to Atlantis. Images of the Tower of Babylon and its confusion of tongues, the vice, the depravity and the collapse of civilized values are consonant with our modern world.

Finally, the great work of the Russian Immanuel Velikovsky is evidence for cyclical cataclysms more than for the existence of Atlantis. His books describe multiple axis shifts of earth caused by collisions with asteroids or comets that affected life. He collected evidence from widely diverse fields. His central theme is that the Biblical story of the Exodus describes an Atlantean cataclysm.

Images of floods, cataclysms, and Atlantis have such a deep hold on our imagination because humanity possesses a collective memory, programmed into our genetic code, through resonant patterns in time.

Chapter Three — Eternal Recurrence

For the earth once more begets what it's begotten of old.
Goethe

Cyclic history naturally evokes the concept of eternal recurrence – the exact repetition of events in time. We experience recurrence in the *sentiment du déjà-vu*, which is the feeling of exactly experiencing a particular situation that has happened before. Scents, sights, tastes or other sensations open floodgates into previous experiences. Such feelings happen to everyone at some time in life, and many of us experience constant access to such apparent alternative worlds.

Recurrence is an ancient idea symbolized by the snake, called the *ouroburos,* biting its tail. In modern physics, the curvature of time is a property of the cyclic nature of the universe and implies that repetition occurs at many levels of reality. Molecules break down into their component atoms (they essentially 'die') and reassemble into new molecules, essentially creating a new molecular body. Cells in our body die and are replaced daily; our cellular body is completely replaced every few years, but the variation from body to body is so slight that it apparently recurs just as it was before and carries the exact same habits, form, constitution and health. The mechanism of this astonishing continuity, a kind of biological reincarnation, is recurrence, described in detail in books by P D Ouspensky, Rodney Collin and Maurice Nicoll.

Ouspensky illustrates recurrence as a cyclic wave for each day, a sequence of such waves making a year, which is itself one wave within the lifetime of 77 years, which is a wave within the lifetime of all humanity. When seen end-on each cycle is a circle, but when seen side-on, from a higher dimension, it is a continuous wave like the solar system seen in its temporal dimension. Each wave is independent of the whole when seen as a circle, yet is a whole in itself and parallels the waves below it and above it. The basic nature of sine curves is that they appear as circles seen from a higher dimension. These ideas, which are more than 60 years old, are remarkably similar to modern theories of the physics of multiple universes.[40]

This idea also relates to a concept called transfinite points. One point contains an infinite number of points. A line contains an infinite number of points bounded by transfinite points at the beginning and end. The circumference of a circle contains an infinite number of points without a beginning or end. A plane contains an infinity of lines and a solid contains an infinite number of planes. In the transition to higher dimensions, each moment contains an infinite number of possibilities. As a plane contains an infinity of lines, a moment of time contains an infinity of histories and futures.

Pythagoras taught eternal recurrence. His character Eudemus envisaged a complete return in every detail and identified two kinds of recurrence: one is the 'repetition in time' of the natural order of things such as seasons, or day and night, produced by cycles of the sun, moon, earth and the planets; the second is 'repetition in eternity', where identical things exist in a number of existences.

Plato's *Phaedo* describes the triple repetition of lives. Knowledge is recollection, implying a previous time in which we learned the information. Our soul has had a previous existence in the same body – a proof of the immortality of the soul.

> *Now into the same place from which each Soul cometh, she returneth not until ten thousand years have been accomplished; for sooner is no Soul fledged with wings, save the Soul of him who hath sought after True Wisdom without deceit, or hath loved his comrade in the bonds of Wisdom. The Souls of such men, when the third course of a thousand years is finished, if they have chosen this life three times in order, being fledged with wings do they then depart.*

Plato implies that the Soul incarnates many times with periods of thousands of years in between, and that we live hundreds of lives, each one three times, and that True Wisdom is the only escape from recurrence.

The Stoics believed man to be a microcosm of a Universal Being, who periodically reincarnates into a world governed by cycles.[41] After the destruction of each world, individual souls return to the divine home from which they emanated. Cosmic life is an infinite series of identical world cycles, populated by the same souls.

Even the New Testament implies the basic Gnostic tenet that Jesus taught recurrence. His crucifixion and rebirth was a return after three cosmic days. Christ spoke of recurrence: 'Ye shall see the Son of man ascend up where he was before',[42] and, 'I will come again, and receive you unto myself'.[43] The church later eliminated references to recurrence, but the Gnostic gospels retained them. The Gnostic *Treatise on Resurrection* states: 'Do not suppose that resurrection is an apparition. It is not an apparition; rather it is something real. Instead one ought to maintain that the world is an apparition, rather than resurrection.'[44] Resurrection is the moment of enlightenment, revealing what truly exists and a migration into new life, a secret teaching transmitted directly to the disciples. In the *Wisdom of Jesus Christ* disciples gathered on a mountain after Jesus' death; he appeared, smiled and offered to teach them the 'secrets (mysteria) of the holy plan' of the universe and its destiny.[45]

Many medieval philosophers believed in the idea of cyclical world ages and supported recurrence, such as Clement of Alexandria (c. AD150-220), Arnobius (280-340), and Joachim of Floris (1145-1202). Giambatista Vico put forward a scheme of cyclic civilization in his *Scienza Nuova* (1725).

Nietzsche accepted eternal recurrence because of the necessity for a finite number of centres of force which:

> *In infinite time would realize every possible combination an infinite number of times. Since between every combination and every other combination all other possible combinations would have to take place, and each combination conditions the entire sequence of combinations, a circular movement of absolutely identical series is thus demonstrated: the world as a circular movement that has already repeated itself infinitely often and plays its game ad infinitum.*[46]

Nietzsche saw recurrence as a means for transcending cause and effect and liberating the soul.

> *This world: as force throughout, as a play of forces and waves of forces, at the same time one and many, increasing here and at the same time decreasing there; a sea of forced flowing and rushing together, eternally changing, eternally flooding back, with tremendous years of recurrence, with an ebb and flood of its forms; ...this my Dionysian world of the eternally self-creating, the eternally self-destroying, this mystery world of the twofold voluptuous delight, my 'beyond good and evil', without goal, unless the joy of the circle is itself a goal; without will, unless a ring feels good will toward itself.*[47]

If the logic and sentiment of modern civilization opposes the idea of eternal recurrence, Pythagoras, Plato, Aristotle, Jesus and Nietzsche are formidable references to its reality. The recurrent nature of subatomic phenomena weighs heavily in favour of a recurrent model of reality, and it is impossible to ignore the implications of the concept. J B S Haldane wrote that 'there must he a general recurrence of events' because 'everything must recur'.[48]

The only time track we know is the one along which our life is lived in time; one reality among an infinity of possibilities. Following another track would make us a different person, living another life. Most people never consider that there are other possibilities because they limit their awareness to only one. The present moment contains infinite possibilities and histories. There is an eternal All, available at any moment to any individual. Ouspensky said:

> *Time does not exist! There exists no perpetual and eternal appearance and disappearance of phenomena, no ceaselessly flowing fountain of ever-appearing and ever-vanishing events. Everything exists always! There is only one eternal present, the Eternal Now, which the weak and limited human mind can never grasp and conceive.*[49]

The world contains infinite possibilities, but our mind only follows one. All possibilities are available, but we do not see or know them – only the actuality as lived.

> *Not only is it impossible for things to be other than they are, it is even impossible that the initial situation of the universe could have been other than what it was. No matter what we do at a given moment, it is the only thing that is ever possible for us to be doing in this moment.*[50]

Ouspensky postulated a fifth dimension that he called 'eternity', a further dimension beyond time that contains all possibilities and that recurs infinitely. The universe perpetually recurs within eternity. To understand eternity is to discover the evolution of the universe within. The temporal universe is a mental process, not a sensible object. The universe is available equally to everyone.

Ouspensky applied the principles of eternal recurrence to individual life. Life is a circular process. At death, incomplete life energies disseminate and pass outside of linear time only to reassemble again at the original conception instant in the womb of the same mother, impregnated by the same father, and at the same time. The unique set of circumstances that define a life belong nowhere else in the universe of space and time but back to their original beginning. Life is a loop recurring in time, repeated infinitely.

Plato observed that, although souls have choices, most souls out of force of habit return to repeat the experiences of their previous life.[51] The impure soul passes through the river of forgetting, the River Lethe, and in a new life, which is a repetition of the last life, cannot remember what he or she was, or why life events seem so familiar. The Orphic mysteries' function was to initiate the soul to remember by drinking the water of the Lake of Memory. The choice lies in this life, because this life is a synthesis and summation of all lives. Only by remembering our personal past, which is the past of all individuals and of the universe, can we ascend to enlightenment and be free from the endless wheel of rebirth. Collin stated that we must fully recognize the futility of recurrence before the tasks of penetrating consciously into the unknown and unimaginable dimensions that lie beyond can he undertaken.

Cosmoses

Time perception is relative to the length of the lifetime of the perceiver. The word 'cosmos' describes self-evolving wholes that are complete in themselves and divine images of the universe. Cosmoses exist throughout the universe, greater cosmoses reflecting greater degrees of consciousness and intelligence and giving birth to smaller cosmoses. The Gurdjieffian hierarchy of the chain of cosmoses is: Universe (the Absolute), galaxy, solar system, Sun, Earth, Nature, humanity, an individual human, cell, molecule and electron (see the Table of Rodney Collin's times and cosmoses). The duration and relative dimensions of each cosmos differentiates level from level.

> *Each new dimension represents movement in a new direction. A point of no dimensions, such as the point of a pencil or lighted cigarette in the dark, when moved, traces a line. A line – the spokes of a bicycle-wheel or crayon, for example, when spun or moved at right angles to itself (or a disk spun on its axis) traces a plane. A solid, such as a man, when extended into the past and future, traces a lifetime. A lifetime, extended at right angles to it, brings us to the idea of parallel times, of time-repetition or eternity outside of time. The totality of such repetitions, projected in yet another direction, implies an absolute whole, the realisation of all possibilities, everything existing everywhere.*[52]

A point has no dimensions, a line one, a plane two, a solid three; a lifetime four, a life repeating eternally five, and All has six dimensions. The dimensions in each successive cosmos slide along a scale. A man perceives a cell as a point of no dimensions, while to nature, man is a point, and to the sun, the earth is a point. The lifetime of a cell is a solid to man, as it is his body, just as the lifetime of nature is a solid relative to earth. The lifetime of cells constitutes a human, and the solid of all men and women in history is

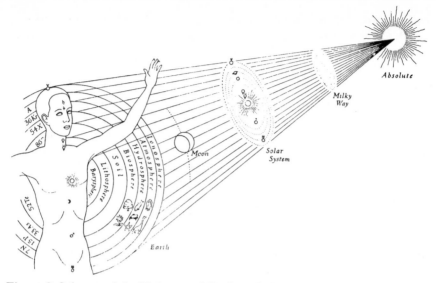

Figure 8: Scheme of the Universe of Rodney Collin
The individual as a reflection and microcosm of the unity of the absolute being of
the universe. (From Collin, *The Theory of Celestial Influence*)

humankind. 'Remembering his life as a whole, man sees himself as
Nature sees him. Thus, memory, for man, is the key to perceiving
himself and his surroundings as they are perceived by a higher
cosmos.'[53] Every cosmos links with every other by relative size and
time sense and length of life. The scales of forms from electrons to
galaxies are in this way reconciled into a perfect whole, rather than
occupying incommensurable niches as in contemporary science.

All living beings are conceived, born, mature and die in time, and
therefore all cosmoses are alive – they live their own lives in their
own relative time. Just because a rock or a galaxy has a vastly greater
duration does not mean that it is not alive. After all, we are
composed of atoms that resemble galaxies and we are alive. All
dimensions are interdependent and mathematically connected. Time
is the key: the period of rotation about the vital centre of a greater
world creates it. In Kepler's Third Law, the relation between
distances from the sun (line) and periods of rotation about the sun
(time) is the relation between square roots and cube roots. All
cosmoses conform to the same general plan. Linear space develops
by cubes as time develops by squares, as Table 1 shows.[54]

Human perception is usually limited to three dimensions out of
the many available. Three primary principles govern the
relationships between cosmoses. The 'law of three' relates each
cosmos:

Cosmos	Moment	Breath	Minute	Hour	Day	Week	Month	Year	Lifetime
Electron	—	—	—	—	—	—	—	—	1/1500 s.
Molecule · 28,000	—	—	—	—	1/1500 s.	1/300 s.	1/50 s.	.25 s.	18 sec.
Blood-Cell · 4,800	—	1/1500 s.	1/90 s.	2/3 s.	18 sec.	1.75 m.	7 min.	1.5 hr.	6 days
Man · 28,000	1/30 s.	3 sec.	1 min.	1 hr.	1 day	7 days	29 days	1 year	76 y.
Nature · 365	.25 hour	1 day	18 days	3.25 days	76 y.	537 y.	2150 y.	25,800 y.	2.25 my.
Earth · 7,800	3.125 days	1 year	18 years	1075 y.	25,800 y.	187,000 y.	750,000 y.	9.33 my.	750 my.
Sun · 100,000	75 years	7000 y.	135,000 y.	8 my.	200 my.	—	—	—	5.6^{12} y.
Milky Way	7.5 my.	700 my.	13,500my.	—	—	—	—	—	5.6^{17} y.

Table 1: Rodney Collin's Table of Times and Cosmoses
Each level of existence in the universe is considered an organism in its own right, with a lifetime of relative stages like all other organisms. Each organism, from the electron to the Milky Way, is governed by the same mathematical laws, as the table shows. (From Collin, *The Theory of Celestial Influence*)

a. To its past (the next smaller cosmos) by attraction;
b. To its future (the next larger cosmos) by radiation, and;
c. To its present (itself) by time, this combines the effect of receiving the past and projecting to the future.

The relations between the three cosmoses are exponential powers of ten. A perceiver can only understand the cosmoses directly above and below with any clarity. Beyond these limits, only those who manifest transcendent (beyond time) reality have access. For example, we are aware of our cellular body, our own existence as a human and a general awareness of Nature as a whole, although our centre is individual ego-existence rather than body or Nature. Only exceptional beings are able to extend their awareness into the molecular world, the electronic world in the microcosm, the earth, the sun, or the galaxy in the macrocosm.

Collin describes the relationship as that between a breath, a day and a life. A breath is $1/28,000$th of a day (three seconds), a day is the present, and a life is about 28,000 days (77 years). As nature is the next higher level of perception, a day for a man must be a breath for nature, and the life of the Earth equivalent to a breath of the galaxy, and similarly other cosmoses relate to each other. The relativity of time allows the human to relate to and understand the entire universe.

The Darwinian Cataclysm

Cyclical cataclysms and the evolution of life on the earth are inseparable systems, but have received little support from scientists since Darwin. In 1849 the anthropologist: d'Orbigny stated:

> A 'first creation' appeared after the Silurian Age. After its total annihilation by some geological cause and after the passage of a considerable span of time, a second creation took place at the Devonian stage. Thereafter twenty-seven successive creations repopulated the entire earth anew with plants and animals, geological upheavals having each time destroyed all living nature. These are certain but incomprehensible facts.[55]

D'Orbigny believed that since there was positive proof of successive geological periods punctuated by cataclysms, and that identical species existed in these periods, there must have been extinctions followed by the recreation of species. Even now, there is an astonishing lack of solid evidence to corroborate the evolutionary theory of Darwin. The idea of a gradual, systematic evolution is obsolete because there are no traces of the intermediate forms of any species, and if there is no proof, how can the hypothesis be sustained? The anthropologist Hoffman states that the catastrophes in previous ages were not gradual, but the work of a moment. Animals and plants died out suddenly as the conditions required for their existence ceased to exist.

Georges Cuvier (1769-1832) classified animal and plant kingdoms on the same principles used up to the present day, and held that the various species and types of animals do not exist independently, but are closely interrelated. 'Every living organism forms a whole. No part can change without changes in the other parts.'[56] Cuvier proposed a static order of species, each relegated to a specific time and place, each wiped out in turn by a catastrophe. Floods, volcanoes, and earthquakes on a worldwide scale destroyed the land and remade the whole. Entire races disappeared, leaving only traces.

Cuvier's successor, Charles Lyell (1797-1849), postulated the Uniformitarian Theory that stated, first, that it was necessary to assume uniform natural laws in time and space. This is an a priori claim all scientists must make about the world – that nature acts in the future as it has acted in the past, and that it is not capricious. Second, he stated the obvious – that geological processes are uniform through time. However, is it obvious? Lyell's two other laws were highly suspect and intended to disprove catastrophism. The third is that present processes alone were admissible to explain nature, and that geologic change is slow, gradual, and steady. His fourth concept was that the earth has been the same since its creation. What is fascinating about Lyell is his view that 'the fossil record is representative of only one part of a great year – a grand cycle that will occur again when the huge iguanodon might reappear in the woods, and the ichthyosaur in the sea, while the pterodactyl might flit again through umbrageous groves of fern trees.'[57] The late Stephen Jay Gould of Harvard agreed that catastrophists take a literal view and see the direction of history.

Louis Agassiz (1807-1873) accepted Cuvier and catastrophism and annotated Lyell, accepting that the 'summation of present causes over geologic time cannot account for the magnitude of some past events'.[58]

Darwin's *Origin of Species* of 1859 spelled the decline of the catastrophist view of history, even though his strongest champions, Professor Gray, Thomas Huxley and Haeckel, refused to accept the idea of natural selection – that the fittest survive. Today, 140 years later, proof has not been forthcoming and evolutionary theory is under even greater pressure than in Darwin's time because the fossil line consists for the most part of gaps. Nonetheless, the majority still believe Darwin's unworkable theory under the leadership of such retrogrades as Richard Dawkins.

The death-knell of an ecological cyclic reality was the acceptance of Darwin's linear view of evolution as a development of successive organisms, each one better adapted to its environment, culminating in humanity as the apex of the evolutionary scale. Natural Selection is the mechanism by which evolution acts – the 'survival of the fittest' means that the fittest of each generation tend to survive to transmit survival traits to their offspring. Characteristics that are not survival-proven gradually disappear from the inherited pattern of the species.

Proof for Darwinian evolution is fragmentary and contradictory at best, primarily in the case of humanity, where there should be traces of a succession of intermediate beings connecting the higher primate apes to modern homo sapiens. As is well known, no such 'missing links' exist. The gaps in the fossil strata containing the proof are so large as to totally refute the theory. Charles Fort spent a lifetime collecting and publishing data that are inexplicable to science, and had a unique and amusing statement about Darwinism:

> *As for Darwinism: The fittest survive. What is meant by the fittest?*
> *Not the strongest; not the cleverest – weakness and stupidity everywhere survive.*
> *There is no way of determining fitness except in that: a thing does survive.*
> *"Fitness," then, is only another name for "survival."*
> *Darwinism: That survivors survive.*

How do geologists determine the age of rocks? By the fossils in them.
And how do they determine the age of fossils? By the rocks they are in.[59]

The fossil record does not validate Darwin, and on the contrary shows fossils with no significant change over 10 million years. 'Punctuated equilibrium', where well-defined groups of creatures adapt sporadically interspersed with long periods of little or no change, is an alternative. Niches in the sequence of organisms are filled by other beings that adapt to the niche. Once in its niche, an organism does not change. The obvious analogy is to the structure of the atomic shells. When we knock an electron out of an inner ring, another electron from the next ring out moves into its place – but the overall structure of the atom remains the same. The implication is that the sequence of life forms is set, and that development fills up the available categories, an idea that sounds very much like the Greek concept of metempsychosis.

The genetic code is a record of all past reproductions. The great problem is that the programme of the present-day organism resembles a text, proof-read and corrected for two billion years, continually improving, refining and completing itself, gradually eliminating all imperfections, but without an author. Natural selection may choose only among organisms in existence. However, how can this be when it appears that each molecule is specifically engineered? Even sophisticated modern genetic technology is far away from understanding the origin of the process of life in time, considering 98% of the human genome 'junk DNA' because they have no idea what it contains. What is this junk but our history?[60]

Dangerous modern genetic engineering uses the common bacterium e. coli as raw material. The fact that such a non-specific organism has the capability to approximate human genetic information poses an interesting point. Every life form on earth uses that same basic genetic structure. The differences are the result of differential utilization of the base coding sequence in time. Just as in physics all particles are composed of the same set of four quarks in their three modes ($4\times3=12$), so the genetic code uses the four acid bases in their three forms (also $4\times3=12$ combinations).

The parallel to the four elements in three modes of astrology is clear. Genetic code resonates with the movements of the planetary bodies and its formal pattern existed in an energetic pattern from the beginning of earth's history, and in turn derives from the information carried by the planets. The form of a solar system determines the form of life in residence there.

The idea, common to the esoteric view of creation, such as that of the Theosophists, Alice Bailey, Steiner and the Eastern religions, that before incarnating in the human body the soul passes through planetary existences is formally correct. It implies that:

– The code was operational at the start
– The code did not evolve
– All life forms have the same source
– There is a spiritual and physical link between all beings throughout the universe

The Divine Plot uses astrological language to describe the pattern in time that guides development in physical, emotional (astral), mental, spiritual and cosmic realms, which satisfies the requirements of prevailing theories of evolution. The major problem is the definition of terms, because those used by previous cultures have been inadvertently 'discovered' and renamed by modern science, albeit in a simplistic form. A primary example is that fragments of an idea previously called 'reincarnation' have been renamed 'genetics'.

Catastrophe Theory

The most recent advances in astronomy imply that catastrophe theory is the basis of our cosmology. Physicists accept the Big Bang theory of creation, and apply similar ideas to genetics and evolutionary processes. The change in species is not caused by external influences such as natural selection, but by catastrophes. Our genetic code is virtually the same as that of apes – biochemical comparison of the 44 proteins and enzymes common to both chimpanzees and human beings show them to be 99% identical – thus bringing into question the mechanism of how we separated from apes, if that is indeed what happened. The genes of humans and chimps are as similar as the genes of sibling species of other organisms, so much so that it requires biochemical analysis to tell them apart.[61]

The radiation that accompanies comets, earthquakes or the proliferation of nuclear weapons could be the required catastrophic agent of large-scale biological change. Random variations do not produce variety, but circumstances as exist today in the world might. 'Numerous catastrophes or bursts of effective radiation must have taken place in the geological past in order to change so radically the living forms on earth, as the record of fossils embedded in lava and sediment bears witness.'[62] The similarity of species in early life is taken as proof that evolution works backwards from humanity to the other animals.

Nature's favourite form seems to be that of the circle. A straight line is an abstraction and becomes a segment or arc of a circle in the context of space. Closely seen matter resolves into orbiting electrical charges. The spherical properties of the universe determine space and time. Galaxies rotate in stately waltzes in a universe that spins as it expands. The conclusion is that man's life and social forms follow circular principles. The cycles of birth and death, of the disintegration into the earth and the arising of new life from the earth, the rise and fall of dynasties, of nations, of civilizations, of species all tend, to support this view. Why should the development of man alone in the universe follow a straight path from slightly differentiated living matter to miraculously complex intelligent forms and proceed forever in a linear manner to further and further progress? Is it not more probable that his destiny, like that of everything else, is to follow a circular course, and that as he approaches an apogee, the forces of life will spin him back to his beginnings?[63]

The theory of catastrophism, like chaos theory, is a 'controversial new way of thinking about change – change in a course of events, change in an object's shape, change in a system's behaviour, change in ideas themselves'.[64] Professor Rene Thom of France's Institute for Advanced Scientific Studies proposed a mathematical explanation of the processes of change. While science can explain gradual change, it has never been able to describe spontaneous change, where discontinuity is the rule. Changes of form (in processes as well as in objects) are real, and the aim of science is to grasp the universal 'ceaseless creation, evolution and destruction of forms'.[65] Number has two functions, and the mathematics and geometry of catastrophe theory are qualitative rather than quantitative, which allows a description of the similarities between tree branching patterns, a river system, and a nerve cell. Thom believes that the qualitative features of all natural processes are recurrent, an assumption not shared by science generally. Thom recognizes the inherent stability of physical systems that continuously pursue a process of change throughout their lives. He compares the genetic legacy of each individual with its necessary parallel in the ecological stability of the species.

Invoking Lyell, scientists assume that two experiments can produce the same quantitative results, but they cannot, because the circumstances can never be reproduced, nor can external influences be eliminated. The Earth moves hundreds of thousands of miles through space and time every day through the movement of the solar system through time. The requirement that experiments be reproducible is a central fallacy of modern science, and Thom's goal is to describe qualitatively repeatable observations and through them the origin of forms, which process he calls 'morphogenesis', the same term later used by the radical Cambridge biologist Rupert Sheldrake.

Morphogenesis includes 'mind' in its frame of reference as the most complex system – by definition, because it must be at least one degree more complex than that which it perceives or imagines. Our concepts are mathematical models or topological maps of universal processes, which we use to shape our world. Catastrophe theory is a way of leaving behind the static reality of Newton and entering the relativistic world beyond, which Thom calls 'the landscapes of change'.

C H Waddington, a palaeontologist, embryologist, geneticist and evolutionist, realized in investigating the development of species through time that the contours of the landscape of change are multidimensional. Biochemistry alone cannot explain morphogenesis – he wanted a theory that would topologically describe biological forms. Thom at that time (1962) was developing a model that created a mathematical 'cross-section in time' of an integrated process. All genetically governed beings follow the same stable pathways and 'every organism's form represents a partial record of the processes of development and metabolism'.[66]

Thom formulated seven elementary catastrophes and many mini-catastrophes inherent in every system, any of which could potentially incite the whole system to jump from one state to another. The great conceptual leap is that different systems, at different scales, could have similar processes of change but different sets of causes. Basic structural geometric patterns recur in many processes in nature. Sudden and forced systemic change happens in atomic structure when one knocks electrons out of inner electron rings and outer electrons rapidly jump from ring to ring to fill up the missing inner spaces. Packets of energy (quanta) exhibit similar qualities of rapid change when stressed instead of smoothly changing nature through the spectrum of energy.[67]

Catastrophe Theory is a paradigm that may be applied to many areas, such as biology, sociology, psychology, behaviour, mechanics, politics, economics and other processes. 'The old idea of Man, the microcosm, mirroring the world, the macrocosm, retains all its force.'[68] The inclusion of these ideas with astrology, metaphysics and psychology yields The Divine Plot and Life Time Astrology.

The Changing Scientific View

Sir William Ramsay's work related perception to time and eternity. As we undergo mental transformations, we imagine worlds – that is to say, we construct mental cosmologies.[69] The universe is in our mind and may *be* our mind. According to the level at which the universe is perceived, greater and greater dimensions of actualization become available. There are recurrent mental cycles and recurrent universes as we recreate them every time we imagine them. Our universes are successive layers of perception reached during our inner journey, reflecting successive layers of what we perceive to be the physical world. The only obstacles to transcending the temporal universe are therefore within us.

A new understanding of the world is emerging that echoes eastern religious and western mystical cosmologies. Since the time of Newton, the scientific method has maintained an empirical approach to the universe, verified by repeatable experiments, evaluated statistically. Science requires objective observers and the separation of the object or event observed from the whole within which it exists. It is now clear that there is no such thing as an objective observer because the observer is inseparable from what he or she observes. No part can be isolated from the whole in the way required by science. As an example, the light required to observe subatomic events itself alters the sensitive structure and nature of the events. The presence of a measuring device itself alters what it measures. Similarly, optical microscopes show images in their own form, rather than seeing a small object for us. We see the optics rather than the object.

The physicist Werner Heisenberg demonstrated that the observer alters the observed by the act of observation, and the consciousness of the observer affects degree of that alteration. Mind can and does affect space and time because the space-time continuum is a product of the mind that perceives it. The traditional view of the world as a 'great machine' is changing to the world as a 'great thought'. Scientific laws that describe events in the large-scale macro-world do not adapt or work in the micro-world. Scientists can predict the behaviour of groups of particles or events, but cannot observe one particle and its movements. Either the macro-world has different laws than the micro world, as many suggest, or science is making a profound mistake, which is what I believe. What if the continuity of measurement is at fault? It is using additive series to link logarithmically disparate worlds. Scientists are forced to subscribe either to the statistical quantum mechanical view of reality or the causal reality of Einstein, but the true state of affairs includes both, and must be able to describe both.

Scientists searching for successive generations of elementary particles, believing that their mechanisms determine the nature of the universe, are only belatedly discovering that matter is ultimately composed of patterns of energetic events. We cannot break the universe down into isolated parts, but must understand it as a whole. The relative perspective that enlivens each cosmos provides a unification missing from even the New Physics.

Particles are patterns of energy in constant movement, interaction, and transformation, and the universe is a web of relations rather than an accumulation of particles. In the past matter and mind were understood as mutually exclusive rather than integrated, as they are in Eastern religions or Western mysticism. Mind affects space and time, and in a very basic way the whole space-time continuum is a product of the mind that perceives it, a concept that has led to great confusion inside and outside science.

Measure, Meditation and Maya

For the Holy One hath weighed the world (aeon) and with measure hath he measured the times, and by numbers he hath numbered the seasons, neither will he rest nor stir until the number be fulfilled.

Esdras Gospel, Nag Hammadi Texts[70]

David Bohm worked with Einstein and states that to take any physical theory as an absolute is to fragment knowledge about the universe, because the mere act of so doing differentiates one from the universe. The solution is for the observer and the observed to become 'merging and interpenetrating aspects of one whole reality, which is indivisible and unanalysable'.[71] We must view the world as a universal flux of events and processes. The nature of the world is historical process. The world is a whole in which we, as the observer, occupy the central place amid the formation and dissolution of energy and life. We must search for formative causes or overall patterns of reality, the structure and order that underlies what is, as distinct from the atomistic and fragmentary view of the modern sciences, empirical psychology and biology, where a mechanistic rationale for life is sought in the structure and function of DNA molecules. Although DNA is admittedly powerful in its functions, what made it in the first place? DNA is virtually identical in the earliest organisms from the earliest life a billion years ago as modern human DNA. How can this be?

Thus we arrive at the very odd result that in the study of life and mind, which are just the fields in which formative cause acting in undivided and unbroken flowing movement is most evident to experience and observation, there is now the strongest belief in a fragmentary approach to reality.[72]

The fragmentation of the modern world influences social, political, economic, ecological and psychological crises in individuals and society. We even convert so-called 'holistic' principles into absolute knowledge rather than as theories of perception.

Bohm states that notions of measure play a key role in determining a world view. Instead of measure as an objective standard unit, measure has a deeper significance as an indicator of conformity to harmonious reality. The deeper sense of measure is as a proportion or ratio acting in universal relationships. To understand ratio is to understand the innermost beauty of something, its essence in time. The words medicine, moderation and meditation all have the Latin root, which means 'to measure'. A meditator creates a quieting process where fragmentation diminishes and unification is encouraged. Inner measure is necessary in healthy, spiritual life. Measure in Greece and Rome was the underlying harmony of the world as expressed in music, art and architecture. The notion of measure as a human quality was expressed by Pythagoras as 'man is the measure of all things'.

In the West, measure has been desacralised by a science and technology dependent on measurement, while the Eastern focus is on the immeasurable qualities of religion and philosophy. The idea that only what is measurable is real is a fallacy, but measure can help bring about order and harmony when treated by the wise. The Sanskrit word meaning 'measure' is the root of 'Maya', the illusion of reality. The integration between East and West, religion and science, lies with the integration of opposite and contradictory ways of experience. Bohm beautifully states that the original and creative insight within the field of measure is the action of the immeasurable.[73]

It is important to distinguish between number as quantity or as a Platonic idea – two oranges is a measurement of quantity, while the meaning of the number two as duality is immeasurable. Numbers are meaningful carriers of patterns and proportions, as well as being quantities of objects. The Greeks had a word for the two equivalent aspects of time: 'chronos' is objective and quantitative, while 'kairos' is subjective and qualitative.[74]

Number is a device used to organize the world. In school, the significance of the dates of events often means more than the events themselves. To historians, Western European history is linear and has no rhythm or proportion, but in the East, history is seen as circular, recurrent, and relative.

Spengler mentions the rarely noted opposition between 'chronological' and 'mathematical' number. In the time scale I present, number is the guiding force in history, but it does not correlate to the 'years' BC and AD to which we attach events. It was only in AD525 that Dionysius Exiguus proposed the AD sequence, and as recently as 1681 Brossuet suggested the idea of BC years. The accepted system of identifying dates has not been in operation for long. The Jewish calendar measures time in lunar months, and Moslems measure their lunar years from the Hegira of Mohammed in AD622. The latent measurement of history enables a different perspective on historical facts, what they signify, what they point to and how they relate harmonically to other facts and times.[75] Spengler states that:

> *Morphological relationships inwardly bind the expression-forms of all branches of a Culture. Beyond politics, these relationships allow us to grasp the ultimate and fundamental ideas of Greeks, Arabians, Indians and Westerners in mathematics; the meaning of their early ornamentation; the basic forms of their architecture, philosophies, dramas and lyrics; their choice and development of their arts, the details of their craftsmanship and choice of materials. We can uniquely appreciate the decisive importance of these matters for the form-problems of history.[76]*

In Spengler's terms, there is no theory-enlightened technique of historical treatment beyond the realm of physical cause and effect, and physics has never addressed itself nor been applied to history. By the standards of physicists or mathematicians, historians are careless about the way in which they assemble and order their material and pass on to interpretation. Kant restricted himself to establishing rules governing the relationship between human cognition and the world: for him, knowledge is mathematical knowledge. Kant never applied his categories of consciousness to the historical process, nor did Schopenhauer, who utilized the Kantian categories and spoke contemptuously of history. Both limited themselves to understanding cause and effect. Few of the great individuals of history have even attempted a synthesis such as Spengler proposes, although many would have liked to. Spengler identified other necessities, such as the 'logic of space', which is the organic necessity of life, called Destiny, and the 'logic of time', which suffuses mythological religions and artistic thought and constitutes the kernel of all history, but is unapproachable through Pure Reason. Spengler stated in 1926 that the theoretical formulation of these new logics was still to come. We will try to apply a mathematical order to history that fits the conditions of Spengler.

The Form-Creating Mechanism

Our 'being' exists through a series of events in life, changes of form and phase, yet we retain our identity, even though change is the essence of life. The historical process reflects a continual transmutation of self as it seeks manifestation in the world. Adam and Eve in Eden are symbolic of the original male and female reality. The transformation is from mythological deities to god-heroes sired by the gods and humans, to heroes with god like attributes, to hereditary kings and queens descended from the gods, to humans with heroic qualities, then finally to components of the individual. The theme of the world is the awakening of individual consciousness and differentiation from nature.

Everyone relives the historical process in life, but the question is how we can learn from the fact. We inherit many strands of ancient, primordial historical reality encapsulated in our body, emotions, mind and spirit. The instinct to hunt, kill and survive remain: when suppressed, they are dangerous. In modern societies where the primitive has been outwardly eradicated, aggressive instincts find expression in vicarious violence: sport, war, pornography, television and cinema. The barbarism of wars, terrorism, religious fanaticism and racism are widespread examples. The urge results from hundreds of thousands of years of instinctive survival following millions of years of primate reality – the veneer of civilization is only a few thousand years old. Instincts precede individuality and are a shared base, regardless of race, religion, nationality and sex. What differentiates us is the way in which we express our common heritage and our closeness to the origin.

The memory of our past lives are stored in the brain, heliacal genetic code, body substance, soul and spirit – at every level of interaction with the universe. Esoteric knowledge describes levels as 'bodies' of increasing fineness and closeness to god. Every person has physical, emotional, mental and spiritual bodies. In each system, the number of such bodies and the terms used to describe them change, but the principle is clear in all systems. As we age, we naturally transfer awareness to higher and finer bodies. Thus, in gestation, the physical body is created within the mother, in childhood the emotional body is created within the home and family system, and in maturity the mental body is created within the world. If an individual is able to extend reality beyond the initial three bodies, a transpersonal or transcendent body is available. Each body encompasses the previous bodies as successive shells of reality. Our body may he represented as proportional interpenetrating circles and forming a link between heaven and earth.

The ascent through the bodies in life parallels the evolution of humanity. The earliest reality was physical; emotions evolved that differentiated humans from the animal world; mind evolved; and finally the realm of the spirit, out of which all arose, became the goal. All four bodies are inherent in us from the beginning. It is more a matter of utilizing each successive vehicle for experiencing the world than creating them. Complete reality is existence on all levels.

We do not know how and where memory is stored. There is increasing evidence that the brain is merely a receiving apparatus, rather than a receptacle for information. We know that we use only a small proportion of our brain – less than 10%. What the other 90% does is unknown. That control resides in brain centres can be demonstrated

Figure 9: Fludd's Microcosm reflecting the Macrocosm
The cosmic macrocosm reflects the human microcosm, which are bound together
by a spiral cord that resembles the DNA molecule and the spiralling solar system.
(From Robert Fludd, *Utriusque cosmi historia*, 1574)

when certain parts of the brain are damaged and an equivalent set of
bodily functions are impaired, but if the damage occurs at an early
enough age, other parts of the brain can take over the functions of the
damaged part. A strict localization is impossible.

The biologist Rupert Sheldrake proposes *A New Science of Life* that
supersedes the mechanistic view that the genetic code is the only form-
creating and guiding mechanism for organic life. His hypothesis of
Formative Causation states that every organism possesses a non-
physical morphogenetic (form-creating) field that organizes the
coming-into-being of its developing biological system. Specific
morphogenetic fields are responsible for the characteristic form and
organization of systems at all levels of complexity, not only in the

realm of biology, but also in the realms of chemistry and physics.[77]
Morphogenetic fields are ordered patterns derived from the field of
all past systems transmitted through a developing organism. The
genetic code acts like a computer program that requires the existence
of a programmer, implying that time and space structure physical and
chemical interactions. The 'interactionist' theory postulates that past
mental states influence properties of mind, rather than through the
physical storage of memory within the brain. Sheldrake's work
resonates with Jung's concept of a collective unconscious, and he
suggests an inherited collective memory containing archetypal forms.

Previous systems influence subsequent similar systems by morphic
resonance, acting through vibrational frequencies. Systems select, out
of a mixture of vibrations, the particular frequencies they need.[78] All
living systems, from atoms to organisms, have their own characteristic
vibrational rates and internal rhythms. The spatio-temporal pattern of
former systems superimposes a characteristic vibrational structure
onto present systems with a similar form. Resonance is non-energetic
and energy-less and mass-less; it could be 'just as effective over ten
thousand miles as over a yard, and over a century as an hour'.[79] Physical
form, character, instincts, and learning processes are influenced not
only from the past, but also from future systems that do not yet exist.

The principle such as morphic resonance carried through the
medium of time is central to the mechanism of The Divine Plot. The
effect of all past systems creates a matrix from which individual forms,
characteristics, and ways of learning derive their initial creation. The
gradation of time with an exponential time scale is a way to describe
developmental stages of time for an individual, the collective, the
physical universe as a whole and correlate them to stellar rhythms. The
fact that Sheldrake proposes a non-physical resonance that nonetheless
influences the development of all organisms refutes a primary
objection to astrology. Scientists have rejected astrology because there
is no physical or energetic explanation of its mechanism.

In recent years the concept of nonlocality in physics demonstrates
that information can be transmitted across vast distances in the
universe without an apparent physical explanation, which seems to
reinforce both astrology and morphic resonance. Astrology is a
language that may be transmitted by a process such as morphic
resonance, and in turn is a language that relates to the structure of
DNA and to planetary movements. Everything is a pattern in time.

> *This life is the way, the longest sought after, the way to the incomprehensible, which we call divine. There is no other way.*
>
> Carl Gustav Jung[80]

Chapter Four — Life Time Astrology

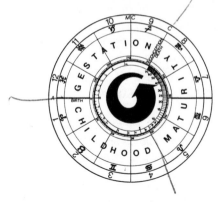

The most ancient system for integrating the cosmos with the individual is astrology. My work is a restructuring of contemporary astrology to include modern understanding of the universe, as described in my books, *The Round Art, Life Time Astrology, Astrology and the Art of Healing* and *A New Vision of Astrology*. Our starting point is the relativity of time that we experience every day.

Everyone knows that the earth orbits around our sun, a star suspended in space, and the moon orbits around the earth. Every year the earth returns to the same spot in its exorable path around the sun, just as every month the moon returns to its similar position in the sky. In reality, these statements are not true. The sun moves around the galactic centre at more three-quarters of a million kilometres per day, pulling the planets along with it, which is 20,000 kilometres per hour. The planets trace a spiral path around the moving sun – the inner planets spiral tightly and the outer planets tag along. The sun revolves around the centre of the Milky Way galaxy, currently at 28° of Sagittarius, in 250 million years and the entire flattened spiral galaxy itself moves through space. The simultaneous spiral, rotational and orbital movements of earth, sun and galaxy combine to propel us through space (and time) at an astonishing rate. It is shocking to picture such great movement while the tea on the table maintains its apparent stillness.

The astrological horoscope is an angular slice through this spiralling circus at a specific time and place of birth. Everyone lives within the same spiral but from different relative vantage points. The spiral projects backward into the past and forward into the future.

There is a formal connection between the movement of the solar system and the structure of the DNA molecule – they are both spirals. DNA encodes the knowledge of life in the galactic model. In Figure 10, the path of the sun is a straight line. When the path of earth is the central viewpoint, it is a spiral within the sun's apparent spiralling path.

The form of the resultant double spiral is similar to the genetic code
DNA that carries the mechanism of life and controls growth in time.
The 97% of so-called 'junk DNA' may carry a history of all humanity
encoded in its spiral form. The pattern of the solar system in time in
the macrocosm reflects the pattern of the DNA molecule in the
microcosm. In *Cosmic Cybernetics*, Dr Theodore Landscheit refers to
remarks by the physicist Jacques Bergier:

> *If Ducrocq, Hoyle, Narlikar and Costa de Beauregard are right, then the universe is
> just as well organized and functions just as precisely as a DNA molecule in the nucleus
> of the cell. Just as one has succeeded in discovering the genetic code, one should also
> be able to find the astronomical code. The communication of information is not
> restricted to living organisms; it is also an integral part of the universe, just as matter
> and energy are.*[81]

The DNA molecule bears the form pattern of every cell and the
entire organism of which the cell is a component, resonating with its
cosmos. When our parents mate, the genetic code of their offspring is
a combination of the separate genetic memories of the parents. The
'individual' is a set of characteristics defined by the gender, psychology,
physical appearance and many other qualities, derived from the
combined qualities of both parents, four grandparents, eight great-
grandparents, and so on. Through childhood, experiences resonate
with the basic genetic molecular coding. When the child becomes an
adult and reproduces, the second-generation offspring combines both
the inherited characteristics of the grandparents and the experiential
permutations derived from the parents' experiences. Every living being
carries previous lifetimes stored in the collective genetic memory
matrix. The differences between individuals are due to varying
emphasis within the same coding process.

The general characteristics of each species and the differences that
distinguish individuals from one another transmit modifications of
level and reproduction maintains them. For example, molecules are
self-replicating. A molecule experiences a life cycle of conception,
gestation, childhood, maturity and death, finally replicating copies to
replace itself in its own image. Such efficient reproduction ensures the
continuity of the organism – its continuing existence depends upon
repetition in time. Molecules parent other molecules in their own image
– molecules only make variations when errors occur. Molecules are
composed of atoms, so the replication of a molecule is when a parent
molecule organizes atoms in its own image, and when a molecule dies
(changing form is death in the molecular world) it reverts to free atoms.
All the molecules in our entire molecular body replicate, yet it takes

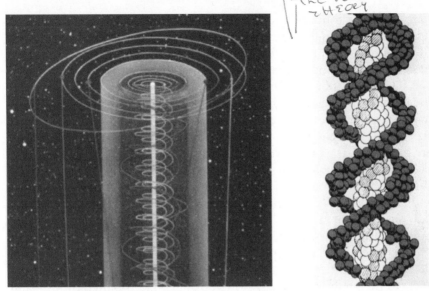

Figure 10: Spiral Solar System
The Sun's path is a core around which the planets spiral through time. A horoscope is a slice taken at the time of birth. On the right the DNA molecule resonates with the solar system as a similar form in time. Microcosm and macrocosm vibrate.

many cycles before there is any change apparent in the body as a whole. The eyes temporarily sag after a drinking bout, but recover 12 hours later. We continually die and are recreated repeatedly, breaking down into our constituent atomic and molecular parts and reassembling again. Yet in the life of the species, many generations of individuals repeat until there is any noticeable change and some parts of the population literally 'live in the past'. The millions of spiralling electronic impulses in a strand of DNA resonate with the movement of the entire galactic mechanism through time. The question is, how can we understand the cosmic process and apply it to our personal life?

Astrology is Knowledge of Time

The experiments in biological time of Pierre Lecomte du Noüy (1883-1949) are a foundation for the relationship between astrology and biology. During the First World War, de Noüy analyzed the rate at which wounds healed according to the age of the wounded, and discovered that metabolic processes, reflected in the rate at which the body consumes and processes oxygen in healing, slow down with age. The older the wounded man, the longer healing takes. He calculated that the apparent passage of time for a 20-year-old and 50-year-old man would be four and six times faster than for a five-year-old child.[82]

Biological time is the relationship between metabolism and perception. Metabolism is the rate at which an organism processes food and oxygen, based on relative body weight, respiration rate, food consumption and age. The perception of the passage of time is primarily determined by the number of images the brain receives in any given time period. When metabolism increases, the rate at which images are processed increases. If six images per second are normally processed, but in an excited state nine are processed, the brain overestimates duration and signals that one and one-half seconds have passed – it would feel like time is passing slowly. When metabolism decreases, we receive only three images per second and the brain underestimates the passage of time because it seems that only one half of a second has passed. As metabolic rate slows down, time appears to pass faster.[83]

At conception, the rapid 'molecular' time scale of the ovum determines our metabolic rate, until at death metabolism ceases. As we age, our metabolism gradually slows down, counterpointed by local and temporary modulations. This is why time seems to pass so slowly in childhood, but faster and faster as we age, until near death time passes so quickly that we cannot keep up with it. We can characterize youth and old age by fast and slow metabolic rates. Months in gestation seem like years in childhood and decades in maturity. Excitement and stimulation increase metabolism, temporarily inducing the time perception of youth, while boredom and depression decrease metabolism, like old age. We continually modify our time sense by internal and external stimuli including diet, sensory input, drugs, psychological and emotional states, and physiological factors.

Metabolic rate is proportional among organisms of differing sizes. Rodney Collin, basing his work on Gurdjieff and Ouspensky, found similar proportions between a lifespan and a breath for organisms at many different scales. He related Man, Nature, Earth, Sun and the Galaxy, and found that each cosmos had a similar mathematical relationship with the others. At each level of being, a lifetime and its speed seems to have the same relationship, whether a galaxy or an insect. A gnat has a lifetime of one day, but it lives its life 30,000 times faster than a human does. The gnat responds to information and perception at its accelerated time. Sound waves would be slow pulses, relative to the gnat's time. In spatial terms, when the gnat hears a human voice from the length of the garden, it comes from 1,700 miles away. The gnat moves at a speed close to the limit of human perception, but it sees a human as an almost immovable object. A gnat in a rainstorm perceives the particles of water moving at the same rate as we perceive the advance of a glacier. Air is liquid to them, and water is solid.

The psychology of memory is foreshortened according to the same mathematics as metabolism. We compare each present perception to the memory of all previous days of our life. With each passing day, more memories are added, and as we grow older the collection increases. Each day relates to the whole, yet also reflects and contains the whole. For example, the first day of life is $1/1$, or 100% of the whole, and influences registering then are very important. The second day of life is compared to memory of the first, making it $1/2$ of the lifetime. The third day is $1/3$, then $1/4$, $1/5$ and so on, until at one year old each day is $1/365$th of the whole, and at 30 years old each day is only $1/10,000$th of the whole. Each successive day is a smaller and smaller proportion of the whole life. As we age, time appears to contract, to compact and to pass more quickly. The mathematical expression describing the compaction of life in time is a logarithmic progression.

Life Time Astrology

The lifetime of a human ovum is one lunar month, and the average lifetime of the cellular body is 1,000 lunar months, or 77 years. The timescale of the ovum is 1,000 times faster than the timescale of a person at 77 years old, and the lifetime of the ovum is $1/1,000$th that of the cellular body.

A lifetime can be subdivided using a logarithmic scale to the base 10 with the lunar month unit. The sequence 1, 2, 3 and 4 of an additive scale equals 1, 10, 100 and 1,000 in a logarithmic scale. Intermediate divisions occur at 10 lunar months after conception (nine calendar months), at birth; at 100 lunar months after conception (seven years old), when the personality is formed and childhood is generally considered to be complete. The end of the process is death. The divisions create three developmental 'octaves' of life – Gestation, Childhood, and Maturity – that are unequal in calendar time but perceptually equal.

Conception	Birth	Childhood's End	Death
1 LM	10 LM	100 LM	1,000 LM

Gestation	Childhood	Maturity

During Gestation the physical Body is created within the mother. The fertilized ovum travels up the fallopian tube and attaches itself to the wall of the mother's uterus, where its further development ensues. During gestation we pass through many developmental stages directed by our genetic code, which guides the creation of our physical body. While we gestate we perceive everything our mother thinks, feels, senses and intuits, and there is a reciprocal communication from us to her. These earliest influences are integrated into our body.

At birth we are transferred to a new environment in the air. Childhood begins with the circumstances of birth, when gender, physical appearance, manner of delivery, the effects of those present and their actions combine to create our Personality. During the seven years of childhood our personality is created within the home and family system. As the circumstances of gestation determine physical reality, the circumstances of childhood determine emotional reality.

During Maturity we integrate our personality with our body and project their combination into the outside world to work out our various possibilities. Creation of the Soul is determined by an ability to act out our life objectives and to understand our being in time as a whole. As the Body is created within the mother and Personality within the family, the soul is the whole of life created within the world as a reflection of the universal process of all life. To identify with the soul is to transcend life.

The three octaves describe the transformation of personal reality and consciousness. Gestation is pre-personal and subconscious (collective unconscious), Childhood is personal and self-conscious, and Maturity is transpersonal and super-conscious. Throughout life we relive the evolution of consciousness of all humankind, from pure instinct to transcendence.

The triple octaves of Gestation, Childhood and Maturity occupy the circumference of the horoscope circle. The circular representation of logarithmic time grades the houses of your horoscope from conception to death and combines the mechanism of biological time with the astrological horoscope.

In our horoscope the Ascendant, which is equivalent to the birth moment, orients the octaves to the houses. When the three octaves are further divided into four parts each, the periods in our life when certain developments occur correspond to the succession of 12 houses in the horoscope. These astrologically defined phases exactly match the rigorously derived phases identified by the psychologist Piaget in his clinical studies (see Bibilography – Ruth Beard, *An Outline of Piaget's Developmental Psychology*). The meanings of the houses are derived from the developmental ages of the average person.

The houses are numbered in a counter-clockwise direction from our Ascendant. We must go backwards four houses in a clockwise direction to the cusp of the 9th house for conception. Ahead of the Ascendant four houses, at the cusp of the 5th house is seven years old, the end of childhood and the beginning of maturity. Maturity extends from the cusp of the 5th house to the cusp of the ninth house. Conception and death coincide at the ninth house cusp.

Conception and death, the beginning and end of life, seem unrelated to each other except as limits to life, but there is a profound connection between them. At conception the fertilized ovum links into a code, which determines the development of our entire life – our pattern in time as the formative cause of our existence. At that moment life is all potential. At the instant of death the entire life passes before our eyes in an instant; a dramatic replay of our whole life, which constitutes a 'last judgement'. At death our life is all actual as all its potential has been utilized. The principle that any moment between conception and death is a stage in the transference of potential to actual reality is essential to the analysis and interpretation of the horoscope. In the ancient world the beginning and the end were symbolized by Alpha and Omega, the first and last moments, and as the ouroburos snake forming a circle with its tail in its mouth. Both are symbols of the wholeness and eternity of life.

A traditional problem of astrology is that the sign Scorpio and the 8th house are attributed to death, but they are only two-thirds of the way through the sequence of signs and houses. Sagittarius and the ninth house are attributed to self-realization and rebirth. In the Life Time scale the borderline between the eighth and ninth houses is both the moment of conception and of death. The eighth house is the termination of life and the ninth house is the origin of life. Life is a circular process, where beginning and end are linked. To quote T S Eliot:

> *What we call the beginning is often the end*
> *And to make an end is to make a beginning.*[84]

When the logarithmically graded time scale wraps around a circle, conception coincides with death, closing the circle (see the diagram at the start of this chapter). At conception, the soul enters the space-time continuum and the spiralling solar system, leading to the creation of the astrological pattern that resonates with the genetic code as derived from its morphogenetic fields, and creates and maintains the physical body. The pattern activated at conception, of which the genetic code is the physical manifestation, determines the form of life in time, which is at this point 'all potential' – none of its actuality realized.

The life energy enters into the space-time continuum where it becomes subject to more rigid laws than in its previous domain of spirit, which signals an incarnation – birth onto the cross of matter and the wheel of karma. At death a life is all actual, all its potential has been utilized, and the identical code registers as a last judgement, flashing before the dying. All events in life are stages in the transformation of potential into actual reality.

When we superimpose this logarithmic time scale on the horoscope and subdivide it into 12 developmental stages, they are the 12 houses, the pattern of life in time. The positions of the planets describe:

- Events in life occurring at specific times from conception to old age;
- Archetypal and individual psychological mechanisms that determine character and behaviour;
- Influential persons in life and their equivalent inner mechanisms;
- Glands, organ systems and their release cycles;
- Mythic behaviour patterns resonating with us psychologically.

Integrating biological time with astrology creates a revolutionary picture of the whole life, based on mathematically derived principles; a valuable tool in psychotherapy, healing, psychiatry, the raising of children, in relationships, executive placement, and work on the self and individual awareness for personal growth.

We reconstruct the patterns and sub-patterns of life using the log time scale. The path around the periphery of the horoscope circle symbolizes the events and mechanisms of life activated at spiritual, psychological, emotional and biological levels, often simultaneously. We reconstruct the events of gestation, from the mother's point of view, and the long-forgotten events of early childhood, together with the people who participated in or caused them. We see both the outer environment and inner psychology in the horoscope in symbolic form. Life is cyclical and knowing the origin of behaviour patterns is a great help in understanding the present and future on multiple levels of consciousness. Life Time Astrology is an analytical tool and a way for making future projections.

The Signs of the Zodiac are symbols of a twelve-fold process of months in the year and developmental stages in life. The interpretation of the astrological horoscope is a description of your lifetime from conception to death, following the sequence of houses numbered from one to 12 in counter-clockwise direction. The sequence of houses is archetypal when the first sign Aries coincides with the 1st house. The following table shows the signs of the zodiac, their equivalent houses and seasons of the year, and the general characteristics that define them.

Table 2: The Zodiac Signs

♈ *Aries the Ram*   Cardinal Masculine Fire Sign   00°-30°
21 March to 20 April   Germinating time; unfolding energy. Self-assertion; initiatory energy; adventure; daring; impatience; the personality.

♉ *Taurus the Bull*   Fixed Feminine Earth Sign   30°-60°
20 April to 21 May   Invigoration and strengthening; form creation; preservation. Physical world; matter; fertility; security; finances; stewardship; form; endurance.

♊ *Gemini the Twins*   Mutable Masculine Air Sign   60°-90°
21 May to 22 June   Diversity; multiplication; vitality; adaptability. Instinctive mind; imitation; communication; duality; versatility; mobility; facility.

♋ *Cancer the Crab*   Cardinal Feminine Water Sign   90°-120°
22 June to 23 July   Mothering; fecundation; fertilization. Feeling; emotions; mother; home and family; the unconscious; dreams; protective urge.

♌ *Leo the Lion*   Fixed Masculine Fire Sign   120°-150°
23 July to 24 August   Ripening; summer heat; full energy; extraversion; harvest. Self-expression; personal love; games; pleasure; ruling; vanity; arrogance.

♍ *Virgo the Virgin*   Mutable Feminine Earth Sign   150°-180°
24 August to 23 September   Ripe fruit; orderly storage and collection; selection. Discrimination; work; perfectionism; health & hygiene; analysis; prudence; diet.

♎ *Libra the Balance*   Cardinal Masculine Air Sign   180°-210°
23 September to 24 October   Balance & adjustment; thanksgiving; social equilibration. Partnership; marriage; public relations; enemies; persuasion; sublimation; yielding.

♏ *Scorpio the Scorpion*   Fixed Feminine Water Sign   210°-240°
24 October to 23 November   Vegetation death; seedlife; survival; endurance. Death & regeneration; passion; separation; others; losses; inheritance; metaphysical.

♐ *Sagittarius the Centaur*   Mutable Masculine Fire Sign   240°-270°
23 November to 22 December   Hibernation; advent; inner life; meditation; expansion. Realization; higher mind; religion & philosophy; sport; freedom; action; rebirth.

♑ *Capricorn the Goat*   Cardinal Feminine Earth Sign   270°-300°
22 December to 20 January   Preservation; patience; reality; self-concentration. Perfected matter; ego objectives; organization; power; success; society; government.

♒ *Aquarius the Waterbearer*   Fixed Masculine Air Sign   300°-330°
20 January to 19 February Waiting; fasting; Lent; observation; planning; abstraction. Social consciousness; humanitarian; collective; progressive; cold; altruism; Utopian.

♓ *Pisces the Fishes*   Mutable Feminine Water Sign   330°-360°(0°)
19 February to 21 March Swelling seed; purifying rain; serenity; potential. Sensitivity; receptivity; self-sacrifice; psychic; karma; seclusion; hospital; dreaming.

The horoscope is the unfolding of life from its potential pattern. The ages of the beginning and end of the 12 houses in life are determined mathematically. They have an archetypal timing based on the average lifetime, but for every individual unique house durations and their appropriate ages are determined by the place, date and time of birth.

The ages at which the houses begin closely match the developmental phases identified by the psychologist Piaget and the stages in the evolution of consciousness as described by Ken Wilber in *Up From Eden*. In each house, all previous development is assimilated and integrated to higher levels of awareness and consciousness, and psychic energy is transferred to ever higher levels. Due to the mathematics of the logarithmic time scale, the duration of each house is almost equivalent to the entire preceding time from conception to the beginning of that house. Although each house is almost twice as long as its predecessor, it takes the same time to experience each one in turn. For example, the six-year time during which one experiences primary education in the 5th house from seven years old to 13 is almost equal to the entire preceding time back to conception.

The Process of Life

The Life Time Astrology time scale corresponds to and may be the root of the general house attributions of traditional astrology. Traditional astrology is restricted to perceptive character study or the investigation of psychological mechanisms in individuals, but the whole remains an enigma. The leap to a logarithmic biological time scale is like the change from the static Newtonian world view to Einstein's Relativity. As such it is important to understand the process of the time scale.

First, a logarithmic scale is unique because it does not begin with zero, but one. As soon as unity is reached, it can be seen to contain another smaller-scale whole. In the smaller numbers log scales approach but never reach zero, a fact that evokes the mystery of creation: the cellular body is created from the united ovum and sperm. It could not have been created from nothing, unless one accepts a Biblical idea of spontaneous creation. The mathematical properties of logarithms are critical in Life Time Astrology and The Divine Plot.

All ova exist in the mother *in potentia* within weeks of her own conception, passed down directly from her mother, all the way back in the first ovum. This process parallels the transmission of matriarchal mitochondrial DNA. Each ovum is directly connected to the first life and is therefore eternal. During gestation the ovum repeats the metamorphosis of all life through the evolutionary scale, which is therefore the collective property of all humans. We carry the history of life within every cell in our bodies.

The Ascendant sign of the zodiac on the eastern horizon at birth is the starting point of life. In Life Time Astrology the birth moment does not begin life, because conception point is moment of creation.

The beginning of the 9th house and the sign Sagittarius is the conception-creation point in individual life.

Life is a process that has a definite duration: it begins with conception and ends with death. In order to understand what life means, we must realise that it is a Process in Time. Every intermediate moment in life from conception to death is a stage in the transformation of our potential into actual reality. The sequence of 12 houses in our horoscope describes this process.

Within each of the three developmental stages in life, there are four intermediate houses. The 12 houses describe the transformation of life energy and reality. During each house in turn we work to fulfil the demands of an appropriate development, then move on to the next developmental stage. Our energies are continually transferred into more complex and more challenging channels as we age. When opportunity is rejected or misunderstood, the focus shifts backwards on earlier stages about which we know and within which we are comfortable. Regression is a return to the habits and attitudes of an earlier time in life: if we cannot extend our involvement in the world, we retreat and channel it into something to which we do have access. When marriage (7th house) is too challenging, there is a regression to the competition of secondary school (6th house); or when a child finds the demands of elementary school (5th house) overwhelming, there is a regression to the baby talk and thumb-sucking of early home life (3rd house). Regressions are not always permanent, but the principle operates in us all.

The duration of each house in sequence mirrors its importance in life, as they successively occupy more time. The houses in gestation last weeks, while in maturity they last decades. Life is cumulative and as we age, memories of all past experiences accumulate within our psyche, whether we are able to recall them or not. The experience of each house is built on a foundation of experiences from all previous houses, so we must remember earlier developments and incorporate them into new attitudes. The old is never discarded, but becomes the foundation of the new.

The mathematics of the time scale is such that each house in turn is almost equal in duration to the entire preceding time, from the beginning of the house all the way back to conception. There is a proportion approaching unity between the house we are in right now and our entire life up to the beginning of that house.

We all pass through the same sequence of developmental stages. Of course, mechanisms learned and formed in each stage can happen out of sequence, and the ages at which the houses begin vary from person to person.

Since we all develop at varying rates, the following table shows the Archetypal Ages of the houses presented average ages. The positions of the house cusp positions in our horoscope determine the exact duration of the developmental times to which they correspond. For simplicity, we should understand the average times and process first; then the real variations in timing may be applied to our horoscope.

Table 3: The Archetypal Ages of the Houses

House	Archetypal Ages	ASC+°	Key Words
	GESTATION		
9th	Conception to + 7wks	240°-270°	Mother's self-realization
10th	+ 7wks to + 12wks	270°-300°	Recognition of conception
11th	+ 12wks to + 22wks	300°-330°	Idealism and planning
12th	+ 22wks to Birth	330°-360°	Isolation and sacrifice
	CHILDHOOD		
1st	Birth to 7mths	0°-30°	Personality and self-assertion
2nd	7mths to 1yr 8mths	30°-60°	Physical sensory reality
3rd	1yr 8mths to 3yrs 6mths	60°-90°	Mobility and communication
4th	3yrs 6mths to 7yrs	90°-120°	Home and family emotional system
	MATURITY		
5th	7yrs to 13yrs	120°-150°	Self-consciousness and education
6th	13yrs to 23yrs 5mths	150°-180°	Discrimination and health
7th	23yrs 5mths to 42yrs	180°-210°	Partnership and world affairs
8th	42yrs to Death	210°-240°	Separation, metaphysics, death

When the horoscope is divided into 12 houses using the time-based Placidean House system, each house registers at a specific age. Houses smaller than an equal 30 degrees show developmental phases that are compacted, while larger houses show longer than average times of development.

The Ascendant sign at birth determines the sequence of signs and their relationships to the stages of our life. In the beginning just knowing the ascending sign in a horoscope is enough to describe the stages of a life accurately. Eventually it is critical to know which part of a sign is on the Ascendant as a fine-tuning mechanism.

The Ascendant defines the relationship between the horizon and the zodiac. The rotation of house ages and 12 sign qualities shows the permutations of viewpoint available to us. It is possible to have any of the 12 signs in any of the houses, but the sequence of signs and houses remains the same. Each house is occupied by one, two or three signs, depending on its length. For example, the 5th house is the time from seven years old to 13 years old and is occupied by the signs Pisces and

Figure 11: Life Time Astrology
When the time scale is wrapped around the horoscope, each planet can be dated from
conception to old age. Here is the archetypal alignment with Aries corresponding to
the 1st house, Taurus the 2nd, and so on. In actual horoscopes the houses are
unequal and the ring of signs and houses rotate against each other uniquely.

Aries. The Pisces part of this house, up to the age of 10 years old,
shows feelings of isolation and sacrifice at school, but when Aries
begins at 10 years old, there is an increase in personality strength and
self-assertion. The qualities of the signs are adapted to the times of the
houses and their archetypal developmental objectives. Aries qualities
produce self-assertion at the time in life when its sign registers. In the
7th house it would affect partnerships, in the 11th house it would affect
planning and idealistic attitudes.

If we have Aries on the Ascendant at birth, we experience the
sequence of houses in synchronization with the traditional signs, as
Aries is on the Ascendant at sunrise on the Spring Equinox.

Throughout life developmental phases would be archetypal. We would have earthy Taurean characteristics in its natural time of seven months old to one year, eight months old, and Libran balancing qualities in the 7th house time of partnership. With the opposite sign Libra ascending, each house would be occupied by its opposite sign quality. This would describe a character associated with Libra – that is, balancing qualities, equilibrium and partnership.

In the following description of the archetypal sequence of the 12 houses we must understand that everyone experiences variations of the same sequence. We all make use of the same set of cyclical qualities, but at different times in our lives and for different durations.

The signs that occupy each house are the primary influence on our character. They carry the quality that provides the background framework of the developmental stages. The second factor is the planets in residence which further qualify the meaning of the houses. The more planets in one house, the more complex and important is the corresponding time in life. The planets are influences we receive from other people, mechanisms within ourself, and the relationship between the two. The planets catalyze an event that binds a developmental age, signified by the house, to the quality described by the sign. The precise role of the planets will be discussed later.

The Process of Life begins at conception, the only true beginning of life. The importance of this earliest time of life cannot be overstated. All other astrological systems, even those which attempt to grade the horoscope circle, do not even mention conception and gestation, much less recognize their importance in interpretation and in life (see the systems of Dane Rudhyar and Bruno Huber). Most current psychological theories ignore development prior to birth. As a result, the description of the events of gestation initially seems foreign, although women who have had children understand easily. The feminine perspective is essential to wholeness.

We are conceived by our parents, carried within our mother for about 10 lunar months and then born. All autonomic and regulatory body systems are created during gestation; the influences we receive are incorporated into our physical body and affect us always.

The function of the Process of Life is to describe life through time, but very few individuals ever contemplate the reality of their lives in this way. The only time we are likely to do so is just before we die.

Most of us are trapped within a present moment, which knows neither past nor present as we have forgotten the past and dread the future. While 'live in the present' sounds a profound statement, our life is a process. To attain a larger perspective and to transcend time, we must understand the peaks and troughs, the incidents that counterpoint the ebb and flow, and the people who interweave their lives in ours. To be whole, we must reconstruct our life from conception to the grave.

(For ease of understanding, the zodiac sign that corresponds to each house is shown in brackets.)

The Octave of Gestation

The Octave of Gestation begins with conception on the ninth cusp and ends at birth on the Ascendant (first cusp), during which time the body is created within the mother. During gestation the foetus repeats the entire evolutionary process from a one-celled ovum to being fully human at birth. Hereditary characteristics from the parents combine to determine the qualities, shape and health of the body. In gestation influences are transmitted through the mother to the developing child and are carried somatically within the physical body.

9th house   **(Sagittarius the Centaur)**

Conception until seven weeks after conception
(Higher mind, meditation, religion and law, long journeys, foreign influences, philosophy, psychology, initiation, self-realization.)

During the fertilized ovum's lifetime of one lunar month, the time scale is molecular and the entire pattern of our life in time has registered. The three spiral germ layers of the ovum form a pattern similar in time to the three major developmental stages or Octaves of our cellular life. In fact the lifetime of the ovum is a microcosm of our lifetime, compressed 1,000 times.

By the end of the first lunar month, the fertilized ovum has travelled up the fallopian tube into the mother's uterus and attached itself to the uterine wall. By the end of this house our major bodily systems are fully operative, the liver can process waste and the embryo technically becomes a foetus.

The medical profession assumes that a mother cannot know of her child's existence until at least 38 days after conception. Obviously, many women know that they are pregnant soon after, if not at, conception. The more sensitive a mother is to the subtle energies of her psyche and body, the greater the likelihood that she will have discovered her baby's existence early on in the 9th house, and the more sensitive her child is to these influences.

A mother has already begun a dramatic hormonal transformation that changes not only her body but her life. All her attitudes register on us during this time: the way in which she realized that something was happening, what symbolism her thoughts took, who she turned to for verification and the overall quality of these circumstances provide a key to our own orientation mechanism within the world. A mother's attitudes towards religion, parental wisdom and individual philosophy during this first phase of gestation are very intense and important, as the women's movement recognizes.

The 9th house is the ability to orient oneself within the world as a reflection of our mother's realization of our existence.

The Midheaven (MC)
Seven weeks after conception or 33 weeks before birth
The Midheaven (MC) registers at approximately 49 days after conception. By this time the development of our bodily components is essentially complete: sex is determined, the face is fully human, features are recognizable, and we live and move within the amniotic fluid. Around the forty-eighth day the first true bone cells replace our cartilege skeleton. When this physical development is reached, a mother becomes aware that she is pregnant.

Hindus and Buddhists believe that the soul enters the physical body 49 days after conception. The now human body accepts its karma (traces of past lives), a metaphor for its genetic inheritance and astrological pattern in time which has become tangible. During this first stage of gestation the early brain components, the R-complex, the limbic system and the neocortex are developed, recapitulating their historical sequence.

The MC is our ego and is symbolized by the position of the Sun at noon, when it is hottest and brightest. The ego is the centre of consciousness, our objectives in life and our ability to exercise will in life. It is the focus of all conscious activity. The quality, strength and complexity of our ego is determined by the sign of the MC and the planets in aspect to the MC. When the MC is in Gemini, for example, our objectives are often doubled; when in Capricorn, they are practical and material; when in Leo, they are speculative; when in Pisces, they isolate us or expose us to external influences. Planets near or in aspect to the MC show objectives we manifest.

Before this time even if a mother intuits or dreams that she is pregnant, she does not know for sure. The moment of verification is distinctive as a differentiation of our foetal reality and her own consciousness. A mother becomes conscious of her child in the same way that we become conscious of ourself. Whether she makes this discovery as a result of her own realization, requires outside opinions or doesn't trust herself, are all metaphors for our own route to self-discovery in life.

10th house   (Capricorn the Goat)
7 weeks until 12 weeks after conception
(Perfected matter, concrete relationships, organization, father, public affairs, fame and fortune, ambition, aspirations, pragmatism.)
By the time our mother has realized the fact of our existence, we are a miniature version of our grown self in many ways – development during the 10th house is quite mechanical, as are our movements.

The 10th house is traditionally our parents and often begins with our father being told of our existence. Our mother announces the change in her life, the adoption of new physical conditions and begins to prepare the environment for the new arrival. Practical matters to be handled at this time include the choice of doctor or midwife, dietary and physical regimes, whether to deliver in hospital or at home, mechanically or naturally. There are many decisions to be made, adjustments in life-style to be considered and practical issues to be confronted.

All our parents' concerns foreshadow our ability to make arrangements and our way in the world. When our mother is reluctant to tell our father about her pregnancy, it will follow that we resist making ogur creative objectives known to the world. When our parents broadcast the fact, we will expect great publicity to attend our life objectives. A neutral response would imply little impact on the outer world and little direction. If our parents did not want us at all, we will feel threatened by the world. The realizations and actions that follow can range from open to totally suppressed, and from natural to superficial. An instrumentally determined pregnancy would predispose us to a life influenced by machines. The way our mother deals with our existence determines our attitude towards life objectives.

The 10th house is our ability to confront reality as determined by our parents' reactions to the discovery of our existence and their subsequent actions.

11th house   (Aquarius the Waterbearer)
12 weeks until 28 weeks after conception
(Altruism, selflessness, humanitarianism, idealism, planning, friends, group relationships, social matters, abstraction.)

At the beginning of the 11th house, movements change from being marionette-like mechanical actions to being graceful and fluid. The increasing rhythm of these movements coincides with the 'quickening', when the mother recognizes the movements within. The placenta is of primary importance now as an intermediary between the mother's body and the foetus. None of the mother's bodily systems directly exchange with that of the baby – rather, the placenta exchanges carbon dioxide for oxygen, waste for nutriments and provides minerals, vitamins and hormones for foetus and mother. The umbilical is a closed loop carrying separate blood and the vessels filter out large cells, unwanted whole protein and bacteria (see Bibilography – Flanagan, *The First Nine Months*).

The middle period of gestation is occupied with plans. Our mother projects all possible variants of gender, appearance, character and life onto us, running through infinite possibilities one after the other. The variety and breadth of her viewpoint reflects our increased movements inside her. Practical matters have been largely resolved, the reality of the pregnancy has been accepted, but limitations of activity and increased size do not occur until the end of this time. The mother is in a unique position to free herself from the outer world and focus on her inner world. Her relationships become less sexual due to the natural satisfaction of her state, and she creates and maintains altruistic friendships with those around her. Talking with other women who have carried and birthed children benefits her and may culminate in an interest in groups and organizations that teach, assist, comfort and understand her state, feelings and thoughts. Her responses to the possibilities of this time can range from ignorance of any relationship at all to a profound recognition of the interconnections permeating every step in the gestation process. She can focus on herself or on the universal state of childbearing and birthing.

Towards the end of this house she not only feels different than others, but is physically, emotionally and mentally separate from her former self. This can lead to a unique understanding of others, compassion and sympathy for people in general and progressive thinking, all transmitted to us.

The 11th house is our ability to abstract and detach ourself from the physical world and ascend into the realm of ideas and plans.

12th house   (Pisces the Fishes)

28 weeks after conception until birth
(Self-sacrifice, extreme receptivity, psychic activity, sensitivity, karma, destiny, escapism, institutions, isolation, loneliness.)

At this time our mother begins to gain weight, which in turn restricts her mobility. The amniotic fluid is exchanged regularly while it cushions us, supports us, facilitates exercise and evens our temperature. We live within this watery capsule totally protected from the outside world. Our mother becomes more and more dependent and her sensitivity to external influences increases as psychic contact with us increases.

As birth approaches, the self-sacrificial element of the 12th house is stronger. Examinations by doctor or midwife become more regular, as does the realization that birth itself is approaching. As our mother's psychic faculties, fantasies and dreams are all in full operation, total absorption in birth is complete. While husband, friends, midwife, doctor and other children support her, she realizes that she will give birth alone. The acceptance and release of her deepest instincts coincides with our final development. The inability of the uterus to expand any further begins pre-delivery time. Our mother is totally alone, yet carries us within her. Her choices of birth technique and circumstances reflects our later reliance on or independence from the inner life or the outer life. The more she bypasses her own instincts and relies on mechanical direction, the weaker our instinctual contact will be.

The last eight weeks of gestation are particularly important because the 10 degrees immediately above the Ascendant are the hidden elements of our personality; those influences, dreams and fantasies that lie or even remain just near the surface of consciousness. The mechanism is derived from the distortion of the Sun at sunrise. Instinctive maternal responses represent the best possible outlet for these influences, and natural birth tends to allow these instincts their proper role. With the end of this house, the Octave of Gestation is complete and our transition into an independent existence in the air follows.

The 12th house is the relationship between forces acting on us from outside and our inner psychic attitudes.

The Octave of Childhood

The Octave of Childhood is from birth until about seven years old, when the personality is created within the home and family system. Planets in childhood are mechanisms of behaviour learned from or projected onto parents, family, brothers and sisters, and others who affect the development of the personality. Personality is an emotional body composed of instincts, feelings and values. Childhood is related to the early development of consciousness when humanity was still integral to the natural world.

Ascendant or Rising Sign – Birth

The Ascendant registers when the first breath is drawn at birth. The manner of birth and its implications determine the way in which personality functions. The body which formed during gestation is tangible and physical, but personality – the essence of which is formulated at birth and develops throughout childhood – is a process. It is a mask that contains instincts, habits, mannerisms, expressions and fantasies, and is our vehicle of adaptation to the world.

Personality is determined by the nature of our birth, physical appearance, gender, and the actions and projections of those people present or affecting the birth from a distance. The zodiac sign on our Ascendant shows the atmosphere and attitude existing in the birth environment. Cancer shows warmth, maternal influences and emotional reactions as environmental and then personal qualities. Scorpio shows separations in birth and subsequent treatment. Taurus determines a totally physical view of birth and of the personality. (A complete listing of signs on the Ascendant and its influences appears later.)

Planets near the Ascendant show people apart from the mother who are present and become direct components of one's personality. Often sub-personalities are derived from the delivering doctor, young anaesthetist, worried grandfather or pushy grandmother. Planets in aspect to our Ascendant show people who have an indirect influence on our birth. If the aspecting planet is below the horizon, the influence on our personality is unconscious; if it is above the horizon, it is conscious. These influences might emanate from a nervous father at home or younger children wondering what was happening. All the influences coming directly from those present and those making distant projections determine the sub-personalities we possess. Once these influences have been identified, we can discover exactly who these individuals were.

As personality is a process, the process of birth itself is a key to understanding the Ascendant. When birth is rapid and easy, the resultant personality manifests itself fluidly both in short and long-term situations in life. Whether in the local pub or in lifelong working associations, personality flows easily. A difficult labour, which requires great effort by the mother, produces a hardworking personality. The longer and harder the labour, the more stress and strain on the personality. When a doctor or midwife must help delivery, our personality requires assistance from others to assert itself. When birth is accomplished by forceps or caesarean section, we require the physical intervention of another (doctor) to allow our personality to function. When an entire team of doctors and hospital staff is necessary, the resultant personality needs collective situations for awakening personality, such as mass movements, gurus or religious revivals. The more people present at a birth, the greater the collective influences on the personality.

In addition to the physical conditions of delivery, our attitudes are determined by the reactions to our birth and to us of those present. Modern birth movements stress the importance of who is present at birth and the general atmosphere of all births. Anaesthetics, local or general, produce numbness, vagueness or great sensitivity to certain influences. Induction exposes our personality to an overstimulation by external forces and generates a compulsive attitude. We would feel that others were compelling us through external circumstances to emerge from within, before our time. These birth 'complications' are interventions in what should be, but rarely is, a natural process. The medical profession has accepted and encouraged such intervention as routine, and as a result is implicated in problematic and violent personalities exhibited by many people today. The degree and manner of involvement of those present at our birth determines the closeness or detachment of our personality to others. If the doctor was hurrying things along so that he could play golf, our personality would reflect this by continually rushing into self-expression.

The Ascendant also governs the personality aspects of physical appearance, gender and initial health. When the mother is surrounded by her family and friends, there are many sympathetic supporters who respond to us at birth. Reactions to our gender and appearance should be various and full, although in institutional births these responses are lacking. The closer we are to others at birth, the more related we feel to our gender and body.

The implications of birth and subsequent treatment have such a profound influence on one's whole life-view that attitudes towards childbirth affect entire generations of children. Natural methods and the increasing awareness of women and men create natural awareness in children. Rigid, suppressive, assembly-line birth techniques produce zombies and disaffected youth.

The Ascendant is our personality, which is derived from the manner of our birth and the influences of those participating in and surrounding it.

1st house (Aries the Ram)

Birth until seven months old
(Self-assertion, the personality, shape and appearance of the physical body, early family environment, independence, selfishness)
The 1st house is the time during which we assert ourself in the world. Primary concerns are nourishment, warmth and attention. The ability to communicate these needs, the difficult and harmonious adaptations we experience, and our treatment within hospital and home, determine our ability to assert ourselves during life. If we are coddled, watched and surrounded by a supporting family and parents, we expect such

support throughout life. During this time of mother-child bonding, if we are rejected and left in the back room, we feel isolated whenever we try to assert our personality.

During this time we are not free to move your own body and others must see to our wants, which are basic and self-oriented. As we do not focus light properly until about three months old, we identify others on an energetic level, then on a visual level, accepting those who satisfy our needs. Our instinctive reactions to mother, father and others are related directly to satisfaction, and our personality reflects these external influences.

Since personality is an adaptive mechanism, the primary activity during this time is to adapt to life. Our instincts have total domain and gratification must be immediate. The 1st house is the ability to assert one's personality within the family.

2nd house   (Taurus the Bull)

Seven months until one year, eight months old
(Physicality, undifferentiated matter, pure substance, the senses, perception, security, property)

In the 2nd house we are immersed and imbedded in the physical world. Our body is a primary object and everything is investigated as it enters our space. Objects are tasted, touched, observed and put down. Often this stage begins when we are weaned from mother's milk and begin taking solid food. Our focus is centred on pure sensation, before the subject-object split in perception which characterizes the next house.

As bodily control increases, the range of sensations is extended. Bad tastes, unpleasant odours and textures are rejected and good tastes and pleasant sensations are appreciated. Objects possessing the strongest sensations are preferred. The broader the range of sensual material to which we have access, the freer and wider our sense of physical security. This includes physical relations with parents, brothers, sisters and our environment. Everything, including the body, has an object-like quality at this time, and flexibility and response to the physical world is now defined. Senses do not yet striate into levels, but remain open to each new object and sensation; being touched and touching in turn are primary transactions. When access to objects is limited, our connection with the world is restrained. As these mechanisms determine our eventual attitude towards property, possession and the physical world, the freedom of sensation is vital.

The 2nd house is the ability to apply energy to the purely physical world and relate to the use of our senses.

3rd house   (Gemini the Twins)
One year, eight months until three years, six months old
(Instinctive mind, communication, movement, adaptability, mimicry, siblings, diversity, short journeys)

In the 3rd house we apply energy to objects in order to communicate. Many things are perceived simultaneously, whereas previously only one object could be accepted at a time. The relative positions also begin to matter. Objects fluctuate between being extensions of our reality and possessors of their own independent life. This subject-object duality is the most prominent characteristic of the time, and leads to differentiation.

We associate the sounds learned in the 2nd house with actions. Even sounds themselves seem like possessions to be played with. Names of people and things are identical to the people and things themselves; a name is our access to the person or object it describes.

We learn to walk and this animates our world as the range of impressions increases dramatically. Dependence on others lessens and the ability to connect thoughts to actions allows us to communicate with them. Nearby people are models on whom we pattern our attitudes. As the speed of adult perception is logarithmically so much slower than ours at this time, our primary models are other children. When adults read a newspaper, it seems to take them aeons. A balance between child and adult models achieves the widest range of experience in communication. When those around us communicate with words, we follow suit if we can. When parents baby-talk, for example, we learn an irrelevant vocabulary, for whatever means of communication we observe, we mimic and integrate.

Whenever the outer world becomes too difficult to understand, we enter a parallel inner world of magic. If words are misunderstood, we simply label the object with our own words or sounds. Such natural difficulties in communication send us back into the 2nd house stage of sucking or physical contact, and we blame the words themselves. The verbal faculty relies on transferring rhythmic sucking and chewing movements into language. Singing, dancing and games ease this transference of energy into the communicative sphere. The more time we spend alone, or the more problematic language becomes, the more highly developed our fantasy world.

The 3rd house is our ability to communicate.

4th house   (Cancer the Crab)

Three years, six months, until seven years old
(Parents and the mother, family, feelings, home life, receptivity, heredity, intuition, the psychic world, personal life, belonging)

In the 3rd house language is still basic and unexpressive, but in the 4th house we react to our ability to communicate. We realize that words produce particular responses from parents and siblings – some words produce laughter, others a reprimand. Home should be a place where the full range of communication may be presented, but permitted actions and reactions determine our emotional 'set' for life. The valuing mechanism is emotion: our feelings about home, church, country or nature are conditioned by those prevailing within the family, and made manifest by our parents. We recognize that our family has its own views of the world, or that family views bear little resemblance to those of the world outside. When a questioning of family attitudes is not permitted, our feelings are reserved from expression. This is a reversion back into the 3rd house, where certain words had no value and merely described objects.

Our parents influence our feelings as their attitudes are guidelines whether we accept or reject them. Our emotional patterns are a blend and compensation of our parents', and we realize that the family system is held together by feelings which are not necessarily consistent nor just. We can relate more strongly to one parent than the other, but must gradually take their relationship with each other into consideration. The ability to comprehend these complex relationships determines the kind of home and family system we seek or avoid in later life. The parent with whom we create the strongest bond is often the carrier for our eventual marital role. In single-parent families, one parent must portray both roles.

The Sun and Moon are the influences of our father and mother in the horoscope and their placement conditions these parental-emotional valuations. The position of these luminaries can exaggerate, parallel, negate or have no effect on this house according to their positions.

Emotions are the glue of family relationships, and our feelings are important for our family as well as for us. When our feelings are blocked or unexpressed, we revert back to the 3rd house of instinctive thinking – we just don't feel at home.

The 4th house concerns feelings about our ability to communicate within home and family.

The Octave of Maturity

The third Octave of Maturity is when the body and the personality are combined, integrated and projected into the world to work out one's various possibilities. The soul is rediscovered through self-consciousness and the function of life in spiritual, family and occupational objectives in maturity, culminating in a mental body or philosophy of life. The developments of maturity parallel the creation of civilization and individuality in history.

5th house   (Leo the Lion)
Seven years until 13 years old
(Self-consciousness, creativity, pride, affections, love of the self and others, acting, confidence, education, publications, speculation)
We develop our personality in the first four houses of childhood and in the 5th house exteriorize ourselves into the outside world and become self-conscious. This coincides with primary education.

The major expressive device is game-playing, as games are a natural way of expressing our ability to relate to others. The particular games we choose or are forced to play define a range of possibilities: some games provide us with a channel for our energies, while others do not allow expression. Some of us prefer to make up our own rules, some only play by commonly accepted rules, some must receive their rules from others, and some refuse to allow others to play with them at all. The kinds of games we play and our attitude towards rule-making determine our personal relationships. Those friends with whom we play and establish rules are those with whom we form affectionate contact. Personal relationship is the acceptance of game-playing.

Games may exchange energy, demonstrate physical proficiency or intellectual superiority, provide an outlet for emotions, or any of these in combination. The best games contain all of these. The framework within which relationships develop is school, where we learn the rules that our social class, religion, geographical area or country hold to be important. We choose to abide by certain conventional games, while others are ignored or resisted. The open-mindedness of games contracts with the rigidity of school discipline. A well-adjusted child balances the two.

Once out of our parents' domain, teachers and those who play games for a living become primary role models for action and thought. This often tends to hero-worship of ideal individuals. The preoccupation with school or games sets a pattern which we follow in later life, especially in sexual relationships. When game-playing and school are difficult, there is a regression to the security of home and mother in the 4th house.

The 5th house is to accept and play games as a way of expressing ourself and forming relationships with others.

6th house   (Virgo the Virgin)

Thirteen years until 23 years, five months old
(Differentiated matter, distillation, discrimination, puberty, diet and health, secondary education, work, service)

The 6th house is the discrimination and physicality of self-conscious adolescence. Puberty accompanies this time during which the transition to secondary education is completed, and the great struggle is between the games we learn and the reality of the world.

Parental identifications which were transferred onto teachers or heroes during the 5th house are now assimilated. The medium is the body, as our role-playing now involves sexuality – the way in which we relate to our body determines the nature of work relationships. If we are governed by sensual responses to objects, including our body, then we expect to work for or to serve others; if we control our sensations, we can expect to manage and be served by others at work. Our degree of physical involvement determines the intermediate ground between the two extremes. We have to make choices, accept responsibility for our own decisions and create a physical reality.

Many of our choices are physical: we must choose clothes, diet, hygiene and information. Our health reflects the overall balance of physical necessities. Difficulty in decision-making leads to disease. The many games and speculations available in the 5th house become limited and we must decide on what is essential.

It is not possible to separate ideals from realities before this time, so complete control over the world seems possible until tangible impediments intervene, such as mental or physical limitations, lack of financial mobility or class barriers. Systems that we learned contrast and permute with the actual mechanism of the world of school or job. Game-playing attitudes and techniques must be channelled into working situations. Flexibility is valued where specialization formerly was encouraged. We either accept or reject control over our own life.

Relationships that obeyed rules become subject to experimentation beyond familial and social codes. Sexuality is mainly fantasy at the beginning of this house, and the fantasies either are eliminated in favour of real physical relations or remain fantasies forever. Often our choices are binding, as when we produce children from early sexual experiences. To resist experiment produces naivete, but unreasonable experimentation produces premature commitments. The ability to synthesize the impressions of early life, to organize ourselves into a consistent whole rather than a collection of parts, is the object of this time. Criticism towards others counterpoints our self-criticism; we may be accurate and objective about others, but not about ourselves. If we cannot make choices or organize ourselves, we revert back to the gameplaying attitudes of the 5th house.

The 6th house is the ability to adapt to the world in physique, health, work and sexuality.

7th house   **(Libra the Scales)**
Twenty-three years, five months, until 42 years old
(Sublimation of self, balance, partnership, the public, obligations, enemies, justice, communal and business relationships, sociability)
Now we are directly opposite the time when our personality registered at birth in the logarithmic time scale. The way we see ourself is the opposite of the way we really are, and the polarity promotes objectivity.

Our personality was conditioned by parents, brothers and sisters, and early environment, and now must be reconciled with the outside world. The equilibrium we seek between inside and outside manifests in our choices of partnerships, both marital and professional. We leave the subjectivity and unconsciousness of the lower half of our horoscope and emerge into the upper, conscious and objective hemisphere. The synthesis involves blending both positive and negative traits developed and enacted during our first 23 years, five months.

Partnerships are a summation of our appearance, parental relationships, education, ability to communicate, attraction, ambitions and conflicts. Our partner is the balancing agent in this complicated equation as someone who seems to possess the characteristics we lack, yet desire to possess. These characteristics are projected onto our partner, whether or not they actually carry them. Often it is more important to discover what we think and feel about a partner than what they are really like.

The 7th house is opposite the 1st house, which governed self-assertion in the months after birth. We seek a partnership that counterbalances the strength of our personality. It is the process of partnership which is important, and the growth it allows and encourages is all-important. We act out and become familiar with the opposing characteristics of our partner, and they gradually integrate into our being, just as a parallel process occurs to them. Excessive strength or weakness in either partner reflects a similar imbalance within each partner.

Business relationships parallel our personal relationships: efficient business requires that employees sublimate their individual drives for the good of the whole. Yet every individual wishes to advance and maintain his or her own influence. The individuality of each partner dovetails with the collective job. The higher up in business one progresses, the more necessary is an image of the whole operation.

At present marriage is a contractual agreement, subject to moral and legal controls. Subsequently, many marriages are transactions where little beyond sharing lodging or children is held in common by way of growth and evolution. The rules of behaviour within relationships should allow both partners the latitude to grow, yet also must hold them together in common interest. This is true whether heterosexual or homosexual relations are involved. It is necessary to define roles and then play them. The success of relationships hinges around foresight determining the interweaving demands of each individual as well as the whole marriage. The liberation of women and men from stereotyped family roles is important, but it must be remembered that it is we ourselves who make and break these roles and rules.

When our personality is very complex, it becomes necessary to expand beyond a nuclear relationship. This may mean a succession of growth partnerships or a desire to form a relationship with the world itself. Public figures often sacrifice personal relationships in favour of their career.

An inability to relate to others forces a regression back into the unconscious lower half of the horoscope. We may then find that partnerships become work (sixth), game-playing (fifth), protection fourth), childlike (third), purely physical (second) or alone in self-assertion (first). At best, all the elements described by the early houses are present in a blended form.

The 7th house is the ability to form permanent relationships.

8th house   (Scorpio the Scorpion)

Forty-two years old until death

(Life processes, karma, separation, death, regeneration, occultism, metaphysical beliefs, shared resources, legacies, perversity)

The 8th house is the last house and governs the gradual withdrawal from life. As it is opposite to the 2nd house entrance into the physical world of the senses, the 8th house is the release of our grasp on the sensual world; we experience the results of our life's work and all outstanding debts are paid. By the end of this time we should have 'made our peace' with the world.

This is old age, when we must gradually relinquish or delegate control over our own affairs. The end of the 7th house is the time of maximum acquisition, but as we progress through the 8th house the desire to accumulate must be transformed into a willingness to let it all go. Detachment from the world accompanies ageing. A dependency on the feelings, thoughts, will and even physical support of others increases. After a lifetime of being in control, it is hard to relinquish direction of our affairs.

The gradient of energy declines during this last phase of life, and our activities reflect this. A healthy increase of interest in metaphysics, religion and the intangible is a way of transferring the focus away from youthful gratification towards the symbolic acts of old age. Friends pass away; old places do not seem the same; the activities of middle age are tiresome; the physical world dissolves into an internal, spiritual world that lies behind appearances. In senility, the inner world literally encroaches on and dominates the outer world.

The primary effect of ageing is that our time sense becomes so highly compacted as our metabolism slows down towards a stopping point that the world appears to fly by. All we can do is sit and watch it happen. By the time we have reacted to a situation, it has passed. The mind moves faster than the body can react. While driving, we see our automobile hitting the post but cannot act in time to avoid it. The deterioration of the senses is the slowing down of perception – our understanding just cannot keep up with the speed of perceptions around us.

The 8th house and the death that terminates it represents the most critical time of life. We should be able to detach ourselves from the world gracefully. The necessity to release control and property, when understood, generates the conditions for a positive death. When matters are left undone and grasping is prominent, death is painful torment. The primary objective is to channel our diminishing energies into their intangible places, to pass on our understanding of life and the world to those who are younger, and to maintain an interest in the last great transformation.

The 8th house is the separation from life as we approach death.

The Transcendent Octave

How can a man be born when he is old? Can he enter a second time into his mother's womb and be born? Jesus answered, 'Truly, truly, I say to you, unless one is born of water and the spirit, he cannot enter the kingdom.'

John 3:4-5[85]

The process of life from the ninth cusp-conception point until the end of the 8th house of separation and death defines our mundane life. Life is a circle in time. As T S Eliot stated so beautifully:

We shall not cease from exploration
And the end of all our exploring
Will be to arrive where we started
And know the place for the first time.

In order to understand life, we must see it in its entirety in time. The joys, sorrows, meaningful moments and trivial enjoyments, the complexity and simplicity, the loves and fears, protagonists and allies must all be unified into a Life. Until we comprehend the whole, we cannot pass beyond ourselves.

Most people live mechanical lives: they are conceived, born, mature and die. When we see them walking down the street, we do not have to be an astrologer to predict where they came from or where they are going. They never attempt to extend their reality beyond their physical, personal situation. Their actions and feelings are dictated to them by the world, and they are locked into time and cannot, nor do they wish to get out. They may struggle briefly in early life, but ultimately they bow to the pressures of the world in order to conform.

The life just described is similar to the horoscope circle because they both exist in one plane. Like the sheet of paper on which the horoscope is drawn, the circle becomes a line when you hold it at certain angles. For most, life is a continuously repetitive orbit round the circle. At its most mechanical, life is a straight line of definite length, but with no height or width. Time acts as an absolute constraint and flexibility is minimal if not non-existent as a mechanical life is lived around the periphery of the horoscope circle. At the end of life is the return to the beginning, but without the knowledge that it has happened.

The two-dimensional version of reality is similar to the way we understand the solar system as static. As we have seen, the planets spiral around the moving Sun. The orbiting planets and moons appear to spiral around the central bright path of the Sun like filaments enwrapping a live wire. Through time the spiralling circus of our Solar System makes a complex cylinder.

Figure 12 illustrates the horoscope extended into a cylinder of life, where conception is at the bottom and the transcendent octave at the top. As we live the cylinder fills up with memories, and the present moment is the surface. Within and without this cylinder the planets spiral, reflecting and synchronizing with our life pattern in time. Most perceive their life as only the surface of the cylinder above a murky fluid, while the realized individual perceives a crystal-clear cylinder forwards and backwards in time and is able to go beyond its confines at will.

The diagram of the solar system through time is distinctly similar in structure to the genetic code DNA-RNA, which is also a pattern that functions in time. The language of astrology is a sister to the language of genetics. The 12 basic units of DNA are divided into four bases, similar to the 12 astrological signs and four elements. Both the spiralling path of the solar system in time and the double helix spiral of

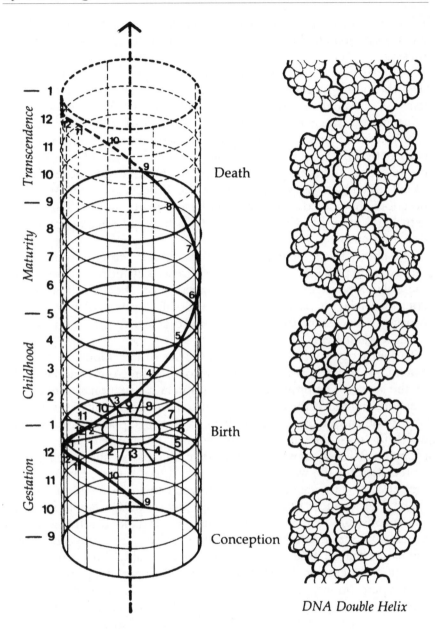

Figure 12: Cylinder of Life Time Astrology
When the horoscope is extended in time along the central axis, conception is at the bottom and transcendence at the top of the cylinder. As we age, the cylinder fills with perceptions and memories. The present is the surface of the contents, which most take to be the whole. Outer life events are at the surface of the cylinder, while inner events are within the cylinder.

DNA are energy patterns, which carry and record the form of the entire developmental process of life. A slice through DNA is a coded message called a gene, which guides biological assembly and development, just as an astrological planetary position with its aspects describes a life mechanism and the event through which it expresses itself. Consistent to Rupert Sheldrake's revolutionary concept of morphic resonance, the formation of organisms is not determined by DNA alone. There is a developmental pattern within time which is carried by DNA on the physical level. Similarly, the planets do not create events, but merely act as carriers of the large-scale development of all individuals, presented here as the Process of Life. Astrology describes the pooled memory of all past humans, and the symbols of astrology are the signs which describe the twelve stages of development.

The ability to understand all life presupposes an understanding of our own life process. To describe our life as a cylindrical spiralling of the solar system extends the perspective of the two-dimensional circle we take to be the form of the solar system. An analogous process is necessary to move our life to a higher level of reality; a Transcendent Reality.

To gain access to the Transcendent Octave of development, we must extend our reality beyond the confines of the three-dimensional world of the senses. The process of conception and gestation describes our creation, and this is the pattern of our transcendent reality as well. The way in which our parents conceived us is a metaphor for the way in which the masculine and feminine sides of our nature blend together creatively. The way in which our mother realizes that she is pregnant is a precedent for the way in which we first discover our creative nature; the process of pregnancy describes how creativity manifests itself.

The Transcendent Octave is the higher level of Gestation, so if we can reconstruct our gestation, we can understand the transcendent process. If our gestation was fluid and satisfying for our mother, then the same will be true of our transcendent reality. Problems during gestation reflect blockages which may constrain us from utilizing higher perceptions, or an attempted abortion is a tendency to end the creative process prematurely. The events of gestation provide a pattern which we enact in living out our creative potential in life.

The Gestation Octave both begins and ends life in time: it completes and encloses the circle, yet provides the possibility of being free of the circle. The point of access to the Transcendent Octave of the horoscope is the 9th house conception point/death point. The way we are conceived is a pattern of the way we enter the transcendent octave, and we must pass the barrier of death before we can leave the confines of mechanical life. The passage of this barrier is initiation.

Initiation

Initiation was a ritual to which both women and men were exposed. The initiate was removed from his or her parental home, stripped of childhood identification and subjected to severe tests of patience or strength. Often the initiate was required to find and kill a totem animal, which meant a life or death struggle. On successfully passing the test, the initiate was educated as to the history and inner tradition of the whole tribe or religion. He or she received a new name, a new identity and status as an individual.

One object of initiation was to force the initiate to realize that it is essential to accept a higher purpose (that is, the survival of the entire tribe) that transcends personal value in life. Strength lies in the whole life or whole tribe or whole culture, and not just in one part, an idea that would be helpful today. The shock of the physical test and pain increased the force of the ideas imparted. Initiation provided a direction and purpose to life, which was lacking in the unconsciousness of childhood.

The classical initiation process is extinct, but there are ways in which the initiation process is available to us. One of the most obvious initiations is the bearing and birth of children; the women's mysteries of virtually all cultures in the world. The initiation began with a young girl's first menstruation and culminated with the birth of her first child. Women's mysteries were as painful and traumatic as the more overtly violent men's mysteries and possibly even more powerful.

First menstruation is a biological signal that a woman is of age and can conceive. It is an evocation of the ripening of the ovum from which the woman herself was conceived. As the ova ripen within her young body, so she herself is ripe for life. Menstrual blood was sacred, and elaborate taboos, usually in the form of isolation, were observed to protect a woman and her tribe from each other. The first sign of creation within her was met by a ritual separation – a symbolic 'death' in relation to the tribe. She could never be the same again. Similarly, gestation is an initiation process to the mother.

When a woman conceives her first child, she irrevocably changes the pattern and orientation of her life and she 'dies' to her former life. Her thoughts, feelings, intuitions and senses during pregnancy are an inner change which accompanies her outer, physical change. The element of life or death affects both her and the child she will bear, especially at birth. A woman can know what it feels like to risk her life for another.

A woman relives the process of her own gestation when she is pregnant. Through the Life Time Scale her own gestation may be outlined as a base on which to build an initiated reality for herself and her child. It is less necessary to manipulate the child-carrying process than it is to understand who she is, the implications of her behaviour, and the choices she makes. Initiation is the ability to accept responsibility for creativity beyond our own life.

The initiation of man is a very different process, although of similar roots. Men cannot carry or bear children. The mysteries of creation are idealized, abstracted and ritualized. The act of male orgasm is a dying release and the struggle of the one sperm out of millions to survive the trial in reaching the ovum is highly symbolic. The test of strength in initiation evokes these procreative acts, providing a springboard to a higher purpose in life.

There are many ways in which to experience initiation. Since it is the symbolic death of a previous life attitude, the process can occur through near death; by physical shocks or accidents; by emotional traumas; intellectual crises of conscience; with psychedelic drugs or plants; through meditation; or through the religious impulse. Events of this kind are never planned, but are accidental. Sometimes the effect of peak experiences are immediately suppressed or forgotten, but once we have seen the vulnerability of life, we are never the same again. This is true whether or not we choose to act on the experience.

The actor or actress who is able to eliminate personality to don other roles fulfils the conditions of a metaphorical death and rebirth. The historian who studies past civilization eventually transfers his 'reality' back into a former time. His success is dependent on leaving the contemporary world view in order to adopt the viewpoint of a chosen historical era, then to synthesize the two worlds separated by time.

Psychedelic plants and drugs also remove one from 'normal' reality in space and time. As psychedelics increase bodily metabolism through their chemical action, the resultant trip is quite literally a journey back into life. Faster metabolism is a quality of youthful perception, and as it increases our perceptual age decreases. We see the world as we did as a child. Astrologically we travel clockwise back against the natural direction of the signs and houses, towards the Ascendant and further, into gestation. Potent doses send us back into the womb. The loss of personality experienced with psychedelics occurs when we pass back through our own birth! When psychedelics are properly understood and administered, they provide an opportunity to relive life and experience existence without personality – to transcend ordinary life.

Our own sexuality links conception and death. Orgasm is a symbolic death; an opportunity to experience our conception during life. The connection between sexuality and creativity is determined by the nature

Figure 13: Alchemy and Mitosis
The action of the snake within the alchemical retort echoes the action of mitosis, when genetic material separates and rejoins to create new life during conception. (*Rosarium philosophorum* alchemical manuscript)

of the sexual act between our parents, which is evoked whenever we make love. Sex is an initiation, as the practice of Eastern tantric yoga verifies. Reconstruction of the sexual act that conceived us is a primary key to our own creativity, sexuality and entrance into the transcendent octave of reality.

In Gnostic alchemy, heaven and earth have a womb-like shape.[86] The alchemical process as shown in *Alchemy* by Johannes Fabricius is not as the transmutation of gold, but a transformation of the psyche. Jung discovered parallels between the process of psychic growth and the visions of the alchemists. Fabricius shows that alchemical diagrams that seem bewildering dreamscapes are accurate diagrams of the processes of conception, fertilization, meiosis and mitosis, up to the moment of birth (see Figure 13). We recapitulate the evolution of the spirit since its incarnation in matter when it creates us; reliving it is realization.

Many primitive legends and folklore carry the belief that at death our entire life flashes instantly before our mind's eye. Near-death experiences (NDEs) tend to validate the phenomenon known as 'panoramic memory'.[87] With the last registration of the life pattern at death, life is actual and all its potential has been realized. All life is continually available except that we lose sight of the whole while it is happening.

The remembrance of life at death is the Last Judgement of Egyptian and Christian religion.[88] The weighing of the soul at death in the underworld is a powerful archetypal image. The last judgement is an assessment of the value of life to the soul as a determining factor for its next incarnation, similar to the quest for transpersonal reality. The factual raw or fine material, the content of life (the prime material of the alchemists), must be understood so that it can be transmuted to a higher level. The death of the former reality is a requirement for the transcendent process to ensue. Death signals not just the extinction of the physical body, but also a transmission of life energy beyond individuality into the 'realm of the mothers' of Goethe's Faust.

Psychoanalysis, psychotherapy and other analytic processes can be initiations, as we track our life backwards towards gestation with the benefit of a trained guide. Glimpses of the whole can happen through association, hypnosis, the recreation of archetypal situations via psychodrama, movement, words or symbols, and can occur through the presence of a sympathetic listener. Correct bodily movement in athletics, running, stretching, dance and sex often provides a breakthrough into transcendence. Yoga, martial arts, Tai Chi, meditation and other techniques developed in the East are specifically oriented towards the identical aim of unity.

Initiatory processes induce reality beyond the physical and release creative potential. The process of using the logarithmic Life Time Scale is another means to this end. It is most helpful as a pattern, which may be used together with other techniques. Once the breakthrough into the higher octave of transcendence has been accomplished, the four gestation houses take on greater additional meaning.

The Higher Octave Houses

The time of gestation, which begins with conception and ends with birth, is a pattern of our own creative processes and potential transcendent development. As transcendence, creativity and sexuality are three aspects of the higher life, the energies that drive these processes are the same.

The nature of our conception can be reconstructed using Life Time Astrology. Our father and mother are the masculine/feminine, positive/negative and sperm/ovum combinations that produce us, and each parent contains both polarities. It is possible that our father was active or passive, that our mother was passive or active, or any permutation of the two opposite roles of the life force. Whichever parent was responsible for the impulse to conceive us registers as the creative motivation in our life. Our other parent represents mechanisms within us that are acted on. The manner of our parents' courtship and seduction mirrors our own creative mechanism. It may have been accidental, planned, one-sided, equivalent, bored, highly sexual, asexual, purely physical, extremely emotional, intellectual, violent, detached, attached, athletic or lazy. Whatever the circumstances, our access to creativity will reflect the nature of conception as a relationship between our parents.

The physical act of conception is a metaphor for our ability to make creativity manifest in the physical world. Either parent may have had the primary inclination to create, but not the necessary strength or will to follow through. Analysis of our conception moment provides a key to our own sexual motivation as well as to our creativity.

The Higher Octave 9th house
The higher octave of the 9th house reflects the first seven weeks of gestation, when our mother gradually realized that she was pregnant. This also occurs after our first initiatory, creative or sexual experiences. The feeling of pure life pulses through us, as though no one had ever made love, painted a picture or realized the implications of their beliefs before. The breakthrough made running long distances a higher octave of physical activities, and we must push through impulses to stop before the breakthrough is made. The 9th house refers to the religious, philosophical and psychological perspective within which a larger perspective of our life and views may be contained. A mother's ability to understand her new creative state sets a pattern of behaviour for our transcendent, creative and sexual experiences.

The Higher Octave MC
This reflects the moment our mother realizes she is pregnant. This is the moment our ego registers, our mother becomes conscious of her new objectives and the soul enters our physical body. The quality of our mother's consciousness is equivalent to the nature of our own self-consciousness in life. Our mother's projections and reactions at that time, the people she consulted, their reactions and her ability to broadcast her successful creativity determine the strength and quality of our ego. If she required a doctor to tell her that she was pregnant, we will need such verification from a

protective figure like a family doctor or psychoanalyst to justify our own life objectives. In previous times the mother or other women would have recognized pregnancy, but in the modern world pregnancy is usually determined by chemical test or doctor's examination. The return to natural methods is important in more than the obvious ways! If our mother kept her pregnancy secret initially due to confusion over paternity, we would keep our life aims secret. Our mother's reaction to pregnancy is a direct metaphor of our place in the world.

The Higher Octave 10th house
The higher octave of the 10th house reflects our parents' organizational abilities in the world after accepting the fact of our conception. Their responses and actions show how we organize and manifest life objectives in the real world. Higher perceptions from the 9th house must be integrated into our mundane life. If our parents stress practical matters during gestation, our life will be conditioned by practical matters. If they espouse more profound attitudes, our life philosophy emphasizes higher values.

The Higher Octave 11th house
The higher octave of the 11th house sees our mother forming idealistic attitudes reflecting her relationships with others. Her involvement with or abstraction from those around her, especially group values, determines the pattern of our collective life in the world. Our mother once transcended physical concerns in gestation to purify and project high values onto us, and we must extend our world view beyond mere security. Once we have stepped beyond physical reality to higher aims in the 10th house, we must transmit them to the public. This starts with our immediate family, extends to local groups and then the public at large. The contrast between personal and collective ideals generates higher Utopian aims, communal activities and inventive social systems.

The Higher Octave 12th house

The higher octave of the 12th house reflects a receptive and sacrificial orientation of our mother in the last phase of gestation. Once we transmit our ideas into the world, we must reap the consequences of our actions. In contrast to the physical transformation of the 8th house, these ultimate karmic influences describe the spiritual impact of our life and its ideals on others, inwardly and outwardly. This indicates to what extent we are willing to sacrifice ourself, even physically, to higher aspirations. If a mother is willing to obey even the most subtle signals emanating from us during the last phase of pregnancy, we can respond sympathetically to the finest spiritual values.

With the completion of this last house, life is complete on all four octave levels of existence; Gestation, Childhood, Maturity and Transcendence. All potential we accepted at conception has been translated into actuality and the process of life is complete. In reconstructing life with the Life Time Scale, our understanding of it in time is complete.

Travelling in Time

While the transcendent octave may be a return to the beginning, the centre of the horoscope is also the transcendent centre of the Self, always available to us. The eternal presence of the transcendent is the energy that drives the process.

Life history is recorded and stored logarithmically in a code based on metabolism, therefore any action or influence that affects metabolic rate is potential access to individual and collective life history, and vice versa. Emotional states increase metabolism, as in childhood, and when in the throes of intense emotion, we are childlike. In contrast, depression decreases metabolism, as in old age, and the depressive feels prematurely old and tired. Psychological states are stored at their appropriate age in life experience. When a developmental stage becomes a barrier, we tend to regress back into previous states that were more comfortable. Thus, there is a counter-clockwise movement in time and a clockwise movement back to the source in gestation. The entire process revolves around the centre of the horoscope and the psyche.

Psychotropic drugs alter our time sense by affecting metabolism and create apparent time-travel back into life.[89] LSD increases molecular metabolism – we seem to become younger. We project parental identities onto whoever is nearby. Critical events of childhood and transcribe them into the local environment. Adults act as a young child, backtracking the process of growing up. As the effect of the psychedelic becomes stronger, earlier and earlier circumstances and modes of perception register. As the child learned to walk and communicate, the feeling is that those abilities are being lost, until eventually the helplessness of the newborn infant is experienced. We scrutinize visual phenomena with which we are familiar as an adult as if for the first time, and our senses are intensified.

If the dosage is sufficiently high, we pass through our own birth in reverse. The compression into a protective yet terrifyingly claustrophobic space within the mother mirrors those influences that accompany our own birth. When born by a traumatic surgical delivery, the trauma is re-enacted, as in Janov's Primal Scream Therapy. As the birth moment signals the creation of the personality – a way of seeing ourselves – the reversed psychedelic experience eliminates personality and announces the entrance into the womb. Once within the womb, the incredibly vivid psychic tapestry of intrauterine life replaces the formerly objective outside world, which vanishes. Psychic contact replaces direct perception, and a transit through the collective unconscious replaces the mundane realities of daily life. Gestation repeats the evolutionary process, and so in the psychedelic experience we travel back in time.

When we take a particularly potent dosage, the journey may extend all the way back to the time of the registration of the MC, when the ego entered our evolving physical matrix and the embryo became human for the first time. We commonly call the process 'ego-loss'. In the earlier 9th house the various brain structures form as vestiges of primary evolutionary forms. The hallucinated journey back through the primary states is sometimes horrifying – it is the Bardo states described so vividly in Tibetan Buddhist texts. Quite literally, we experience unfamiliar life forms in the primordial saurian world, the primeval swamp and, still earlier, the pre-planetary existence of earth material. The final stage of the psychedelic experience is a return to the burst of energy at conception that echoes the Big Bang and that the Buddhists call the White Light. The White Light is unity, wholeness and pure bliss. We gradually feel the impulsion of incarnation, begin to seek a womb, and the experience is repeated back – a recreation of the life and a return to reality.

The psychedelic experience is a journey back through the space-time process of life and parallels the perceptions of millennia of mystics and seers as an investigation of the origin of the psyche.

Chapter Five — The Cast of Characters

The 10 planets represent the *cast of characters* in our life. The characters are parents, siblings, relatives, doctors, neighbours, friends, lovers, enemies, associates, partners, children and others of importance. Each character enters life, plays his or her role, then leaves at a time corresponding to an equivalent planet's position in the horoscope. Some roles are permanent, some sporadic, but most are played by a succession of characters. The Sun is originally our father, then becomes a teacher, then an employer, then we become a father ourself. All characters influence our whole being and play their part in forming our character. A key to the discovery of our essential nature is to use Life Time Astrology to identify and understand all the characters, their various guises, their times of appearance, and their meaning as they enter and leave life. Each of the 10 planets registers at a specific time, manifests through an outer event or an inner realization, and is carried by a character or characters. The event, the character and their interaction are reflections of our being.

When we relate to someone, an image of them is created within that reflects the way we see and feel them. Through time, they and we change, mutual attitudes change and our internal reflection of them changes. A central development in life is the balance of the way people really are as opposed to our attitude towards them.

Since life begins at conception, some of the central characters – parents, family and their friends – precede us onto the stage of life. Initially they do not realize our potential existence and play their parts uninfluenced by us. We have no control at all over those who determine the earliest and deepest levels of our identity. A primary paradox of life is that by the time we question those who affect our gestation and childhood, their influence is already past. For better or worse, parents and the events surrounding conception and gestation cannot be changed. Only an understanding of them and attitudes towards them can alter. To discover why we are who we are, we must put our past into perspective by determining who was present in our early life, how and why they behaved as they did, and what it all means.

The most important correlation of planets to characters is that of the Sun to father and the Moon to mother. The Sun is not only our father, but also all the ways in which we relate to him and to the idea 'father'. The Sun is anyone with whom we have a paternal relationship, as well as the father within. The concept 'mother' means much more than the personal qualities enacted by our own mother. It includes all mothers and all maternal feelings. Our mother has her own unique personal qualities, but she also partakes of the mother archetype. She may not even carry any of the receptive, nurturing or protective qualities, but she shapes all attitudes to such qualities.

The planets function as *archetypes*. Archetypes are patterning structures that carry and transform psychic energy, and are the symbolic expression of instinctive processes like love, hate, fear, flight, nurturing and repulsion that are inherited from all humanity. Each planet is an archetype through which instincts are channelled. Likewise, each planetary archetype carries both the positive and negative characteristics available. Venus is loving and lovers, but also the rejection of relationships when badly aspected. Venus may also generate its opposite Martial qualities in frustrated love.

Each planetary archetype is carried by many people in life. For example, in the early part of life all maternal qualities are projected onto a mother by child-parent bonding. Gradually we experience others who possess motherly qualities, like nannies, grandmothers, aunts and teachers. Our own mother is the primary subject of the mother archetype, but we discover that there may be other women more protective, receptive or open than our own mother: our mother may possess none of these qualities! The total feeling towards all our 'mothers' is eventually the basis of our own personal value system; the mother in us. We all possess mothers, fathers, brothers, sisters and the entire range of people we know inside ourself.

As we age, our attitudes towards parents, friends, siblings and others change as they themselves change. With movement through our horoscope houses in succession, planets in residence are affected by the qualities of the developmental stage signified by each house. The nature of each planet and its characters change according to the house of residence and the sign qualities occupying the house. Venus in the 12th house could be a midwife or mother's friend; Venus on the Ascendant could be a nurse or mother's helper; Venus in the 2nd house could be a favourite object or toy; while Venus in the 3rd house could be a sister or playmate; and so on.

Figure 14: Planetary Personifications
These cartoon figures show general planetary correspondences within the family. The Sun is father; Moon is mother; Mercury is baby; Venus is sister; Mars is brother; Jupiter and Saturn are grandparents. The outer planets show generational influences: Uranus is explosive events; Neptune sensitive situations; Pluto is forceful circumstances; and the Node is groups, including the whole family. (Illustration by John Astrop)

The house of residence changes the quality of events in addition to changing the character indicated by a planet. Since Venus is relationship, the house and age of Venus' registration qualifies the type of relationship in question. Venus in the 3rd house at two years old is communication with a sister or playmate, while Venus in the 7th house at 32 is a love relationship.

A planet's house position qualifies whoever carries its affect. Early in life, events are most often caused by those around us; therefore, the planets are other people. Later in life, events are more likely to be a result of our own actions, if not directly caused by us. Mars accidents would happen to us when in the 2nd house, but would be caused by us in the 6th house. It is important to know whether we or others cause the critical events in life, even though we ultimately must take responsibility for them all.

The sign location of a planet qualifies its action and character. Each planet rules a sign or signs and their equivalent house or houses. When a planet resides in the sign it rules, it functions at its purest and most archetypal. The Moon rules the sign Cancer and the 4th house, both of which govern mother, home, family and emotions. When we have the Moon in either of these positions, our maternal relationship is archetypal. Mercury rules the positive Gemini and the 3rd house of communication, walking and talking; and the negative Virgo and the 6th house of discrimination, criticism and decision-making to define our position in the world.

Table 4: Planetary Rulerships

Planet	*rules*	*Positive Sign and House*			*Negative Sign and House*		
Sun	rules	Leo	&	5th House			
Moon	rules				/Cancer	&	4th House
Mercury	rules	Gemini	&	3rd House	/Virgo	&	6th House
Venus	rules	Libra	&	7th House	/Taurus	&	2nd House
Mars	rules	Aries	&	1st House	/Scorpio	&	8th House
Jupiter	rules	Sagittarius	&	9th House	/Pisces	&	12th House
Saturn	rules	Aquarius	&	11th House	/Capricorn	&	10th House
Uranus	rules	Aquarius	&	11th House			
Neptune	rules	Pisces	&	12th House			
Pluto	rules	Scorpio	&	8th House			

When a planet resides in the sign opposite to the sign it rules, such as Venus in Scorpio or in the 8th house, it is in detriment and it functions negatively.

Planets located above the horizon in a horoscope are conscious and those below the horizon are unconscious. Venus represents a relationship, so Venus above the horizon is a conscious relationship and Venus below the horizon is an unconscious relationship. The naturally objective, active and vital Sun, when below the horizon, still carries those qualities but we are unaware of possessing them. When the naturally subjective and receptive Moon is above the horizon, our maternal side is prominent but we are conscious of its behaviour.

Planets located in the left, eastern half of a horoscope are self-oriented and planets in the right, western half are oriented to the outer world. Jupiter as the indicator of life philosophy would be exclusive when in the left side and inclusive when in the right side of the horoscope. Planets near the Ascendant in a horoscope affect personality and planets near the MC affect objectives and aims in life.

Aspects are geometrical relationships between planets and will be explained in the next chapter, but they should be mentioned here. Planetary influences can operate alone, but usually affect each other mutually, combining planetary influences. Saturn is inhibition and Venus is relationship, so the Saturn/Venus aspect is 'inhibited relationship'. Planets naturally combine with each other, just as in nature the elements are rarely found in their pure state, but abound in compounds and complex combinations with other elements.

When any planet is in one of the double signs Gemini, Cancer, Libra, Sagittarius, Aquarius or Pisces, there is more than one individual carrying the planetary influence and a duality results in the equivalent event.

The planets are considered either masculine, feminine or neuter. Women and men are composed of both masculine and feminine qualities, and the overall balance of masculine-feminine varies dramatically through life. Women exhibit objectivity, consciousness and vitality, in the same way that men exhibit subjectivity, unconsciousness and passivity. If masculine planets are dominant by sign and house position in our horoscope, masculine qualities predominate whether or not we are biologically male or female. The planets are paired in masculine-feminine dyads, which depend upon each other for wholeness. The only exceptions are Mercury, which signifies neutral intelligence, and Uranus, which is originality and independence.

The Sun is the ability to understand and integrate all influences in life into a conscious and objective whole, while the Moon promotes feelings and emotions that generate the internal value system in life. The Sun differentiates as the Moon integrates. The geometrical aspect between the Sun and Moon in our horoscope describes the nature of our parents' relationship, as well as forming a pattern for our own relationships and the masculine–feminine balance within us.

Mercury is the ability to establish communication with both father and mother as a gauge of our intelligence and balance. It is a neutral planet as it combines masculine and feminine, and left and right brain halves.

Venus and Mars are the feminine-masculine polarity manifest in the physical and sexual realm. Venus is passive sexuality that wishes to relate and to be possessed, while Mars is active sexuality that wishes to alter the object of its affection – a desire to change.

Jupiter is a masculine expansion of horizons and Saturn is a feminine contraction of concentration. Their polarity is that of philosophy, religion and psychology versus materialism, pragmatism and science.

The three outer planets take so long to pass through each sign that they indicate transpersonal or generational mechanisms within the psyche. Uranus takes about seven years to pass through each sign; Neptune takes about 14 years; and Pluto takes about 22 years. Everyone experiences a complete cycle of all the inner planets through all 12 signs by the age of 29 years and six months when Saturn has completed its cycle. The planets from the Sun to Saturn are the personal characteristics everyone shares. The three outer planets show influences that affect the masses and the equivalent inner understanding of collective values some people possess.

The Sun   (Rules Leo and the 5th house)

The Sun in a horoscope describes our relationship to the masculine, conscious and vital forces of life as determined by attitudes towards our father. The Sun is this relationship, not the father. As our first physical contact with our father occurs after birth, it is rarely as direct as bonding to our mother. The masculine principle becomes most evident when we begin to focus light clearly at about 80 days after birth and remains objective, rational and detached. This timing reflects the Sun's first complete cycle of 365 days after conception (280 + 85). Although the Sun is often considered the most important planet in a horoscope (or as the only planet in so-called 'Sun Sign Astrology'), this is not the case. Many of us have weak, absent or multiple fathers. The Sun as our father, although central to our life, is also a component of the whole.

With age we realize that our father is not the only man in the world; there are other men stronger, more intelligent, more objective and more masculine. This signals the transformation of the Sun influence beyond those attached to our actual father. The solar image and our vitality depend upon finding ever higher forms upon which to project our life focus and to which to apply energies. Sexual energy, libido, psychic energy or kundalini metamorphoses into purer channels as we age. The energy of sucking in the 1st house transforms into chewing in the second, talking in the third, emotional give-and-take in the 4th, gameplaying in the fifth, competition in the sixth to sexuality in the 7th. When energy is blocked from transforming itself into the next higher level, symbolized by the next house position of the Sun (or any other planet), it regresses. When we cannot find the next gradient of energy, it regresses to a previous house. When there is no outlet for sexual energies, we must return to games to express them.

The Sun symbolizes the gradual process of becoming conscious of Self, energy and life.

In early life, the Sun is carried by those who organize or control our environment. This may include, in addition to the father, masculine qualities of the mother, grandparents, housekeepers, uncles, doctors, priests and those who exert influence upon the mother. Early paternal projections transfer to teachers, heroes, actors, athletes, politicians, idealogues, celebrities, royalty, impressarios, the wealthy and anyone in authority. From the beginning of Maturity at about seven years old until the Descendant point at 23 years and five months, these projections happen often and are natural. Past the Descendant it is time to begin repossessing these paternal projections: we must become a father ourself. The quality, variety and number of paternal projections made in early life define our own masculine nature. Our father and his surrogates provide models of consciousness, and the degree of awareness depends upon understanding this relationship, whether we are male or female. We can and must be aware of our father and his role, even when he is unsympathetic, absent, unconscious or instinctive.

The Sun in a horoscope is vitality, objectivity, consciousness, organization, decisiveness and spiritual focus.

The Moon   (Rules Cancer and the 4th house)

The Moon in a horoscope is the ability to value, to feel and to reflect emotions. The structure and intensity of our instinctive value systems is derived and influenced by the way in which we relate to our mother. She carries us within her during gestation and bonds to us at birth. From that time on we begin to differentiate ourself from her. Feelings about one's mother are continually in flux, like the changeable but repetitive lunar phases each month. The time of the Moon's registration in a horoscope shows the time when we relate to her most strongly. In early life she is an extension of our own reality, but with age she occupies a relative position in our affections.

Early maternal projections surround us within the womb yet are also transmitted by grandmothers, aunts, midwives, female doctors, emotional people, women in general and the feminine component in our father. From birth, the Moon signifies everyone who protects, nurtures and feels towards us, including nannies, medical people and males within our environment. From school age, lunar projections are displaced by teachers or girlfriends, just as home and family are displaced by school and classmates. Beginning at the Descendant, the Moon becomes a pattern for feelings about partnership, sexuality, mating, raising children and the world. Ultimately we must integrate maternal feelings into our whole being. When the traditional childraising function is rejected, variants emerge to take its place, like finding others to protect or being protected emotionally, an instinctive return to sport, nature or the land.

The Moon moves rapidly and functions as a connecting agent and catalyst in a horoscope. She reflects and values the other planets and establishes the tone of emotional life through events that bring out our feminine nature.

 Mercury **(Rules Gemini and Virgo, the third and 6th houses)** Mercury is an ability to communicate with and mediate between mother and father outwardly, and our feminine and masculine natures inwardly. Our intellect, intelligence, mental and nervous processes are determined by the fluidity of this communication. As communication requires the acquisition of visual and audial languages, it is essentially imitative. We communicate as we observe and hear others around communicate. Our mind interweaves masculine-feminine by the connecting bridge between the left brain hemisphere, which has domain over logical, analytical, mathematical and verbal functions with linear masculine qualities, and the right brain hemisphere, which has domain over holistic, mental, artistic and spatial functions associated with feminine simultaneous qualities. When Mercury registers, it shows at which age mental development is most critical. Mercury in the 3rd house is adaptable communicative mind, while Mercury in the 7th house is comparative, balancing and team thinking.

During Gestation, Mercury is an indicator of our mother's expression of her changing mental state and may represent her brothers or sisters, friends, confidants or our siblings. In Childhood, Mercury connotes other children and teachers – those after whom our own communication methods are patterned. Mercurial influence is also carried by books and the media, especially by television in the present world. Later manifestations include business sense, criticism, scientific work and individual self-expression.

Mercury is a gauge of our breadth of communication formed in early childhood, which is modulated by parental relationships. Even when parental attitudes openly conflict, they must combine within us. Mercury ranges from quick wit and easy superficiality to scathing criticism and serious scientific logic. Mercurial events are adaptations, changes of mind, perceptive insights, learning and teaching phases of life.

Venus　　(**Rules Taurus and Libra, the second and 7th houses**)
Venus represents relationships, harmony, love and personal aesthetics as determined by an ability to accept physical situations in life and to make them work, whether furnishing a room, adorning oneself, choosing a partner or making love. Venus is integration and physical attraction.

During Gestation, Venus shows a mother's relatedness to herself and others. Venus may be older sisters, friends of our mother's, or any women who guide her through gestation and birth, such as midwives, those who teach or espouse natural childbirth and those who write about these subjects. In Childhood, Venus indicates other children, aunts, friends of our mother, or even our mother herself. In Maturity, Venus describes woman friends, lovers, artists, mates, anyone attractive physically or those involved with beauty, art, clothes and appearances.

Venus indicates relationship to the physical world as amplified by the character of our sexual contact. Relationships with others mirror our understanding of the feminine reality within and the ways of projecting it outside in associations, artistic involvement and indulgence.

Mars　　(**Rules Aries and Scorpio, the first and 8th houses**) ♂
Mars represents the masculine sexual reality and physical situations that we cannot accept and that we desire to change. Mars is never satisfied with what is, only with what can be altered to suit its

affections. Mars resists absorption and is assertive, initiatory, passionate, energetic and conflicting. Sexual energy can be channelled into the physical world, but if no outlet is available Mars is violent, overbearing and ruthless.

During Gestation, Mars indicates doctors, medical examinations, men in general, aggressive midwives and our parents' sexual contact. At birth, Mars is often the doctor in his role as surgeon and intervening agent. In Childhood, Mars is active children, men, athletes, medical people, brothers, uncles or craftsmen. In Maturity, it is the acceptance of any of the former occupations or roles and those who change the world. On the sexual level, Mars is men to whom we are sexually attracted and the masculine aspect of women that attracts us.

Mars is an active desire to change the physical world into our own image, to produce progeny and to assert our own will. The degree of competitiveness in our persona mirrors the strength and nature of inner masculine reality. Mars events are accidents, creative moments, changes, alterations of attitude or situation, transactions we initiate, crises, resoluteness and enterprising moves. When Mars has no viable channel, it becomes violent, angry and self-destructive.

Jupiter   (Rules Sagittarius and Pisces, the ninth and 12th houses)
Jupiter represents expansive influences which are optimistic, positive, generous, enthusiastic, cohesive, philosophical, psychological or religious. Even in negative connections, although being indulgent and lazy, Jupiter is our life view and those who provide patterns for optimism.

During Gestation, Jupiter indicates religious influences, grandparents, socialites, prominent people, spiritual or psychological advisors and beneficial midwives or doctors. When registering at birth, Jupiter represents anyone who enlivens or is wise. In Childhood, it indicates surrogate parents, nannies, aunts or uncles, grandparents, early teachers, religious trainers or merchants. A registration of Jupiter in Maturity shows those people who determine our world view, psychologists and therapists, advisors, successful or notable people, politicians and those associated with education.

Jupiter indicates expansiveness, openness to new influences and a willingness to adopt educational, religious or psychological standpoints in life. We grow towards the goals we set for ourself; the higher the goals, the greater the possibilities. Jupiter events are expansion in work or philosophy, the advent of wealth and the appearance of people who help us. It is the ability to accept higher tasks that transcend our material appetites.

Saturn (Rules Capricorn and Aquarius, the 10th and 11th houses)
Saturn is a self-regulative counterbalance to Jupiter and tests, limits, concentrates, structures, orders, focuses, crystallizes, contracts and conserves. Saturn is acceptance of material and unavoidable restrictions of life. When we resist life's responsibilities, restrictions increase, while the willingness to confront reality enables us to focus and centre ourself.

During Gestation, Saturn is restrictive grandparents, serious doctors, pessimists, the authorities and those who inhibit our mother. Registering at birth, Saturn shows over-regulators of the birth process, emotionally restricting people present and the seriousness of the atmosphere. In Maturity, Saturn represents teachers, employers, elders, bank managers, authorities and those who seek to form and crystallize our reality. Saturn symbolizes those older, more depressive, more concentrated and more restricted than us.

Saturn is the acceptance and perfection of life through discipline, tests of strength, seriousness, confrontation and resolution of the problems of ageing. Saturnine events are inhibited crossroads, paralysing circumstances, illnesses, troubles and difficulties resulting from changes.

Uranus   **(Rules Aquarius and the 11th house)**
Uranus is the ability to step beyond the purely personal characteristics of the seven inner planets. Uranus represents originality, eccentricity, uniqueness, intensity, inspiration, inventiveness and rhythm, which allow you to integrate diverse influences that initially seem divisive, unusual or disconnected. It is the part of you that wants to be unique and free of the fetters of physicality.

During Gestation, Uranus indicates anyone who responds in an original way to a mother's pregnancy, including medical practitioners, midwives, childbirth instructors, other women or those who disrupt her natural rhythms or introduce new rhythms such as breathing exercises. When Uranus registers at birth or in aspect to the Ascendant, it indicates medical technicians, doctors, anyone who changes existing patterns and acts independently. In Childhood, Uranus shows rebels, eccentric playmates, independent friends and ambitious people. During Maturity, Uranus represents eccentrics, independent people, reformers, inventors, dancers, technicians, inspired people and fringe medical practitioners. Uranus symbolizes anyone who breaks down our established life patterns in unexpected ways and provides prototypes for our own independence.

Emotional and mental rhythms condition material rigidity and Uranus is the potential to integrate and balance new output. Uranus events are sudden, traumatic, unusual, eccentric and often happen in rhythmic phases.

 Neptune   **(Rules Pisces and the 12th house)**
Neptune represents our psychic, sensitive, imaginative, mediumistic and intuitive nature derived from the finer levels of reality and mirrored in dreams, fantasies, idealism, Utopian projections and imagination. Neptune shows our sensitivity and receptivity to the spiritual impulse as well as our illusions; the domain of drugs, psychic experiences, ESP and dream states. These are mechanisms that allow existing but hidden principles to rise to the surface of consciousness.

During Gestation, Neptune is those near our mother who sense that she is pregnant or act as mediums for her; as often others divine our innermost psychic states before we ourself do. Psychic friends, dreamers, mystics, gurus, dieticians, drug dealers and anyone who exerts psychic influence upon her are also covered by Neptune. At birth, Neptune is anaesthetists, hospital nursing staff, the watery medium of birth itself or sensitive participants. An amusing parallel is that the Neptune influence attracted in induced or anaesthetic births is similar when babies are born into pools of water, as one modern practice. Neptune registering in Childhood indicates dreamers, idealists, doctors treating childhood illnesses, fantasy characters, dream images and invented roles, as well as the omnipresent teddy bear or doll. In Maturity, Neptune is those who live in fantasy, illusion, dreams, sickness or sensitives, mediums, tricksters, psychics, astrologers and mystics, in addition to those who are sensitive and who dispense drugs.

Neptune symbolizes those who make us aware that the higher and finer levels of consciousness and reality are available, and teach how to gain access to them. Neptune events are difficult to describe as they are vague, internal, dreamy, psychosomatic or spiritual.

Pluto   (Rules Scorpio and the 8th house)

Pluto is contact with the masses and transformation, which involves the destruction of existing behaviour patterns and environments as a necessary prerequisite for regeneration. Often Pluto refers to world events that disrupt people and society – world wars, economic collapses, mass movements and super-power politics. Pluto is the effect on us of the world in which we live, specifically historical transformations. Most of us are affected by mass events without understanding what they are. Pluto shows our relationship to the influences that affect entire generations as well as our own parallel, internal changes. Changes of residence, school, attitude, partnership and other dramatic alterations of importance are governed by Pluto.

Pluto in Gestation shows world events affecting a mother's pregnancy, her contact with public figures such as medical specialists, authorities on childbirth, and even indirect contact with public influences through books or media. Being born during a world war, raised according to Dr Spock or delivered by the LeBoyer technique are examples of such influences. At birth, Pluto is people who exert influence, take charge or transform us. Pluto in Childhood is bossy people, parents or teachers. In Maturity, Pluto indicates figures who carry generational influences such as politicians, musicians, actors, propagandists and all those who affect us through public opinion.

Pluto is the part of us that responds to the challenges and trials of the masses and participates in public events, either actually or as a surrogate of mass movements for friends or acquaintanceships. Pluto events are gradual but extreme, exceptionally powerful, critical and carry long-lasting influence.

The Moon's North Node   (Rules Gemini and the 3rd house)

A line drawn through the long axis of the Moon's elliptical orbit round

Earth intersects the ecliptic at two places: the ascending North Node (which is more often used), where the intersection is from south to north, and the descending South Node. The Node moves backwards through the Zodiac in a complete cycle of 18 years. In our horoscope, the Node is adaptability, associations, family and groups.

The Node in Gestation shows the influence of groups upon a mother, particularly her family. At birth, it is the total influence of everyone present, including nurses, hospital help, and so on. Natural childbirth or women's groups often reflect the Node. In Childhood, the Node is other children and our family; in Maturity, clubs, social or political organizations, friends, circles of associates and all other groups of people.

Planetary Timing

The house cusps and sign cusps are dated in the time scale from conception to 99 years old. An identical process is used to find the registration age of every planet in a horoscope. An easy technique is to photocopy the circular dating disk (see Appendix B) onto transparent acetate and align it with the horoscope so that the figure 0 (the birth moment) in the inner ring is on the ASC. Dates during Gestation (the ninth, 10th, 11th and 12th houses) are graded in months before birth. Dates immediately after birth during the first year of life are graded in months, then the scale is graded in years. When a house cusp falls between two years, estimate the date in between. In most horoscopes the conception death point does not correspond to the dating disk. Conception point is the actual location of the 9th cusp in the horoscope, not the point on the disk! This reflects the fact that most births are either shorter or longer than the exact full term. A more accurate dating table and information about a computer program that creates a list of dates can be found in Appendix B.

Chapter Six — Aspects of Life

Aspects are angular relationships between planets, which connect and blend planetary qualities according to their precise angle as seen from Earth. The pattern of aspects in any horoscope shows how the planets integrate with each other. As aspects link planet to planet, they also connect events to each other, the people to each other and components of our own nature to each other. The simplicity or complexity of life is mirrored in the quantity and quality of aspects. Many aspects indicate the potential for combining many parts of ourself, while a small number of aspects show fewer natural interconnections.

The journey round the outside of our horoscope is a process in time. The outer events of life follow each other in a counter-clockwise direction from cause to effect. The centre of a horoscope is the centre of our being – the hub around which events turn and the totality of all qualities we possess. In the east this is called the wheel or round of samsara (illusion). The periphery is movement through time but the centre is timeless. The strength of aspects is determined by their penetration into the centre and by the nature of the planets combined. Individual aspects are differentiated by their angle and type of reception. Similarly, radio reception is influenced by the angular relationships of planets in relation to the Earth: 60° and 120° angles produce disturbance-free fields, while 90° and 180° angles produce disturbances and static (see the work of John Nelson of RCA in the 1960s), just as their equivalent angles produce either harmony or static in the horoscope.

The *Conjunction* (see Figure 15a) is an angular relationship of 0° and is the aspect of unity, when two or more planets occupy the same position in the zodiac. Their qualities are blended and they register at the same time in our life, which can make it difficult to differentiate them. When one planet is in aspect to a third planet, the other usually is also. The closer planets are to each other, the more firmly they are bonded and the more closely integrated are their qualities. Conjunctions are totally bound to the periphery of the horoscope and are in the causal sequence of life.

The *Sextile* aspect is an angular relationship of 60° degrees, one sixth of the circle, and is a peripheral aspect, only penetrating one eighth of the way into the centre (see Figure 15b). As each sign occupies 30° degrees of the circle, sextiles skip signs. A planet in Gemini makes sextiles to planets, forwards to Leo and backwards to Aries. A planet in Scorpio makes sextiles backwards to Virgo and forwards to Capricorn. Sextiles are movement slightly ahead or behind. Masculine and feminine signs alternate through the zodiac, and sextiles connect feminine to feminine and masculine to masculine. The sextile is the aspect of mental or sexual relationship and tends to involve surface rather than essence.

The *Trine* aspect is 120°, penetrates half-way into the circle, and mediates between the periphery and the centre, resulting in fluid communication, balance and support (see Figure 15c). The trine is communication which is neither superficial nor central; close contact, but not too close! The trine connects planets of the same element and their ease of relationship is due to this similarity. Earth sign Taurus trines the other earth signs Virgo and Capricorn, and the air sign Gemini trines the other air signs Libra and Aquarius. The structure of the octaves of the time scale is based upon triangles and the trine aspect connects a development in one octave with the equivalent stage of another octave. A planet in the self-assertive 1st house may trine another planet in the self-exteriorizing 5th house or the self-realizing 9th house. The octaves describe the creation of the physical body (Gestation), emotional body (Childhood) and mental body (Maturity), so a trine relates a facet of one body to a similar developmental stage of another body as emotion-to-physical or physical-to-mental or emotional-to-mental. The trine is the most balanced aspect, but also the most static.

The *Square* aspect is 90°, one fourth of the circle, and is shown as a right angle pointing at or embracing the centre (see Figure 15d). The square connects planets on the periphery, which tension the centre but are capable of resolution and produce movement. As the sextile and trine are pacific, the square is a source of motivation and forces changes of direction. Squares connect signs of one gender to signs of the opposite gender; feminine to masculine and vice versa. The masculine Leo is square to the feminine material Taurus and the metaphysical Scorpio. The contrast of gender is disruptive, but its influence provides creativity and energy, just as in life.

The *Opposition* aspect is 180°, one half of the circle, and is the relationship of two planets directly opposite each other (see Figure 15e).

Figure 15: Aspects

Aspects are defined by their penetration into the centre of the horoscope. (a) is a conjunction in Taurus, which is bound to the periphery; (b) is a sextile between Mars and Mercury, which is peripheral; (c) is a trine between Uranus and Neptune, which penetrates halfway to the centre; (d) is a square between the Sun and the Moon that tensions the centre and forces a change in direction; (e) is an opposition between the Node and Mars that passes through the centre and splits the horoscope in two.

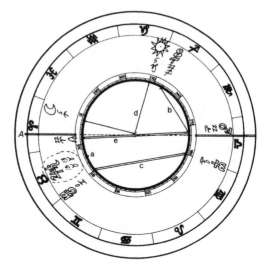

The opposition creates maximum tension, which leads either to polarization or reconciliation. The energy passes from one end to the other directly through the centre, and as opposites attract each other, there is both an antagonism and complementarity at the same time. The events, people and mechanisms involved are opposed in quality, character and time of life, just as both opposites are represented within our psyche. Usually our focus is upon one of the opposites, forcing the other to be suppressed or projected onto someone or something else outside us. If we cannot integrate the feminine in ourself, we project its contents onto an available woman. The natural polarity of life gives rise to the necessity of the integration of opposites as a way of generating the greatest energy. There are many minor aspects which may be used in addition to these and which are harmonics of the major aspects. The *Semisquare* is an angle of 45°, one eighth of the circle and half a square. This aspect carries tension, like the square, but performs a mediating function. The *Sesquiquadrate* is an angle of 135°, midway between a square and opposition. It also carries tension but does not penetrate as deeply as a square or opposition. The *Semisextile* of 30° is one-twelfth of the circle or one complete sign – this is the most peripheral aspect and indicates superficial connections. The Quincunx or *Inconjunct* of 150° is midway between the very static trine and very tense opposition, and so is variable and irrational.

Complex Configurations

When more than two planets aspect each other, complex configurations result which can be identified by their shapes.

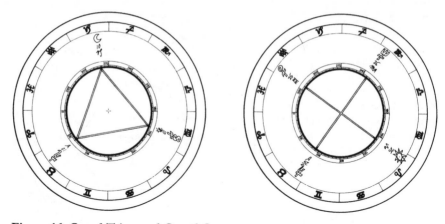

Figure 16: Grand Trine and Grand Cross
This 'earth' grand trine is a rigid shape with the Moon trine Saturn trine Mercury, which encloses the centre and is physically static. The 'fixed' grand cross is two oppositions mutually in square, each planet in two squares and an opposition, all in fixed signs of the zodiac.

In the *Grand Trine*, three planets are mutually trine to each other, making an equilateral triangle within a horoscope. They are usually in the same element and are identified as Fire, Air, Earth or Water Grand Trines. The Grand Trine is often considered the most positive shape possible, but as a triangle is a rigid shape in geometry, it often shows balance to the point of boredom. The Grand Trine surrounds and encloses the centre of our horoscope, as though we are so balanced that it is impossible to penetrate to your essence. An Earthy Grand Trine would has planets in Taurus, Virgo and Capricorn, tending to an obsession with physicality, tangible organization and possession.

The *Grand Cross* is composed of two opposing pairs of planets in mutual square, making a cross that dominates the centre of the horoscope. Every planet in the Grand Cross is in square to two others and in opposition to one, producing maximum tension through the horoscope and the life. This shape registers in one of the three modes; cardinal, fixed or mutable. A Fixed Grand Cross has planets in Taurus, Leo, Scorpio and Aquarius, none of which are willing to yield or change. Unless extraordinary outlets or understanding are made available, the internal tension is so great that the planets involved govern the person totally.

The *T-Square* is an opposition with a third planet in mutual square. It carries tension, but as the planets all reside in one half of the horoscope, its resolution is often easier than the Grand Cross. T-Squares also fall in modes of cardinal, fixed or mutable. A Mutable T-Square could be composed of planets in Pisces, Gemini and Sagittarius, all double signs and all very ambiguous. It is not uncommon to have series of T-Squares in a horoscope.

The way in which all the planets in our horoscope combine is analogous to the way in which we relate to the various parts of ourself and to others: the aspects represent possible channels of communication. The conjunction is similarity of view and attitude; the sextile is an exchange of superficial views; the trine is transmission between friends who connect well but never approach central or difficult issues; and the square shows mutual agitation through different but not opposite views. The opposition manifests different views that polarize and result in the dominance of one party over another or a stand-off. Where there is no direct aspect between planets, there is no direct communication.

We can imagine that our horoscope is activated in the following way: Pretend that we are throwing a grand party and inviting everyone critical in our life from past and present. We adopt a vantage point outside the room and simply observe the interactions between the characters. Certain people know each other already, but others have existed separately. The interesting factor is who relates to whom, and what the tenor of the gathering as a whole is likely to be. This gathering reflects the internal and external organization of our horoscope and our life! In a horoscope with few aspects and many unaspected planets, we would expect to see a roomful of people milling around, feeling uncomfortable, without attempting to intermingle at all. A well-knit horoscope with many aspects would produce a convivial and spirited gathering where everyone gets to know everyone else. Of course, the most interesting speculation of all would be if we assumed that everyone was obliged to talk about their relationship to us.

Aspect Patterns

The planets naturally form chains of aspects in a horoscope. It is possible for every planet to be aspected to every other planet, or connected through a chain, although this is rare. A chain is formed when two or more planets are in aspect to one base planet without being in aspect to each other. In John Lennon's horoscope, Pluto and Uranus are in aspect to the Moon, but not in aspect to each other. When Uranus is interpreted in the time scale, the operable aspect is Moon trine Uranus; when Pluto is operable, the aspect is Moon opposition Pluto; but when the Moon is being interpreted, the aspects are Moon trine Uranus and Moon opposition Pluto. The Moon, Lennon's mother, is the link between his ability to change (Uranus) and his ability to be recognized by the masses (Pluto). Thus the Moon is a link in a chain that includes Uranus, Pluto, a square to Mercury and a trine to Neptune.

Chains of planets are webs of relationships in life. At certain times they dramatically connect events, people and parts of us. The aspects are not 'good' or 'bad' as traditional astrology judges them; they simply describe the varieties of communication possible within our whole life. A very easy communication between two isolated trine planets may be less desirable than a web of five planets connected by squares of tension and superficial sextiles. Each event in a horoscope (and life) is connected with certain other events, and sometimes the connection is more interesting than either event itself. To segregate any event or person from the whole of one's life is misleading and may be damaging.

Groups of planets function like a psychological *complex*, which is a network of emotionally charged active associations that accumulate and discharge energy. Complexes are natural structures and are pathological only when they lack integration or are suppressed. Just as most people have a number of complexes, so there are usually series of planetary groupings within the horoscope that do not connect with each other.

In John Lennon's horoscope (see Figure 17) there are three clearly defined constellations, which we can call A, B and C. Constellation A is composed of the Ascendant opposed Sun, two very important positions that are isolated in tension from the rest of the horoscope. Constellation B includes the MC, Jupiter and Saturn, Venus, Mars, and Mercury. Constellation C includes the Moon, Uranus, Neptune, Pluto and again, Mercury. Mercury, showing Lennon's ability to make connections, is a very important element in the horoscope as it is the only link between these two major constellations.

Complexes vie with each other for momentary control. As we age, we move around the horoscope, into and out of the influence of our various complexes continuously. When we are under the influence of one complex, the others seem to disappear, but in the course of time they reappear and become dominant again. Aspect relationships come into and out of influence when any of the planets of which they are com posed is activated.

Within a constellation, energy flows along the path of least resistance. When two planets are in opposition, but mediated by a third planet in trine with one end and in sextile to the other end, the opposition can be avoided in favour of the easier, but more superficial sextile-trine route. In Lennon's horoscope, the Moon/Pluto opposition can be avoided by moving from the Moon along the trine to Mars and then along the sextile to Pluto, which would be interpreted as avoiding a feminine, emotional, one-sidedness (Moon opposed Pluto) by making

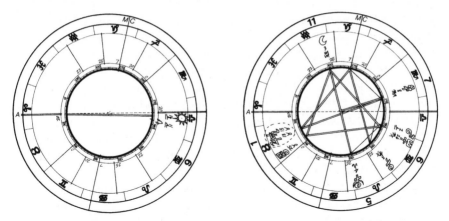

Figure 17: Horoscope Constellations A (on left) and B + C (on right)
The opposition between the Aries ASC and the Libra Sun is separate from the rest
of Lennon's horoscope: the energy can only reverberate back and forth between the
two. On the right a complex constellations links the other nine planets together.
Constellation B is composed of the MC, Jupiter and Saturn, Venus, Mars and
Mercury. Constellation C is composed of the grand trine with the Moon, Uranus,
Neptune and Mars, and the t-square involving the Moon, Pluto and Mercury. This
places great importance on the Moon (the feminine) because it is common to both
the grand trine and the t-square. Mercury carries even greater importance because it
is the only link between the two major constellations.

communication with other men (Mars) in work relationships (6th
house) and showing great vigour and ambition (Mars sextile Pluto). In
these cases, energy is capable of moving along either of two paths – the
healthiest situation of all. There should be a choice between tension
and equilibrium as often as possible for true growth, and a recognition
that these choices are available. The more aspects to any planet, the
more variations of the archetype the planet carries and the broader the
view available to us through the planet.

The number of planets in each constellation, the number of
individual constellations, the planets which connect sub-constellations,
and planets which stand alone – all these criteria are significant in
evaluating our life pattern.

Orbs

Aspects are strongest when the angle between two planets is exactly 0°,
60°, 90°, 120° or 180°. A planet's orb is the distance on either side of an
exact aspect, where the quality of the aspect still functions. Orbs vary
according to the size and importance of the planets involved, the aspects
involved and the system of interpretation used. Astrologers earlier in this

century sometimes used orbs of up to 15° on either side of the planets, making every planet aspect every other planet! It is important to understand planetary movement, because the horoscope 'freezes' the continual movement of the planets at the specific time and place of birth, but the planets themselves continue to move on their way. The faster a planet moves, the faster it passes into and out of an aspect, the shorter the duration of its effects and the weaker its potency. The slower planets move, the longer their influence and the stronger their effects. The Sun moves about 1° per day, the Moon about 13° per day; therefore the Moon moves 13 times faster than the Sun through the zodiac. You must expect the effects of the Moon to be proportionally less tangible. Pluto takes several months to pass through one degree, so the Moon moves about a thousand times faster than Pluto! This is why the Moon is seen as a trigger of other, slower-moving aspects. The slower the planet, the narrower its orb of influence. Table 5 shows suggested orbs for the planets.

Table 5: Planetary Orbs

Planet or Personal Point	Orb (in degrees)
Sun, Moon,	±8
Mercury, Venus, Mars, Ascendant, Midheaven	±5
Jupiter, Saturn, Uranus, Neptune, Pluto	±4
Node	±3

As a planet moves along the signs into the orb of another planet or angle, its effects gradually increase up to the point at which the aspect is exact and maximum effect manifests. When a planet moves into orb it is *Applying*. From exactitude, the planet then leaves the orb and gradually decreases in strength – this is called *Separating*. In Figure 18, the Sun is in 15° of Cancer and its orb extends from 7° Cancer (97° absolute longitude) to 23° Cancer (113°). Planets passing through this zone or in aspect to this zone combine with the Sun's influence at 7°, culminate at 15° Cancer and leave its influence at 23 degrees.

Within the context of the Life Time Scale, the orb takes on additional meaning. Movement around the horoscope determines the speed of our perceptions and the duration of an orb in calendar time varies accordingly. An orb of 5° in early childhood represents two weeks, while the same 5° orb at 60 years old covers more than six years. Events come and go more rapidly the younger we are; the older we are, the longer events take to manifest. This echoes the fact that wounds heal much faster in youth than in old age (see Bibliography – du Noüy, *Biological Time*), and the results of other experiments in human time perception.

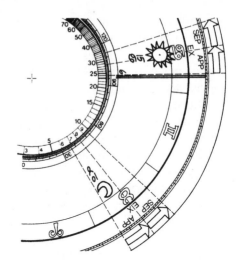

Figure 18: Dating Aspect Orbs
This shows a sextile aspect between
the Moon and Sun. Planets aspecting
the Sun come into orb at 7° Cancer,
become exact at 15° Cancer and pass
out of orb at 23° Cancer. You can see
the ages at which the planets come
into and out of their orbs.

If we allow the standard 8° orb on either side of the Sun, and the
Sun registers at the age of 28 years old (as in Figure 17), the Sun would
influence you from 24 years, four months, until exactitude at 28 years
and end at 33 years, five months. The same aspect in gestation would
apply, become exact and separate within days! The timing of orbs
must be considered in evaluating all aspects when we use the Life
Time Scale. The formation and after-effects of events in maturity take
longer and longer.

Interpreting Aspects

Each aspect is an interaction or process through which two planets are
combined and permuted. Interpretation is created by linking planet-
via-aspect-to-planet. If Venus represents relationship and is connected
by tensioning square to Saturn as inhibition, the resulting interpretation
of Venus square Saturn is 'a relationship tensioned by or producing
inhibition'. If Saturn registers earlier, the inhibition precedes the
relation ship but if Saturn registers later, the relationship produces the
inhibition. In our personal life, it is essential to understand this kind of
valuation. The people or parts of us involved are the personifications
of the planets; as Venus is a beautiful or harmonious person and Saturn
is an old, serious or depressed person, so Venus square Saturn is 'a
beauty inhibited by or inhibiting a more serious person' or 'the part of
us that wants to be attractive is inhibited by our seriousness'. An aspect
links sets of ideas, states or people indicated by the connecting planets.

The action of an aspect is qualified by the age at which it registers.
Venus registering at three months old in the 1st house square Saturn is
'you as a baby being restricted by grandparents' or 'your sister is jealous

of the attention you are getting from elders'. If Venus occurs at 13 in the 6th house square Saturn, 'your parents inhibit your choice of girlfriends' or 'you are discouraged from taking art (Venus) by a scientifically oriented advisor (Saturn) at school'. The nature of each developmental house must be attached to the interpretation of planets.

The signs of the planets qualify the interpretation. If Venus is in the security-minded Taurus and Saturn in the social Leo, Venus square Saturn is, relative to Venus at 13 years old, 'a young girl wanting security feels tension with an older man with good social connections'.

The connection of planet–aspect–planet qualified by house, sign and age is an association process that describes astrological events accurately and becomes easier with practice.

Sensitive Points

Sensitive points – the positions of exact aspects to a planetary body around the horoscope, whether or not these points are occupied by other planets – are important in Life Time Astrology because they show all the dates and ages at which natal planets and personal points register. Figure 19 shows the 11 common sensitive points to a natal planet around the horoscope. Whenever any of these points are occupied or passed over by planets, the energy of the base planet – in this case Jupiter – is released. If Jupiter in the birth chart is a generous protector, whenever Jupiter's sensitive points are activated, a similar protective influence is made manifest, either within or without. By using the time-scale disk, every sensitive point may be dated exactly in life at the times when each planet and personal point can be expected to produce an effect in life.

Every planet in a horoscope has its birth position and seven major sensitive points. The total number of active points in a horoscope translated into dates in life makes 96 (12 × 8). When the 30°, 45°, 135° and 150° minor aspects are added, as they are on the Life Time Astrology printouts described in the Appendix, there are 192 points (12 × 16). Sensitive points are distributed either uniformly or in bunches, depending upon the closeness of aspects in the birth chart. Many exact aspects make tight clusters of sensitive points, which produce active and potent series of life events separated by less active time gaps. Events that happened many years ago continue to vibrate within us, just as events that are to happen in our future are vibrating in us now.

Sensitive points cover the entire circle of life, but there are so many of them, it is unreasonable to use them all. They are useful when we wish to fill in apparently empty spaces and times between the

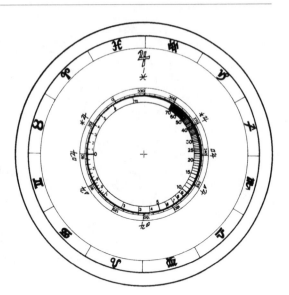

Figure 19: Planet Sensitive Points
Jupiter at the top is near the MC in early gestation. Its sensitive points are exact aspect points around the circle that resonate with the early event signified by Jupiter.

registration of natal planets. To illustrate this, process we will calculate the sensitive points that register between Pluto at five years old and Venus at nine years, two months, in John Lennon's horoscope (see Figure 20). The sequence of sensitive points are as follows:

Natal Pluto	*4 Leo*	*4 yrs 11 mths*
Square to Mercury	8 Leo	5 yrs 05 mths
Sextile to Node	11 Leo	5 yrs 08 mths
Square to Saturn	13 Leo	6 yrs 00 mths
Square to Jupiter	13 Leo	6 yrs 00 mths
Sextile to Sun	16 Leo	6 yrs 05 mths
Trine to Ascendant	20 Leo	6 yrs 11 mths
Square Uranus	25 Leo	7 yrs 09 mths
Natal Venus	*3 Virgo*	*9 yrs 02 mths*

These sensitive points are interpreted as being in Leo with Mercury, Node, Saturn, Jupiter, Sun and Ascendant in the 5th house and Uranus in the 6th house. In addition to the interpretation of each planet in its sign and house position qualified by the aspect, the intervals between pairs of planets may be used to describe the intervening time. The interval between sensitive sextile Sun at six years, five months, and the sensitive trine Ascendant five months later at six years, 10 months, is described like a Sun/ASC aspect. The interpretation of the sensitive points and their intervals adds a detailed dimension to the sequence of natal planets in a horoscope.

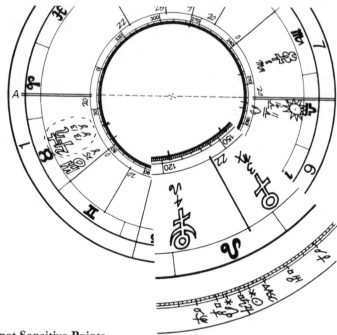

Figure 20:
Sequence of Planet Sensitive Points
The sensitive aspect points fill out apparent gaps between the registration of Pluto
in Leo and Venus in Virgo. Each gap is interpreted like an aspect between the two
planets bounding it.

Time Scale Constellations

The logarithmic time scale grades the entire periphery of the
horoscope by age: all planetary positions, personal points (ASC & MC)
and sensitive points are located and dated in sequence, producing 91
major formative events in life.

Each constellation is considered in relation to a natal planet located
at a particular age. In Chapter Three we learned how to locate and date
the planets from conception to the end of our life – now it is necessary
to determine the sequence in which the aspect combinations are to be
interpreted.

There are two sets of considerations for describing a constellation of
planets. First, the planets in aspect to a base planet register either before
it (back towards the conception point/9th house cusp) or after it
(towards the 8th house) in time sequence. The locations of aspecting
planets show the 'history' of each constellation in sequence. Second,
the proximity of the sensitive points of the aspecting planets in relation
to the base planet show both the strength of aspect (closer aspects are
stronger aspects) and the sequence of the unfolding of the

constellation, as the sensitive points register either before or after the base planet.

An analysis of the structure of some of the constellations in a horoscope illustrates this process. An analysis of the Moon in Aquarius and the 11th house at 31 weeks before birth includes aspects to Uranus, Pluto, Neptune, Mars and Mercury. The Moon is first paired with each of the other planets according to whether their sensitive point falls before or after 3° Aquarius. The eventual registration time of each aspecting planet is indicated:

1.	Trine from Uranus (25° Taurus) at 10 mths old to	25 Capricorn
2.	Trine from Neptune (26° Virgo) at 14 yrs 9 mths to	26 Capricorn
3.	Trine from Mars (2° Libra) at 16 yrs 8 mths to	2 Aquarius
4.	*Natal Moon at*	*3 Aquarius*
5.	Opposition from Pluto (4° Leo) at 5 yrs to	4 Aquarius
6.	Square from Mercury (8° Scorpio) at 34 yrs to	8 Aquarius

This is the sequence in which the aspects to the Moon unfold. Each aspecting planet either evokes earlier events or is a preview of later events. Since the Moon is in Gestation, all of its aspects happen later, indicating the first registration of a very powerful lunar–maternal influence. This would amplify the importance of gestation events! The strongest planets in this constellation are the closest aspects in the sequence: Moon–Mars and –Pluto, –Mercury, –Neptune and –Uranus. Their hierarchy of strengths should be taken into consideration when interpreting this constellation.

The next position in Lennon's horoscope is his Aries Ascendant, to which the only aspect is an opposition to the Sun in Libra (see Figure 15). When two planets or one planet and a personal point (ASC or MC) are in aspect with each other but unaspected to the rest of the horoscope, they tend to vibrate back and forth. The energy flows from one end to the other and back again. This creates tension through the opposition in Lennon's case and a trapped outlook. As the Ascendant is the birth moment and the Sun registers at the age of 21 years, 10 months, these two periods are critical in his life.

When the planet chosen as base registers in later life, as Mercury in Lennon's horoscope, an additional timing must be included in interpretation. Planets in aspect to Mercury cover a period of time before and after the actual registration of Mercury. As we age, the orb of aspecting planets becomes indicative of the fact that later events take quite a long time to develop, manifest and then to have their after-effects assimilated. Mercury has aspects from the MC, Moon, Jupiter/Saturn conjunction, Pluto and Venus. These planets register as follows, with the addition of the dates of registration of their sensitive points:

1.	Sextile from Venus (3° Virgo) to	3 Scorpio at	30yr 07mths
2.	Square from Moon (3° Aquarius) to	3 Scorpio at	30yr 10mths
3.	Square from Pluto (4° Leo) to	4 Scorpio at	31yr 02mths
4.	Sextile from MC (7° Capricorn) to	7 Scorpio at	33yr 00mths
5.	*Natal Mercury at*	*8 Scorpio at*	*34yr 00mths*
6.	Opposition from Saturn (13° Taurus) to	13 Scorpio at	37yr 03mths
7.	Opposition from Jupiter (13° Taurus) to	13 Scorpio at	37yr 07mths

The Mercury constellation lasts from 30 years seven months (May 1971) until 37 years, seven months (May 1978), or seven years! The sequence of planets is absolutely critical in interpreting constellations, as profound differences between horoscopes with constellations containing similar planets occur when the sequence varies. Each constellation describes a very specific series of planetary events, which is reactivated whenever any planet subsequently passes over the base planet. The sequence of planets is the most important information conveyed by the horoscope!

This type of aspect analysis must be done for every planet in a horoscope. Each planet is analyzed by sign, house and age; its aspects are determined; the aspect combinations are collated in the sequence of their sensitive points; the original registration times of all the planets are noted; and finally, the interpretation is connected.

This method of analysis is similar to the way in which memory functions. We live life sequentially. Certain periods or events in life carry clusters of associations, which preceded or resulted from the primary event. Each of those events in turn has its own past. Whenever similar events, clusters of events or even fragments of events happen, we remember the entire constellation of influences again. Since sensitive points provide the times when primary events and their constellations are likely to emerge again into consciousness, it is useful for understanding the timings and mechanisms of all events in life.

Aspect Interpretation Tables

Appendix A includes the tables for interpreting planetary aspects. They are as simple and inclusive as possible, because the first necessity is to have material from which to associate freely and with which to build accurate events and people in our horoscope. Every pair of planets has: basic principles and events that are likely to occur; possible negative manifestations when there are squares, oppositions or when they are in unfavourable houses or signs; and personifications of each pair of planets. Remember that all events have both an outer and inner significance and influence upon us. The crotchety old man indicated by Saturn may be inside us already at 21 years old!

The use of pairs of planets and personal points is essential to understand the workings of Life Time Astrology, but the aspect combinations are so exhaustive that they require an entire book to themselves. The best book is *The Combination of Stellar Influences* by Reinhold Ebertin (distributed by the American Federation of Astrologers). Its interpretive material is so complete that it has 184 pages and 1,117 categories of aspects alone! Figure 21 shows two facing pages of *CSI*. Ebertin's Cosmobiology Institute in Germany has verified all information with case histories collected by thousands of astrologers.

The left-hand page of *CSI* shows the base pair of planets to be combined, in this case Saturn/Uranus, together with their Psychological, Biological, Sociological Correspondences and Probable (Event) Manifestations. On the right-hand page are the other planets that can be combined when in the same constellation or when they activate the base pair by transit or direction. The introduction of a third planet makes the interpretation much more specific.

Ebertin bases his system on *Cosmic Structural Pictures* – groupings of planets related by mathematical formulae – where a planet exactly halfway (on the axis) between two others, at the *midpoint*, shares the qualities of both. This is a shift away from static traditional astrology and prepares the way for Life Time Astrology, which treats life as a dynamic web of relations. Using *CSI*, it is possible to compare up to ten planets or personal points with any primary pair of planets. Ebertin's text is essential for more advanced work.

With the survey of aspects, all structural techniques for interpreting the horoscope are complete. All that remains is to combine them to interpret your life story.

0866   ♄ / ♅   S A T U R N / U R A N U S

P r i n c i p l e
Irritability and inhibition, tension.

P s y c h o l o g i c a l   C o r r e s p o n d e n c e :
+   The ability to cope with every situation, the power to pull
    through and to endure, perseverance and endurance, inde-
    fatigability, will-power, determination.

-   Unusual emotional tensions or strains, irritability, emo-
    tional conflicts, rebellion, the urge for freedom, a provo-
    cative conduct, an act of violence.

C   A self-willed nature, tenaciousness and toughness, ob-
    stinacy, strong emotional tensions or stresses.

B i o l o g i c a l   C o r r e s p o n d e n c e :
Inhibitions of rhythm, heart-block, Cheyne-Stokes' breathing.
Unrhythmical processes. - A sudden loss of limbs (a chronic
illness in this sense); operations accompanied by the removal of something. (Removal of intestinal parts, spleen,
amputation etc.)

S o c i o l o g i c a l   C o r r e s p o n d e n c e :
Violent people.

P r o b a b l e   M a n i f e s t a t i o n s :
+   Growth of strength caused through the overcoming of diffi-
    culties, difficult but successful battles in life for the purpose
    of overcoming a dangerous situation. (Operation).

    Kicking against tutelage and against the limitation of freedom,
    the tendency to cause unrest within one's environment, a
    quarrel, separation, the use of force, interventions in one's
    destiny, the limitation of freedom.

Figure 21: The Combination of Stellar Influences

The left page describes the Principle of the combination Saturn/Uranus, the
Psychological Correspondences, Biological Correspondences, Sociological
Correspondences and the Probable Manifestations. The right page describes the
interaction of Saturn/Uranus and each of the other planets and personal points.
(From *The Combination of Stellar Influences* by Reinhold Ebertin)

SATURN/URANUS ♄/♅

0867= ☉   Physical exposure to severe tests of strength, the power of
            resistance, rebellion, inflexibility. - Separation.

0868= ☽   Strong emotional tensions and strains, states of depression,
            inconstancy. - The sudden desire to liberate oneself from
            emotional stress, separation from members of the female
            sex.

0869= ☿   The making of great demands upon one's nervous energy,
            the ability to hit back hard under provocation, the ability to
            organise resistance, the act of separating oneself from
            others. - Necessary changes.

0870= ♀   Tensions or stresses in love-life often leading to separa-
            tion.

0871= ♂   An act of violence, the occasionally wrong use of extraor-
            dinary engergy, undergoing great efforts and toil. - A
            violent or forced release from tensions or strains, the
            stage of challenging others for a decisive contest or fight. -
            Injury, accident, deprivation of freedom.

0872= ♃   The ability to adapt oneself to every situation, a fortunate
            release from tensions. - A sudden turn (in destiny), the mis-
            fortune to get into difficulties. - Losses, damage to
            buildings, motor damage.

0873= ♆   The inability to face emotional stresses, falsehood or malice
            caused through weakness. - A resolve to resign oneself to
            the inevitable, the abandonment of resistance, weakening
            strength, separation, mourning and bereavement.

0874= ♀   An act of violence or brutality. - The desire to overcome
            a difficult situation through extraordinary effort. - Re-
            bellion against one's lot in life, harm through force majeure.

0875= ☊   The inability to integrate oneself into a community, provo-
            cative conduct. - Joint resistance to a common opponent,
            separation.

0876= A   Being placed in difficult circumstances, the fate of standing
            alone in the world. - The suffering of difficulties caused by
            others, experiencing emotional suffering together with
            others, mourning and bereavement.

0877= M   Making the highest demands upon one's own strength, re-
            bellion, provocation. - The act of separating oneself from
            others.

Aspect Interpretation

When we use interpretation tables, they list the range of possible manifestations of each planet in every sign of the zodiac, in every house of the horoscope and in aspect with every planet. Each planet in a horoscope must be evaluated by combining these three categories:

1.   Planet in sign (the quality of the planetary operation)
2.   Planet in house (the time and developmental stage of life)
3.   Planet in aspect to other planets (connections to other events at other times in life)

Within each category there are a range of possible manifestations, ranging from the most positive to the most negative. The astrologer's choice is based upon the following criteria.

First, each planet has a quality that can be naturally difficult or easy. The planets Sun, Venus and Jupiter are positive in most circumstances; Mars, Saturn, Uranus and Pluto often show tension, negative energy or difficult situations; and the Moon, Mercury and Neptune are neutral and easily influenced. In addition, the outer planets, Uranus, Neptune and Pluto, carry generational influences that everyone receives.

Second, the types of aspects involved in connecting planets must be considered. Conjunctions are neutral aspects of unity, where the quality of the planets joined are simply compared to each other. Sextiles and trines produce supportive or positive connections, which equilibrate the planets combined. Squares and oppositions produce tension, which tend to static in combined planetary influences.

Third, the location of the planets in a horoscope condition their interpretation. Planets in gestation represent very deep and archetypal influences, which have a primary effect upon the body; planets in childhood represent emotional influences, which are familial in origin and are carried in the personality, while planets in maturity are mental and affect the individual soul or entire being. The octaves range from the general to the specific through a lifetime. Planets near or in aspect to either the MC or the ASC are of particular importance as they condition our world view and personality, respectively, and convey this importance within a constellation.

Fourth, the traditional system of rulerships of planets indicates the strength or weakness of a planet by sign and house position. Planets are strongest in those signs (and equivalent houses) that they rule and weakest in those opposite signs and houses. The other signs and houses are neutral. For example, Venus rules the active sign Libra and the 7th house, and the passive sign Taurus and the 2nd house, and is weak in detriment in the active sign Aries and the 1st house, and the passive

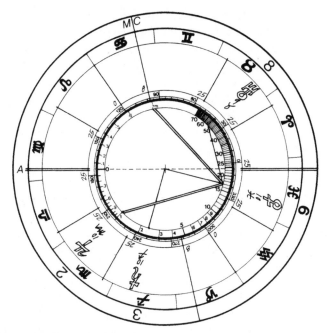

Figure 22: Aspect Interpretation
Venus in Pisces is the base planet in this constellation, and registers at 17 years old. The MC trine extends back from seven months before birth; the Jupiter trine goes back to one year old; the Saturn square comes from two years and four months old; and the sextile to Uranus extends ahead to 53 years old. The Venus configuration synthesizes the earlier events and leads to the Uranus manifestation later in life. Using the date disk in Appendix B, all aspect combinations may be evaluated and dated in this way.

sign Scorpio and the 8th house.

In Figure 22 we interpret Venus as a base planet. Venus is in Pisces and the 6th house, is trined by Jupiter and the MC, squared by Saturn and sextiled by Uranus, and registers at the age of 18 years old. By sign and house position Venus is neutral. Venus in Pisces would be 'longing for love, romance, feeling oriented' and Venus in the 6th house would be 'work loving, puritanical, modest'. The combination indicates a romantic longing for love is hampered by a puritanical love of work. As Venus registers at 18 it refers to a young woman or lover. The aspecting planets are evaluated separately, and then accumulated and blended into an entire picture. Venus is a positive planet in its own right. Uranus is a tense generational influence connected by a positive sextile; Saturn is negative and also in a very tense square aspect; the MC is objective and conservative (in Cancer); and Jupiter is positive and connected by a supportive aspect. Therefore, we have two positive planets, including the base planet Venus, two neutral and one negative.

In the Aspect Tables each planetary pair has positive keywords, negative keywords in brackets, and personifications of those involved in the aspect. As our base Venus registers at 18 years old and is in the octave of maturity as is Uranus, the MC is early in the octave of gestation, while Jupiter and Saturn are in the emotional octave of childhood affecting the personality, the event is emotional but with a strong bearing upon the overall life direction. The four combinations are:

1. *Venus trine MC*: The neutral keywords are 'objective Love, attachment; artistic inclinations' with the personification being 'an artist, an admirer, or a lover', showing an affair, and evoking the conservatism inherent in the mother when she discovered she was pregnant. This could well show a concern about an unwanted pregnancy.

2. *Venus trine Jupiter in Scorpio*: The slightly above neutral keywords are 'popularity, good form sense, happiness' with the personification being an 'artist, social person, expansive lover', implying a relationship. As Jupiter registered at one year old when there was positive contact, then separation (from an uncle), this implication is carried here. A more positive constellation could indicate marriage, while a more negative could imply laziness and arrogance.

3. *Venus square Saturn in Sagittarius*: The keywords are 'reserve, economy, loyalty to an older person, fear of illegitimacy' in the person of an 'older lover, lonely people, widower'; the lover is older and there may well be the threat of an unwanted pregnancy, producing reserve. Saturn originates in the 3rd house and shows a foreign grandmother inhibiting communication when the subject learned to talk.

4. *Venus in Pisces and the 6th*: The subject is an art student, open and receptive, wanting love and affected by outer circumstances.

5. *Venus sextile Uranus*: This aspect projects ahead to 53 years old and shows 'arousal, eccentric impulses, musical and artistic talent' carried by one who is an 'artist, musician or eccentric lover'. It shows a later relationship in life that mirrors the early one, but the roles change and this individual is the Uranian older lover of a young student.

The total picture shows the subject at 18 years old involved with an older artistic teacher in an elicit love affair. She is wary of committing herself for fear of illegitimacy, but this situation sets a precedent for a later eccentricity at 33 years old when she is sexually more adventurous.

Chapter Seven — Your Story

There is unity between the events that begin and end life. At the instant the sperm fertilizes the ovum, a complex life pattern registers and begins its exorable unfolding. The nature of life – physical, emotional, energetic and intellectual – is largely determined at conception and our experiences and environment qualify this inherent reality. Many who have almost died report that the events of their life flashed before their mind's eye at death. This describes the same pattern in time at the moment of its completion.

In other words, at conception, life is all potential; at death, all potential has been made actual and life is finished. The life process is the translation of potential into actual reality and at every moment past actualities are balanced against future possibilities. The fulcrum point from which you experience this phenomenon is the Present. Life may be compared to a transformer which takes raw energy from the earthly environment and transforms it into finer and finer energies through time, until the process is complete and the body is released at death.

The horoscope is the graphic representation of your life pattern from conception to death. Movement through the horoscope follows life and is *Your Story* – a tale involving everything essential in your life. The rules that govern your story are those which govern all stories and are not generated by particular psychological schools, religions or nations. Your Story is the playing out of your version of timeless archetypal patterns, which the code transmitted to you at conception. Since birth you have continually told, retold, altered, permuted, remembered and forgotten your life story. What you tell your partner, children, friends, bank manager, psychoanalyst and yourself are variations of your story. Every time your stories are told, you alter them minutely to suit the audience and the occasion. The only information you have about anyone else you know, or have known, is carried in memory in the form of a story. Obviously the stories you tell about yourself, your past, your family and your parents are totally true! Everyone else is subject to elaboration, to bending the truth to improve content, interest and intelligence, but you yourself do not. But you do! Without an objective view of your life derived from the astrological information in your horoscope, you are left with a view of life as you have told it and distorted it.

The only memories you are likely to have before the age of five are vague scenes of spring days seen from rocking prams, reminiscences of parents and relatives, photographs posed for family scrapbooks, or nothing. If events are remembered at all, they tend to be superficial in respect to your real being. Yet you possess clearly demarcated characteristics, which were formed during the earliest times of life. Of the time during gestation even less is known, as you must rely upon the verity of aged parents for all information. How do you know that what you remember or are told by your parents is true? They also alter their stories through many years of retelling them to verify their roles as responsible parents and to play down their own shortcomings. The more culpable they might have been, the more likely they are to have forgotten the associated stories. When there was chaos, it was your fault. In remembering and retelling stories about your early life, they redefine their role in your life and extensively redefine your reality by their stories.

To see and understand yourself clearly, you must recognize habitual ways of remembering, and go back to the beginning and reconstruct your life. Reconstruction is integral to psychoanalysis because therapy starts at the present and works backwards into the past. The past is gradually recovered through recall, dream analysis, free association, memory stimulation, psychodrama or hypnosis, and as the analysis goes deeper, the importance of the emerging contents increases. Gaps in early life are often the subject of years of probing and much of the confusion derives from what you 'know' about early events. Is what you know true?

For analysis to be helpful, it is essential to eliminate spurious stories and discover the real motivations of your past. Life Time Astrology is unique because the order in psychoanalysis is reversed – instead of regressing backwards into life, you recreate your life from the beginning in the order in which it was lived.

The object of an astrological analysis using the Life Time scale is to recreate the pattern and subpatterns of life. The resulting objective view of the principles and people can be compared to memories, and more importantly, the connections determined by the aspects show how the events in your life interweave. We can understand life as a process in time, which continues into the future rather than as an isolated present moment cut adrift of true meaning.

A central issue in astrology is that of contradiction. It is not possible to describe character with absolute statements as though it never changes because no behaviour is static – it is always being modified by age and circumstances. Everyone possesses contradictory feelings, thoughts, intuitions and sensations. To be realistic, astrology must present all sides of your being, at the times when they come into play. Life Time Astrology does just this. As you reconstruct your life with your horoscope, squares and oppositions or combinations of incompatible planets describe contradictory views, events and parts of you which you always carry within. At one time of life, you feel one way about your mother, while at other times you feel the opposite. This is true of relationships, life's work, children, and virtually all areas of reality, including attitudes towards yourself. Instead of constituting a threat, the tensioning and opposing parts of your nature and life are essential to the whole. You must accept all contradictory parts, understand them and work with them, rather than trying to make them disappear.

In the psychology of Jung, all components of the self of which you are unconscious or unaware constitute the shadow. As well as including the dark parts of your nature, the shadow carries all the characteristics you do not want to see in yourself. The usual solution is to project those unwanted characteristics onto people around you, who then become, in your mind, responsible for them. Similarly, events in life that demonstrate your failings are also repressed or attributed to others. When any person or event in life becomes more important than the whole, the strong emotional charge carried is a sign that the shadow is in operation. The inner experience of coming to terms with the shadow (that is, the negative sides of nature and life) is enacted by everyone in life. In Life Time Astrology both sides of your nature are presented in their proper sequence. If the position of Mercury indicates great intelligence, while its opposition to Saturn shows inhibited mental development, rather than trying to decide which you 'really are', you should realize that you are both of these at different times. At times when Mercury is operative, you are very intelligent but at the times when Saturn is dominant, you are inhibited. You can benefit from knowing when each of these situations are in operation. If you can accept vices as well as virtues, you are on the path to the unification of the whole self.

Ground Rules

You must accept that life is a story told from your own point of view. Others may set the scene before your arrival, but you are the central character. As you grow into the central role, others may temporarily pre-empt centre stage, or even occupy it for long periods of time, forcing you to accept 'bit parts', but even then you retain your own unique vantage point.

Your story must be consistent. The characters and characteristics as defined by planets, signs, houses and aspects must be created realistically. Each character must have an identity and must develop with the story.

The signs of the zodiac represent a sequence of behaviour patterns. In life you live through all 12 signs and have an opportunity to act out many permutations of viewpoint and behaviour. The difference between you and others lies in the fact that *everyone passes through the various signs at different ages,* and that the planets amplify certain signs and not others. Aries describes 'self-assertion'; it is crucial whether you pass through this sign at the age of two or 42.

The houses of the horoscope describe the exact phasing of the developmental periods in life. As you age from conception, you pass through the 12 houses in sequence. The change in time sense as you age means that each house occupies a time period almost equal to the time from the beginning of that house all the way back to conception. During each house, you recapitulate your entire previous existence.

The signs overlaid upon the houses describe the qualities that govern each developmental period. The three octaves are three *acts of life* (Gestation, Childhood and Maturity) and each act contains four scenes (houses).

The first act is gestation, when your mother is the central character and your father, grandparents, doctors and midwives play supporting roles. Each scene of gestation follows the transformation of your mother, and the signs through which she passes are the sets against which she plays her part. If she passes through the isolating 12th house occupied by the physically secure Taurus, you would feel physically secure when isolated and dependent upon others.

The second act is childhood, which begins when you first appear at the 'curtain-raising' moment of birth. During childhood you gradually adapt your personality amid the characters who set the scene in the first act, possibly joined by other young characters as the family expands. You vie increasingly for better dialogue and more spotlights. If, to continue the example, you have demonstrative and extravert Leo qualities during the communicative 3rd house, you would become very powerful as soon as you learned to talk and express yourself.

The third act is maturity when, after establishing a physical and emotional milieu, you work out all your various possibilities in the world. Gradually the earliest members of the cast relinquish their roles and their lives, and by the end of the drama they have exited from the stage and you have taken over all their parts, retaining them as the memories of a lifetime. The culmination of the play is the departure of the central character, you...

The fourth transcendent octave does not occupy its own stage time, but lies within the higher meaning you are able to impart to the drama as a whole.

The planets are the cast of characters. In the beginning, the primary characters are all the 'others' who produce, nurture and allow you to develop many parts. They are the prototypes of your range of roles; early directors and script-writers who determine the pattern and breadth of your first parts. Gradually you integrate their influence into the whole of your role. The Saturn grandfather who attended your birth and worried in the adjoining room becomes the hidden seriousness, which only those who know you well can see. The times when planets register in the sequence of houses and signs show exactly when each character makes his or her most important contribution to the whole, as well as those other times when they influence you. As the Saturn opposition showed a fretting grandfather, when Saturn actually registers at 24 years old, you worry over the birth of your own child. The quality of life depends upon your ability to identify these significant characters and to integrate their roles willingly into your total character.

The aspects are relationships between house development phases, sign qualities and planetary characteristics, all bound together in your life. The aspects show the web of relationships, which tension and equilibrate your being, and they define the pattern and rhythm of the events of your life through time. When there are many more squares and oppositions in the horoscope, life is tense, testing and difficult, but also potentially powerful. When trines and sextiles dominate, life is easy and comfortable but may lack drive, ambition and liveliness. An even blend between the two shows enough balance to provide a stable base to your activities, yet the requisite tension to generate movement and diversity.

Interpretation is information derived from the logical combination of signs, houses, planets and aspects, with which you are now familiar. The most effective way to order and convey this mass of information is as Your Story. The fluency of the story depends upon understanding the basic mechanisms of astrology, so when you cannot remember the meaning of a sign, house, planet or aspect, refresh your memory. With practice and repetition, you can interpret horoscopes at a glance.

The description of Your Story proceeds octave by octave from conception to the end of life, or a predetermined age in the future. You begin by interpreting the relationship between your parents leading up to conception, then conception itself. As you advance through the houses, the positions of the planets determine the rate of movement. Houses without planets are passed over, while houses with concentrations of planets show important developmental periods. In the next section it will be shown how all components of the horoscope are approached and blended together. The house-by-house process of life is broken down into octaves and the planetary characters and characteristics are also described for each octave.

Each house section is accompanied by example horoscopes, which show how to interpret life events accurately. In each case, only the relevant planets are shown to eliminate confusion, although in practice all planets combine to generate the astrological whole.

Setting the Scene

To begin, you must set the scene for your entrance. It would not do to start anywhere else except the time before you are conceived. First you must identify which of your parents had the impulse to conceive you, why they had this impulse and the nature of the relationship between your parents at this time.

Conception includes the ovum's lunar month of ripening, which begins with your mother's last menstruation; it is fertilized midway through its cycle and ends when the fertilized ovum attaches itself to the uterine wall, when the cellular body begins developing. In a clockwise movement from conception (9th house cusp) in the horoscope, the circle is the pattern of events that happen to your ovum. The lifetime of the ovum is a microcosm of the process of cellular life. Since fertilization occurs at an intermediate point in the ovular cycle, you can see in the horoscope how your parents participated in your conception.

The prelude to the story is the relationship between your parents just before conception. The Sun is your father, the Moon is your mother and the point of conception is the cusp of the 9th house. Gestation begins at this point and continues in a counter-clockwise direction. To discover which parent was responsible for the impulse to conceive you, you must move in a clockwise direction backwards from conception point until you find either the Sun or the Moon. If you find the Sun first, your father was responsible for conception, and if you find the Moon, then your mother was responsible for your conception.

The body is created during gestation, and conception is the creative act that begins gestation. The description of how your parents acted to conceive you also describes the way in which you yourself create; that is, the sexual act of your conception is a metaphor for the principle of creativity in your life. If the Sun-father is primary, the masculine influences within you precede the feminine, but if the Moon-mother is first, feminine influences are primary in your creative and sexual life. Both women and men have an equal possibility of feminine or masculine origin and creative influence at conception.

Now that you know which parent has the initial impulse, it is essential to discover the attitudes of your parents. This information is carried by the Sun and Moon in specific signs, houses and in their mutual aspect, if there is one.

You first determine whether the originating parent is conscious or unconscious of the desire to produce a child. This is indicated by the position of your Sun or Moon: either above the horizon, indicating consciousness, or below the horizon, indicating unconsciousness. Both luminaries above the horizon imply that both parents are conscious of the desire for a child, or even the possibility of a planned conception. If both are below the horizon, the probability is that your conception is instinctive, unplanned and accidental. One above and one below indicates that the conception combines the conscious being of one parent and the unconscious being of the other.

The eastern left hemisphere of the horoscope is the logical and rational physical realm of the self, and the western right hemisphere is the holistic and artistic realm of the not-self. The placement of each luminary/parent reflects whether they acted selfishly or selflessly. The left-right divisions in the horoscope could even describe the relative importance of your brain hemispheres!

The sign elements of the Sun and Moon are further definitions. In Earth signs parental reasons for conceiving a child are material; in Air signs as a means of communication; in Fire signs as an energy exchange or common creation; and in Water signs someone to feel for or about. Parental motives influence not only your prenatal state, but reflect the motivating force behind your creative activity throughout life. The elements correspond to the four psychological types of Jung: Fire with Intuition; Earth with Sensation; Air with Thinking; and Water with Feeling. The types of creativity as determined by the prenatal influence are important in discovering your own creative role in life.

The location of the Sun and Moon by sign and house constitute a major determining influence upon your masculine and feminine natures, as of course we all have some proportion of both. The sign of each luminary describes the *quality* of their creative influence and the house describes the *developmental stage* to which your parents respond. The following key words demonstrate the meanings of the signs and houses:

Table 6: Preconception Parental Designations

House Sign	Octave and Interpretation
	Childhood = Emotional Body Through Personality
1st Aries	Self-expressive, impulsive, self-centred, spontaneous (selfish, demanding, restless, tempered, tactless)
2nd Taurus	Possessive, productive, physical, sensual, secure (indulgent, stubborn, jealous, grasping, withholding)
3rd Gemini	Expressive, communicative, mobile, adaptable, active (superficial, nervous, dualistic, moody)
4th Cancer	Familial, protective, sensitive, devoted, receptive (touchy, greedy, timid, overemotional, inferior)
	Maturity = Mental Body Through Soul
5th Leo	Playful, impressive, self-conscious, leading, controlled (egocentric, fixed, conceited, dramatic)
6th Virgo	Orderly, diligent, discriminative, practical, perfected (critical, pedantic, suppressed, naive, hypochondriac)
7th Libra	Harmonious, balanced, consistent, related, just, united (indecisive, vain, unreliable, shallow, lazy)
8th Scorpio	Penetrating, wilful, separate, passionate, intense (fanatical, repressive, jealous, destructive)
	Gestation = Physical Body Through Body
9th Sagittarius	Realized, free, exploratory, mobile, sporty, religious (material, split, careless, extremist, hedonist)
10th Capricorn	Pragmatic, rational, logical, selfish, disciplined, tough (serious, inflexible, reserved, cautious, inhibited)
11th Aquarius	Idealistic, humanitarian, sociable, civilized, intuitive (detached, cranky, frigid, rebellious, unreliable, inane)
12th Pisces	Solitary, reserved, absorptive, patient, secretive, open (druggy, inhibited, negligent, doubting, sacrificial)
	(Negative indications are in brackets.)

The house position shows the sequence of parental involvement, as you have seen. The house position by octave shows which 'body' is being influenced by which parent. For example, the Sun in Leo and the 12th house would be leading, impressive and controlled when interpreted by planet in its house, but in the 12th house the Leo characteristics of the father are of the physical body, are solitary and reserved. The father would be dominant, but dominated by external influences; he appears strong in a weak situation. This is how the masculine nature would function. The Moon is in the orderly, naive and discriminative sign Virgo, but also in the expressive, impulsive and spontaneous 1st house. Your mother would appear less dominant, but at this time would be very active and the feminine side would be stronger than it appears. As these parental influences bracket the Ascendant, the resultant character would show a personality carrying the above masculine and feminine sides. If the horoscope is a man's, he seeks a wife (or partner) who is really passive but behaves actively to compensate for his own dominant act, which covers up inner security. If the horoscope is a woman's, she seeks men who appear to be active in the world but who are trapped by circumstances. It is important to stress that these descriptions mirror your choice of partners, but only show the character of your parents *from your viewpoint.*

At this stage, the parents are described before either of them is aware that a conception is about to take place. The Sun or Moon, or both, when situated exactly on the conception point, indicate instant realization that a conception has occurred. Luminaries directly opposite or in square to the conception point show resistance to conception and in constructive sextile or trine aspect show active support for the conception.

An interesting fact about families is that the differences between individual children of the same parents are partially determined by the way in which the parents act out their relationship before and during each child's conception and gestation. Parents also age from child to child. 1st children are inevitably seen in a different perspective from subsequent children. Each child of the same parents has its own unique circumstance and life, even in multiple births, when there can be different parental reactions to each child. If either parent is acting out of character during conception, the resultant child carries divergent characteristics from either parent.

The mutual aspect between Sun and Moon shows the relationship between your parents before conception. If connected by trine or sextile, they possess a stable relationship and communicate well. If in opposition, they may disagree about having children; in square they disagree but are capable of resolving the tension; if conjunct, they have similar views and motives; and if there is no aspect, their relationship is indirect at the time, or that their communication is slight. It is essential to realize that you are describing their relationship at a specific time. They may have intimate contact before conception, which is continued after conception, but were out of touch with each other when you were conceived. Your being reflects the state of your parents' relationship throughout this time.

At this point you have established your parents' motives separately and now you must discover how conception occurred.

Conception Point

The conception point is the cusp of the 9th house and shows the nature of the sexual act, as well as the prevailing atmosphere within which it occurs. The nature of conception is a metaphor for the way in which your own creativity arises. If your father is passive and your mother active (as shown by sign and house locations of the Sun and Moon) in this moment, creative drive originates in your feminine nature. The sign on the conception point shows the element/type governing creativity. The previously established characteristics of your parents before this time are combined through the medium of conception.

Follow the procedure described in this section when reconstructing your own preconception time and conception itself. Locate the luminary responsible for conception, describe it by element, sign and house; then locate the other luminary as the parent acted upon, describe it by element, sign and house; then describe their mutual aspect relationship if there is one; finally analyze the element and sign on the ninth house/conception point with the previous information in mind. This prepares you for the interpretation of the octave of gestation.

Octave of Gestation

Gestation is from conception until birth, during which time you develop from a fertilized ovum to the complex being that is modern man. Influences received from the outside world through your mother interact with internal genetic processes as you pass through the cellular realities similar to simple organisms, invertebrates, reptiles, later mammals and primates. Each stage leaves traces in your final character as woman or man, especially in the convoluted structure of your brain. Biological history is carried within us all, as well as the residue of all our ancestors. Gestation is the *'collective unconscious'* of Jung – a primal inheritance common to all humanity, which forms the basic material of every individual psyche. These contents are undifferentiated instincts of survival carried by all humankind.

Throughout gestation your mother is subject to influences from you within her and from individuals and situations around her: her reality during gestation blends these influences. You must identify the origin of the influences that affect her and you during this time.

Planets in gestation, and planets that aspect them, show influences that affect your mother or signify other individuals who carry them. The four houses of gestation describe stages of intrauterine development described from your mother's viewpoint. Her activities change during the process of the four houses, but the planetary characters tend to remain constant. The number and strength of planets in gestation (or aspecting planets) show whether you relate to your body directly or indirectly. Once gestation influences and the people who carry them have been identified, you can determine what effect they have upon her and you. As gestation is a collective substratum within the psyche, influences registering here have a very deep and powerful yet general impact upon your reality. In the following description of the planets and their personifications in gestation, remember that they are qualified by their sign, house and aspects and that they refer to both outer and inner influences.

The Sun during gestation is your father – an indication of your mother's consciousness of what is happening to her, her vitality, and paternal support for your mother. Since gestation is described from your mother's viewpoint, the Sun may also be her father or father-in-law, particularly since grandparents often have strong reactions to their children's children. The Sun can also be the doctor who diagnosed your mother's pregnancy, who advised her in gestation, or delivered you, according to where they register during gestation. Generally, aspects to the Sun show relatives on your father's side of the family or his associates. When the Sun is in the double signs Gemini, Cancer, Libra, Sagittarius, Aquarius or Pisces, it is likely that your mother split her masculine projections between your father and her father, her husband and another man; her husband and the doctor, or when there is a question of paternity. Those born during the Second World War in countries where conscription was common, and allies or occupying forces abounded, are especially subject to this question. Positive aspects to the sun show paternal support for the pregnancy, while tension aspects indicate paternal disagreement or resistance.

The Moon during gestation is your mother herself – her feelings and emotions about gestation and the quality of her instincts. She must totally alter her life because of your existence and be in tune with the creative energies within her body. Since you interpret this time from your mother's viewpoint, the Moon is also her mother or maternal support. When women conceive and carry children, especially for the first time, they tend to identify with their own mothers in ways previously impossible. The Moon in gestation also implies particular genetic influence transmitted via your mother's family. When both Sun and Moon register during gestation, the luminary closest to or in closest aspect to the conception point shows the deepest genetic influence. The Moon is also other women to whom your mother responds or respects: midwives, woman doctors, friends, mother figures, those who teach birth exercises, counsellors or other women who are mothers themselves.

Mercury during gestation shows your mother's thoughts – her ability to communicate what she thinks and her perceptions of gestation, culminating in her understanding of the creative process. Mercury is reflected outside by friends of hers who stimulate communication, cleverness and perception, as well as siblings and family. Their function is to stimulate thinking about the gestation process, its implications and creative matters generally. Mercury also shows intellectual attitudes to which your mother is attracted, such as talking and reading, which stimulates intellectual roots in the expected child. Mercury also shows anyone who adopts your mother's viewpoint, represents her or performs a mediating function.

Venus during gestation shows beauty, harmony, love, adaptation, relationship and sociability, which manifests in your mother or someone to whom she relates. Venus often indicates a female friend, associate or sister of your mother's who acts as a prototype for your appearance, taste or relatedness. Venus is passive sexuality as mirrored in her relations to others in general, and your mother's reaction to her own appearance as it changes during the nine months.

Mars during gestation indicates a desire to change, activity, conflict, and will as personified by doctors, midwives, aggressive people in general or those with whom your mother has sexual contact. Whether medical advice and personnel are threatening is shown by the position of Mars by sign and aspect. If squared by Mercury, your mother thinks nervously about the coming delivery, and if opposed by Saturn she resists the restriction of gestation or is worried by the possibility of physical injury during birth. A prominent Mars at this time shows a forceful intervention in her own destiny and a wilful response to this challenge of the pregnancy and anticipated birth.

Jupiter during gestation is your mother's ability to accept gestation philosophically through her own religious beliefs, her particular psychology, or through those who protect her during this time. Jupiter is carried by those who are generous, supportive, optimistic and expansive; typically aunts, uncles, grandparents, counsellers or the religious. Expansion in your mother's viewpoint and her physical size are indicated when Jupiter registers, and its influence is noble, good humoured and broadens her horizons.

Saturn during gestation is worrying, pessimism, restriction, and seriousness, which is often imposed upon your mother by doctors, grandparents, financial restrictions, and in some cases the father himself. Saturn are personifications who are older, sicker, negative, depressive or limited in perspective, and who obviously or inadvertently transmit these qualities. Your mother may have to continue working, be isolated, be in the care of her parents, depressed or forced to economize, so the impact of Saturn is to narrow her perspective, not necessarily in a detrimental way. Constraint upon relations with others may derive from illegitimacy, unwished cohabitation, forced tightness or social limitation, or from within your mother herself. Saturn has its strongest effect when it is near the MC or ASC, reflecting an actual or expected limitation of mobility and life as a result of the creative act of gestation.

Uranus during gestation institutes reform ranging from expressive creativity to disruption transmitted by revolutionaries, reformers, creative people who do things their own way, and friends who are independent or inspired and encourage your mother to be so herself. As Uranus is the first of the generational planets, its influence is often carried by more than one person. The sexual-creative appetite shown by Uranus becomes very active during gestation and unless sated manifests as rebelliousness or secretive behaviour. A change in rhythm is Uranus' most frequent indication and eccentricities in thought, action and diet result, if not accidents, which threaten your mother's well-being. As a generational influence Uranus also governs prevailing birth and gestation attitudes of the public, birth technology, and those who support new techniques or modern scientific attitudes.

Neptune during gestation increases sensitivity on physical and psychic levels to events in the outer world and to inner attitudes. Neptune often refers to your mother's increased fantasy, dream and psychic life due to your presence within her and the profound communication possible. She is especially sensitive to the effects of diet, drugs, tobacco and the psychic influence of others, particularly in the early stages of pregnancy. Increased openness and vulnerability transform usually dominant women into dependency or unreasonable expectations, if not outright idealism. Often Neptune has no real outer cause and is carried by your mother, or feels as though it is emanating from within her, although there is no way to know for sure. The lack of tangibility characterizes Neptune influences, which are transmitted by those around your mother who dispense food or drugs, those sensitive to her needs and others who have similar ideals.

Pluto during gestation is dramatic transformation, and fanatical, magical or extreme influences, which derive from the world at large. Great experts and those who propagandize through the media, books and classes, from Dr Spock to Michel Odent, could be such influences. Pluto exaggerates the force of any house within which it resides and shows collective disruptive force as more dominant than that of individuals. The effects of war, changes in residence, near accidents during gestation, traumas in relationship and radical alterations of lifestyle are all Plutonian.

The Node during gestation is the urge to unite with others, socialize or adapt to blood ties, groups of other pregnant women or friends. The Node is your parents' families and other relatives collectively, as well as any groups or alliances.

The 9th house (naturally Sagittarius)
Conception until seven weeks after conception
The moment of conception is the cusp of the 9th house and its domain is from conception until your mother realizes that she is pregnant about seven weeks later. These influences function after she has conceived but before she know this fact. She experiences the early stages of hormonal biological changes, which eventually affect her. Although it is possible for your mother to 'feel' or even to 'know' that she is pregnant during conception itself, the earliest time doctors believe pregnancy can be detected (by them) is 38 days after conception. Planets in the 9th house show influences intimating pregnancy, which are received by your mother in the process of discovering that you exist and which set a pattern for your self-discovery in life. The 9th house feels foreign, strange, alien, sentimental, spiritual and active.

When the Moon, Venus or the psychic planet Neptune register in the 9th house, there is 'woman's intuition' that something is happening; this may emanate from your mother, her mother or friends. When any of these planets occur just after conception, your mother experiences sudden and dramatic emotional and physical changes. When planets occur just before the MC, your mother senses that she has conceived, rather than exhibiting true psychic powers.

The Midheaven (MC)
Seven weeks after conception or thirty-three weeks before birth
When the MC registers, the ego enters the physical body and your mother accepts the reality of pregnancy. By this time you possess all human systems, sex is determined and the face is fully human.

When you are born near the Equator or at certain times during the day, the MC is exactly 90°, a square aspect, from the ASC; the archetypal relationship between the personality/ASC and the ego/MC is a tension between your view of yourself and your life objectives. At all other times, the MC leans towards the ASC/eastern side at the left or the DSC/western side at the right. The MC leaning towards the ASC shows self-oriented ego-consciousness, while the MC leaning towards the DSC shows ego-consciousness oriented towards the not-self or the outside world.

The element of the sign on the MC shows the way in which your mother discovered she was pregnant. If in a fire sign, it was intuited; in an earth sign, sensed; in an air sign, thought; or in a water sign, felt. On a higher level, this is the way in which you discover your own Ego direction in life. For example, if your mother realized her pregnancy because *she felt* she was pregnant, you can expect to evaluate your position in the world by the way you *feel*.

The sign of the zodiac on the MC further qualifies your mother's realization of her new purpose. The cardinal signs Aries, Cancer, Libra and Capricorn show that she initiates action in response; the fixed signs Taurus, Leo, Scorpio and Aquarius show firm and resolute acceptance; and the mutable signs Gemini, Virgo, Sagittarius and Pisces show a desire to change whatever conditions or attitudes exist already.

Planets in conjunction to the MC show people directly influencing the mother and the qualities of which your ego is composed. The stronger the planets and the closer the conjunction, the more powerful and specific is your ego. The Sun directly conjunct the MC means that the goal in life is the establishment of your own individuality, while Uranus on the MC means that your mother responds in an eccentric and original way, producing original and eccentric objectives for your life.

A number of planets near the MC indicates multiple objectives and egos. When there are planets on both sides of the MC, ego-consciousness alternates between selfish to selfless motives. Remember that the registration of inner planets (Sun, Moon, Mercury, Venus and Mars) show influences and events coming from people around your mother or from her, while outer planets (Jupiter, Saturn, Uranus, Neptune and Pluto) show activities attributable to more than one person or large scale events. Those born during the Second World War in Europe with Uranus or Pluto on the MC reflect the influence of deeply violent transformative events on their mothers at the time.

Aspects to the MC show people your mother told and those who have an indirect effect upon her as personifications of secondary manifestations of your ego. Aspects from planets below the horizon show unconscious or inner influences, while from planets above the horizon they show conscious or outer influences. If the MC happens to be in one of the double signs, indicating multiple influence already, these objectives become quite numerous. With no planets conjunct the MC, but many planets in aspect to the MC, you would have many secondary objectives in life but a difficulty finding your major focus.

In some cases, there are no planets conjunct the MC, nor any aspects to the MC. The sign governing the MC then becomes the objective, but there is little other support from the remaining planets. This would imply single-mindedness, which reflects the mother being left to her own by others upon realizing her pregnancy. When she wishes to keep her pregnancy a secret, there are tell-tale signs. The isolated signs Scorpio and Pisces show a desire to reserve judgement, and planets conjunct the MC but no planets in aspect indicate recognition of the pregnancy, but a lack of interest in spreading the knowledge.

When Mars, Saturn, Uranus, Neptune or Pluto conjunct or aspect the MC traumatic events during gestation may be expected, especially when these planets or aspect points register after the MC. This is because planets after the MC show repercussions of the mother's realization of pregnancy. Mars usually indicates a doctor, easy aspects imply that the doctor reassures the mother, while difficult aspects suggest that the doctor is threatening, unhelpful or even damages her. Chemical tests or talk of induction register as Neptune influences, as do dangerous drugs such as thalidomide and others that are supposed to relieve symptoms of morning sickness. Saturn shows restriction or intense concentration resulting from the realization, often through, or as a result of, someone older or more serious. Pluto indicates an extreme transformation accompanied by drama, disruption or even violence. Uranus shows alterations in the mother's rhythm, eccentric circumstances or her desire to continue to be independent in spite of obvious dependency.

When more than one of these planets combine in a difficult square or opposition aspect to the MC and also connect to the surgical Mars, there is a possibility that abortion is contemplated or attempted. It is obvious that when such attempts are made, they are unsuccessful because the horoscope involved presupposes a survivor, but it is necessary to judge the severity of the attempt by the specific planets that make direct aspect connections and the closeness of the aspects. Neptune aspects imply fantasy and uncertainty; Mercury aspects imply a questioning of the situation; the Node is a sampling of friends as a primary response. All these metaphors are carried directly in the ego.

To interpret inner and outer MC events, be sure to examine the planets, aspects (using their sensitive points) and the MC itself in order, moving in a clockwise direction from conception point towards the birth moment Ascendant. When the correct order is followed, the mother and everyone significant in the discovery of your existence and, by extension, your ego-consciousness, can be reconstructed. The events and individuals involved foreshadow the pattern of development of life's objectives.

After finding the influences acting on your mother at the MC, you must take her specific response and carry it into the three houses comprising the remainder of gestation: the 10th, 11th and 12th houses.

The 10th house (naturally Capricorn)
Thirty-three weeks until 28 weeks before birth
The 10th house reflects the repercussions after your mother realizes

that she is pregnant, as the first function is to communicate her situation and attitudes to the world. Her ability to make your existence known determines your life ambitions. The more effectively she and your father organize this communication, the greater chance you have of finding your own position in the world.

This house governs perfected matter and practical concerns – during this time the parents must orchestrate all necessary practical tasks for confronting gestation. Selecting a doctor or midwife, a location for the coming birth, an attitude and technique for childbirth itself, finding a space at home for the baby, planning for the welfare of the mother and making the necessary financial considerations must all be done by the parents.

Planets in the 10th house show who influences your mother during this crucial period. You must remember that from this time on your mother is likely to see doctors, nurses, midwives or childbirth experts and her other associations in a different light than usual. She must assert herself and require that decisions made during this time are consistent to her thoughts and feelings.

Symbolically, this time sees the mother applying the objectives determined at the MC into the 'real world'. As the 10th house is traditionally considered paternal or masculine, she may struggle for her own way or for control over the circumstances of the birth from her husband or her doctor. A mother's ability to manifest her own objectives physically is an indication of an eventual authority and ability to achieve one's aims in life.

Many planets in the 10th house show multiple influences on your mother and subsequently various goals in life. An absence of planets in the 10th house shows a natural and uneventful expression of the recognition by the mother of her pregnancy and would indicate general goals without specific personal patterns or definite ideas.

The 11th house (naturally Aquarius)
Twenty-eight weeks until 17 weeks before birth
In the period represented by the 11th house, the pregnancy is accepted and material matters are resolved, yet it occurs before the mother has any outward appearances of pregnancy. The mother decreases her usual labours and her primary function is to prepare for birth, including communicating with her mother and friends who have already had children. She occupies herself with plans and ideals common to expectant mothers and becomes more careful of her diet, clothing, activities, social life, sleeping and sexual habits – in short, she reconsiders and revalues everything about herself.

While it is perfectly natural and acceptable to have sexual intercourse well into gestation, the 11th house is often characterized by a decrease in sexual appetite: your mother's procreative drive is temporarily satisfied. It is a unique situation. Her activities and thoughts centre around her unborn baby, and much of her time is spent musing, planning and speculating about what the child will look like, act like and live like. The mother continues to function in the world but her concentration is both inside herself and outside in the future. Planets in the 11th house show your mother's friends, family and acquaintanceships who affect her ideals. Since you remain quite mysterious to her, she must idealize her experience of you. You begin moving inside her but remain more an idea than a reality.

An 11th house devoid of planets indicates that the mother formulated her ideals and attitudes herself, without any prominent exterior influences. This would imply little interest in group and other collective contacts in life.

The 12th house (naturally Pisces)
Seventeen weeks before birth until birth
At the beginning of the 12th house the mother starts gaining weight, which increases her sensitivity to psychic reality as well as to her own emotional state. Her inner focus gradually becomes dominant over exterior circumstances, while her dependency upon others increases towards the birth time. The image of Pisces, the sign equivalent to this time, is that of two fishes swimming in opposite directions but tethered together at the tail, symbolizing that the inner world of the mother and her outer world are linked emotionally. The mother's primary function during this stage is to reconcile these two worlds. Increased movement within her balances her decreased outward activity and reflects the psychic rapport between mother and unborn child. As birth nears, the mother's commitment to the inner, relinquishing her own way in favour of her child, her submission to doctors, hospital examinations and her limited mobility all contribute to the self-sacrificial element that permeates this house. It is only in recent years that expectant women are becoming aware of how they can regain active control over this critical time in their lives and their children's lives.

All those with whom your sensitized mother communicates carry profound influences upon your psyche, especially the hidden elements. These include her family, friends, medical advisors, midwife and even hospital staff, so it is essential to identify from whom these influences derive and what they imply to you, so that you can decipher the hidden components of your psyche. In traditional astrology the 10° immediately above the Ascendant represent hidden parts of your personality. In the time scale these 10° cover the seven weeks before birth and planets registering within this zone are integral to your personality. These influences precede your birth and their ramifications precede every assertion of your personality throughout life. This is often responsible for the unconscious tension we all feel just before important meetings, tests, introductions to new people, performances or events that place focus upon our personality. The importance of the awareness of expectant women during this time cannot be underestimated. Her various responses may determine the difference between a difficult or a sublime personality in her offspring.

As birth approaches, the mother becomes aware of the many possible birth circumstances. The best monitor of the pre-birth situation is the mother's conscious and unconscious perceptions. She should be naturally directed to eat the correct foods, to exercise at the proper times and in the right way, and to begin to orient herself to the daily cycles which eventually determine the time of birth.

When a birth is natural, there is either the Sun, Moon, Mercury, Venus or Jupiter just before (above) the Ascendant or an absence of planets. Mars or Saturn registering just before birth usually show a doctor or midwife responsible for the delivery, the influence on the delivery and the effect on your personality. The implication is that force (Mars) or constriction (Saturn) are elements in delivery technique. The use of force would make the mother resist; and the use of constriction, as in the stirrups in common use in hospitals, would make her tighten. These influences are transmitted directly to your personality.

The registration of Uranus and Pluto, or aspects from them, signal drastic changes in attitude or physical circumstances just before birth. Since both planets are usually generational, the changes are from all the people present at birth – for example, hospital staff, friends, family or midwife taken as a whole.

Neptune in the 12th house indicates the degree of sensitivity of your mother right before birth. The traditional interpretation of Neptune/ASC is impressionability, illusions, sensory deception or drugs and it accompanies induced births or those where anaesthetics are administered. The use of drugs at birth are substitutes for your mother's natural sensitivities and are at tempts to dull or eliminate her reactions to the birth process. Neptune indicates detachment and extreme sensitivity in the personality resulting from such a birth.

The Node in the 12th house describes your mother's associations leading up to your birth as a substratum of your eventual personality. The feeling of belonging to or being separate from a group of sympathetic friends, associates or hospital staff mirrors your personal attitude towards such groups and their ideas.

The Ascendant
Birth

The Ascendant registers at the moment you take your first breath and is the transition point between gestation and childhood. The description of birth as a *'process'* parallels the development of your personality as a process. Personality is not a 'thing' but a pattern of actions and acts which repeat themselves in a seemingly infinite number of variants during life.

Birth circumstances include everything that happens before, during and afterwards and the personality, which registers at birth, is a combination of those many influences patterned in time. Personality is a mechanism by which you act out instinctive and unconscious contents, and is strongly influenced by the atmosphere around your mother at birth. The zodiac sign on your Ascendant symbolizes this synchronistic relationship. The accompanying list of Ascendant signs and their associated environments and characters. The planets that rule each sign qualify the general qualities of the signs themselves.

The range of interpretations describe personalities derived from the nature of the birth environment. The choices as to which words are most apt are made in relation to the planets around the Ascendant, the circumstances described in gestation as leading up to the birth, and the planets that are in aspect to the Ascendant.

Planets conjunct your Ascendant show people and influences directly affecting your birth and personality. When a conjunction is *before* (above) the exact ASC, external influences affect the initiative part of your personality, and when *after* your ASC the influence is strongest after birth and is an after-effect of your personality. The closeness to the Ascendant shows the strength of a planetary connection. The closer the orb, the more direct and integral the influence.

Table 7: Ascendant Birth Interpretation

Aries	Restless; energetic; self-assertive; rash; aggressive; selfish; impatient; and from Mars ruling, surgery and surgeons; aggressive doctors or midwives; impatient people; forceps injuries; hospitals.
Taurus	Stability; quiet; secure; domestic; sensual; beautiful; attractive; homely; and from Venus ruling, women; midwives; attractive people; artists; loving, attentive people; children.
Gemini	Changeable; ambiguous; adaptable; superficial; mobile; talkative; observative; dualistic; nervous; and from Mercury ruling, children; crowds; thinkers; gossips; hurriers; talkers; conversationalists.
Cancer	Moodiness; homeliness; simplicity; maternity; passivity; warmth; conservatism; reliance on others; sensitivity; and from the Moon ruling, feeling people; the instinctive; midwives; women; mothers; nurses; breast feeders; feminists.

Leo   Authoritative; confident; open-minded; joyous; self-confident; open; active; proud; prominent; game-playing; and from Sun ruling, warm; domineering; purposeful; boldness; extrovert.

Virgo   Naive; virginal; stable; critical; nervous; hospitals; reserve; clean; hygienic; sterile; cautious; attentive; pedantic; and from Mercury ruling, intellectual; medical students; doctors; nurses; observers; critics; digestive problems; collaborations; teams.

Libra   Balanced; harmonious; homely; lively; authoritarian; easy; vain; attentive; chatty; moody; obliging; social; and from Venus ruling, youths; women; nurses; midwives; woman doctors; beauties; friends.

Scorpio   Disharmonious; humid; hotheaded; cautious; industrious; passionate; separative; violent; surgical; impulsive; dangerous; brutal; forceful; and from Mars, surviving; surgeons and surgery; Caesareans; technicians; forceps; brutality; danger; force; and from Pluto ruling, tragic events; endurance; large hospitals; forceful deliveries; violence; circumcision.

Sagittarius Enthusiastic; athletic; joyous; good humoured; expansive; foreign; natural; scattered; social; messy; lively; adventurous; talkative; religious; and from Jupiter ruling, expansive; doctors; grandparents and relatives; religious hospitals; nuns; nurses; foreign hospitals and countries; tolerance.

Capricorn Concentration; seriousness; practicality; long labour; inhibition; hard work; goals; reserve; pragmatism; anxiety; physicality; and from Saturn ruling, will; restraint; doctors and surgeons; older people; strictness; paternalism; masculinity; slowness; methodicality repression; unemotional; materialistic; expensive.

Aquarius   Communal; abstract; friendly; detached; sociable; progressive; sympathetic; inventive; eccentric; idealistic; Utopian; planned; and from Saturn ruling, realised plans; seriousness; older doctors or grandparents; and from Uranus ruling, inventive, technological, instrumentative; original; unorthodox; mechanical; rebellious; scientific; changeable; rhythmic.

Pisces   Self-sacrificial; lacking confidence; externally influenced; anaesthetic; depressed; vague; lazy; comfortable; peculiar; passive; asleep; weak; drugged; induced; gentle; simple; and from Jupiter ruling, institutional; isolated; contented; visionary; wasteful; religious; and from Neptune ruling, psychic; dreamy, drugged; idealistic; Utopian reserved; sensitive; mystical; escapist; overemotional; vague.

Table 8: ASC/Planet Interpretation

Aspect	*Personifications/Influences*
Sun/ASC	Father, men, doctor, grandfather. Relationships to men, recognition, popularity, personal attitudes to others, self-confidence, physical relations, the public, masculinity.
Moon/ASC	Mother, grandmother, midwife, nurse, women. Personal feelings about others, feminine influence, maternity, protection,

breastfeeding, sensitivity, receptivity, adaptability (alkaloids, induction, anaesthetics, drugs, watery birth).

Mercury/ASC Friends, talkers, nurses, young children, gossips. Thoughts at birth, definition, talking, changing views, ideas, criticism (sense stimuli, nerves).

Venus/ASC Women, sisters, nurses, girls, attractive people, lovers, midwife. Harmonious personality, loving atmosphere, art, adornment, beautiful surroundings, easy birth, pleasure, even-tempered (good complexion, general appearance, proportions).

Mars/ASC Surgeon, doctor, midwife, men, fighters, aggressors, male children. Fighting, teamwork, forceful success, physical strength, restlessness, decision (surgery, force, circumcision, violence, episiotomy, forceps, facial scar, accidents, Caesareans, birth apparatus).

Jupiter/ASC Doctor, midwife, uncle, aunt, grandparents, team, positivists, priests. Easy birth, pleasant experiences, agreeable manner, compromise, generosity, correct acts, successful operations (large baby, jaundice, difficult breastfeeding).

Saturn/ASC Doctor, hospital staff, grandparents, serious people, inhibitors, lonely people. Isolation, restriction, inhibition, seriousness, experience, hindrance, depression, seclusion, (separation, isolation, long labour, birth apparatus, skin trouble, blockages, tension, amputation, sensory disfunction, facial mark, premature birth, stillbirth, lack of attention).

Uranus/ASC Excitable people, innovators, originals, technicians, orderlies. Excitement, originality, scientific birth, movement, rhythmic, incidents, disquiet, sudden events, unexpected circumstances (quick birth, short labour induction, machines, monitors, headaches, forceps, accidents, sensitive skin, responsive nervous system, circumcision).

Neptune/ASC Anaesthetists, nurses, psychics, sensitives, druggists, mediums. Impressionable, sensitive, insecure, peculiar contacts, disillusionment, sympathetic, exploitation, (inducement, anaesthetics, alcohol, drugs, peculiar birth, dreaming, water birth, sensory deception, malformations, incubators).

Pluto/ASC Doctors, staff, powerful people, authorities, fascinating people, those in control. Fascinating personality, ambition, psychic forces, unusual influences, readjustment, dramatic changes, radical alterations (force, Caesarean, forceps, brutal birth, forced birth, physical transformation, surgery, accidents, circumcision).

Node/ASC Family, friends, nurses, colleagues, fellows, social workers. Collective contacts, personal relations, family influences, social contact, teamwork, relating (respiration, metabolism, hospital birth, anti-social behaviour).

To understand personality through an analysis of birth requires a description of a sequence of influences before, during and after the birth. The sequence shows how your personality reveals itself in action and development over long periods of life and in short-term situations. Great attention to the mother in the pre-birth stage of labour followed by the child's removal immediately afterwards signifies a focus upon gaining the energy to assert the personality, followed by a rapid decrease in attention following its assertion. The sequence of events at birth is crucial to the description of the process of your personality. Planets conjunct or in aspect to your Ascendant show people present at birth, the influence they convey and their effect upon your personality. When the Ascendant or any planet is in one of the double signs (Gemini, Cancer, Libra, Sagittarius, Aquarius or Pisces) the personifications and effects are doubled and show more than one person and influence. The table shows the planets and their effects as influences at birth. Each person/planet shows as an aspect or sub-personality of your whole personality. The planets in this situation are like traditional planet/Ascendant aspects.

When the planets are combined, they mutually affect each other. When Mars and Saturn are both involved, it is a difficult labour (Saturn) requiring the assistance or intervention of a doctor (Mars). If the difficulty of Saturn were complemented by a positive Jupiter aspect, it would mean that the labour was long and hard, but that there were no complications. If Mars and Saturn are in sextile or trine to the Ascendant, the surgeon performs a supportive role. A trine from Saturn can be an older person who lends support; a square from the Moon is a woman or grandmother exerting a tensioning influence.

Your birth is described by combining who was there (as determined by the planets) with the atmosphere at the birth (from the ASC sign).

Octave of Childhood

At birth you enter the Octave of Childhood, which extends to the age of about seven years old, during which time you create and adapt the personality which registered at birth. Because influences during childhood are received through the medium of the family, it is necessary to understand your childhood home and relationship to your family in order to understand the nature of your personality. These houses are below the horizon in the horoscope, so their influences are subjective, unconscious and accountable to influences beyond your immediate control.

Your personality develops against the already existing structure of your parents' relationship to each other and to others within your family. Your own development during childhood is rapid compared to the more static framework of your family. You must continually contrast your instinctive grasp of relationships to the attitudes your parents project onto you as rules of behaviour. This interchange creates a value system by which you live your life.

Planets in childhood and their aspects from the other two octaves represent people around you and those upon whom you base your personality. They are models of behaviour to be accepted, rejected, excluded or integrated. Since most childhood influences are carried by those within and accessible to your family circle, your attitudes are highly conditioned by the prevailing familial reality. You may or may not be free to adopt your own opinions and ways of behaviour; this depends upon what is acceptable to your family. One of your primary tasks during this time is to understand what the family is and what its attitudes are.

Freud believed that a child recapitulates the development of all mankind during childhood. The four houses of childhood describe a collective development (we all must enact it), which is also individually unique. The early developments of mankind are mythological, and childhood events carry a mythological and fantastic atmosphere – even your parents' stories play their part in defining your personality.

The Sun during childhood is the vital relationship to your father. His influence during gestation is indirect, but during childhood you gradually realize his relative importance within the family. This is often because most fathers have little direct contact until their children begin to speak or even later. When the Sun registers at this time your father exerts a strong influence upon your personality. Due to natural contact with grandfathers and uncles during childhood, there is a likelihood that they also participate in the solar qualities. Aspects from the Sun to planets in childhood show indirect paternal qualities. As in Horoscope 15, the father is missing at birth, but later in childhood, at one year old, the Moon and Mars are square to the Sun indicating a permanent separation.

The Moon during childhood is your early feelings about your mother and feminine continuity from gestation, where it was of primary significance. As in gestation maternal qualities are the medium within which you are physically created, in childhood mother is more a protector and guide to personality development. Immediately after birth, you cannot differentiate yourself from your mother because of necessary and natural survival instincts; you are bonded to her. Only gradually do you begin to separate from her and her influence. By the end of childhood you have distinguished yourself from her and from other women, but early on she can be interchangeable with nannies, grandmothers, aunts, surrogate mothers and even older sisters.

Mercury during childhood is communication, as even in the womb you receive and evaluate sounds and words. The primary manifestation of Mercury is other children and the effect they have on you, unless Mercury is in aspect to either the Sun or Moon, when the main communication is with one of your parents. Mercury indicates children at home, while aspects from Mercury to planets in childhood are children outside your immediate family. Other planets aspecting Mercury qualify its personifications. For example, when Mercury and Saturn are in aspect to a planet in childhood, the communication may come from a talkative grandparent.

Venus during childhood represents adaptation to or relationship with young women or children who affect your love or aesthetic sense. In aspect to the Moon, Venus can be the aesthetic quality of your mother. Venus is people and objects you accept readily and to whom you are willing to accommodate yourself. Drawing, painting, music, taste in clothes and the general look of your family's world either clashes with (for square or opposition aspects) or supports your outlook.

Mars during childhood is the desire to go beyond parents or to react against your family. Mars is active, wilful and can be destructive, yet mobile and intense, as its function is to activate and break up static situations in order that creativity may issue from them. Mars also governs accidents and feverish childhood diseases caused by or restricting active mobility.

Jupiter during childhood denotes expansion or support from family friends or those outside the family, and religious attitudes prevalent at home. Generosity and optimism keynote the events and people described by Jupiter and transmitted by them.

Saturn during childhood shows restrictions defining and limiting your development. It is the tendency to isolate yourself, withdraw and concentrate upon your own way, and is carried by those whom you observe doing this themselves. The influences are serious, concentrated, pessimistic or negative and may derive from financial situations and locale as well as individuals. The family doctor is often indicated here.

Uranus during childhood is eccentric, unusual, disruptive or independent tendencies which do not conform to your family's rules or perspectives. Restless, highly strung, erratic and rhythmic influences predominate as vehicles for Uranus' pattern-breaking effects.

Neptune during childhood is sensitivity, receptivity and psychic links in feelings of your family and others. Fantasies, imaginary friends, toys or animals which generate their own identities, dreams, and the world of make-believe are defined by Neptune. Often Neptune is not equivalent to a real person or animal, but is accumulated among many imaginary figures or counterparts of family members. The connection to these fancies is exaggerated during illness or times of weakness.

Pluto during childhood is association with and relation to the public outside your family, often conveyed by propaganda in the media. Contact with news and famous individuals through television exposes you to accepted opinion and the rules of the world at large. Pluto also carries prevailing attitudes towards child-raising, from popular viewpoints to rejection as shown by violence and abuse.

The Node during childhood is the ability to adapt to your family and associated relatives, neighbours and friends as an overall unit.

A predominance of planets in this octave indicates that the ability to create your personality within the family situation is central to and a governing factor in the formation of your world view.

The 1st house (naturally Aries)
Birth until seven months
In the first seven months after birth you are totally reliant upon your mother for food and support, and she becomes an extension of your will. The demands you make upon her are instinctive and require immediate gratification, and she responds instinctively to meet your demands. The quality of this interchange is defined by the sign or signs occupying the 1st house. Fire signs show immediate assertion; Earth signs are physical links; Air signs are communications; and Water signs are emotional attachments. As each house is usually intersected by more than one sign (and element), the mother/child relationship goes through a change at some point amid this house.

For many decades it was standard practice to separate newborn children from their mothers directly after delivery. The detached and brutal practices include being handled by rubber-gloved hands, being powdered with various chemicals, held upside down and spanked, circumcised, umbilical cords cut before natural separation time, being wrapped in sterile tight sheets, incubated, and many others. All these practices were considered the standard and thought to be essential to antenatal health. It is now clear that most of these practices are as harmful as they are unnecessary. The traumatic act of separation for hours after birth interrupts the natural bonding of child and mother. The effects of a generation of these practices upon the Western world shows in the widespread violence and alienation in world youth.

The women's movement has been responsible for the recognition and alteration of these unnatural practices, and a return to natural childbirth practices is well under way. The education of women during pregnancy, exercises to promote natural delivery without anaesthetics, support from other women, monitoring by midwives instead of doctors, delivery at home in positive surroundings and conditions, close physical connections with the mother even before the umbilical cord is naturally severed, and an encouragement of breastfeeding are all integral to public knowledge. In fact, the return to natural birthing practices is called 'alternative' birth!

The manner of antenatal treatment is often indicated in the horoscope. A square or opposition from or to the Moon is separation from mother. Saturn near or in aspect to the ASC is separation, inhibition or restraint caused by a doctor or others. Mars is brutality or aggressive treatment, surgery or rough handling, as well as force in delivery itself. Uranus shows technology, erratic behaviour, accidents, abrupt transition, changes in rhythm or the unexpected. Neptune is drug treatment, the use of and response to anaesthetics, induction, substances administered through breast milk or bottle, or gasses. Pluto is a threat to life, alteration caused by other children or influences from the hospital or the outside world. The Node is adaptation to the family in addition to the mother's exclusive control. Jupiter governs dietary matters and general hygiene.

The first five degrees are influences related to the post-natal period of one month. The remaining degrees of the first house describe bonding to those who tend you, those with whom you have close personal contact, and those who represent extensions of your personality. The archetypal Aries qualities of this house create a world as a contiguous whole surrounding your centre, an attitude which those with Aries Sun or Moon retain forever. The variety of people present during the 1st house time determines the multiplicity of assertive sub-personalities, as distinct from your personality itself. The primary criteria are that your appetites are gratified, your nappies dry and your demands for attention met. At this stage positive influences cannot be differentiated from negative influences as they are all integrated into your world.

The elements of the signs in the 1st house define your assertive direction. Fire requires energy from others; Earth, physical contact; Air, verbal and audial response; and Water requires emotional feedback. Cardinal, Fixed and Mutable modes of the elements determine whether your environment is initiatory, stable or changeable. Having a fixed water sign Scorpio in the 1st house shows a child who requires stable emotional attachment against which to assert its personality. Gemini would require a continually changing, highly communicative atmosphere, reflecting its mutable air qualities. The signs in this house show the kind of environment within which you assert yourself.

Planets in residence and their aspects combine with or undermine the element and sign in the house and determine whether or not the prevailing atmosphere is supportive or obstructive. The 1st house shows those individuals who were essential in your earliest home environment and how you adapted to them.

The 2nd house (naturally Taurus)
Seven months until one year and eight months
The 2nd house is your emergence into the physical world as a separate object among other objects. Generally, you are weaned from mother's milk and begin eating solid food at about this time. You contact the physical world and learn to utilize natural resources, including objects, sounds, people and behaviour. Your level of access determines your later attitudes towards material and the physical world.

Planets in the 2nd house show people and influences that determine and qualify your physical reality. The Sun or Moon indicate that parents are primarily identified as being object-like, or that they are the bearers or custodians of objects. Venus is accommodation to the physical world and Mars is the desire to change it. Mercury is thought about objects or their use in communication; Jupiter is the will to obtain more; and Saturn is a limitation with their presence. Often planets here symbolize family members and reflect a tendency to adopt or resist physicality depending upon prevailing family attitudes and circumstances, like the improvement or disintegration of your father's business and material attitudes.

The signs in this house define your attitude towards material matters and your body. Earth signs are natural here; Air signs reflect the physical world as an abstract idea, as words or as the material for communication; Fire signs use the physical world as the background for self-expression; and Water signs relate to their feelings about things. Emotions concentrated upon parents are similar to feelings about objects, such as an obsession with teddy bears, rugs, blankets and thumbs. The object is the only respite from a threatening world.

The 3rd house (naturally Gemini)
One year and eight months until three years and six months
In the 3rd house you learn to walk, talk and communicate in other ways. These extensions in movement amplify your range of influence and the variety of experiences you encounter. As language is primarily imitative, it is critical to identify who influenced you at this time, how you learned to communicate and what influences were transmitted to you. Your world is unbound from the obsession with objects of the 2nd house and directed to people, primarily children like brothers and sisters.

Planets in the 3rd house show the nature of communication as symbolized by people within your home and family. Luminaries show parents as primary models of communication. Mercury, Venus and Mars are almost always other children with whom you identify or spend time. Jupiter and Saturn represent aunts, uncles, grandparents, housekeepers or nannies who either expand or limit self-expression. Although Jupiter and Saturn are usually identifiable as specific people, sometimes Jupiter is the expansive side of all relatives and Saturn the limiting side of them, or they may symbolize the expansive and limiting parental sides of your family structure. Uranus and Pluto show dominant changes in your environment coming from the world, as through the media, or from the inside. Neptune is sensitivity or insecurity about movement, change and communication. The Node shows collective values where no individual is a primary model, but rather the whole family or group.

As there is a powerful fantasy element during this time, most of your family carry prominent inner images within you sometimes related to, but often a distortion of, an objective reality. Nicknames, family jokes and special characteristics imagined or real fall into this category. The more planets in this house, the more complex and potentially dualistic your communication, as there are more models with whom you connect. Sometimes imaginary figures seem real, just as real people seem obscure. Planets in the 3rd house with aspects to or from many planets outside the house indicate that most models are from outside the immediate family system, or that the family transmits ways of behaviour deriving from the world outside.

The Gemini archetype of the twins doubles personifications in this house. The Sun produces double father images literally or as the working father versus the homebody father, while Jupiter produces doubled sets of grandparents.

An absence of planets in the 3rd house indicates a lack of specific models for communication, which can result from being an only child. As usual, the signs occupying the house determine the type of adaptation and diversity of communicative power. Fire signs communicate intuitively through energy exchange; Earth signs with physical means like drawing, building, toy manipulation or touch; the natural Air signs are verbal and use movement; and Water signs seek to express feelings through gestures and words.

The 4th house (naturally Cancer)
Three years and six months until seven years old
During the 4th house you realize that you produce effects in others and responses in yourself due to your communicative abilities. The range

and nature of these responses defines your emotional reaction to the family: the way you feel about them is a reflection of how you feel about yourself. You begin to try out the range of contents and question the beliefs and behaviour of your family, especially your parents. The nature of this informal yet critical inquest determines the firmness of your own family circumstances later in life.

Planets in this house show emotional models and the tenor of your feelings. Although the 4th house is traditionally associated with the parent of the same sex (the father for a male and the mother for a female), there are other criteria that determine the general emotional slant. One factor is the gender of the sign on the cusp of the house. If the sign on the cusp is a water or earth sign, then the emotional dominance is feminine, while if a fire or air sign, the dominance is masculine.

The other factor is the planets in the house. Obviously, when either the Sun or Moon are here, the equivalent parent is the emotional prototype, as is the case when the Sun or Moon aspect any planets here. When the Sun is in a feminine sign or the Moon in a masculine sign, the identification is blended. When either luminary is in one of the dual signs, the identification is dualistic, which generates a tendency for multiple relationships later in life as a response to multiple parental attitudes here. Mercury shows changeable thoughts and the necessity to think about the way you feel. Venus and Mars are usually sisters and brothers or other children who provide physical, non-parental influences. Jupiter and Saturn are the grandparents, aunts or uncles, surrogates, relatives, priests and doctors who determine emotional family values despite being outside the immediate family. Uranus is the urge to break away from the home and family, or eccentric behaviour within the family. Neptune is extreme sensitivity and psychic contact within the family as a whole, or instability when not recognized. Pluto is restlessness, revolutionary influences, a need for isolation, and often changes in residence or alterations of the family situation, such as those caused by world affairs. The Node indicates very close contact with the family, including grandparents and the parental home and homeland. An empty 4th house shows an undifferentiated home life where the influence is unconscious and instinctive. When there are only one or few planets in this house, but many aspects from planets elsewhere, you seek family organization and its equivalent feelings from outside sources.

Fire signs in the 4th house are active, individualistic and intuitive attitude towards family and home; Earth signs value physical security and visual contact; with Air signs the spoken parental views count more heavily than the reality; while for the natural Water signs the feeling of home and family are optimal.

As this house is the summation and termination of the Childhood

Octave, it also determines the emotional response to your ability to create a personality within the home and family, the root of your emotional set and tone for life.

Octave of Maturity

By the end of the 4th house you have received a body during gestation and a personality during childhood. During maturity, you must combine body with personality and project the resultant combination into the outside world. You gradually leave the influence of parents and family and adapt to increasingly greater and broader contexts. The early stages of this octave occur during school years: the 5th house being primary education and the 6th house being secondary education and/or early working life. The 7th house from 23 years, five months, until about 42 is the time of partnerships and most important contact with the world, and the 8th house is the gradual withdrawal from life leading up to death. The first two houses of this octave are unconscious, being below the horizon, while the last two are conscious, being above the horizon. This reflects an increasing control over life and the gradual creation of objectivity with age.

As in gestation you create a body and in childhood a personality, the function of maturity is to contact and accept your soul. Your soul actually enters its physical vehicle at the registration of the MC, just after conception, but remains latent until you synthesize attitudes in life to its command. *Soul* is the ability to see and understand life as a whole in time, as reflected by the entire horoscope circle of life. This corresponds to modern concepts of 'holistic health' – seeing the body, personality and soul as integral components of a meaningful whole. This also involves understanding life as a process instead of as a series of insular present moments strung together like beads on a necklace.

There are hypotheses current in the medical profession that ascribe to time perception the major cause of stress-related diseases such as heart disease, hypertension and cancer (see Bibliography – Dossey, *Space, Time and Medicine*). Revolutionary cures for these killers are related to the new perception of time inherent in the Log Time Scale presented in this book. Development in gestation is primarily physical; development in childhood is primarily emotional; and development in maturity is primarily mental. Your state of mind determines your health, welfare and the quality of all relationships. The ability to see yourself as a whole being in time is essential for a healthy, holistic life.

You must understand the part you play in life. The events, characters and settings of the first two life stages of gestation and childhood teach you certain ground rules and ways of acting. In maturity you must accept your part and play it out with maximum comprehension, feeling, joy and, above all, life.

The planets registering in maturity are particularly important because they describe higher manifestations of each planetary quality. Your entire previous life is the background for this third stage of development and planets have a particularly potent effect. Whereas in the earlier stages the planets are primarily other people in your life, in maturity the planets are distinctly you and events are determined and acted out by you. One object of maturity is to transcend personal models, to integrate them all into your whole, and to transpersonalize life. You must go beyond environment, heredity, parents and friends into the sacred and timeless realm of wholeness.

The Sun during maturity is the conscious paternal focus of your vitality. During maturity the influence of your father declines as you take over the fatherly reality in your own creative life. The gradients of this transition are from a protective father at the end of childhood, to the teacher in the 5th and 6th houses, to the father in you in the seventh and 8th houses. The Sun during this time represents the drive towards recognition, acknowledgement, personal focus and strength. The goal involves individuality and self-esteem as well as the ability to meet the practical goals in life of success, health and the creation of a family life.

The Moon during maturity is the transference of the maternal image from your mother to those with whom you have the deepest feeling connections. Your mother's influence is strongest and deepest in gestation, protective during childhood at home, and during maturity begins to reconstruct itself in your own homing instinct and choice of partner. As you detach from your mother, you find and accept the soul. The motherly influence becomes integrated into your whole as you bring feelings into line with the will to exist in the world. The Moon is feelings and protective instinct, and on the higher level the Moon is emotional reality as a whole and the summation of your hereditary disposition.

Mercury during maturity is communication with friends, students, workers, associates, salesmen, agents, mediators, intellectual leaders, organizers, friends and their effect upon your mental reality. The context for communication you create around yourself is echoed in the people with whom you express your thoughts. The intermediary function of getting your ideas out into the world may be delegated to others or may be an integral part of your own reality. After your daily life is structured, you quest for higher ideals that reflect a transcendent view beyond ordinary life. Mercury can also refer to the passing of life structures onto children, or through intellectual products like books or other creative acts.

Venus during maturity is the relationship to your loves, those you find and who find you attractive, mistresses, artists, musicians and sexual partners. Venus is also the milieu of these contacts in social life, entertainment, cultural venue and friendly relationships. Venus is also children.

Mars during maturity is the desire to change your world with athletic, sexual, mechanical, skilful and aggressive activities. Initially Mars energies are projected onto physical fitness, athletic competition and sexual investigation, which later transforms into the desire to focus energy within business, marriage and associations. Doctors, surgeons, craftsmen or soldiers fall under Mars' jurisdiction. When energy is blocked during these houses, it becomes rechannelled into physical therapies, sexual relations outside marriage or, if it is not redirected, it is forced inwards until it creates the physical afflictions that affect many people towards the end of their lives.

Jupiter during maturity shows your life philosophy and those from whom and with whom it is formed and used. The influence can be religious, psychological, philosophical or financial, and promotes expansion and optimism. The expansion first takes the form of being able to feel a part of groups and schools, and later is the possibility of growing beyond the institutions of life. Jupiter may be officials, religious people, gurus, psychologists, psychiatrists, those of high character, wealth and esteem, speculators, healers and all people who carry fortunate connections.

Saturn during maturity describes life systems that define your responsibilities, sense of security and community, and ability to establish and fit into collective patterns in your home and society. Saturn is those who maintain these organizational systems, like doctors, bank managers, employers, partners and associates, as well as those who are serious, older, strict, conservative, hard-working and mature. Towards the 8th house, you possibly become a grandparent or older person and represent the existing or declining order.

Uranus during maturity represents sudden changes, inventions, independence, erratic drives and all influences that serve to break up rigidity and patterns in your life. The carriers of these influences are reformers, eccentrics, inventors, unusual teachers, therapists and unusual associations or partners. The impact of Uranus ranges from submission to teachers or gurus to exerting a transformative influence upon your own life and that of others.

Neptune during maturity is the gradual transformation of youthful fantasies and ideals into sensitivity followed by detachment. Concern for society is envisioned by romantics, sensitives, mediums, spiritual people and rejected by alcoholics, mediators, hypochondriacs and seducers. Drug experiences and mystical reveries, confusion and wondering, all contribute to Neptune's influence.

Pluto during maturity is your relationship to collective values and changes in society. The influence is carried by those people in personal and public life who understand or force collective values. You may either be altered by a changing civilization or be a transformer yourself. Pluto symbolizes revolutionaries, transformers, those who exert psychic or magical influence over the masses, the media, politicians, gurus, domineering partners or employers and those who force change. Pluto's registration often generates changes in job, residence, partnership and overall view of life.

The Node during maturity indicates teamwork, your family, and the alliances, collaborations, marriages and partnerships you form. Professional associations, political parties, labour unions and groups all show Node influences.

A predominance of planets in maturity shows that the focus of life is to become stronger and more important.

The 5th house (naturally Leo)
Seven years until 13 years

The 5th house is a higher level of the 1st house, where you asserted yourself, and you now exteriorize yourself into the world outside the family and become conscious of who you are. The primary device in this understanding is game-playing: organized ways of exchanging energy, feelings, ideas and intuitions. The random and self-centred play of childhood becomes more involved and the choices of friends, school subjects, sports and diversions all describe and are affected by the games you play. Giving, taking, winning and losing are all part of personal relationships; ultimately the object is to enjoy and receive fulfilment from games rather than placing paramount importance upon winning, although many people would contest this interpretation.

Civilization rests upon playing by the rules adopted by ancestors. During primary education you learn these rules, their history and application. Your approach to game-playing in school and at home determines the kind and quality of relationships you form in the world.

Planets in the 5th house are those with whom you play and after whom you pattern your own games. Positive signs show an active and extrovert approach to games, while negative signs show a passive and introvert approach. The luminaries include not only parents, but new prototypes such as teachers, heroes in books and media, and older children. The Sun asserts the importance of game-playing and is a person after whom this trait is patterned. The Moon denotes imaginative, emotional and romantic motivations in play and is carried by those who feel this is important. Mercury loves change and nurtures the idea of the game as central. Venus focuses upon creative activities and the entertainment value of games and their rules, but Mars is aggressive, physical, competitive and unruly. Jupiter wishes to extend the importance of play and promotes a broad range of activities, while Saturn concentrates upon specialities, suppresses creativity through conservatism, wishes for security and associates with older children. Uranus creates original games that diverge from accepted rules. Neptune dreams and fantasizes more readily than it acts, expects ideal situations and tires easily of the reality of games and rules. Pluto dominates, rules and forces others to join and play games to which they might not otherwise be exposed, or popular games. The Node tends to play and accept rules adopted by everyone else without dissent. If you have no planets in the 5th house, it shows a lack of importance of schooling and games in your life.

Fire signs in the 5th house indicate an intuitive, instinctive and active approach to games; Earth signs rely upon physical stability and might, or may be the child who owns the ball and knows they will be included in the game; Air signs discuss and treat games as ideas and continually alter the rules to suit their needs; and Water signs take the results of games emotionally and value the role of the participants seriously.

The 6th house (naturally Virgo)
Thirteen years until 23 years, five months
At the beginning of the 6th house puberty is at its height and the body comes into focus. Suddenly sexuality is a central factor in the game-playing of the previous house and the rules of the games change dramatically. The choices you make and the way you make them become binding, as during the time of secondary education you determine your future direction and work relationships. The general tenor of your choices are physical as you select diet, clothing, activities and work disciplines, and systematically regain control from your parents, who formerly made such decisions for you.

Planets in the 6th house determine attitudes towards school and work, teachers and employers who guide you and friends whose choices affect your own. The Sun here promotes paternal ambition, which is either a reflection of or a reaction against father, which may be competitive or supportive. The Moon stresses feelings over practicality, serving, the functional aspects of life and changeable moods that affect logical decisions. Mercury appreciates detail but does not see the whole clearly, producing nervousness when choices must be made. Venus shows reliance upon school and work relationships and an ability to adapt easily, while Mars focuses upon efficiency, vitality, hard work and a desire to succeed. Jupiter is opportunistic, philosophical and loyal. Saturn is conscientious, selfish, serious, responsible and concentrates on security. Uranus institutes original methods in school and work, new techniques, and implies changes in focus. Neptune drifts idealistically, makes sacrifices to causes and is influenced by prevailing situations, especially when under the influence of drugs or alcohol. Pluto is attraction to large-scale occupations, large universities and mass movements in education or technology. The Node is association with others for guidance and protection.

Fire signs in the 6th house indicate that choices are intuitive and based on the energy they carry; Earth signs show decisions based on tangible values, financial gain or possessions; Air signs value the ideas behind work more than its rewards; and Water signs feel their way into certain types of school or work where fine valuations are essential.

The 6th house governs school and occupation. Table 9 describes occupations congenial to planets here.

Table 9: Planets and Occupations

Sun	Administrator, stars, politicians, leaders, speculators, company directors, public figures, royalty, the famous.
Moon	Midwife, cook, gardener, vintner, sailor, brewers, collectors, dealers, domestics, hoteliers, landowner, obstetricians.
Mercury	Teacher, journalist, writer, reporter, clerk, accountant, agent, mediator, artisan, architect, solicitor, cabbie, educator, optician.
Venus	Artist, musician, entertainer, actor, nurse, broker, associate, clothier, cashier, furnisher, jewellers, restaurateur, treasurer.
Mars	Surgeon, builder, designer, engineer, fireman, adventurer, athlete, butcher, manufacturer, machinist, soldier, physiotherapist, police.
Jupiter	Lawyer, judge, banker, physician, insurer, clergyman, foreigner, merchandiser, official, professor, publisher, sportsman, trader.
Saturn	Scientist, doctor, banker, farmer, archaeologist, osteopath, businessman, cattle-raiser, miner, dentist, geologist, plumber, potter.
Uranus	Astrologer, radio/TV, musician, technologist, electrician, healer, fliers, cartoonist, electronics, feminist, mechanic, physicist.
Neptune	Chemist, anaesthetist, astronaut, dancer, distiller, medium, psychic, navy, oiler, photographer, poet, psychologist, wizard.
Pluto	Revolutionary, undertaker, taxman, atomic scientist, insurer, outlaw, prostitute.

The 7th house (naturally Libra)

Twenty-three years and five months until 42

As you approach the cusp of the 7th house, exactly opposite the Ascendant/personality, a more objective attitude towards life begins as you complete the lower, subjective half of the horoscope of childhood and the first half of maturity. The domination of parents, family and birth circumstances must be recognized, worked through and resolved through partnerships. Partnerships sublimate the self-oriented first 23 years of life by requiring you to give away to others as much energy, emotion, material and ideas as you have received – all in order to balance out life.

Planets in the 7th house show those with whom you have emotional or work partnerships, new people encountered once you enter the world, and attitudes to such contacts and realities. The Sun represents a strong capable, close and conscious relationship and the person with whom you form this relationship. When in double signs, you can expect to have more than one partner. The Moon stresses domestic and emotional sides of partnership, and can indicate an instinctive partnership. Mercury is changeable and indicates more than one partner – often a choice of one younger, more intellectual or nervous – and describes those who mediate between you and the world. Venus shows deep physical attachment in relations where affection, love and aesthetics dominate. Mars is independent, selfish, aggressively sexual and impulsive in making and breaking relationships. Jupiter values social status and financial advantages in relationships, often prospers in more than one relationship as a way of expanding a world view. Saturn is responsible, conscientious and concentrated yet limiting re-lationships to older and more inhibited partners. Uranus is a wish to remain independent despite rapid attraction, and a romantic attitude which produces unexpected situations that form and dissipate quickly. Neptune is a dream of ideal partnership and attracts those admired from afar, often with ensuing disillusionment; or platonic unions where sacrifice is required. Pluto indicates relationships as a bridge to public affairs; mass values often determine the degree of cooperation, thereby producing great changes of attitude. The Node represents special aptitude for groups, circles of friends, communal cir-cumstances, clubs and politics as outlets or substitutes for collective expression of views. No planets in the 7th house show partnerships and partners as a continuation of earlier attitudes, people, events or identifications.

For most adults, the 7th house time after 23 years and five months is the region of the horoscope in which they are most interested. This house is the collection of the entire planetary pattern from previous ages all the way back to conception, and your last chance to affect or become aware of your destiny. By the time of your entrance into the 8th house, you will not possess enough energy to rectify laziness here. In many cases, the actual positions of planets in the horoscope are such that there are no planets in the 7th or 8th houses (which cover only

17% of the entire horoscope wheel), in which case the sensitive points are essential for describing the process of maturity and for prediction beyond your current age. Sensitive points are harmonic registrations at the exact aspect points of planets in the horoscope projected into an area you wish to study more closely. Even when there are already planets in the 7th house, it is important to identify and interpret sensitive points.

To fill this area with as many sensitive points as possible, you should use the minor aspects of 30° and 150°, and possibly even those of 45° and 135° degrees.

In Figure 23 a highly creative person enters the initiatory Aries on the 7th house cusp, indicating a new beginning and creativity until 42 years old. The benefic planets Venus and Jupiter register at 24 years, 10 months, and 27 years, five months, and the malefic planets Saturn and Mars register at 39 years, one month, and 40 years, eight months, but we want to discover what happened in the intervening time. The planets themselves describe the transformation of a creative man (Venus conjunct Jupiter) with innovative powers (Aries) to a condition of inhibition and a separation from these powers as a result of excessive sexuality (Mars sextiled from the Sun and MC, and squared by Pluto), increased flirtations with danger (Mars square Pluto) and re-straint (Mars conjunct Saturn). He is surrounded by beneficial and helpful people early on (Venus and Jupiter), but increasingly attracted aggressive and binding people (Mars and Saturn).

The sensitive points in this horoscope are the semisextile (30°) to the Moon at 9 Aries at 28 years, five months; the semisextile Uranus at 18 Aries at 33 years, five months; the opposition Node at 23 Aries at 36 years, 11 months; and the sextile from the Sun at 25 Aries at 38 years, six months. Even though there are no planets at these points, the sensitive points are treated as though there were. The sequence of planets and sensitive points is shown in Table 10, with the intervals between planets interpreted as aspects between the two limiting planets.

Table 10: Sensitive Point Sequence

1. Natal Jupiter (08° Aries 46 at 27 yrs 05 mths). Magnaminity, a philosophy of independence, expansion, of self.

2. Jupiter to 30 Moon. Happiness, social conscience, travel, negligent emotions.

3. 30 Moon (09° Aries 54 at 28 yrs 05 mths). Impulsive partnership, acting without thinking, strong personality.

4. Moon to 30 Uranus. Emotional tensions, instinct, sudden events in partnership.

5. 30 Uranus (18° Aries 08 at 33 yrs 05 mths). Restlessness, reforms, blinding zeal, violence, dreamy enthusiasts, eccentric partnerships.

6. Uranus to 180 Node. Shared experiences, incidents, upsets with others in

partnerships, activity, restlessness.

7. 180 Node (23° Aries 10 at 36 yrs 11 mths). Ruling others, submission, striving to lead others (groups), teamwork is difficult.

8. Node to 150 Neptune. Idealism, sensitive groups, antisocial, deceptions.

9. 150 Neptune (24° Aries 55 at 38 yrs 03 mths). Realised inspiration, rich feelings, confusion, no aims, insane–mad ideals.

10. Neptune to 60 Sun. Sensitivity, delicacy, imagination, uncertainty, weakness.

11. 60 Sun (25° Aries 20 at 38 yrs 06 mths). Leading others, enthusiasm, courage, lust for power, boldness, advance through ruthlessness.

12. Sun to natal Saturn. Inhibition, separation, absorption, seriousness, work, suppression, concentration on a partnership.

The sequence of sensitive points and their intervals, all in the sign Aries and the 7th house describe the 'coming out' into active homosexuality. The process starts creatively, becomes highly emotional with the Moon, then erratic and unusual with Uranus. The registration of the 180° Node sees a transference into a gay community, which exaggerated the idealistic content (Node to Neptune), culminating in the registration of the Sun (literally, a man in his life), and then the final link into the Saturn/Mars conjunction astride the 8th house cusp, showing physical threats and violence in relationships. Any zone of the horoscope, but especially the 7th and 8th houses, can be analyzed as this sequence has been.

The 8th house (naturally Scorpio)
Forty-two years old until death
After the drive for security and success in the world has been sublimated during the 7th house, the 8th house is the time of withdrawal from and meditation upon life. As you gradually release control over affairs, the favourable direction is towards a metaphysical reality, a broader and less materialistic perspective of life. During this time there is a natural decline of the senses, which were manifested during the opposite 2nd house: energy lessens, physical problems become central, senses weaken, mind is more and more internalized and private, and finally even your emotional grasp is eliminated. Your time sense is such that events which in early life would have come, manifested themselves and left in weeks now take years. Injuries and illnesses that formerly were brushed off become major liabilities. Financial shortcomings become critical problems that only get worse. You lose family and life-long friends who cannot be replaced and are even difficult to remember. The most important guide to this time is to relinquish control gracefully, as it is inevitable. The 8th house is the time of separation and death.

Planets in the 8th house indicate attitudes to metaphysical reality, to

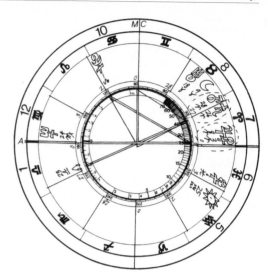

Figure 23: The 7th house
To fill in the space between
Jupiter and Saturn, we use
sensitive points from other
planets. The sequence of
sensitive points is the fabric of
our life in time.

the physical situation during the last phase of life and, when indicated, the manner of death. The Sun in the 8th house shows that the centre remains hidden until the latter stages of life and a gain in strength, insight, and inner emotional stability with advanced age. Additionally, an interest in metaphysical arts and a deep will, which survives all physical danger, is symbolized by the Sun. The Moon denotes extreme sensitivity and striving for truth beyond physical circumstances, financial dependence on women or protecting family, as well as an emotional old age. Mercury shows a mind specifically interested in metaphysical ideas, pursuits, secrecy and ideas derived from others and a lively old age. Venus indicates relationships that produce gain, the importance of art, and intense feelings towards the loss of physical appearance. Mars indicates a sex drive into late life, persistence in retaining energy, aggressive independence until the end and a tendency to die quickly. Jupiter is hopeful, confident and philosophical about life and death while indicating a natural death. Saturn resists relinquishing physical energy and property, and is hampered by these matters, yet is so disciplined and rigid that a long life can be indicated. Uranus is more eccentric and independent with age, shows psychic values and telepathic phenomena, possibly a deep vision into the mysteries amid changeable physical conditions and points towards a sudden end. Neptune increases sensitivity and also vulnerability, physically and financially; its nervous component increases the likelihood of death by wasting away, undiagnosed or psychosomatic disease, in drug therapy or in hospital. Pluto shows an attitude that accepts the necessity of death and regeneration manifest in an interest in occult subjects and arts, and can expect a great change in attitude and feeling late in life.

The Node shows increasing attraction to communes, monastic situations, withdrawal from the world, groups, societies or larger communities of people with similar views. No planets in the 8th house show that the last house in life is almost entirely affected by events and circumstances which have resulted from earlier acts or attitudes, as karmic repercussions of past life deeds.

Fire signs in the 8th house exhibit great energy and vitality once life's business is finished, reaching a peak while others decline; Earth signs concentrate upon physical fitness and financial resources; Air signs are withdrawn into the thoughts and memories of life; and the Water signs have strong and deep emotional responses to the ability to contact the soul and complete life.

The famous modern guru Bhagwan Shri Rajneesh suddenly, after achieving enormous popularity, wealth, following and recognition, left his Indian base and sought refuge in the US under threat to his life from illness and political resistance. His popularity is indicated by the succession of Mars, Mercury, Venus and Moon in Capricorn, the sign of recognition and fame. The Venus and Moon conjunction is the essence of love and devotion liberating tensions, sexual inhibitions, eccentricities and musical energies by the square of both planets to Uranus (licence). The prominent material undercurrent is shown by the Capricornian sign quality. At the registration of Saturn opposed Pluto the great change occurs at 49 years, two months, and the hardening-up process has critical effects on his health. This is the configuration of a magician and adept, but also of a martyr.

The 9th house cusp/Death Moment

As life is a process, so all events in life are processes within a process. Conception, birth, the transition from childhood to maturity, and death are changes in state that every human being experiences. The 9th house cusp is archetypically the death moment. Due to the mathematics of the Placidean House division system, it is possible and often happens that this cusp registers as early as 40 years old, or past the age of 100 years old. The ninth cusp is the symbolic death point and is not to be taken literally!

In some horoscopes there are many points at which life may be threatened or possibly terminated. Determination of the exact time of death is the most difficult analytical question in astrology, and the astrologer has a responsibility to leave an open mind on this issue. Unless circumstances are exceptional and knowledge about the manner and time of death is necessary or helpful, this issue should be left open. Dangerous times should be identified, but not stated as possible death.

When the ninth cusp registers in life, it must be understood as a great transition. The transition is either a revelation which terminates existing life values and patterns, an insight into a different and higher level of reality, or a negative step away from life into a more mechanistic reality. This cusp can coincide with retirement, the onset of senility, a radical change in life like moving into a rest home, the death of a long-time partner, a change in residence after a long and stable home life or a physical disability which forever alters one's lifestyle as in the case of heart attacks, diagnosed cancers and other crises. On the more positive side, it can indicate a new awareness of life's mysteries, an involvement with communal organizations that relieve isolation, or even being taken into the care of others. In earlier Eastern societies, this would mark the time when a man, after having completed his life as a husband, father and householder, gives up his possessions and leaves to wander the high Himalayas as a wandering monk until death. This is the time of stepping beyond the world, exemplified by the 9th house values of higher mind, religion, psychology and philosophy.

Sometimes the 7th and 8th houses are expanded instead of compacted, and there are planets which register past the age of 100 years old, yet are still within the 8th house. This implies an influence which carries on after death either in the world or within the family.

Planets that register after death indicate posthumous recognition or a lasting effect upon those who survive the individual. This is often the case when people die early in life, yet have planets registering afterwards. Their emotional, spiritual or even mental existence remains to have an influence on family or society.

Transcending Your Story

A majority of people occupy life simply surviving. Their lives are significant only to themselves; they never attempt to extend the focus of life beyond the immediate situation. It is possible to extend your reality beyond the 'mortal coil' and transcend the story of your life. To do so, it is necessary to remain awake to the positive and negative events, people and processes of life, and to integrate them all into a complete whole.

Most people, when asked to remember and date the important events of their lives, can only locate graduation from school, marriage, births of their children, the date of divorce and others of like kind as being critical. The times in between simply drop out of the whole. Their lives are shallow and bleak, and events are only the outer manifestation of a missing inner life. All meaning has disappeared from life, leaving a series of legal transactions instead.

Humanistic psychology regards the process of personal growth as the focus of life. The manifestation of a full, active, successful life is paramount, and the individual resulting satisfies their social, personal and hereditary conditions totally. While these goals are elusive to all but a few people, there are lessons learned in life through the horoscope that point to higher levels of awareness and understanding. Once life is mapped out and its events and personifications defined, you can see that it is continually alive within and is being relived and re-experienced daily. Past events and dead parents remain with you throughout life as lessons and guides. The basic information of life – the dates, places, people and times – and the meaning of the whole is brought into every subsequent life situation. If you remember nothing, you learn nothing. Only by recognizing the past in your present and future can you move beyond the mundane. You are trapped by the past until you understand it clearly enough to recognize and transcend its games. Every event, problem, difficult person or relationship, every recalcitrant child you raise, creates possibilities for transcendence. Often, the greater the difficulties, the more you must try to remain awake and find the higher value of experiences. All difficulties in life reflect problems within, which have yet to be resolved, and identify parts of the whole of which you are not yet aware. Wholeness requires the identification of those missing parts.

The only way to move beyond life into the transcendent realm is to make use of what you know about yourself to help others to a clearer understanding of themselves. The best way to communicate unity to others is by example. If you live life accepting adverse conditions in the same manner as beneficial circumstances and learn and grow from everyone around, you set such an example. When you can maintain equilibrium in spite of difficulties, you do not avoid confrontation nor become complacent amid plenty: you can live life consciously.

When awareness exists, events indicated in the future lose their terror. Often people try to make what appear to be difficult combinations of planets in their future go away because they wish to avoid problems. But you cannot make difficulties go away. If a Saturn registration, indicating restriction, limitation and concentration, is due at a certain time, the nature of Saturn determines the correct attitude. To try to throw a party or to expand socially is contrary to the message of Saturn. If you throw a party, people will have prior arrangements or will feel inhibited while there. If you try to go out, the car will have a flat tyre. The restriction will operate whatever you do. If you approach the situation creatively, you realize that if you stay at home alone and confront those problems that you have avoided, the concentration of Saturn can work for you. If you do not use the concentrating energy of Saturn on your own terms, its effect registers against your will. It is better to use the difficult influences of the planets rather than leave yourself open to their influence when you least expect or want it. If a difficult Venus aspect is about to operate, indicating a confrontation with a woman, the confrontation cannot be avoided, but the woman with whom you have the confrontation can be chosen, including the woman within you. It can be the woman associate at work with whose work you are dissatisfied, or your wife. You can choose to use the influence to confront the situation in a creative way, but if not, it will rebound back at you. This principle operates with all the planets and in all events in your life. You must try to understand the demands of life and use all situations maximally.

Ordinary people believe they are living creative and fulfilling lives, but often they repeat their past ad infinitum. The only way to move past early childish patterns, determined by parents, is to observe your reactions and actions. Only then can you rectify life patterns by using them consciously. This is the object of Your Story: to transcend your role, the other characters and the entire situation of life by choosing higher consciousness – being awake.

Chapter Eight — Divine Time & History

We live life in time. We may transcend time in spiritual or meditative experiences, but only temporarily. As the fourth dimension beyond the three spatial dimensions of the physical world, time contains all space and by extension, all material reality.

Life Time Astrology, shows that an individual life signified by the horoscope is a recapitulation of all life in the universe. The progress of spirit and soul through earthly incarnation is the descent of unity and its entrance into physical form. The creation of physical form repeats in every being from the dawn of time, and the process exists within form itself.

The lunar month unit of Life Time Astrology corresponds to the lifetime of the ovum. The common thought that the ovum is 'created' each month in a fertile woman is like Aristotle's belief that the human embryo develops out of an admixture of menstrual blood and male seminal fluid, with the male merely providing the stimulus to growth to the already-developed embryo. It was not until 1827 that the biologist Karl Ernst von Baer discovered and saw the ovum. A woman does not create the ovum each month any more than menstruation is an expulsion of an ovum. All the ova that a woman brings to fruition are present soon after her own conception. The ovaries contain more than a quarter of a million immature cells, one or more of which ripen each month within alternate ovaries.[90] The ripened human cell was first seen in 1930, and the events of the first seven days after fertilization were not understood until the 1950s. The intricate cell structures that shape heredity were only partially understood in the 1960s.

The ova do not originate in the mother, but in the extra chromosome that women possess from their own conception. In this sense, the ovum is eternal. However, it can only be so because it is impossible to create life from nothing. The ovum is eternal, and carries the memory and structure of all previous life within it, ready to provide information when required. Every ovum is similar to the ovum that created the first life. Each ovum recurs an almost infinite number of times, carrying all its predecessors' histories within it.

Each cell contains genetic material sufficient to build and monitor all genetic structure in the body. The 100,000 genes that describe and create a specific cell are only 3% of the genetic material. Geneticists consider the other 97% 'junk DNA', meaning that they do not know what it does.[91] The parallel between the brain and the genetic code, each using only a tiny fragment of its capacity to create and maintain life, leads one to suspect that the remainder is devoted to other functions and 'bodies', the whole of life and all history, which is carried within, although this differs from the accepted mechanistic and materialistic views.[92]

Freud's idea that ontogeny (the life of the individual) recapitulates phylogeny (the life of the species) is borne out. We experience childhood in a state of consciousness similar to the collective mythological reality of humanity thousands of years ago, after the emergence of consciousness. Individual life reactivates patterns established millennia ago. We do not learn the deeper instincts of sexuality, hunger, sleep, and anger from parents, but they are contained within the psyche. Jung identified two types of inherited characteristics as a *'personal unconscious'* which is all the memories derived from childhood, and a 'collective unconscious' shared with all other humans. We are influenced by many levels of reality, in varying degrees, and simultaneously.

The principle of recapitulation is central to depth and transpersonal psychology, and to Astrology.

I. The *Octave of Gestation* from conception to birth reflects the time from Creation to the origin of consciousness, and is the collective unconscious. We repeat the process from fertilized ovum to birth and all such influences are stored somatically within the physical body as instincts.

II. The *Octave of Childhood* from birth to seven years old reflects the mythological time of human pre-history, from when humanity first became conscious until the emergence of the first historical individuals, and is the personal unconscious. We carry familial influences in our emotional body.

III. The *Octave of Maturity* from seven years old until death is analogous to the development of civilization in history, from the first historical individuals to the realization of the renaissance. Influences derived from the educational life process are stored in the mental body as a worldview.

IV. The *Octave of Transcendence* is the higher level of creative being, which reflects gestation but lies outside of individual time. The historical parallel is the age when humanity realizes its existence and function within the cosmos. We carry the search for the origin of life in the spiritual body as a craving for transcendence.

Each successive developmental stage in life becomes longer and longer, taking almost as long as the entire preceding time back to conception. In history, each successive stage is shorter than its predecessor's. When we compare an individual life to all history, we must reverse the direction of expansion and contraction. Individual developmental stages get longer as we age, while collective developmental stages get shorter as history proceeds. The two opposite flows of time mutually compensate the historical perspective of time. Since history and the individual times flow in different directions, they compensate for each other, which accounts for the fact that although most people recognize a variation in the flow of time, very few would actually posit it as a natural law, and fewer still as a central mechanism of the universe. The scientific community ignores the obvious compaction of time.

A profound picture emerges once we understand history, both individually and for the species, as exponential and circular rather than additive and linear. It is easy to find cultures that espouse both systems of grading history. Buddhist and Hindu cycles of great ages decrease in length towards the present as examples of the first, and the Precession of the Equinoxes of 25,000 years in the Platonic Year is an example of the second.

Hindu and Buddhist world ages decrease successively according to the ratio 4:3:2:1. The belief that each age reflects the same events as the former but in less time indicates a progressive deterioration. The length of life decreases as does the quality of life. The Chinese also had theories of a fall from a 'Golden Age' recorded in the *Record of Rites* of Li Chi in AD100 and, before that, by Huai Nan Tzu in 200BC.[93] There are significant advantages and logic to both linear and exponential systems of describing history – The Divine Plot includes them.

The Acceleration of History

We assume that the universe develops at a constant rate, but this is not the case. Turn-of-the-century historian Henry Adams studied the relationship between science and social history, being familiar with electromagnetism, the laws of thermodynamics, the then recent discovery of radioactivity, and the dilemma of Michelson and Morley's time equations, as well as the pace of modern history. Adams plotted the rising curves of scientific discovery rates, coal output, steam power,

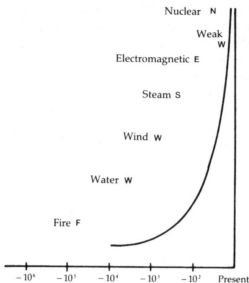

Figure 24: Acceleration of Time
A graph combining the exponential increase in energy sources, similar to those plotting the discovery of elements, agricultural and industrial outputs. Together they generate the curved law of acceleration of Henry Adams.

mechanical and electrical usage and many others, and said: 'Any schoolboy could plot such curves and see that arithmetical ratios were useless; the curves followed the old familiar law of squares'.[94] The curves rise more steeply as they ascend from the base line of time.

The logarithmic time base line of Adams' chart gives equal space to the last millennium as to the preceding 10,000 years. It not only serves geometrical convenience, but also reflects the compression of the past in memory. 'Acceleration is the law of history.'[95] Conclusions drawn from statistics on energy use and changes in phase in history related to thermodynamics indicate that at a constant logarithmic progression, humanity will reach a limit of possibilities by the year 2025, by Adams' most optimistic projection.

Adams likened the life of humanity to the passage of a comet that traverses the infinite without origin or end. Occasionally an object of curiosity lying in its path attracts it, which forces it to condense its velocity as it curves past. This image implies that evolution has already passed its perihelion and is moving retrograde already. According to Adams, by 2025 humanity will have overbalanced its ability to integrate by an increased ability to disintegrate.

H G Wells voiced similar ideas just before the first nuclear bomb tests:

Events now follow one another in an entire untrustworthy sequence. Spread out and examine the pattern of events and you will find yourself face to face with a new scheme of being, hitherto unimaginable by the human mind. This new cold glare mocks and dazzles the human intelligence, no matter how this intelligence under its cold urgency contrives to seek some way out or round or through the impasse. The writer has come to believe that the congruence of the mind, which man has attributed to the secular process, is not really there at all. The two processes have run parallel for what we call Eternity and now abruptly they swing off at a tangent from one another – just as a comet at its perihelion hangs portentous in the heavens for a season and then rushes away for ages, or forever.[96]

The world is accelerating past its breaking point. Events in the modern world verify these 80-year-old and 50-year-old predictions. Shortages of food, energy and natural resources, coupled with an exponential increase in population, have followed the most negative predictions.

Hermann Kahn and The Hudson Institute predicted logarithmic increases *In the Year 2000* for measuring Gross National product projections, Postwar Economy Growth, Rate of Increase of Energy in Particle Accelerators, GNP Extrapolations, Populations, Total GNP, Individual Country Production, Population from 8000BC to AD2000, GNP per capita, Population per GNP, United States GNP per capita, Japanese GNP per capita, and many others.

Bertalanffy, the founder of General Systems Theory, gives exponential growth as a basic law of nature. The great eras in the earth's prehistory are all shorter than their predecessors. The time scale of evolution is not a clock marked by equal intervals, but more like a stone falling to the ground.

J G Bennett, in *The Dramatic Universe: History*, confronts the problem of historical time scales, presenting accelerated progress as an idea no one doubts. 'Statistics show that the output of science and technology has for a long time been increasing at an accelerated pace. Moreover, accelerated progress seems to be a law of nature.'[97] Bennett constructed a graph of the logarithmic nature of the great eras.[98] He calls acceleration 'objective eschatology', but runs into a problem when he carries his time scale any nearer the present than 100,000BC. His mathematics prevents measurements except those remote from the present. In the larger sense, the rate of development went out of control 100,000 years ago. Humanity's entire existence occurs within a mere hyphen of nature. Bennett does allow, however, that the acceleration must continue into historical time – even through to the present, stating that, 'We should expect the completion of the eighth (and last) Era within the next half a million years and perhaps very much sooner.'[99]

The concept of an exponential (logarithmic) spiral of life and time is not new. Descartes proposed it in 1638, as did Bernoulli, the biologist

J B S Haldane, and even Charles Darwin. Exponential spirals govern the growth pattern of the nautilus, many varieties of shells, flowers, trees, and even galaxies.[100] Organisms that utilize the divine proportion in its natural form continue to grow and expand while maintaining the same shape, making the name 'spira mirabilis' appropriate.

Many great scientists and thinkers have used logarithmic scales in an attempt to describe the natural world. Hans Kalmus proposed a logarithmic scale to study the numbers characteristic of generations of various levels of organization from virus to man through the geologic ages. Rolland Fisher uses a logarithmic spiral of 'biological time' for describing increasingly rapid events in learning processes through time.[101] J B S Haldane observed that since the existence of humanity, the natural evolutionary rate has increased exponentially, a frequency of change that affects the length of generations and could be a factor in the extinction of species.[102] Nigel Calder graded history from Creation to AD2000 with a logarithmic scale because it allowed him to collate great spans of magnitude. Proportional scales are more relevant than linear yearly scales alone. The detail available is greater, the closer one approaches the present; in terms of human population it compensates for the rapid increase in growth, and brain size is proportional to lengths of time and lifetime.[103]

None of these theories takes full creative advantage of a log scale applied to individual and collective history.

The Divine Proportion of Time

Wherefore He resolved to have a moving image of eternity, and when He set in order the heaven, He made this image eternal but moving according to number, while eternity itself rests in unity: and this image He called Time.

Plato[104]

The two most important proportions used in The Divine Plot are the *golden section* and the *logarithmic scale*. According to Pythagorean number symbolism, the golden section is five-based, the number of creation, and the logarithmic scale is 10-based, the number of diversity and completion.

The golden section proportion is the ratio 'phi' (1.618:1), derived from the projection of a half-diagonal of a square. Kepler called it the '*divine proportion*' because it is pleasing when used either mathematically or aesthetically, and he used phi to describe planetary orbits. The phi proportion generates an additive and geometric series, where each successive number is the sum of the two previous numbers and is the product of the previous number multiplied by 1.618.

Figure 25: *Lapidus multiplicativa Auri*
An ancient alchemical formula shows that
the final stage of the transformation
involves multiplication by a factor of ten to
produce 'the golden stone'. 'And if one
part of it (the stone) in the first place
converts with its bodies a hundred parts in
the second it converts a thousand, in the
third ten thousand, in the fourth a hundred
thousand, in the fifth a million, into the
true sun-making and moon-making.'
(*Philosophia reformata*, Frankfurt, 1622)

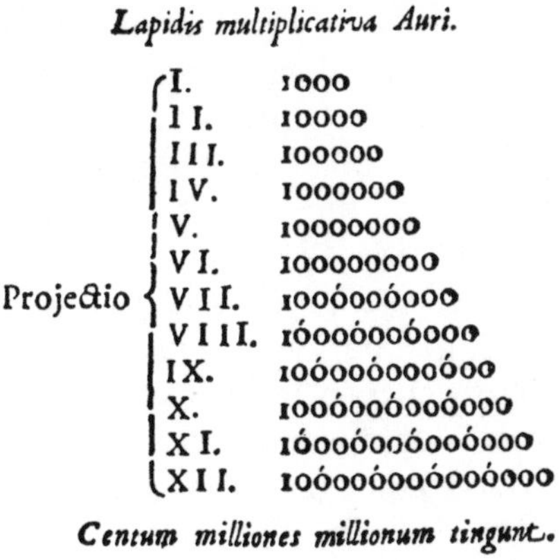

Lapidis multiplicativa Auri.

Projectio

I.	1000
I I.	10000
I I I.	100000
I V.	1000000
V.	10000000
V I.	100000000
V I I.	1000000000
V I II.	10000000000
IX.	100000000000
X.	1000000000000
X I.	10000000000000
X I I.	100000000000000

Centum milliones millionum tingunt.

The golden section is the geometric basis of the pentagram and
pentagon worshipped by the Pythagoreans, and later by magicians and
mystics of the middle ages and the renaissance. The pentagon is a
regular five-sided figure that, when we extend its sides, forms the
pentagram star. Both yield many phi relationships.

The golden section is a linear, planar, and spatial proportion. We may
divide lines into segments proportioned by phi; we may divide planes
into golden rectangles as in painting; and in architecture and sculpture
we may use phi to define the internal and external proportions of
buildings or sculptures.

What is the equivalent of the phi proportion in time? The proportion
that governs the growth of nature, civilizations, and individual men
through time is the base 10 logarithmic proportion. Base 10 logarithms
constitute are golden section of time.

Ten represents the ten in one, ten integrated by one.[105]

In the Buddhist Hwa-yen Sutra, Fa-tzang characterizes two aspects of
the enlightened condition by the numbers one and ten. One is the Unus
Mundus (One World), unity and all-embracing Self, and 10 is the form
in which unity manifests in the multiplicity of existence, a pervading,
continuous identity. Marie Louise von Franz interprets numerological
correspondences psychologically in an attempt to explain the
paradoxical multiplicity and unity of the Self that denotes psychic
wholeness, because numbers form the midpoint between the spiritual
and the material (extrasensory). The log progression 1, 10, 100 and
1000 embodies the operative force that creates matter through the
emanation of a divine dynamic.[106]

Egyptian sacred scientists attributed the number 10 to the synthesis,
the origin of phenomenal nature and its aim.[107] The Platonically

inspired Sixth Ennead of Plotinus proposes a tenfold division of existents, dividing every element of the world into 10 genera.[108]

The Tree of Life of 10 sephira of the mystical and numerological Hebrew Cabbala is based on Kether the Crown (unity) emanating the qualities of the Universe, stepping them down to Malkuth the Earth (multiplicity). 'Planetary lives are composed of ten dreams of a hundred years each, arid each solar life is a thousand years; therefore is it said that a thousand years are in the sight of God as one day.'[109]

The alchemical table *Lapidus multiplicativa Auri* (see Figure 25) shows the process of multiplicatio, whereby the base material is converted into the divine gold by factors of 10, called true sun-making and moon-making.

The Incan's sophisticated mathematics used rope-adding devices utilizing base 10 logarithms.

The Round Art and *Life Time Astrology* identify the base 10 log sequence as the proportion of biological time governing growth and metabolic processes in humans. Rodney Collin utilizes the base 10 log sequence 1, 10, 100 and 1,000 as divisions of lunar months defining the developmental stages of human life. The mathematical proportions of metabolism and memory affect and modify perception time of the sequence of life. When we integrate the logarithmic-lunar sequence of biological mechanisms with the perception of the linear-yearly sequence of astrological signs, it mathematically combines linear and circular, additive and exponential realities, which together determine perceptual space-time. We use the same circular matrix for both systems, reflecting the circular, repetitive and recurrent mechanisms that operate in the year, in one's life and in all life.

The three necessary criteria for a mathematical matrix for The Divine Plot are:

1. An **Additive** scale of cyclic recurrent years independent of subjective time values, measured in seconds, minutes, hours, days, calendar months or astrological signs, equinoxes and solstices, years, millennia and precessional cycles of 25,000 years.

2. A **Geometric** scale of base 10 logarithms, reflecting the subjective compaction of biological time and memory as humans, humanity, civilizations, nature and the universe develop through their life cycles.

3. A **Circular** matrix around which the additive and geometric systems may be placed, so that the beginning and end of cycles coincide, satisfying the necessity of recurrent lives, ages, civilizations, world ages and universes.

Chapter Nine — The World Age

For the Holy One hath weighed the world and with measure hath he measured the times, and by numbers he hath numbered the seasons, neither will he rest nor stir until the number be fulfilled.[110]

The cycle of a World Age parallels an individual life. The consensus among anthropologists is that humans became conscious about 50,000 years ago, at the time human pigmentation occurred.[111] Richard Leakey states that Homo sapiens is 50,000 years old.[112] At that time, the supremacy of the Neanderthal ended as the more advanced Cro-Magnons eradicated them over the next 15,000 years. The transition is interesting because no earlier traces of the Cro-Magnons, from whom all modern humanity developed, exist. The 'missing link' is still missing. The conquering Cro-Magnons interbred with the beetle-browed, hairy, short, stocky and powerful Neanderthal, creating intermediate characteristics, which remain in the present Homo sapiens stock. Their brain capacity was nearly the same, but the Neanderthals were closer to proto-primates in habit, appearance and social structure, while the mysterious Cro-Magnons were virtually identical to modern humans. The situation is reminiscent of Creation as described in the apocryphal scriptures, where the sister and first wife of Adam, Lilith, created a race of half-humans by mating with degenerate angels. It may be the origin of the myth.

The World Age of humanity began 50,000 years ago, but its duration must be determined. Projections relating to population explosion, the inability of humanity to distribute the food necessary to feed the world, the threat of destruction from nuclear energy and weapons, and ecological collapse all seem to focus around the year 2000. It is also a common target date for the 'end of the world' as predicted by many prophets, including Nostradamus and the raving

Jehovah's Witnesses.

The Jewish Jubilee Cycle is 50,000 years. The rabbis gave an added importance to the year AD1000 as the beginning of the last thousand-year Jubilee Year, which would make AD2000 the changeover of world ages. These cycles are repetitive – the end of one age is the beginning of the next. Jose Arguelles chooses the end of the 20th century as the 'end of history' and the beginning of 'post-history', a quantum leap to the next level of planetary consciousness.

The astronomical-astrological mechanism of the precession of equinoxes also corresponds to the duration of about 50,000 years as two equinoctial cycles – a night and day of creation similar to the night and day of Brahma.

If 50,000 years is the duration of the World Age from the origin of consciousness to the end of its cycle of manifestation, by applying base 10 logarithms, the unit of measurement is determined to be one-thousandth of the duration, or 50 years. Fifty years in history is equivalent to a lunar month in individual life, just as 50,000 years is equivalent to 1,000 lunar months (77 years). The feminine lunar unit in individual life balances the masculine solar unit in collective life. The last 50-year period represents the death experience of humanity, the 'last judgement', a compacted reliving of the entire life cycle and an ovum seedtime of the next world age. The beginning of the last judgement is 50 years before AD2000, or AD1950, just after the explosion of the atomic bombs at Hiroshima and Nagasaki, the year of the first hydrogen bomb tests, and the proliferation and testing of such weapons in the atmosphere and underground. The coherent ecological system of planet received a shock that signals the 'death' of the world age. As has been mentioned previously, it is estimated that population living between 1950 and 2000 is approximately the same as the number of people who have lived in the last 50,000 years.[113] Everyone alive during the whole world age is returning to experience the end and the beginning of a new age.

The limits of the world age of 48,000BC and AD1950 are graded by an astrological sequence from Aries to Pisces. The same log sequence divides history as individual life, but in the reverse direction in time.

1	10	100	1000
—50yrs	—500yrs	—5000yrs	—50,000yrs
AD1950	AD1500	3000BC	48,000BC

The intermediate dates occur at 5000 years and 500 years before AD2000, which places them at 3000BC and AD1500, equivalent to the beginning of Leo and Sagittarius.

About 48,000BC humanity, immersed in the unconscious, nevertheless became conscious and self-assertive. Beings wandered in an undifferentiated state inseparable from the natural world around them, and reality was collective and mythological. They worshipped the gods of heaven, earth, sky and sea.

Five thousand years ago, about 3000BC, humanity became individual and self-conscious. Many early cultures dated the Great Flood at about 3000BC, also the time of the 'eras of creation'. The Jews and Christians believed that God created the world in 3761BC. The first legendary Pharaoh Menes existed at about 3200BC. The original Chinese Emperor Tai Hao existed about 2850BC. The Brahmins compute the beginning of the Kali Yuga (Era of Darkness) as 3102BC. It also signals the beginning of the Bronze Age and the first use of waterpower.[114] It was the time of formation of the great ancient civilizations of Babylonia, China, Egypt and Sumeria. About 3000BC the first individuals were recognized and monotheism reigned. Between 3000BC and AD1500, the classical civilizations of Egypt, Greece, Rome, and China, guided by powerful rulers, determined the development of humanity. By the Middle Ages, the great civilizations had interbred, spread and disintegrated, which led to the dark ages of feudalism, monasticism, crusades, magic and the great plagues.

Five hundred years ago, around AD1500, are the Renaissance and the realization of the self. The death, destruction and decay of classical reality gradually transformed into the Renaissance, the age of humanism. The Enlightenment coincided with the discovery and colonization of the New World, the circumnavigation of the globe, trade routes to India and China, the final fall of Constantinople, the beginning of the reformation of the Church, all abetted by Renaissance individuals transforming government, religion, art, architecture, drama, literature, science and statesmanship.

From the reawakening in AD1500 until the destruction in AD1950, humanity grew and matured. The renaissance provided intellectual and scientific tools for the incredible expansion of the Industrial Revolution and the twin bastions of modern society – capitalism and socialism, the dominant national and international control systems. From their idealistic foundation, both systems steadily gained power until their clash in the wantonly destructive World Wars of the 20th century. The promise of technology and sophisticated politics turned poisonous, contaminating psychology, science and the environment, bringing about with astonishing rapidity the End of a World Age.

The final 'panoramic memory' of the last 50 years of the 20th century is a repetition of the three stages of the World Age, compacted so densely that it is hardly recognizable. Every person in the entire world age has a representative present in the year 2000. The concept seems outrageous, but we must remember that the whole world 10,000 years ago had only about five million people: the present population of London could have more than populated the world.[115]

According to the Pythagorean doctrines of 'transmigration' and 'metempsychosis', there are quanta of souls that continually and in succession animate all living beings. Upon each conception, the soul enters a body, and upon death leaves it – the soul is the vehicle on which the impressions of many lifetimes are registered. The Pythagoreans believed that the animal characteristics of zodiac signs represent a sequence of identities through which the soul progresses towards becoming divine. The quality of a lifetime determines the next incarnation in either ascension to higher life forms, or if the life is degenerate, descent through the lower life forms. The soul travels outside of time, re-entering space-time upon reincarnation in either future or past, relative to the last incarnation.

Every individual living in the World Age is animated by a soul that approaches the last judgement. The type of reality manifested during all recurrences into the temporal continuum – barbarian and cultured, primitive and modern, male and female, spiritual and atheistic – is accumulated and repeated in the company of all other souls, which gives each soul the opportunity to be present at the final moment of death and rebirth of the world soul, of which each individual soul is a manifestation. A vision in the Old Testament Book of Revelations is very descriptive:

> *And I saw the dead, small and great, stand before God, and the books were opened: and another book was opened, which is the book of life, and the dead were judged out of those things which were written in the books, according to their works. And the sea gave up the dead who were in it; and death and hell gave up the dead who were in them: and they were judged every one according to their works. And death and hell were cast into the lake of fire. This is the second death. And whosoever was not found written in the book of life was cast into the lake of fire.*[116]

Christianity absorbed and integrated the ancient doctrines of reincarnation, manifesting in the Last Judgement. Alternatively, the end of a World Age is an opportunity to raise spiritual consciousness to a higher level, to discover the planetary logos and to make an evolutionary quantum leap to a single social super-organism.[117]

The Symbolism of 50

I am the master. The steep mountains of the earth are shaken
violently from their peaks to their foundations.
In my right hand, I hold the disk of fire.
In my left hand, I hold the disk that slays.
I hold the raised weapon of my divinity, the fifty-spoke solar wheel.[118]

Ancient Chaldean magical invocation

There are many numerological supports for making the duration of a
World Age of humanity as 50,000 years, using a base unit of 50 years.[119]

- 50,000 years ago humanity harnessed fire
- 5,000 years initiated the Bronze Age and the use of water power[120]
- 50 years ago we entered the Atomic Age after Hiroshima

The symbolism of the number 50 and its 10× factors pervade nature
and myth, as they do alchemy. The magical number five was sacred to
the Pythagoreans. The pentagram is the classical magical number of
protection and invocation. Brahma is 50 cosmic years old in the present
age. The innermost five electron rings contain a maximum of 50
electrons. There are 50,000,000,000 cells in the brain.

The number 50 appears in many measurements and proportions
embodied in the Great Pyramid.[121] The Pyramid Inch, on which
Egyptian cosmic geometry is based, is $1/500,000,000$th of the earth's
diameter. The King's Chamber sits upon the 50th course of stones, and
contains 100 facing stones. The Queen's Chamber sits on the 25th
course (5 × 5). The two chambers of the Great Pyramid correspond to
two male and female precessional cycles in a world age.

The Egyptians possessed sublime and accurate astronomical
information and integrated it into their culture. The cosmic
archaeologist Schwaller de Lubicz recognized that monuments of
ancient Egypt, when interpreted in terms of number, cycles and
hierarchy, provide insight into higher realms. 'Egypt organised and
administered her civilization upon this knowledge; it is this that
accounts for the structure of her system of calendars, the changes in
emphasis in her symbolism, the ascendance of one Neter (power) over
another and the shifts of the theological hegemony of her various
religious centres.'[122] De Lubicz' observations led to an integration
between the spatial proportion systems of the monuments of Egypt
and the temporal mechanisms of the calendar. These proportions are
central to The Divine Plot.

The great mystery of our calendar is that the cycles of the sun and
moon are incommensurable. The solar year of 365.24 days cannot be

even closely divided by the length of the month, whether the lunar month (when the moon returns to the same zodiacal position each cycle) of 27.3 days, or the lunation cycle (the time from one new moon and the next) of 29.5307 days. Schwaller de Lubicz noted that the Egyptians based their lunar calendar on periods of 25 years, which corresponds to 309 lunar months. A double cycle expresses the Golden Section, comprising 50 years; $618 = (phi-1) \times 1000$. It is interesting that the cycle given by the African Dogon, as the orbit of the invisible companion star of Sirius, is the foundation of Dogon astronomy.[123] The number five is the basis of Egyptian symbolism, architecture and religion, and their calendar and astronomy – the long-searched-for mathematical missing link between Pythagorean number symbolism and astronomy. The integration of the Golden Section phi, a cycle of 50 years, the lunar calendar, and astrological-astronomical correlations is the essence of The Divine Plot.

The Egyptians worshipped the Dog Star Sirius, which they believed to be a sun greater than our Sun, as central to their religion of reincarnation. They celebrated the heliacal (with the sun) rising of Sirius with a 50-day season at the beginning of their year, an evocation of Creation. Because our solar system is in the outermost arm of one of the four spiral arms of the Milky Way galaxy, some astronomers have postulated that Sirius is the greater sun around which our Sun and solar system orbits. This could happen as smaller galaxies have been captured by the Milky Way and spiral within its spiral. Sirius is a double star with one vast low-density star and one smaller, extremely dense star that orbits in a period of 50 years. Its structure looks similar to the nucleus of an atom with its positron and neutron. Rodney Collin thought it natural that Sirius fills the gap in cosmoses between the Solar System and the Milky Way, as the distance of the sun to Sirius is one million times the distance from the Earth to the Sun, falling naturally into the scale of cosmic relationships he proposed in his *Theory of Celestial Influence.*

The African Dogon based their religion on the 50-year cycle of Sirius B in its revolution around Sirius. Mythological parallels show that knowledge of Sirius was widespread in ancient times, beyond the Dogon and the Egyptians. Spiritual and oracular centres like Thebes, Miletus, Dodona, Delos, Delphi, Mount Ararat and Metsamor, were astronomically oriented and the basis of their mysteries was calendrical, mathematical, mythological, and astrological. The stars and constellations of the North reflect the myth of Jason and the 50 Argonauts, the landing of Noah's Ark on Ararat, and the entire geographical structure of religion in the ancient Mediterranean world.

The major star of the constellation Argo is Canopus, which means 'the

Figure 26: Sumerian Fish God Oannes
The Sumerian forerunner of Noah is
both a celestial god and a fish-tailed
amphibian demon from the unconscious.

pilot'. The Sumerians identified the star
with the amphibious descendant of the
gods Oannes in the Sumerian flood
legend – a proto-Noah who assisted
humanity and was the Jehovah of the
Hebrews (see Figure 26). Canopus
correlates with Egyptian, Sumerian,
Babylonian, Hebrew and Greek legends
of the great flood, religious centres of
these cultures and the very creation of
humanity. Deucalion is the Greek Noah,
associated with the central Delphic cults
of Apollo, which controlled music, art,
philosophy,   astronomy,   astrology,
mathematics, medicine and science. The
Delphic mystery ceremonies used a
boat, and at Delphi an omphalos, as
navels of the world. Dionysiac followers
celebrated cults every five years. The
Near Eastern religious belief that Noah
landed on Ararat parallels the Greeks'
belief that Deucalion landed at Delphi.
Temple's conclusion is that these myths refer to beings from Sirius who
fertilized earth in prehistory, although they point numerically to the
mathematics of The Divine Plot.

The symbolic number 50 permeates legends associated by Temple with
the mysteries of Greek and Mid Eastern culture:

- The heroes of Anu were the 50 Anunnaki or assembly of gods, of which
  seven are underworld gods and as such determined destiny.[124]
- There were 50 Danaids, Pallantids and Nereids, and 50 maidens of the Celtic
  Bran.[125]
- The dog of the underworld Cerberus, associated with the Egyptian Anubis,
  the devourer of souls and god of time, had 50 heads.[126]
- The Sumerian god Marduk had fifty names.[127]
- Actaeon and the 50 hounds of Hades, the underworld.[128]
- Thespius had 50 daughters by a celestial union who were priestesses of the

moon, and Hercules impregnated them all in one night or seven nights.[129]
— Gilgamesh, the Babylonian solar god, had 50 companions.[130]

The 50 moon goddesses of the White Goddess relate to the 50 lunations between Olympiads, in turn reflecting ancient esoteric 50-year, 50-month and 50-day sequences. The 50-month sequence also connects with the reign of a sacred king.

— The sacred king Lycaon caused the flood and had 50 sons.[131]
— The myth of the 50-month stag hunt.[132]
— The 50-oared ship of Orestes.[133]
— The primeval earth goddess Gaia had fifty bones, referred by Graves to Stonehenge.[134]
— The 50 stones of Deukalion (Noah).

The asteroid Chiron, named after the Greek centaur healing god, has a 50-year cycle. All these astronomically-based myths utilize the numbers 50 and 100, which are the basis of the time scale.

Prototypes for the 50-year cycle occur in Hebrew mysticism. 'And ye shall hallow the 50th year.'[135] The Hebrews originally divided their year into seven 50-day periods, with seven plus seven plus one bringing them to 365 days. There were seven times seven years in the Jubilee Cycle, plus one year making a Jubilee year every 50 years, and 7,000 year cycles culminating in the Jubilee period of 1,000 years, making a 50,000-year cycle. They celebrated the larger cycles each year in the seven weeks of the Passover Feast of Weeks (Shoves), when Moses received the 10 Commandments (2×5) on Mt Sinai, described in the first five holy books of the Bible, the Pentateuch. The Canaanite calendar also used seven cycles of 50 days. Easter is dated 50 days after the Pentecost, when the Holy Spirit descended as tongues of fire, and its timing reasserts this symbolism.

In traditional Indian teaching, the chakras are force centres in the human body represented by mandalas in the form of flowers, each petal showing a correspondent harmonic frequency and mystic sound. The Svadhisthana or sacral chakra has five petals and the Manipura or solar plexus chakra has 10 petals. In the five lower chakras, there are 48 petals, when we added the two-petalled lotus of the Ajna (brow) chakra; 50 is the number of the perfected personality (see Figure 26). The Sahasrara or crown chakra is the throne of spiritual dominion that heralds the point in evolution when incarnation no longer exists, and has 1,000 petals. In Buddhism it symbolizes the Bodhisattva, who vows to reincarnate until all sentient beings have reached perfection.[136] The product of the two is fifty thousand.

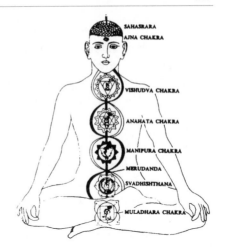

Figure 27: The Chakras
The chakras are energy centres in the form of flowers. In the five lower chakras are 48 petals. When added to the Ajna chakra of two petals, this makes a total of 50 petals, symbolic of the perfected being. The 1000-petalled Crown chakra heralds the ascendancy of Buddhahood over the personality. The product of the two is fifty thousand.

There are 50 numbered sections of Plato's Timeus. There are 50 members of the Brotherhood of the Knights of the Holy Grail.[137]

References to the number 50 in the preceding myths and legends are all relevant to The Divine Plot. We include the time and nature of Creation; the relation between the lunar unit of human life and the 50-year unit of humanity; the relationship between humanity and the gods; the mythological origin of the universal cycle; the organization of cycles and cosmoses; and the origin of humanity.

The Astrological Structure of the World Age

Each successive octave of the Time Scale is one tenth the duration of the preceding octave, yet carries 10 times the density of people, information and energy.

The Logarithmic World Age

Zodiac Sign	Beginning Time	Function
0 Aries	48,000BC (–50,000yrs) *Self-assertion*	Fire – Consciousness
0 Leo	3000BC (–5,000yrs) *Self-consciousness*	Water – Great Flood
0 Sagittarius	AD1500 (–500yrs) *Self-realization*	Pestilence – Black Death
0 Aries	AD1950 (–50yrs)	Fire – Atomic Bomb

In each successive octave, humanity expresses more sophisticated development, higher levels of consciousness and more individuation. The transition times between octaves are 'shock-points' at which human development changes dramatically, often in conjunction with drastic changes in the environment. The idea of gradual evolution with periodical cataclysms, 'punctuated equilibrium', is the most likely explanation of the evolutionary process. The sequence of fire, water, and pestilential shock-points evokes the plagues of Revelations, with the World Age beginning and ending with a trial by fire, initially the discovery of fire, and finally the atomic bomb. In each octave, a new level of reality emerges.

The Time Scale of the historical World Age is an astrological structure divided into 12 developmental stages. The zodiacal signs are a progression of developmental phases with the advantage of allowing geometric and octaval relationships between them. The twofold, threefold, fourfold and sixfold rhythms act like aspects in the horoscope – they connect events in life at various ages. The internal zodiacal geometry connects events at different times in history by parallels of meaning. The set of internal harmonies and rhythms provides the main trans-temporal integration mechanism in history, as it does in astrology.

This approach to history reflects the emphasis of the new physics on the 'web of relations' of history rather than particles embedded within – that is, events of history. It is also non-linear rather than linear, as is the study of history. Phases of historical development are cyclic and interconnected rather than random survival mechanism stacked one after the other. The astrological parallel also brings the stages of history into relationship with the progression of seasons in the year through the solar cycle, with the natural unfolding of the growth cycle, and with the stages of development of consciousness in the individual.

A circular mechanism exists in the working of all natural systems. As Thomas Mann observed:

> *For distance in a straight line has no mystery. The mystery is in the sphere. But the sphere consists in correspondence and reintegration; it is a doubled half that becomes one, that is made by joining an upper and a lower half, a heavenly and an earthly hemisphere, which complement each other in a whole, in such a manner that what is above is also below; and what happened in the earthly repeats itself in the heavenly sphere and contrariwise. This complementary interchange of two halves which together form a whole and a closed sphere is equivalent to actual change – that is, revolution. The sphere rolls – that lies in the nature of spheres. Bottom is soon top and top bottom, in so far as one can talk of top and bottom in such a connection. Not only do the heavenly and the earthly recognise themselves in each other, but, thanks to the revolution of the sphere, the heavenly can turn into the earthly, the earthly into the heavenly, from which it is clear that gods can become men and on the other hand men can become gods.*[138]

The spring sign Aries symbolizes the yearly birth moment and the initial assertion of personality at the dawn of consciousness from 48,000BC to 26,000BC. The table on pages 210 and 211 shows the Time Scale divided into 12 parts, related to the zodiac signs, the seasons, and times in history. The logarithmic contraction from sign to sign makes each sign slightly more than half the preceding sign, a compaction offset by an increased density of population, evolutionary rate and events toward the present.

Astrological rhythms are keys to historical principles that correlate the events, movements, civilizations and individuals, which combine to form the complete historical process.

The most basic rhythm is the binary alternation of masculine-patriarchal and feminine-matriarchal signs through the zodiac. Through the Time Scale, there is a continual flip-flop between the causal, masculine, left-brain view that is linear and mechanistic, and the acausal, feminine, right-brain view that is circular or non-linear and synchronistic. In the historical process, the fluctuations indicate patriarchal societies changing into matriarchal societies, open to closed value systems, and other bipolar social phenomena. The pairs of

---

Table 11 – The World Age

The Time Scale of the World Age of humanity describes the last 50,000 years, from self-consciousness to the atom bomb. The table is schematic because of the intense compaction of information. The horizontal lines are shown in two places in the book. The left-hand column of Astrological Stages, Historical Events, Religions & Mysticism, and Works of Humanity are shown in detail in Chapter Nine – The World Age. Aries to Cancer are on pages 216-7, Leo to Scorpio on pages 226-7 and Sagittarius to Pisces on pages 236-7. The central section shows the Stream of Civilizations, where the earliest civilizations coalesced from Neolithic communities, advanced through their cycles, conquered rivals, joined and comingled to lead to the modern nations known today. Snake-like movements indicate conquests of other streams, and arrows indicate significant shock-points of change of status or direction. The right-hand section shows each of the seven planets as significators for each age. In the first four signs Aries-Cancer, pages 290-91, the planetary prototypes are gods and goddesses shown in four phases of development. The deities of many cultures are shown, while often they were known to many cultures simultaneously under a variety of names. From Leo to the end of Pisces, pages 292-5, the historical individuals emerge from legendary heroes, until the present, when heroes are manufactured instantly. Note that the lifetime of an individual is about one degree in Leo, while it is more than the entire sign in Pisces. The later in history an individual exists, the more likely they are to influence more than one sign developmental stage. The Astrological Reincarnation Time Scale (pages 296-7) is a list of dates related to exact zodiac signs and degrees from which you can translate your horoscope into an exact age in history.

The World Age		Historical Events, Religion and Spiritual History, Works of Humanity
AD1950		
PIS	Institutionalism World Wars; chaos and collapse; isolationism	
AD1910		
AQU	Scientific; nationalism Socialism; idealism; science; evolution	See p. 236-7
AD1840		
CAP	Industrial & national revolutions; capitalism Mechanistic materialism; reformation	
AD1720		
SAG	Renaissance humanism Colonization; enlightenment; philosophy	
AD1500		
SCO	Feudalism; crusades; inquisition & magic Monasticism and Cathedrals	
AD1100		
LIB	Dark Ages; Roman law; barbarian invasions East-West synthesis; Islam and mystic Christians	See p. 226-7
AD400		
VIR	Classicism Greece & Rome; Pantheism; Christianity, Buddhism & Taoism	
800BC		
LEO	Archaic Hero-King religions; Hinduism Civilizations; Egypt and Chaldea; individuality	
3000BC		
CAN	Neolithic grain Goddess cults Religion; cities; nuclear family; Nippur	
7000BC		
GEM	Mesolithic Tribal Cults Language; Villages; Tanist cults	See p. 216-7
14,000BC		
TAU	Upper Paleolithic Earth Mother cults Agriculture and domestication; fertility cults	
26,000BC		
ARI	Paleolithic celestial cults Nomadic consciousness; hunter-gatherers	
48,000BC		

Stream of History									Planetary Gods and Individuals						
South America	North America	Rome	Greece	Egypt	Russia	Persia	India	China and Japan	*Sun*	*Moon*	*Mercury*	*Venus*	*Mars*	*Jupiter*	*Saturn*
Modern	United States	Italian City States	**THE ATOMIC BOMB**				Mughal Emperors	Chinese Revolution / Occupation	See p. 294		See p. 295				
	Colonization			Ottomans											
Aztec	Norse	Rome	**THE BLACK DEATH**	Ayyubids				Ming / Sung	See p. 292		See p. 293				
Mayan			Alexandrian												
Nazca			Crete	Late	Old New		Babylonia	Three Kingdoms							
Olmec															
	Plains Hunters	Neolithic / Mesolithic / Upper Paleolithic	**THE GREAT FLOOD** Gravetian / Magdalenia / Salutrean / Upper Perigordian / Aurignacian [Ice Age / Ice Age / Ice Age] / Perigordian / Mousterian	Nippur					See p. 290		See p. 291				
Paleolithic Old Stone Age			*CONSCIOUSNESS*												

opposites keep short-term balance in the system. The ordered scheme of a powerful and cultured civilization counterpoints the chaos out of which it emerged, and its fall is a precondition for its successors.

Oppositions act across the circle as polarities at opposite times, yet carry great attraction, like the attractive fusion and repellent fission forces in the atomic nucleus.

The four elements fire, earth, air and water occur three times in sequence in the zodiac, once within each octave of the Time Scale, creating a resonant inner structure. The Platonic elements are a numerological system of successively greater densities underlying Nature. For the alchemist and philosopher Robert Fludd, the elements are proportional to each other as they ascend from earth to heaven. The physicist Heisenberg stated: 'In all elementary processes, from which all natural phenomena evolve, four different groups are to be distinguished.'[139] The elements act in a number of ways. In classical terms, fire is energy, earth is matter, air is mind, and water is emotion. According to the psychological typology of Jung, fire is the intuitive function, earth the sensation function, air the thinking function, and water the feeling function. In physics, fire is the energy that motivates the universe, earth the particle nature of reality, water the wave nature of reality, and air the complementarity between particle and wave. When such similar ordering principles operate in the physical sciences as in historical processes, interesting parallels arise.

The elements describe similarity of focus in each octave. The fire signs Aries, Leo and Sagittarius indicate initiatory, creative, energetic, spiritual impulse and concentration upon Self. The earth signs Taurus, Virgo and Capricorn indicate the descent of spirit into matter (the root of mother, matrix), physicality, tangibility and experience of sensation. The air signs Gemini, Libra, and Aquarius combine and mediate between heaven and earth, between energy and matter, creating communication, balance and abstraction through ideas. The concluding water signs Cancer, Scorpio and Pisces end each octave as dissolution of barriers, the accumulation and synthesis of previous developments, and the emergence of feelings about the action of the cycle that ends and creates the possibility of the next higher cycle.

The three historical times of each element show the three-phase development required to manifest the qualities indicated by the element within the World Age. Each element has a cardinal initiating phase, a fixed manifestation phase, and a mutable phase that synthesizes the elemental quality.

Astrology expresses the complexity of human existence, and it provides a viable and rich matrix, model and language of symbols that aid the discovery of the whole within us, represented by our inner historical process. Using astrology illuminates parallels between the individual and the whole historical process we reflect and carry within.

The principle is at the core of psychology. The terminology identifying psychic processes does not limit and define the individual, but rather provides terms that correlate individual behaviour with collective behaviour. We create and define the process of history, while at another level we feel governed by history, mere cogs in a cosmic wheel, vehicles by which history enacts its unfolding, its becoming. History functions in symbolic form and the individuals within act as symbols. We seek our own personal and universal symbolism, the meaning of ourselves and our lives. The quest for meaning proceeds from the symbolic or ideal to the actual or real.

The Time Scale

The 12 signs in history order unfolding developmental stages, the compaction of events, understanding, and population through history. The duration of phases in history contract in the same proportion as the house time periods expand in individual life. The resultant combination of the two temporal processes – the individual life experiencing longer and longer developmental stages, and the collective life compacting – are what make the flow of time seem to be constant. The sense of expansion in the inner world balances the compaction of the outer world. We identify with the outer world and its time or our inner world and its time. Time affects us profoundly, but alters its effects by meditation, life experience, food and drink, psychological states, drugs and in many other ways. Consciousness briefly balances (the Tao) where the two systems equilibrate, which we designate the 'present'. When the Time Scale extends into the past to cycles longer than a World Age, time sense expands, while in the future cycles are shorter, and time is compacted more and more until the speed of light is approached. The movement of time into the future always balances a counter movement into the past. The present moment is powerful because it lies at the junction of past and future.

Each octave describes a developmental phase of history:

- First octave of self-assertion is mythological and instinctive, as the domain of the child.
- Second octave of self-consciousness is individualistic and civilized, as the domain of the adult.
- Third octave of self-realization is collective and conscious, as the domain of the parent.

The duration of every fourth sign (of the same element) decreases by one tenth. For the fire signs the cardinal Aries lasts 22,000 years, the fixed Leo 2,200 years and the mutable Sagittarius lasts 220 years, yet the same number of people live during each sign and developments happen at an accelerating pace.

The length of a human lifetime during the time scale occupies a full stop in the first octave, a tenth of a sign or so in the second octave and entire signs in the third octave, reflecting the increasing mathematical power of human perspective in nature. In the course of the Time Scale, humankind goes from being subject to natural rhythms and life, to having the fate of the natural world in its hands.

Each sign describes the following information:

> – The *Historical Development* related to each phase, the advances of civilizations, the movements of people, the formation, and dissolution of cultures and nations, and the important individuals who affect the eras. The description focuses on the evolution of consciousness within the historical process, both internal to individuals and external to populations.
> – The *Great Works* of culture including literature, architecture, art, earth works, utilitarian or religious objects, inventions and discoveries, particularly those which are symbolic of the civilization of the time.
> – The *Mythological and Religious perspective* describes the first humans who worshipped gods of the sky, natural forces, or the earth, through the descent of the gods. As humankind develops, the gods become intermediaries: many gods unite in monotheism; godlike men and women appear; a son of God is born on earth; humans believe that they themselves are gods on earth; in the end of the world age, there is a lack of belief in God where material wealth, science, popular music, cinema and the artefacts of society are primary objects of worship and devotion.
> – *Evolution of Consciousness* stage as described in *The Atman Project* by Ken Wilber.
> – The equivalent *Astrology Sign* and its stage from Life Time Astrology shows the parallel developmental stage in individual life, the mechanisms that function and the way in which life energy is transformed from stage to stage.

The intention is to create a higher understanding of the history of humanity and spiritual consciousness as a whole, unified, and formally coherent. Throughout history those individuals who have transcended time and history, and influences that support a spiritual overview of history are noted. In the following description of the World Age, the focus is on the astrological principles behind history – the mechanism rather than the dry facts. The octave arrangement shows waves of rhythmic developments rather than a strictly linear process.

The Octave of Mythology
(Aries-50,000BC to Cancer-3000BC)

The first octave of the World Age is the development of humanity in the mythological stage of evolution from the origin of consciousness in Aries at 48,000BC until the recognition of individuality and the first historical individuals in 3000BC at the end of Cancer.

Mythology really cannot be ordered in a linear way, as its essence is dreamlike and random. It transmits information from archaic pre-historic ages, before chronology existed, as oral traditions that vary and distort through constant retelling. Myths pass through many generations and shifts of locale, and they absorb and transmit cultural and historical models accepted by a society.

Original creation myths are roots combined with vague tribal histories – invasions, altered godheads, changed locations, the deeds of heroes and the lineages and respect of ancestors. One of the primary ways of subjugating conquered tribes is to dominate their mythology and alter the oral traditions through new names and hierarchies. The conquering gods become fathers and mothers of the gods of the conquered people. Not surprisingly, Zeus had hundreds of progeny and was involved in virtually all the myths in the Greek domain during their dominant military power over many centuries. Myths contain myriad attributions and complex genealogies, all morphed by the timelessness of the mythological medium. Retrospective mythmaking produces situations where the more powerful and wide the realm of a god, the further back its legends go, until it approaches the Creator gods in power. The mythological substratum also carries the history of our instincts.

Aries   (48,000BC until 26,000BC)

Aries is the birth of consciousness into the world age and the self-assertion of consciousness, analogous to the earliest experiences following birth. The rise of consciousness asserts the instinctual world. The first true humans survived through their consciousness, which differentiated them from the animals. They were physically inferior to carnivorous cave bears and lions, and relied on their superior awareness for survival, banding together in groups to improve their chances.

48000BC   Aries to Cancer

7000BC
Cancer
the Crab

City religion
Feeling and emotion
Matriarchal
Tigress-Euphrates
Nuclear family home
Integration
Neolithic societies
Cities and nations
Mythological religions

14000BC
Gemini
the Twins

Tribal language
Verbal
Patriarchal
Mediterranean
Instinctive movement
Communication
Diversification
Music and dance
Multi-god cults

26000BC
Taurus
the Bull

Earth Mother Fertility cults
Physicality
Matriarchal
European
Fertility
Domestication of animals
Possessions
Bull and skull cults
Tools

48000BC
Aries
the Ram

Celestial nomads
Self-consciousness
Patriarchal
African
Primitive
Self-assertion
Hunting bands
Celestial cults
Weapons

3000 BC

Historical Events	The gods	Works of Humanity

3000	3000 The Great Flood	The gods	3000 Newgrange
	3000 Minoan civilization	Olympians	3100 Cunieform
3500	3102 Death Krisha (Kali Yuga)	Dionysian gods	3500 Sumerian wheels
	3500 Founding of Ur	Home gods	3500 Mesopotamian writing
4000	3600 Taxes	Crain goddesses	4000 Cretan pottery
	3761 Hebrew Era of Creation		
4670	4000 Neolithic Greek city states		
	4004 Bishop Ussher's Creation		
5340	4500 Chinese civilization		
	5000 Nile valley farming		
6080	5800 Tigres-Euphrates settled		
	6000 Gold, copper and bronze		5900 Turkish Bull God temple
7000	6750 Catal Huyyuk		6000 Gold jewellery

7000	7000 Jericho (1st city)	Titans
	8000 Copper Age	Kabiri
7800	Lake dwellings	Hermaphrodites
	Domesticated animals	Twin gods
8800	9000 Denmark hunter-gatherers	Dioscuri
	Mesopotamia cultivated	
9900	Stone Age ends/Icecaps	
	10000 Neolithic Europeans	
11100	North American Plains hunters	
	Introduction of pottery	
12400	Fishing cultures	
	Neolithic rock paintings	
14000	14000 Racial differences emerge	

14000	15000 Microlithic tools	Earth Mothers
	Willendorf Venus figurine	Cyclopes
15400	18000 End of the Fifth Ice Age	Giants
	Grain planting in Africa	Grain goddesses
17200	Herding animals	
	19000 America settled	
19100	Upper Paleolithic skull cults	
	Bow and Arrow huntings	
21200	22000 Landes Venus head	
	24000 Beginning Fifth Ice Age	
23500	25000 Lascaux cave paintings	
26000	Clothing woven	

26000	29000 Interglacial warmth	Creator god/desses
	N American migrations	Celestial god/desses
29000	30000 Ceramics	Primordials
	Trading routes established	Elementals
32000	34000 Last Neanderthal	Asuras
	35000 Lunar calendar	
35500	Advanced hunters in Europe	
	End of Fourth Ice Age	
39300	40000 Blade tools	
	Seafaring cultures	
43000	End of the Old Stone Age	
	47000 Cave Bear cults	
48000	48000 Herbal medicines	

From about 48,000BC to 35,000BC, the primitive Neanderthals, who had been dominant for the previous 120,000 years, were eradicated by the Cro-Magnons. The Neanderthals were short, stocky and beetle-browed, although with a brain size slightly larger than modern man. They survived during the previous Ice Ages by hunting and foraging, moving with climatic changes and creating a workable culture, evidence of which remains in the ochre-pigmentation used in burials, stone implements and cults of the cave bear. Cro-Magnons were virtually identical to modern Homo sapiens, yet anthropologists do not know where they came from. They were super-men who eradicated the Neanderthal so completely that there are only genetic traces left today. The new humans were highly adaptable, even changing physical appearance to cope with their environment.

The first calendars evolved in recording traces of the lunar cycles on bones as early as 35,000 years ago. The moon was magical and its disappearance for three days each cycle was a sacred time, when hunters did not go out and the danger from predators was greatest.

Humankind gathered food from near the habitation and ate it raw. They preyed on and ate small animals, crustaceans and fish, as well as the meat from their hunts for game and woolly mammoths. They were omnivorous by necessity and sheltered in caves when they could oust the dangerous creatures that naturally inhabited them. Flint weapons improved until the invention of blades around 40,000BC. Ice Ages lasted until about 18,000BC, and yearly migrations were necessary to find suitable weather and food sources. The most dreaded enemy was other humans and cannibalism was common practice, because every available source of food and energy was greedily partaken. Survival was the total pursuit.

Aries was the primal time following a cataclysm, when the primary function was instinctive bonding with the world after the shock and loss of memory attending the end of the previous world age. Humans wandered aimlessly over the habitable areas of earth, vaguely remembering a former Utopia and its terrifying end, the dissociation of collapse, the darkening of the sun and the irrationality of natural forces caused by environmental breakdown. A feeling of desolation prevailed. The primary factors were the climate and the vagaries of nature that determined survival.

The mythology of these times concerned celestial deities, Creator, and Creatrix gods. The worship of the elements reflected a one-sided reliance on divine beings – humans crouched in fear before Chaos, Wind, Air, Okeanos and Chronos in his aspect as Time. Celestial sun and moon cults were primary – the sun was born every sunrise and died every sunset, and the uncertainty that it would return each day caused great fear and respect. Eventually sun worship morphed into fire worship, its earthly surrogate. The absolute deities Day, Night, Sky, Earth, Fire and Nature were beyond human control, even the fire in their caves. Feeding the fire was a central ritual and its continuing light and heat the mainstay and protection against the elements and the predators. Celestial cults complemented hunting cults for cave bears or lions and the lesser animals. There were cult identifications of entire groups and for individuals.[140]

The earliest religion, shamanism, enacted with the end of the last world age as an ecstatic process of returning symbolically to the death moment, and the shamans were individuals within whom the true beginning was perpetually re-enacted, intermediaries between the world of spirits and the tribe. The ritual production of fire in shamanic ceremonies represented the fire both at the end of the world and at the same time the birth of the world. The Vedas describe such a ceremony: all fires were extinguished and then rekindled on New Year's Day as a re-enactment of the Cosmic night, corresponding to the fact that the New Year began on the first day of Aries on the spring equinox.[141]

Ken Wilber calls this stage *The Pleromatic Self*,[142] where self and cosmos are undifferentiated and there is a symbiotic relationship to the world. Feelings are oceanic and unconditioned in a paradise of innocence and ignorance. There is no conception of space, time, or objects. Humans are at one with the world.

Aries time is analogous to the time from birth to seven months old, when the infant bonds to mother, learns to receive and focus light, differentiates nothing other than survival.

Taurus   (26,000BC until 14,000BC)

Taurus represents the creation, preservation and consolidation of form. The initial undifferentiated state of Aries led to worship of the Earth Mother and fertility goddesses, together with their related skull cults (connected with the opposing sign Scorpio). The coldest phase of the Ice Age began about 28,000BC and the movement of mammoths south changed cultural patterns in many ways. Tusks and bones provided a new vocabulary of weapons and material for carving Venus figurines (c. 24,000BC), and models for cave paintings at Lascaux (c. 26,000BC) and other southern European sites.

The ice caps limited settlements; traces have been found in Pennsylvania in North America (c. 19,000BC), central and southern Africa, the southern parts of Europe, the Middle East and Eastern Siberia, as well as in Southeast Asia, towards Australia. Groups of humans were small and widely spaced over the temperate zones.

The stabilization of the weather at the end of the Ice Ages at about 18,000BC allowed humanity to settle, which shifted the focus to the cave and engendered many changes in activities. Labour divided into men hunting and protecting the tribe while women tended the fire, cared for children and gathered food. Women discovered that plants growing naturally would transplant to central locations, easing the task of gathering food. Tiny nomadic units gradually enlarged, and as they settled down, they caught and penned animals that surrounded the settlement to graze. The herding and domestication of animals was a revolutionary change at about 18,000BC. Cattle provided milk, offspring, meat and skins for clothing and tents, and eventually horses were beasts of burden. Domestic animals made food available through the winter, which further de-emphasized the hunting function.

Property could not be taken for granted in the former nomadic stage, so here the concept of ownership or stewardship began. The shift in focus to the feminine domain of domestication, cooking, fertility and the increasing reliance upon the earth itself reflected the variety of artefacts found in the Aurignacian and Upper Perigordian eras.

The genesis from hunters to hunter-gatherers paralleled a shift in emphasis from celestial gods to earth goddesses and the resultant society was matriarchal. The earth was the womb, nourished plants, and was the final resting place of the dead; woman was both creator and destroyer of life. Whereas in Aries reproduction was considered a magical act of the gods, here woman was impregnated by Wind and nourished by Rain, just as were the crops – woman was symbolic of fertility. The primary rituals were the plowing, planting or sowing of fields and the harvest and storage of the fruits of the fields. The old custom of the 'bridal bed' in the field to encourage fruitfulness expresses the analogy in a clear form: to make the woman fruitful was to make the field fruitful. Sexual energy transmuted to serve cultivation and fructifying the earth.[143]

Mythologically the Bull, Great Mother and Earth Mother cults merged and diversified until the entire pantheon was feminine – that is, Isis, Gaia, Mother Earth, Venus, Nature, the Fates, Neith, Astarte and many others. The great mother was a pregnant goddess without a face, or a bull with a lunar orb between its horns, or the anthropomorphic deities of these characteristics combined ad infinitum. The godhead moved from heaven to the natural realm of earth. Cults venerated the body, skulls, and earth or mound burials – they were metaphors of the sowing the seed in planting, and moon phases coincided with menstrual cycles.

Wilber calls this the *Alimentary Uroboros*,[144] when the primary structuring of the subjective self-sense forms, albeit collective and archaic. Visceral instincts and rudimentary emotional discharges dominate, yet humankind basks in the arms of the Great Mother. Reality is primary oral, and myths of whales and such originated at this stage.

Taurus is the time from seven months old to one year, eight months, when the infant begins to discover physical sensation, tastes and begins to differentiate the body as a separate object within other objects.

Figure 28: Goddess Isis
Her cultic associations include the serpent crown, horned lunar orb headdress and ankh.

Gemini   (14,000BC until 7000BC)

During the Gemini time language was developed. Writing and numerals on cylindrical, spherical, or conical clay shards in Iran indicated the first attempts to account for numbers of animals, loaves, and so on. The singular functions of hunting, gathering and raising children diversified and became more complex as the declining emphasis on hunting brought men closer into the tribal fold and encouraged a wider development of skills, which increased the quality of life and assured survival. About 12,000BC the retreating glaciers caused a rise in sea level, flooded coastal areas, and forced many tribes to develop seagoing crafts for fishing in addition to their natural food sources. Harpoons and fishhooks existed in Europe and southern Africa as early as 9000BC. An increase in the artistic merit of clay and ceramic pots, the diversity of cultivated grains and grasses, the variety of animals domesticated – all these meant a wider range of things to do and ways to express the self. In the Western hemisphere hunters ranged over North America into South America, eliminating two thirds of all mammal species, stripping the continents of all but bison and llamas among large animals, and condemning the inhabitants to solely agrarian life until the present.

Words and sounds specific to the new activities arose, creating a multitude of variant languages. Communication broadened by trade at market places, the herding of cattle, sea voyages and the multiple functions within each tribe. Instead of each individual duplicating the tasks and skills of all others, the various skills spread throughout a tribe or an area, such that specialization became a positive survival characteristic. In addition to basic survival tasks, certain families also functioned as priests, scribes, farmers, shepherds, weavers, hunters, toolmakers, or builders.

The long-dominant matriarchal cults of the Taurean age were gradually replaced through the principle of the tanist.[145] Initially the power of the Earth Mother did not decline, but the role of her consorts – the male companions of the priestesses – changed. Originally he was chosen from the strongest, most intelligent and best bred to be king for a year, to mate with the priestesses, then to be ritually sacrificed at the year's end, only to be replaced by another consort. Gradually the term of the surrogate king was extended to two years or seven years, then two consorts alternated in the role, until finally the king was able to maintain parity with the goddess, escaping the sacrifice altogether.

The mythologies of Gemini are epitomised by the family of Titans spawned by Uranus (sky) and Gaia (earth), and the many twin gods and goddesses who were companions of the Earth Mother – the dioscuri, the kabiri and the dactyloi – all of whom were intermediaries between the heavenly pantheon and mortals. Hermes predominated as the god of language, communication and the cult of the hermaphroditic gods. The godhead was gradually approaching humanity.

To Wilber this is the *Typhonic Self*, where the physical body feels separate from the physical world, leading to recognition, naming and communicating about the world.[146] The world is ambivalent, potentially dangerous, and differentiating rapidly.

Gemini traditionally means instinctive mind, communication, movement, adaptability, brothers and sisters, short journeys, mimicry, multiplication and diversity. Gemini is the time from one year, eight months, until three years, six months, when a child learns to walk, speak and co-ordinate movements to objects. Speaking is an act of imitation that originates with naming and describing objects and actions. Words represent objects with a mental equivalent, a time Piaget calls the 'preconceptual stage of concrete actions'.[147] Psychologists know that when children at this stage cannot assimilate an object or action name, they accommodate it into fantasy, and give it a symbolic meaning. Reasoning proceeds slowly, with no comprehension of the whole, and each step is dualistic between assimilation and accommodation – fantasy is just as real as reality. The similarity between these developments and the myths of the Titans is striking.

Cancer   (7000BC until 3000BC)

Cancer begins with the creation of the first city Jericho about 7000BC. The creation of market towns came about due to the revolution in agriculture, which freed the population from the bondage of food-producing occupations for the first time. In the fertile river valleys of the Tigress-Euphrates in Mesopotamia (c. 6000BC), the Nile in Egypt (c. 5000BC) and rice-growing valleys in China, societies emerged that differed dramatically from their predecessors because of the class system. With the decline of nomadic life, the city provided a context for stabilization through record-keeping and the hereditary passing down of property and wealth. The institution of the nuclear family and intermarriage led rapidly to a hierarchy of families, the creation of a class system and specialization in society. The city structured itself around the occupations of administration, education, and trades while the division of labour produced sophisticated alphabets, mathematics, and calendars. The geographical segregation of city from countryside generated a congenital problem in future civilizations. The priests became separate and powerful in determining codes of conduct by equating agricultural functions with sacrifices and rituals through their control over the calendrical timing of festivals.[148] Although apparently modern, humanity was still in the grasp of the gods and goddesses. The gods controlled cities and protected them if given their sacrificial due. The agricultural influence swept Europe in the mid-seventh millennium BC.

The technological advances that most enabled change were the invention of irrigation in the sixth millennium BC, of cloth in about 6500 BC, and the very important development of foundries in the fifth millennium BC, when copper and then bronze were made into ploughs and all other implements, particularly weapons. The earliest known foundries were in what are now Rumania, Bulgaria and Yugoslavia, but they spread very quickly. By now both men and women did agriculturally related work, with the men plowing and herding and the women spinning and weaving. The domestication of camels and donkeys as beasts of burden, and oxen as pullers of the plough, were great leaps into the future, especially when around 3500BC Sumerians invented the wheel. They kept dairy cattle and used milk products. The surplus generated by these advances striated the community and created a greater emphasis upon warfare because those previously required to provide food were freed from those functions.

By 4500BC the megalithic builders proliferated all over Europe, stone buildings were constructed for permanence, and by 4000BC there were highly developed city-states and urban cultures.

Religion again became matriarchal and the Triple Goddess reigned over planting, the hearth and burial of the dead, all connected with the quality of home life and living conditions. As humanity became civilized, Dionysian orgies and ecstasies gave expression to the repressed instinctive functions, and the pantheon of Olympian gods ruled over the proliferating breadth of culture. The classical gods of all religions were father and mother to the myriad of creators, creatrix and nature spirits that preceded them. Temples began to appear, housing the godhead for the exclusive use of the city and its inhabitants. The gods were subtly changing from nature deities to symbols of humanity's own collective power, as men began to believe that they were in the ascendancy over Nature. People worshipped hundreds of deities that symbolized the multiplying facets of their existence, and the resultant confusion gave rise to myths such as the Tower of Babel. Cities were repositories of belief systems and languages. The Cancer time ended with a Great Flood, about 3000BC.

To Wilber the *Membership Self* [149] evolved when, after the acquisition of language, a vastly extended emotional life emerged, together with concepts of extended time and a sense of belonging to a tradition embodied by the parents. The emotional set is determined, choices must be made, and rules followed for the first time, as a primary function is to reconstruct reality, as it is perceived.

Cancer the Crab is traditionally associated with home and family, the parents, particularly mother, fertilization and fecundation, heredity, conditions in old age, intuition and the psychic world. The Cancer time is from three years six months until seven years old when a child begins to realize the effect of its ability or inability to communicate and begins to look beyond imitation to create effects in others. Cancer dissolves and assimilates previous stages and channels them into a feeling tone or value, eventually seeing that the family is a structural system within which certain values and feelings are permitted and acceptable. Piaget calls this the Intuitive Stage, when immediate perceptions of the environment dominate and children seek reasons behind the beliefs and actions of family and self. Although primarily feminine-dominant due to the powerful bonding influence with the mother in early childhood, at this time the question of male-female is asserted by the variable identification with either parent or their roles. The domestic situation of home and city, inside and outside, provides models for interpersonal relationships and hierarchical values for life.

The Octave of Civilization
(Leo-3000BC to Scorpio-AD1500)

3000BC was an important conjunction of influences: the approximate date of the Great Flood described in the mythologies of almost all early cultures and the emergence of the first individuals in history.

The Great Flood is both a real event that affected the world's populations and a metaphorical flood of diverse belief patterns, primitive languages, deities and animalistic tendencies that required a filtering process. There were widespread floods from 3300BC until 2300BC all over the world and a major flood occurred due to atmospheric warming in 2900BC.[150] The flood is also symbolic of the necessity for unconscious, natural, animistic components of the psyche to re-enter civilization. Certainly, the rise of the individual in the second octave is the race of Noah and its offspring.

Before Leo, polytheism of the gods dominated, as though humanity existed in the unconsciousness of childhood until this critical trial by water. The sense that individuals represent the godhead on earth occurred about 3000BC, which is the foundation of the great monotheistic religions.[151] Individuals who claimed direct experience of god founded all these religions. These great souls (mahatmas) carried the luminous thread of immortality into the historical era: Tammuz, Osiris, Mithras, Bacchus, Apollo, Adonis, Balder, Orpheus, Krishna, Buddha, Jesus Christ, Quetzalcoatl, Viracocha, and Hiawatha carry parallel strands of the soul into the second octave of the Time Scale.

The most critical development was the discovery of Time. Before Egypt, humanity was ahistorical – like the lunar calendar, a yearly repetition of seasons following each other eternally. The early cultures lived in an eternal present. The Greek Thucydides announced that no events of importance had occurred in the world before his time (400BC). The Egyptians were a notable exception, believing the present to be a bridge between the whole worlds of past and future. The Egyptian religious practices of mummification and representing the soul as the 'ka' figure were transcendental and showed a will to endure, to pass beyond time into eternity.

The primitives needed a perfecting touch, a second creation, to enable them to live as humans. The double task of separating humanity from the immortals and giving completion to mortals fell to Prometheus, the god who brought fire to mortals.

Leo   (3000BC to 800BC)

Both the first civilizations and the advent of monotheism happened about 3000BC. Early Sumerian civilization was a collection of independent city-states in a tentative alliance, but Egyptian civilization unified and centralized. The invasion and amalgamation of Lower Egypt by Upper Egypt was rapid and never subsequently threatened.

Egyptian civilization derived from the Sumerian, but had unique religious beliefs, architecture, administration and writing. The primary difference between them was that Sumerian gods were subservient to the city-states and stood as much for them as for their natural

3000BC   Leo to Scorpio

AD1100 Scorpio the Scorpion	The Middle Ages The Black Death plagues Medieval societies Matriarchal Medieval Europe Inquisition and crusades Separation Feudal and monastic societies The cathedrals
AD400 Libra the Scales	The Dark Ages East-West balance Patriarchal China and Islam Sublimation Law and justice State-religion schism Zen Troubadours
800BC Virgo the Virgin	Classical civilizations Discrimination and rationalism Matriarchal Greek and Roman Distillation Classical learning Culture Christianity and Buddhism Classical architecture
3000BC Leo the Lion	First great civilizations Self-consciousness Patriarchal Babylonian and Egyptian Individuality Organizations Civilizations Monotheism and divine kings Temple monuments

AD1500

Historical Events	Religion & Mysticism	Works of Humanity
1498 Da Gama to India	1490 Harmonia Mundi	1470 Malory, *Morte d'Arthur*
1492 Columbus discovers America	1489 Malleus Malifocorum	1454 Gutenberg, The Bible
1453 Constantinople falls		1370 Chaucer, *Canterbury Tales*
1415 Battle of Agincourt	1370 Brethren of Common Life	1310 Dante, *Divine Comedy*
1348 Black Death plagues Europe	1274 Mehlevi dervishes	1240 Westminster Abbey
1307 Knights Templars massacred	1270 de Leon Zohar	1220 Toledo & Salisbury
1280 Kubla Khan rules	1260 Siena founded	1200 Chinese paper money
1255 Polos in China	1244 Cathars burned at Monsequr	1200 Tower clocks
1215 Magna Charta in England	1226 Fransiscan Order founded	1163 Notre Dame, Paris
1214 Genghiz Khan in Peking	1215 Dominican Order founded	1150 Cambridge University
1198 Inquisition of Innocent III	1125 Cathars founded	1145 Chartres & Angkor Wat
1147 2nd Crusade	1100 Buddhism revived in Tibet	1140 St Denis, Paris
1100 Capture of Jerusalem	1100 Knights Templars founded	1100 Chanson de Roland

Historical Events	Religion & Mysticism	Works of Humanity
1096 European pestilence	1098 Chartres School	1090 St Mark's Clock
1096 Peoples Crusade	1090 Cistercian Order	
1077 Henry IV Canossa Penance	1070 Kabbalistic mss.	1000 Chiming wheel clock
1066 Normans invade England	1057 College of Cardinals	963 al-Sufi, Fixed Stars
986 Eriksson in Nova Scotia	927 Bogomilism	
982 Mayan Empire	750 Religion of Golden Elixir	813 Cluny Monastery
732 Battles of Poitiers & Tours	700 Lindisfarne Gospel	790 Chitchen Itza
711 Moslems invade Spain	632 Koran	760 Ellora Caves
640 Surrender of Jerusalem	622 Mohammed's hegira	745 Han-Lin Academy
092 Roman Plague	604 Gregorian Chant	710 Medina Great Mosque
480 Huns invade India	529 Athenian Schools closed	547 St Vitale Ravenna
429 Vandals conquer N Africa	400 Augustine City of God	532 St Sophia Turkey
410 Alaric sacks Rome	400 Monasticism begins	529 Code of Justinian

Historical Events	Religion & Mysticism	Works of Humanity
361 Julian Mithraism	350 Athanasian Creed	
325 Council of Nicea	277 Mani crucified	244 Hermetic writings
164 Great Roman Plague	200 Christians persecuted	
117 Greatest extent of Rome	150 Sepher Yetzira	127 Almagest/Tetrabiblos
65 Britain invaded, Rome burns	100 Zohar	
0 Birth of Jesus Christ	60 Apocalypse of John	10 Ovid, *Metamorphoses*
51 Alexandrian library burned	33 Acts of the Apostles	
264 Punic Wars	250 The Crucifixion	228 Great Wall of China
325 Alexander in India	495 Code of Mani	432 Parthenon
492 Battle of Marathon	500 Temple of Jerusalem	492 Kama Sutra
597 Babylonian captivity	563 Jainism/Birth of Buddha	742 Sargons Gate
605 Chaldeans conquer Egypt		776 1st Olympic Games
749 Rome founded		8th Homer, *Iliad & Odyssey*

Historical Events	Religion & Mysticism	Works of Humanity
820 Carthage built	810 I Ching	
933 Kingdom of Israel	1000 Egyptian Book of the Dead	
1194 Fall of Troy	1000 Zoroastrianism	
1362 Reign of Ikhnaton	1200 The Vedas	1250 The Lion Gate, Mycenae
1500 Aryans descend into India	1300 Ten Commandments	1500 Karnac, Egypt
1600 Thera volcano	1362 Egyptian monotheism	2000 Avebury & Silbury Hill
1650 Jewish bondage in Egypt	1490 Genesis in the Torah	
1600 Babylon collapses		2170 Great Pyramid, Giza
1800 Bronze Age China		2250 Chinese almanac
2200 Babylonia peaks		2500 Ur Laws
2400 Golden Age of Ur	2900 Rig Veda	2600 Sumerian goat figure
2875 Sargon unites Sumeria		2850 Stonehenge
3000 Iron Age/Troy founded		

prototypes, while in Egypt the gods supplemented the worship of collective human power made manifest through the pharaoh – they believed the pharaoh to be God. The unification of Egypt reflected the mythological relationship of Horus and Set. The ritual murder of Osiris by Set and the revenge of Osiris' son, Horus, originated in the death and rebirth of nature each year, the cereals that the early Egyptians domesticated and the animistic components in themselves they had conquered, but the nature-myth was also adapted to political purposes.

What is interesting is that the myth of Horus-Set is also symbolic of The Divine Plot. After killing Osiris (vegetation), Set (Saturn or Time) cuts his body up into many pieces (the stages of the time scale), each of which he scatters all over Egypt (the world). The pieces are found and reassembled by Osiris' devoted sister and wife, Isis. Osiris comes back to life and hands his kingdom over to Horus, who has avenged him by killing Set. Osiris has a height of 10 royal cubits, is the domesticator of cereals and animals, and the parts of his body are the cities of Egypt (each symbolic of an archetype) united by Egyptian religion. Osiris was the god of the dead; he weighs the soul against a feather at the Last Judgement. The myth that is the primary political force in Egypt describes the creation, destruction and resurrection of the world age. Osiris was also symbolic of the flooding of the Nile and the Great Flood. Osiris was contained in a box similar to the ark of Noah, encased in the trunk of a tree (the world tree).

Plutarch states that, 'Of the stars, the Egyptians think that Sirius, the Dog Star, is the star of Isis, because it is the bringer of water. They also hold the Lion in honour and adorn the doorways of their shrines with gaping lions' heads because the Nile overflows when for the first time the Sun comes into conjunction with Leo.'[152] Isis unites the parts of the divine world. This myth integrates themes of The Divine Plot, including the 50-year cycle of Sirius-Isis, the number 10 and Osiris, the astrological sign of the Lion, the neters (archetypes), the numerical measure of the sacred architecture of Egypt and its origin in astronomical and astrological cycles, and the relevance of myth to reality.

Old Kingdom Egypt was a stable, 1,000-year pharaonic theocracy with an organized kingdom endowed with great natural resources. The society was simultaneously materialistic and desirous of eternal life – a unique combination. Previously humanity lived in an eternal present, but the Egyptians understood time and its mechanisms.

The Pharaoh Zozer built the step pyramid about 2650BC, designed by the architect Imhotep, the father of Egyptian monumental architecture. Over the next 2,000 years the Egyptians continued to create massive pyramids, culminating in the Great Pyramid (see Figure 31), supposedly built in 2170BC. The lack of inscriptions makes its use as a burial pyramid unlikely, but it was a complex and sophisticated astronomical-astrological computer that measured time, was a standard for all measurements of length, acted as surveying apparatus for land apportionment, as an observatory for planetary and stellar movements and, most interestingly of all, could have been a way of organizing Egyptian society.

Schwaller de Lubicz reasoned that the smoothness and tight fit of the gigantic granite blocks was inconsistent with primitive technology – there had to be another explanation.[153] The descending passage, used for astronomical observations, was oriented to Alpha Draconis, the pole star in 2170BC. Because the polar point moves about one degree every 70 years, it would have been necessary either to make a new pyramid every 70-odd years or to change the orientation of the pyramid. Schwaller de Lubicz investigated many other Egyptian antiquities that integrated meaningful fragments from previous buildings, and deduced that the necessity to take the pyramid apart and shift its orientation every 70 years would have taken the entire population of Egypt, and would have provided a perfect task, organized by the Pharaoh and his Architect, for uniting and integrating the population. The building of the Temple is the metaphor of the Masonic rites and mysteries of many ancient religions, and the Great Pyramid could have fulfilled this function. The movements of stone on stone through the generations would have worn down the surfaces of every stone until they fit as precisely as they do today. The pyramid was a manifestation of Egyptian knowledge of time and its symbolic and actual measurement. Victorian archaeologists developed elaborate histories based on the measurements of the Great Pyramid.[154]

Both Sumerian-Akkadian and Egyptian civilizations underwent crises at about the same time in the 2200s BC when unitary political regimes collapsed under pressure from barbarians, but recovered to even greater strength, lasting until the ascendancy of Rome 2,000 years later. The expansion of both powerful civilizations was due to trade, and religion, language and writing were the tools by which they made their influence manifest. They taught the rest of the world.

Similarly, the Indus civilization sprouted, fully formed from its birth in about 2500BC, influenced by the Sumerians, but with unique elements, primarily a previously unknown script and an original and naturalistic art. The drainage, baths, water system and other public architecture of the civilization had a utilitarian quality much like the modern Western standard, but with no known prototype.

Leo religious beliefs were monotheistic, where one being represents, or is, God on earth. Pharaoh descended from the gods and his life was a complex ritual of identification with the gods, providing the people with an image they could see. Pharaoh's life *was* the yearly ritual, just as the succession of pharaohs determined Egyptian history. The king tables of Manetho were among the first attempts to document a history in such a form.

The Assyrian, Akkadian, Babylonian, Chinese, Egyptian and western Aegean empires were solar and masculine. Lion images proliferated in their architecture, especially kingly monuments and vestments. The hero-kings subjugated the pantheon of the Great Goddesses. The first historical individuals were heroes, kings, warriors and prophets, and their prime function was to structure civilization through laws. They were divine and often took upon themselves the functions of the creator. In Central America, the Olmec civilization created massive sacred architecture for the worship of a half-human and half-panther god. The early phase flowered from 1150BC, and later affected the development of the Chavin culture in the Andes. They were 1,000 years behind the Indo-European domestication of cereals, signalling a later shift from hunter-gatherers.

Wilber calls this the *Mental-Egoic Self,* a consolidation of the life around ego, with parental contact becoming relationship.[155] This self-conscious and conceptual stage of development identifies outer models as higher-order personalities and breeds self-control and willpower.

Leo the Lion is associated with self-consciousness, love of self and others, creation, acting, confidence, education, speculation and game playing and the exteriorization of the self, and its time is from seven years to 13, leading up to puberty. Children begin to understand rules at this time learn and invent games that transmit rules and their mechanisms. Piaget calls this the stage of concrete operations, where physical actions are internalized as mental actions or operations, which become models for action ingrained in behaviour. We learn the hierarchy of rules of games, school, society, religion and our culture: they parallel the hierarchy of personal relations outside the family. By the age of seven, children are in primary school, where they learn standards of behaviour and communication. As the child learns to exteriorize, new restrictions arise and controls are more and more specific. The essence of all societies is a hierarchy of classes, elites and orders of succession – education transmits the norm.

Virgo   (800BC until AD400)

Virgo is distillation, discrimination, the critical faculty and ordering processes. The consolidation of kingly Leo time set the stage for the classical civilizations of Greece and Rome, great cultural and political systems that synthesized many prevailing diverse tendencies and

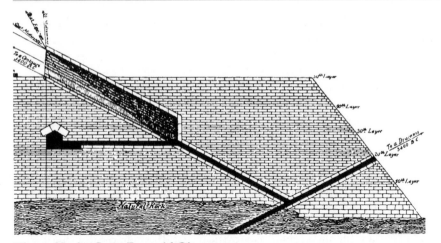

Figure 29: the Great Pyramid Observatory
The Great Pyramid is astronomically aligned and designed. The descending passage aligns with the pole star Alpha Draconis, and its face angle is identical to the latitude of Giza. The King's Chamber is on the 50th course and the Queen's Chamber is on the 25th course, an obvious reference to the equinoctial cycles and world ages.

produced a distilled amalgam. Their military organization conquered the entire known world – first by Alexander the Great in the fourth century BC and then by Julius Caesar in the first century BC. Classical society provided such security and affluence for the population that creativity in science, philosophy, economics, politics, the arts and architecture was truly astonishing. The Greeks integrated a multitude of mythologies, religious beliefs and cultural identities within a common philosophy, language and governmental system.

During Virgo, cultures came into being where Homer synthesized previous mythologies, Pythagoras previous metaphysics, Socrates and Plato previous philosophies, Phidias previous sculptures, Herodotus previous histories, and Pericles former governmental systems. All acted within Greek ideals of concord and freedom. Specific ways of seeing and understanding the world of preceding ages were combined into a working whole, which was extended throughout the vast empire. Technological advances and the increasing sophistication of the war-machine made the Greeks and Romans virtually invulnerable and when their classical way of life finally collapsed after 1200 years of domination, it happened primarily through internal chaos allied with religion.

The Greeks and Romans excelled at systematizing and assimilating the gods and heroes of the areas they conquered. Foreign deities were simply absorbed into the classical pantheon as minor relations or children of the primary gods and goddesses. Prophetic religions arose, based on the teachings of evolved souls such as Buddha, Krishna, Lao

Tse, Confucius, Mani, and Jesus Christ. As Rome absorbed the Greek civilization, so the Roman Empire was the host for Christianity. The combination of Eastern mysticism with the humanitarian ethic and sense of time and history of the West undermined decadent Roman polytheism until it created a schism between two vast halves of the empire that allowed powerful barbarian hordes to wedge them apart as a prelude to total destruction. A similar process happened in the East as the Huns and Mongols from central Asia decimated China after millennia of high culture dominated by religion. The selective process central to the classical civilizations denied the primeval darkness of the psyche and crystalline culture was shattered with the Fall of Rome when Alaric sacked the greatest city in history into oblivion. The primitive craves to be integrated, as it cannot ever be eliminated.

The earlier fertility religions of the Near East were absorbed into Christianity, but certain cults resisted the bureaucratic structure of the early Church and accepted instead the Gnostic ideal – gnosis 'knows by direct revelation'. The Gnostics worshipped the feminine ideal Sophia as a symbol of wisdom and the carrier of the Holy Spirit. By the early third century AD, early Christian fathers chose the books of the New Testament to support the political organization of the Church. They excluded or destroyed those books that were threatening. Similarly, their followers interpreted the direct knowing of the prophets, often by later generations who had no direct contact with the original events and teachings. The naive accepted the surface teachings, while the initiates hid (occulted) their rituals and esoteric teachings.

For Wilber this is the *Late-Ego Self* of creativity, identification and mastering the various personalities while suppressing the shadow elements – that is, all the unintegrated remnants of earlier phases.[156]

The Virgo time in Life Time Astrology is from 13 until 23 years, when puberty brings physical reality back to the fore. The puberty-inflicted youth, having learned the structures and rules of society, must begin to make choices, to distil and define the relationship between mind and body, refining attitudes, habits, diet, clothing and, importantly, ideas. A youth detaches from family protection and recognizes that work is necessary to life. Piaget calls this the stage of Formal Operations, when collaboration and reasoning within and with others leads to simultaneous relationships of differentiation and reciprocity that characterize the co-ordination of individual viewpoints. The use of hypothesis and testing is recognition that the rules and laws of elders are not absolute. Most concrete expressions and experiences translate into verbal and symbolic modes of expression, and rhythmic functions manifest in music, early sexuality and work activities. The choices during Virgo are usually binding and the emphasis is upon specialization and isolation.

Libra   (AD400 until AD1100)

Libra represents balance, sublimation, partnership, the search for equilibrium, law and adjustment, and falls at the midpoint of the astrological-historical time scale, where unconscious influences become conscious for the first time, and where the outward arc returns to completion on the inward arc.[157] The synthesis of classical civilization began with a breakdown into opposites and ended with an East-West fragmentation that led to cross-fertilization. The forced establishment of a unified Christian Church led quickly to the political Rome-Constantinople opposition, further metamorphosed into the age of monasticism exemplified by St Benedict. Fragments distilled by the Greeks and Romans were isolated into feudal enclaves and developed without much overall unity or mutual communication. The branching of previously unified academic, musical and religious studies led to the specialization characteristic of the Dark Ages. The Athenian Schools closed in AD529 and knowledge of humanity almost became the exclusive property of Church theology, a situation that is still largely true.

The feudal kings imposed order through religion and vied with the monasteries and early popes for power. Charlemagne, King Arthur, Alfred the Great and Pepin vied with the popes and monastic authorities for power through a balance of economic advantage. Expanded feudal fiefs eventually became the states of Europe – Germany, France, England, Spain, Holland and Italy – and they related to each other under duress and only because of trade. Trading was the channel of communication and many religious, cultural and scientific innovations spread, specifically the rediscovery of classicism by the Arabic philosophers transplanted in Spain, and the revival of Buddhism in Tibet after its decline in India and China. Seeds crossed from Europe to Asia and backwards and Erikson's voyages to the New World extended the horizon.

In China a similar division in the eastern and western Han Empires led eventually into warring fragments conquered by the Hsiung-nu (Huns), as were the Oxus basin, India, Iran and Europe. The Huns were Tungus or Mongols, incorporating shamanistic beliefs from the earliest shamans of the opposite Aries time in the scale. They had a disruptive influence on the whole civilized world – and where they did not create havoc themselves, the Teutonic Goths, Visigoths and Vandals and Iranian rebels fleeing from them did so – and managed to interbreed and become assimilated into European, Persian, Indian and Chinese cultures. The spiritual vacuum of China paralleled that of the European world, and zealous Mahayana Buddhist missionaries entered China from India and Tibet and supplanted the previously dominant Taoism.

Most symbolic of Libran religion is Islam, received through the Prophet Mohammed's epiphanies from the Archangel Gabriel. The Koran, begun in 610, states that there is only one true God (Allah) and that Mohammed is the most recent and definitive prophet among Jesus, Moses, Elijah and other previous avatars. Islam absorbed its competition and instituted monotheism through its stern law. Within 100 years Islam spread by conquest to the East Roman Empire, Syria, Mesopotamia, Palestine, Egypt, the Persian Empire of Iraq and Iran, the Sasanian Persian Empire, Armenia and Georgia, north-west Africa, Spain, south-western Gaul, the Sind and Punjab, Uzbekistan and Turkey, and was only deterred at Poitiers in 732 from conquering France. The Koran states clearly that all those who live by the word of God must be tolerated and protected, so Christians, Jews, Zoroastrians and Hindus were integrated. But within Islam itself, the struggle for succession to Mohammed caused the Shiite sect, started by Mohammed's brother Ali, to split off – a raw wound to this day.

Byzantine civilization revitalized Eastern Christendom as the Western Christian world was by the Carolingians, culminating in the crowning of Charlemagne as Holy Roman Emperor by Pope Leo III in 800. The order was temporary, as violence erupted with the Vikings, Franks, and Norse rovers overrunning Europe while Erickson reached across the ocean as far as Greenland and the New World. Even in Meso-America, barbarians sacked Teotihuacán (600) and Cholula (800), and the powerful Mayan civilization ended by the ninth century. All over the world, the military might (Aries) opposed the institution of the law (Libra).

The most important structure to emerge was chivalry and romantic love, exemplified by the Arthurian legends of fifth century Britain. The taming of violence by religion and a reverence of the sublime reached its peak as Christian and prior Great Goddess cults combined through the symbolism of the Grail Legend and the magical exploits of King Arthur and the Knights of the Round Table.

According to Wilber, this is the beginning of the ascent of consciousness of the *Mature Ego Self* [158], which integrates all possible personalities, disidentifies from the ego altogether and begins to transform to higher-level unity. All lower levels are synthesized and stabilized in an autonomous, self-actualizing, and intentional being.

Libra the Scales or Balance traditionally governs partnership, communal relations, the public, obligations, sublimation, justice, the law, business relationships, sociability, and enemies from 23 until 42 years old. At 23 we are opposite the birth moment and have experienced the entire lower, subjective and unconscious half of the horoscope. The opposition symbolizes emergence from the unconscious, internal conflict that we fight symbolically, as in the Grail legend. Marriage is the primary process through which opposing qualities may be confronted, married and integrated into a whole, and the marriage of king and queen was a symbol for this, as well as being an actual event. The conjunction of opposites is central to alchemy, which was a predecessor of the psychology of the unconscious. Partnership is initially a sublimation of each individual in favour of the whole relationship, but rapidly attains a higher significance as a model for balancing the psyche and transcending the personal – higher relationship is transformative and aligns with collective values in addition to satisfying personal hungers and ideals.

Scorpio   (AD1100 until AD1500)

Scorpio is the ruthless struggle for survival, passion, death and regeneration, and the transmission of life through the seed. As the opposite Taurus time was sensible contact with the physical world and cults worshipping the Earth Mother, Scorpio time is the reappearance of dark passion in the Crusades and the Inquisition, where bloodshed and warfare were justified by the winner-take-all struggle between Church and State after their uneasy alliances in Libra. Crusaders were fighting fraternities under Church rule abroad, and the inquisition eliminated heretical (read differing) practices at home; in both cases, the aim was the eradication of impurity and evil. Scorpio is the underworld, the incorruptible, discipline and physical and spiritual regeneration, coming as the final dissolution of the classical civilization.

The combination of high culture with historical roots, the tendency for early magical traditions to go underground in an enlightened growth of magic, and the increase in secular power and intolerance of the Church and their henchmen, the Crusaders and Inquisitors, made for a dynamic time. The focus of the Inquisition was the extinction of remaining fertility cults and nature worship, signalling a new materialism. The Crusades were initially great successes of strategy and financial reward by Christian expeditionary forces sent to conquer Moslem Jerusalem, but eventually the Moslems repelled the Christians.

The Norman conquest of England in 1066 proved French superiority in Europe and started a great rise in Western civilization comparable to the rise of Hellenic civilization in the eighth century BC (a sextile from early Scorpio back to early Virgo). The Roman legal system and the Church forcefully implemented the age of chivalry and the ascendancy of the knights. The breakdown of the Roman governmental system into republican city-states or monarchical kingdom-states, however, utilized the rediscovery of Greek language and philosophy.

AD1910   Sagittarius to Pisces

AD1910 Pisces the Fishes	The Great Wars Disintegration Germany, USSR and USA Matriarchal Karmic isolationism Illusion Abstraction Nihilism War devices
AD1840 Aquarius the Waterbearer	Nationalism Humanitarianism Romantic Utopian societies Idealism Bureaucracies and unions Victorian Age Collectivization Socialism-Communism Modern governmental structure
AD1720 Capricorn the Goatfish	Industrial Revolution Physical perfection England Matriarchal Revolutionary materialism Nationalism The Reformation Capitalist machine age Ascendancy over nature
AD1500 Sagittarius the Centaur	The Renaissance Self-realization The Americas Patriarchal New Colonial Worlds Reconstitution Philosophical humanism Wholistic world view Rebirth to higher mind

AD1500

Historical Events	Religion & Mysticism	Works of Humanity
1949 NATO & Mao's China	1950 Assumption of the Virgin	1948 Antibiotics synthesized
1947 Indian independence	1949 Ouspensky Search Miraculous	1942 ENIAC computer
1946 United Nations	1944 Crowley, *Book of Thoth*	1937 Whittle jet engine
1945 Hiroshima atom bomb	1944 Jung, *Psychology & Religion*	1935 Air transport
1939 World War II		1932 Radio astronomy\
1933 New Deal		1930 Pluto discovered
1930 Spanish Civil War		1928 Fleming, penicillin
1929 The Great Depression		1926 Baird, television
1927 Lindbergh flies Atlantic	1922 Tutankhamen discovered	1925 Radio & *Mein Kampf*
1923 Munich putsch	1921 Gurdjieff Institute of Man	
1920 League of Nations	1920 Jung, *Psychological Types*	1915 Cinema
1917 Russian Revolution	1917 Jung, *The Unconscious*	1914 Russell, Principia
1914 World War I	1911 Frazer, *Golden Bough*	1913 Bohr, Quantum Theory
1903 Bolshevik party	1908 1st Psychoanalytic Conference	**1904 Einstein, Relativity**
1900 Boxer Rebellion	1907 Crowley, *Book of the Law*	1903 Wright, airplane
1899 Boer War/Africa partitioned		1900 Freud, Dreams
1894 China-Japan War	1893 Blavatsky, *Secret Doctrine*	1877 Gramophone
1878 Treaty of Berlin	1888 Blavatsky, *Isis Unveiled*	1876 Bell Telephone
1871 Russo-Turkish War	1882 Society Psychic Research	1876 Bayreuth Opera House
1875 Schliemann finds Troy	1876 Muller, *Sacred Books of East*	1872 Mendelkev Periodic Table
1867 1st Trade Union/Serfs freed	1875 Theosophical Society	1867 Nobel Dynamite
1861 American Civil War		1859 Darwin Origin of Species
1857 Indian Mutiny	1865 Society Rosicruciana	1857 1st Oil Well
1854 Crimean War		1851 Crystal Palace
1849 California Gold Rush		1848 Marx Communist
1845 Neptune discovered	1841 Livingstone, African mission	1840 Photography
1839 Brit-Chinese Opium Wars	1831 Second Day Adventists	**1835 Marconi, telegraph**
1832 British Reform Bill	1830 Smith Book of Mormon	1825 Stephenson, railroad
1823 Monroe Doctrine		1807 Gas lighting
1819 Owen Factory Act	1808 Inquisition abolished	1805 1st Museums & Galleries
1815 Battle of Waterloo	1807 Hegel Phenomenon of Spirit	1799 Beethoven, *1st Symphony*
1812 War of 1812		1787 Gibbon, *Decline and Fall*
1805 Battle of Trafalgar	1789 Wesley Sermons	1780 Uranus discovered
1795 The Directory	1780 Order of Asiatic Brethren	1776 Smith, *Wealth of Nations*
1789 French Revolution	1760 Swedenborgian Rites	1776 Paine, *Common Sense*
1787 American Constitution		**1774 Oxygen discovered**
1776 American Revolution		1769 Steam engine
1763 Peace of Paris	1740 Secret Golden Flower	1751 Encyclopedia
1756 Seven Years War		1733 Electricity discovered
1700 Great Northern War		1716 Hydrogen discovered
1688 British Revolution		1675 Roemer, speed of light
1666 Great Fire of London		1666 Newton, Calculus
1642 Australia discovered		1661 Leuwenhoek, microscope
1638 Japan closed (until 1865)		1661 Milton, *Paradise Lost*
1625 Moghul Empire in India	1606 Rosicrucians founded	1623 Shakespeare, Folio
1620 Mayflower Jamestown colony	1577 1st Dalai Lama	1609 Galileo, telescope
1619 Cortez conquers Mexico	1545 Council of Trent	1603 Gilbert, magnetism
1618 Thirty Years War	1542 Francis Xavier in Japan	1599 Globe Theatre
1583 Raleigh Virginia Colony	1539 Society of Jesus (Jesuits)	1574 Fludd, *Utriusque Cosmi...*
1519 Magellan circumnavigates	1533 Agrippa De occulta	
1516 South American Inquisition	1521 Luther Diet of Worms	1520 Machiavelli, *The Prince*
1513 Balboa through Panama	1512 Lateran Council on Soul	1516 Thomas More, *Utopia*

The founding of religious orders such as the Benedictines and Cistercians, the imposed celibacy of the secular clergy and reforms in the Papacy, including its permanent move to Rome, all consolidated the power of the Church. For the first time the Curia of Cardinals elected the pope rather than powerful kings. A parallel shift in power occurred in the Islamic world with the creation of orders of chivalry, the futuwwah, and the dervish sects. The Buddhists revived Buddhism in Tibet in about 1100, and the Mahayana sect spread in Japan and northern China, and the Zen Buddhists introduced their peculiarly militaristic discipline in Japan in 1191. In China, the Sung dynasty was powerful in its neo Confucian doctrines (again, a sextile back to Confucius in early Virgo). The vast and powerful Islamic empires of the Ottomans, Mamluks and Safavis successfully repelled or integrated the Mongol influences and created highly cultured religious societies.

The fanatically religious cultures of the time found expression in the cathedrals of France and England, which were symbols of the domination of the Church and a contrast to the struggles for survival of the populace. Schools of master masons revived almost extinct mythologies and displayed them in the rose windows,[159] in the naturalistic art of Giotto, and the architecture of Brunelleschi and Bramante under the patronage of the Medicis and the popes. Dynastic city-states created contexts for enlightened culture under the Italian Medicis, the Khans of China, and the Mongols in India. There were many reactions to the disorder created by the Crusades, such as the romantic literature of Dante, Chaucer and Cretien de Troyes, all of whom documented the breakdown of the previous order and prepared the stage for the transference of power to the sacred individual. To Wilber this is the stage of the *Bisocial Band Self*[160], the upper limit of membership-cognitive and physical orientation and a stepping-stone to the higher magical through trans-verbal and trans-conceptual reality. It symbolizes going beyond conventional social barriers as the first stage of transcendence, the essential function of Scorpio time in life and history.

Scorpio the Scorpion is associated with the process of life, death and regeneration, karma, occultism, and magic, survival, fanaticism, shared resources and perversity, and occupies the time from 42 years old until death in old age. During the opposite childhood Taurus time one accepts the object-like world of the body and the senses, and here the body must be relinquished at the end of life. We accomplish our outer objectives and rediscover our inner life. The symbolic descent and ascent of the soul in Dante's *Divine Comedy* is a classic description of the Scorpio time and its lessons. Scorpio rules the various means to liberation and the inherent dangers of the failure to liberate oneself from the physical world. The power of Tibetan Buddhism, Zen, Mystic

Christianity and Islam all reflect such spiritual principles. The karmic accumulation of life actions that have not been paid for come back in Scorpio, as they might have been hidden during life, a process symbolized in alchemy by the transmutation of lead into gold; paralleling the transmutation of humanity from the realm of the individual into the next Sagittarius phase of the realized being.

The Octave of Individuality
(Sagittarius-AD1500 to Pisces-AD1950)

The Black Death plague swept Western Europe during the 14th century. It symbolized the dissolution of classical civilization and prepared the way for the humanist age of the Renaissance, which saw humanity's great leap in knowledge and art. Enquiring minds transcended the bounds of the physical world and extended perception into outer space with the telescope and inner space with microscope, an extension to the ends of the known earth. For the first time in history, humankind could map the entire world and place it within the cosmos, artists discovered perspective as a phenomenon of human perception, the entire range of musical tones was understood and heard, and the whole spectrum of colour was exploited in art. In short, humanity reached its limits and attempted to step beyond them.

Sagittarius   (AD1500 until AD1720)

Sagittarius represents realization of the self, higher mind, philosophy, religion, wisdom, foreign influences, and long journeys. After the destruction and fragmentation of Scorpio, humankind rediscovered classical principles as a context for the emergence of higher consciousness in the Renaissance, an age characterized by individuals who gathered, synthesized, combined and manifested many diverse strands of human knowledge and understanding and unified them in great works. The horizon was expanded in every conceivable direction – geographically, intellectually, scientifically, politically and theologically.

Voyages of discovery led to colonial empires for England, Spain, France, Portugal, India, and Russia that allowed cultural trade on a worldwide scale. The colonized countries were raped, subjugated, and assimilated at the behest of missionaries, adventurers and dissidents. A time of physical plenty ensued, with great prosperity in Europe. The influx of previously unknown or rare raw materials and labouring slaves created European treasure houses of wealth. The worldwide expansion also promoted the greatest mental and spiritual revolution since the founding of Rome, a change determined initially by a questioning and then regeneration of Greco-Roman civilization that led finally to the emergence of independent thought.

The Inquisition prosecuted and executed witches well into the 18th century, but many found ways to follow the mystical quest without harassment. Others paid the ultimate price for their beliefs, including Giordano Bruno (1548-1600), who proposed a system of celestial magic and Galileo. Magicians and alchemists necessarily camouflaged their true ideals and philosophies in allegory and metaphor, amid the arts, literature and theology. The integrated celestial sciences of astrology, geometry, and mathematics were divine techniques for communicating with the soul of the world. Robert Fludd showed the human as a mathematical and mystical cipher of the microcosm within which the entire macrocosm lay reflected. He demonstrated that the proportions of the human body were manifest in planetary relationships and intervals of the musical scale, all of which had an integrated relationship with cosmic understanding in geomancy, the art of memory, geometry, astrology, surveying, navigation and others.

John Dee went further with his *Mathematicall Preface to Euclide* of 1570, which presented mathematics as a divine language for describing and attaining power over the natural world. Society considered mathematics a magical art before this time, and it was not taught in the curriculum at either Oxford or Cambridge. Dee demonstrated the dual use of mathematics as symbolic in a Pythagorean sense and as a measurement of quantities, which were to dominate later materialist mechanistic science. Dee was a Hermetic and Platonic philosopher and distinguished between the heliocentric theory of Copernicus, which he understood and accepted as a physical scientist, and the prevailing geocentric (earth-centred) theory of the classical world, which still applied to astrology. He was one of the few men able to grasp the concept of higher worlds of ideas governing the physical plane. Dee was an advisor to the profound Elizabethan court and possessed a more complete library than any university. He was a link in the transition from the Scorpionic magicians of the medieval world to the Renaissance.

The Copernican rediscovery of heliocentricity took 30 years to prove mathematically, but led to a revolution in the skies, while Galileo (1564-1642) was persecuted for inventing the telescope. Tycho Brahe (1546-1601), Kepler (1571-1630) and Newton (1642-1747) were practising astrologers, and were forced to align themselves with the fledgling science and its compromise with the Church. There was an unwritten agreement that science could investigate and describe the universe mathematically, taking over the Church's prerogative, but in exchange science was forced to suppress all speculation about the role of man in the scheme of things – an ominous devil's bargain that still seems to be in operation today. Astrologer-astronomers revolutionized scientific attitudes and formulated the mechanics of universal movements, mathematics, astronomy, physics and cosmology, but the magical component was heretical and eliminated from the scientific worldview. Newton was a scientist and an alchemist, investigating the true origin of the mysteries.

As the exterior world was explored and probed, so was the interior world of the psyche. Leonardo da Vinci (1452-1519) and Michaelangelo (1465-1560) combined architecture, painting, drawing, writing, anatomy, sculpture, mechanics, the technology of warfare and fortification. Francis Bacon (1561-1626) and Shakespeare (1564-1616) created a sublime synthesis of classical drama, poetry and lyrics with sociological, cultural, historical magical and religious material to enthral discerning audiences at the apex of the humanist age. Bacon translated the King James' English version of the Bible and introduced a mystical context and structure that contained a magical, cryptic significance.

The Protestant reformation initiated by Luther (1483-1546), Calvin (1509-1564) and Loyola (1491-1556) created a schism within the Roman Catholic church, which then splintered into myriad reformed sects. An individual and personal approach to God mirrored the importance of logic, as intellectual attitudes became religions. Humanism supplanted organized religion, as Christianity could not control exclusive rights over rational explanations of the world, where observation, objectivity and the scientific method were the primary ways of understanding reality. The religious wars among England, France, Spain and Germany were political power struggles masked by religion.

The striation between science and religion was exemplified by the internalization of the external world by Descartes (1596-1650), the description of a metaphysical basis of reality by Spinoza, and the assertions of Leibniz, Hume and Locke of the mathematical structure of all perception of the world as the domain of pure logic. Medicine advanced due to remembered fear of the Black Death, Boyle's formulation of chemistry, Huygens' discovery of the glass lens, and dissection, which allowed exploration of the connection between the theoretical and mystical beliefs about the human body. The body was a physical object instead of being the seat of the divine soul. The social contract of Hobbes (1588-1679) formalized the materialization of reality.

For Wilber the *Centauric Self*[161] reaches beyond language, membership, culture, egoic logic and will to a higher level of mental reflection. This is a transcultural but not transpersonal beginning of mystical insight.

Sagittarius is a double sign, composed of a materialist centaur body and higher healing, humanist archer. It governs the first seven weeks of gestation, when the brain structure is formed as the mother comes to the realization of her inner creative, and the first stage of initiation when the soul within is discovered.

Capricorn   (AD1720 until AD1840)

Capricorn is the centre of the field of consciousness, the ego, and represents ego-consciousness, spiritual awareness, life objectives and goals, pragmatism, materialism, reality, perfected matter, fermentation, and the rigidity of old age. The ideology of Sagittarius was translated into material form, and humanistic principles were applied to whole societies. For the first time, humanity believed its position as the apex of development and more powerful than nature.

The basic building block of the physical world, the element hydrogen, was isolated in 1716 at the beginning of Capricorn. The discovery of oxygen in 1771 led to chemical formulae and the great diversity of dyes, drugs, explosives and many of the new materials of modern life. Lamarck developed systems for categorizing the natural order of the world, and Franklin, Lavoisier, Halley, Cavendish, and Hershel made discoveries of a structural nature, which created the mechanist-materialist science that exists today. The discovery of electricity in 1733 plunged humanity into the Industrial Revolution, which irreversibly changed the structure of the world. Electricity allowed the invention of machines that drastically affected the nature and speed of production, travel and communication. This directly altered the relationship of man to the environment, culminating in the first steam train of 1825. With the apparent direct control and participation in the world, humanity evinced superiority over the forces of nature for the first time, as well as a sense of being a secondary operator of machines that did the work.

The application of technology to the art of war led to the great nationalist revolutions. The British subjugated India in the 1760s and colonized Australia by 1790. As colonial nations expanded, their appetite for imported material increased beyond bounds, and the desire to subjugate and utilize adjacent territory became obsessive. The previous dominance of Church and monarchy declined rapidly after the new Americans cast off the yoke of European colonization, creating an egalitarian democracy, and the French Revolution established a leadership of the military, a pattern followed by revolutionary movements in South America. Because of the loss of the Americas, the War of 1812 brought separate national European powers directly into conflict over the territorial imperative. Machiavelli transformed the practice of politics and the techniques of power infiltrated Western life, showing the dominance of human mind and will over disorder, as manifest in the structure of the American Declaration of Independence (1776) and Constitution (1787), the founding of the *Encyclopedia Britannica* in 1771, and the total control of warfare and tactics exhibited by Napoleon. The ascendancy of technique over feeling and individuality transformed the spirit of humanity into exploitation of it, and led to totalitarian ethics that reduced humans to components instead of prime motivating forces.

In the intellectual sphere humanity peaked as Kant developed a formal language of cognition through mathematical language. The great German poet and novelist Goethe was also a scientist and politician, a total man who presented parallels between biological and psychological processes, which were later to inspire many other philosophers and natural scientists, including Schopenhauer, who revived Eastern ideas and collaged them into his philosophical systems, reintegrating East and West.

The perfection of the music of Bach (1685-1750), Beethoven (1770-1827) and Mozart (1750-1791) was a highpoint in Western culture, as were the novels of Balzac, Hugo, Scott and Coleridge and the poetry of Shelley and Keats. Romanticism surrounded the tragic lives of Schubert, Byron and Chopin, a reaction against the prevailing mechanist world view.

To Wilber, this is the emergence of the *Low-Subtle Self*[162] in the causal realm where the third-eye pineal gland operates to compose the astral and psychic planes of consciousness. In yoga this is the stage beyond mastery of the physical body that operates on the world.

Capricorn is the time when the mother realizes her pregnancy and organizes the physical world to prepare for the new child as the physical structure of the body forms. The transcendent Capricorn is higher objectives coming into manifestation in the world.

Aquarius   (AD1840 until AD1910)

Aquarius represents idealism, Utopianism, humanitarianism, abstraction, organizations and planning. The established dominance of the material world in Capricorn quickly required the institution of more sophisticated planning, order and an idealization of world mechanisms, especially concerning the public. Basic life hypotheses changed, as the independence and ascendancy of the individual diminished in favour of collective social systems, co-ordinated and working towards similar goals.

The freeing of the underprivileged classes was a main priority, accomplished partially through freeing of the slaves in the American

Civil War, even though economic reasons were a primary reason for the war between industrial North and agricultural South. Tsar Alexander liberated the serfs, and the political commentary and theory of class struggle was advanced by Marx and Engels in *Das Kapital* (1848), leading rapidly to the socialist movement and the formation of the first labour unions. Marx saw history as a process of class struggle towards a future 'Golden Age' of redemption, a view that excluded a transcendental significance from history and was a rejection of the idea that a Golden Age exists at the beginning as well as at the end. The Marxist defence against the horrors of history is paradoxical. Marx suggested that to achieve equality and salvation for the masses results in putting total power in the hands of an increasingly smaller number elites, who are deified with their power.[163] Although Marxism was a reaction against capitalism, it is particularly strange as the capitalist ideals were very similar in many respects.

Unintentional support for political idealism came through Darwin's *Origin of Species*, which outlined a linear evolutionary view of world history as an extension of biology, implying that time is a one-way street leading into an infinite future and that the existing world order was superior to anything that had happened already. These ideal attitudes penetrated the world very quickly after weak initial resistance from those still supporting cyclical world views, and it underscored the revolution against monarchy (originated in the opposite Leo time in history) and colonialism, such as the Indian Mutiny of 1857, the Boer War of 1899, and the Boxer Rebellion of 1900. Few monarchies remained after 1910.

Romantic artists illustrated the modern industrial world with its dank cities of workers, some of whom attempted to structure society by recapturing the past and integrating it into the present. Foremost of these were the socialist William Morris and the Pre-Raphaelite Brotherhood of Victorian England, who brought old handcrafts back into style and accounted the loss of such basic crafts as an undermining of all culture. Spurred on by Schopenhauer, ideas and beliefs from the East flooded into the West through channels as diverse as the *Sacred Books of the East* Series edited by Max-Muller, the Theosophical Society of Madam Blavatsky, the aristocrats of Victorian society and the operas of Wagner. Many exaggerated the chaos, such as Nietzsche, Wilde, Shaw, and the Impressionist painters of the turn of the 20th century. Freud's *Interpretation of Dreams* of 1900 opened the door for psychological explanations for the inability of people to adapt to the new world, and his concept of a suppressed unconscious under the facade of civilization described this time very well.

For Wilber, this is the realm of the *High-Subtle Self*[164], of transcendence, differentiation, and integration through religious intuition, inspiration, and symbolic visions. They are reflections of the highest archetypal forms of being as the summit of consciousness before dissolution into the deity.

Aquarius the Waterbearer is the middle stage of gestation when the mother's concern is humanitarian, selfless, and detached from the world, concentrated within on potential new life and without on ideals transmitted to friends and groups. On the transcendent level, Aquarius is the ability to create and transmit higher reality to the society beyond the range of physical contact through media, books, and information.

Pisces   (AD1910 until AD1950)

Pisces represents karma, the end of life, seclusion and isolation, institutions, dependence upon external conditions, drugs and illusion, the psychic faculty as well as everything hidden. As the last stage of the historical process, it is the final effects of the stream of history and the collision of the many contradictory directions of humanity on the stark reality of life.

Pisces saw the founding of psychoanalysis, the investigation of the unconscious substrata of life, conceived by Freud and Jung, and the Theory of Relativity of Einstein, which drastically altered the perception of the universe by invalidating the mechanics of Newton and forcing a total re-evaluation of the laws of the physical world. Thus, the psychic and physical were relative. The dilemma of the individual isolated by collective society was a metaphor for both fledgling sciences, and was a response to the impending collision of increasingly institutionalized powerful world states with immovable ideologies.

The competition between capitalism and socialism escalated from the Russian, Mexican and Chinese Revolutions of the early 20th century to the full-blown conflict of the First World War. Interim attempts at reconciliation by forming a League of Nations were ineffective. The shift of the industrialized nations to war economy led to great, although artificial, prosperity that forced the Great Depression of 1929. The new power of media allowed Hitler in Germany, Mussolini in Italy and Stalin in Russia to proclaim nationalistic beliefs. With the technological advances of mobility, flight, chemical and explosives allied to the warlike stance, the Second World War crippled the entire planet by the detonation of the atom bombs in Japan.

Every facet of civilization collapsed during Pisces: in music, Stravinsky, Mahler and Schoenberg left classical sounds for atonal and arhythmic composition; in art, the cubists and constructivists shattered the classical sense of form; in philosophy, Bertrand Russell,

Alfred North Whitehead and de Chardin attempted to confront the collapse of society; in literature, James Joyce, Eliot and the existentialists Sartre and Camus exploded the classical conception of language; in entertainment, the celluloid fantasy world of Hollywood movies created an illusory world beyond reality; in science, Einstein, Bohr, Pauli and Heisenberg upset the predictable Newtonian physics and created the technological access to diabolical instruments of destruction.

For relief from the tension and negativism of the world state, many people plunged into excessive indulgence in alcohol, the products of the burgeoning pharmaceutical industries, the distortion of reality of surrealism, the worship of artificially created movie stars, and a dream of stockpiling huge fortunes like the reclusive millionaires. The rush for instant profit, despite the insecurity of a wartime world, forced an abandonment of traditional values, added unpredictable drugs to most foods, produced a destructive military-industrial complex and created a lowest class in Western societies who were, amid plenty, undernourished and poverty-stricken. The shift to dependency upon external values created counter-movements by Steiner, Crowley, Jung, Hesse and Suzuki in a spiritual and magical direction.

For Wilber this is the *High-Causal Self*[165] that leads to Atman, the perfect knowing of formlessness, pure radiance that is trans-temporal, eternal and transcendent. It is the container of all previous stages in the evolution of consciousness and the final transformation. The self dissolves into and becomes co-extensive to the archetypal deity, contacts to a single point, and vanishes into the void.

With the end of Pisces, the world cycle drew to a close in a mood of universal dissolution and annihilation of all positive values. The symbol of Pisces is two fishes swimming in opposite directions, tied together by the tail, representing unconscious forces pulling both down into deeper unconsciousness and up to consciousness. Pisces is the last stage of pregnancy when the mother gains weight, becomes sensitive to influences from the world, and must sacrifice herself for the welfare of the child within. On the transcendent level, Pisces is the final dissolution into the boundless.

The End of the World Age

That ye which have followed me in the regeneration, when the son of man shall sit in the throne of his glory, ye also shall sit upon twelve thrones, judging the twelve tribes of Israel. And every one that hath forsaken houses, or brethren, or sisters, or father, or mother, or wife, or children, or lands, for my name's sake, shall receive an hundred-fold, and shall inherit everlasting life. But many that are first shall be last, and the last shall be first.[166]

The parable of Jesus means that to accept the death and resurrection of the individual and the world age, one must experience the 12 thrones (the 12 zodiacal houses) and judge (live through and identify with) the 12 tribes or stages in the process of the world age. By abandoning identification and thoughts of stabilization in any one stage, we shall inherit everlasting life. Those that are first (most powerful or materialistic) will be last, and the last (powerless or humble) shall be first. Access to spirit is beyond worldly existence. Jesus initially shocked the disciples, but as John observed of Jesus, 'He was in the world, the world was made by him, and the world knew him not'.[167] When we exist in consciousness beyond the purely physical or historical world, we transfer our energies into the spiritual world.

The end of Pisces in 1950, after the detonation of the Hiroshima atom bomb, is the end of the World Age. With the 12 phases of the time scale, humanity has accelerated from the emergence of consciousness to the self-destruction of civilization. The cycle returns to its final point, which coincides with its beginning. Humanity programs itself to believe that the present world is the height of civilization, yet clearly, the powers of destruction are at a peak. What seems like the achievement of the goals of evolution attends a stripping bare of the meaning of life, leaving spiritual vacuum, and nihilism. Collective humanity cuts itself off from its roots, initiating a breakdown into component parts.

At death, the life process passes before the mind's eye in an instant. Gestation recapitulates all history from the creation of life to the moment of birth. In death visions, called by Steiner 'the great panorama' or 'life-tableau', and more recently 'panoramic memory', images of our entire life repeat very quickly. The etheric body is the receptacle of memory, and as it exists for a period of time after the death and dissolution of the physical body, the etheric body is the medium of the death memory.

In the history of humanity, we experience the same process collectively. The entire cycle of history is compressed into one-thousandth of the time – the 50-year unit of the Time Scale. Just as the individual experiences their individual life again in highly compacted form at death, so the world age experiences its history at the end of a world age. The repetition of all history occurs, with every individual returning to experience the whole. Similarly, the burst of energy at conception is identical to the similar shattering of consciousness at death. The last judgement, when the dying civilization experiences the memory loss of the River Lethe, synchronizes with the seed creation of the next world age. Death is required for redemption; two counter-trends create a simultaneous split and synthesis at the cataclysm point.

It is obvious in the world now that such a striation is happening. The collective death moment is the rising of the dead of all ages, the 'second death' mentioned in Revelations. The first death is the death-blow delivered to the world age by the explosion, resultant pollution, and genetic damage of atomic energy and the second death is the culmination of the last judgement in the time approaching the year 2012.

The transition from octave to octave in the time scale is like the 'shock points' in life at conception, birth, the end of childhood and death. In the World Age every individual soul is present during the time of the last judgement, all potentially able to experience the trials that determine the difference between reincarnation into the next world age or transcendence to the right hand of God. It is important to understand the nature of the great confrontation in order to understand the transcendence of history and the way to liberation.

History and all women and men who have ever lived repeat the entire historical cycle. To the extent that one creates a clearly defined historical identity, one is obliged to return in each recurrent World Age to perform the particular role in the same manner, amid the same conditions. The closer the historical individual comes to personal integration, the greater the freedom in choice for following lifetimes.

Paradoxically, the more public one's identity, the less freedom is available to the soul animating the identity. Politicians, movie stars, great thinkers and the famed remark about the apparent inevitability of their lives; they cannot do other than they must in life. While it seems that such lives are more desirable and freer, that notable people have the world as their oyster, the reality as experienced by such people is very different. A strange fate that fame brings is more of a burden than liberation. It is very interesting that the most famous individuals in history, those who have had the most profound influence upon the course of history, seem to be outside of or beyond historical reality. Individuals of whom this is true are Buddha, Lao Tze, Jesus Christ and, closer to our time, Shakespeare. They all 'lived' in recorded historical times that should have located them, but there are controversies about their actual lives. The first three are all avatars, while the life and works of Shakespeare are definitely godlike. A linking factor to all three is a clear understanding of beingness, a doctrine that there is life after death, and that eternal return is inevitable unless one transmits and identifies with the whole.

The *Tibetan Book of the Dead*, the *Bardo Thodol*, is a guide for the 49 days after death, when the soul experiences states from the Clear Light to rebirth in the next womb of the next incarnation. We should recognize the initial state of enlightenment, but the soul typically passes through the state rapidly. Therefore, the first instruction to the soul is: 'Thy own intellect, which is now voidness, yet not to be regarded as of the voidness of nothingness, but as being the intellect itself, unobstructed, shining, thrilling and blissful, is the very consciousness.'[168] The void of the pure light is beyond individual and historic time. The soul loses its confining body and becomes one with the radiant godhead, as every human does upon physical death, and as the entire population does at the end of history. This does so in the universal super-organism envisioned by Peter Russell, the Supermind of Sri Aurobindo, or the Omega of Teilhard de Chardin. The recitation from the Bardo Thodol during the post-death state is an attempt to guide the soul to transcendence, resisting the temptation to attract another womb, and its analogy, a historical time that compels the soul to take up a body. In order to transcend time and history, one must relinquish the craving to return to time and history.

The Last Judgement

AD1950	(–50yrs)	0 Aries	Dec 1999	(–0.05yrs)
		REALIZATION		
AD1500	(–500yrs)	0 Sagittarius	Jul 1999	(–0.5yrs)
		INDIVIDUALITY		
3000BC	(–5000yrs)	0 Leo	Jan 1995	(–5yrs)
		MYTHOLOGY		
48000BC	(–50000yrs)	0 Aries	Jan 1950	(–50yrs)

The 50 years approaching the target year AD2000 is a highly compacted version of the entire Time Scale in one-thousandth of the time, according to the same diminishing spiral. The World Age reached back 50,000 years, 5,000 years, 500 years and 50 years, and divisions within the 50-year period are 50 years, five years, 0.5 years or six months, and 0.05 years or 18 days. The two processes when shown adjacent to each other should align as in the table above.

The events and developments that occur during the original manifestation of the World Age, together with the individuals who participate in them, recur with the object of not being trapped in the historical process (Maya), mistaking it for reality. It is easy for the soul to believe that its home is in the historical age rather than in the limitless realm of the spirit. Similarly, in the passage through the Bardo states various levels of existence appear attractive to and tempt the soul, but they quickly lose their lustre, become grey and lifeless. The soul then descends into lower levels, or 'hells' of existence. The collective mass of society does not understand the illusory nature of reality; is unaware of the concept of Maya. The Darwinian illusion of a linear continuum of preceding ages of history creates a temporal vortex into which a majority of souls are mechanically attracted. The attraction to past forms and patterns is very seductive, and the wandering soul tries to attach itself to a familiar past with which to reattach and reidentify. The same principle is active in ghosts, disembodied spirits that return to the scenes of their earth-life as phantoms. The tremendous renewal, after AD1950, of Hinduism, Buddhism, fundamentalist Christianity, Islam, the worshipping of gurus and religious teachers support this view, and the obsession with the past in fashion, cinema, literature and every other field reflects the eternal return.

The over-emphasis on media is frighteningly similar to the lurid Bardo states. In a 1985 statistic, American children watch an average of 29 hours of television weekly, including 250 acts of violence, not to mention the prevalence of 'video nasties'. By definition, media represents either (a) events that have already happened, (b) events happening somewhere else at the same time, or (c) cinematic fantasies that never have and never will happen. Participation is one-way because the time spent watching television, video-recorder or movie is passive, with no participation other than changing the channel or turning it off. Time spent on such activities is lost forever. The viewer is a captive of the media. Media moguls select objects and times. Illusion interpenetrates reality until it is impossible to discriminate between the two. Is the President of the US really an actor playing a role? A framework beyond our control bounds us. Majority tastes determine the collective mind, if you can call it mind.

A primary manifestation of the power of the past is the world of fashion, the structure of which is to identify with previous times by dressing suitably. Fashion has existed throughout history, but during the recapitulation time of 50 years, the cycles of fashion intensify, until they pass very rapidly and govern masses of people. Fashionistas consider certain eras of history significant and make great efforts to copy every detail of appearance and affectation. Entire subcultures recreate a particular agreed-upon era, like the 1950s, and every garment and gesture is true to that period. The possibility of style reflecting continuing evolution is undermined and the orientation towards the past is total. Each fashion has its own compartment, and when outmoded in weeks or months, disappears as rapidly as it appeared. We must embrace every transition or become unfashionable. Post modernist architecture instituted theme park design as an alternative to creative architecture. Consciously or unconsciously determining the next style allows tastemakers to dictate commercial directions to the public. Since 1950, nostalgia craze has swept the entire Western world until there is little original art or design.

Involvement in the past overwhelms individualistic impulses. Previous times and places seem to be more vital, more real, and easier to imitate, duplicate, and document, as well as to understand. The ability to be present is lost and the automaton is born. Mass-psychological reality has supplanted individual trends, and the follower and conformist are envied. People buy advertising on clothes, perfumes, cars and in many other products as a way of identifying their tastes. Consciousness ceases due to the great pressure to process the increasing flood of information and we overload the senses with input. The room becomes psychically stagnant and the manikins stand around performing, all according to pattern and plan. The world is asleep.

Last Judgement of History

The time from 1950 until 2012 is a microcosm of the entire cycle of humanity and every person has an opportunity to experience harmonics of the eras in history when they were active, to relive collective development in individual life. It is a time of potential synthesis unavailable in the rest of history. Developmental phases are greatly compressed and we repeat history in a higher, denser harmonic. Developments evolved over immensely long eras are compacted into very short periods. Everything compacts, including population, into one thousandth of the time. Developments happen ever more quickly, and more and more information is generated and transmitted. It is estimated that in the 1980s the average Western person is exposed to as much information each day as an educated person was in a lifetime only 100 years ago – quite a staggering statistic.

The higher octave of Aries from 1950 to 1972 evokes our primitive beginnings. Mass-transportation allowed many people to travel, echoing nomadic stages. Everyone abandoned traditional values, the increasing power of science and technology dehumanized life, and this led to Arian reactions epitomized by the 'beat generation', which went on the road to leave the nihilism of civilization behind. The popularity of television encouraged the mindlessness and vicarious experience characteristic of modern life. The activities most prized by the post-war generation were shamanistic and primitive, such as the ecstasy of rock 'n' roll, the rejection of bourgeois materialistic values, fragmented nonverbal communication and, eventually, dropping out. The poetry was reactive, an emphatic free verse as spontaneous and emotional as shamanistic trance ravings. Hippies grew long hair like Cro-Magnon ancestors, returned to nature, moved in groups, crossbred and were addicted to rhythmic, primitive drumming. The reaction against traditional religion was a return to celestial worship, and the practice of astrology was reborn. Young millions converted instantly to revitalize ancient religions and cults revering Eastern gurus. The I Ching became a bible and born-again Christians and Islamic fundamentalists emerged from American slums and the wilds of Africa. The increasing adherence to vegetarianism reflected early nomadic gatherers. At one level, society degenerated and fell into the destructive Cold War split between the USA and Russia, while the undercurrent provided the roots for regeneration.

The primal Aries time led in the more stable, settled and matriarchal Taurus time from 26,000BC until 14,000BC, announced by Venus figurines and Earth Mother cults. In the higher Taurus era from 1972 to 1984 the rebellious generation was domesticated with the shift to health foods and the industries associated with organic revitalization, such as naturally grown grains, herbal medicines and drugs, a search for roots and a return to nature. The counter-trend in the outside world was the mechanization of farming, the scientific programming of livestock and plants, battery breeding and a large-scale shift of country populations into the cities and small towns. As farming machines eliminated the human element from agriculture, people all over the world forget how it is done in the first place. The use of chemical fertilizers and hybrid plants and animals replaced human contact with huge agro-technological combines cultivating millions of acres and raising thousands of animals in mechanical conditions. The creation and rise of the Women's Movement emphasized the shift from left-brain linear logic to right-brain holistic thinking, natural childbirth and a return to organic ways of carrying and birthing children.

The Gemini time from 14,000BC until 7000BC parallels its higher octave from 1984 to 1991, and focuses on communication, language and a change in instincts. Communication is the primary focus of civilization after 1984, with computers and the media being central. Paradoxically, the literacy rate worldwide plummets down as population increases and 'improved teaching methods' like phonetic spelling and New Math contribute to the loss of the basis of language and mathematics. Existing language degenerates through slang and misuse, amusingly called 'Haigspeak' in perverted honour of the US Secretary of State in the 1980s who butchered the English language, evoking memories of the Tower of Babel. Computer technology not only puts millions of industrial labourers out of work, but the primary occupation in the world becomes information and its transmission. The counter current to the disinformation produced by computer logic and the decline of education is in the creation of a new language based on Pythagorean mathematics, the new physics and cosmology, and the decoding of prehistoric monuments. A transformational and transcendent communication network as a counter current is a force for transforming the traditional world and knowledge. Gemini time is tribal and diversifies into New Age business, government, ecology, information technology, politics, education, publishing, media and many others.

The higher Cancer time is from 1991 until 1994, during which time all beings are involved with the emotional reality. The breakdown of cellular family for the masses coincides with the re-establishment of a higher level of heart contact among those who remain awake. The change may occur through a transformation in psychotherapy, higher spiritual impulses or through the shock generated by the decline in order in the world.

The second octave, from Leo (January 1995) to Scorpio (July 1999), evokes the time from 3000BC until AD1500, and is highly compacted into less than five years, during which time the civilizations created in the World Age dissolve into a vague echo of feudal times, complete with world-threatening plagues that sweep humanity.

The third octave of completion, from Sagittarius (July 1999) to Pisces (12 December 1999) is the final breakdown of the World Age into its constituent parts, like the 500 years from the Renaissance compacted into six months.

The options confronting every individual soul approaching the end of the 20th century derive from the historical process. The media explosion and the increased influence of cinema create pictures of previous ages that have highly formative influences on the world. The first octave of development in history was instinctive and unconscious, and the higher octave judgement will see a majority of humanity returning to levels of consciousness similar to the dawn of history, through identification with primitive levels of consciousness. George Orwell predicted the mechanization of the masses in *1984* as a monolithic transcontinental government run by the media in total control. The actor-President of the USA is an uncomfortable echo of Big Brother, especially in his media orientation and the revival of blind patriotism as a primary virtue. There was much discussion in 1984 about how the modern world is unlike that predicted by Orwell, but the similarities are much more subtle and insidious. The burning of books and disinformation Orwell depicted is going on now through the dominance of computers and video, and the only way to transcend the downward trend is to understand the higher octave cultural and historical messages.

The world will not disappear, but existing structures must die before a renewed world can emerge. The dissolution of the outer forms of civilization and their reintegration from the beginning reflects the disintegration of all bodies and beings in both the micro- and macro-worlds.

Aware individuals attracted to particular historical trends, cultural ideas or religious belief systems must retain the integrity of soul in higher transpersonal or transcendent realms rather than identification with physical, emotional, or mental constructs. The Eastern concept of non-attachment to the result of one's actions is a natural law. The barrage of information in the 50 years of the last judgement tempts every soul to form attachments to an individual life, life in general or history itself – all represent the desire to reincarnate. All information is decoded, processed, assimilated and passed through, but not allowed to capture the soul. Attachment to a particular time creates mechanicality, unconsciousness and the impossibility of liberation. In the blunt terms of Gurdjieff, sleep must be fought every step of the way. Awareness of the historical process and dis-identification is the sole way to transcend it.

Everyone contains a spiritual and genetic memory of the entire process of the world age, which we reactivate during the astrological cycles to which living organisms are exposed. Our primary historical roots are in the birth horoscope, which circuits every day when the earth rotates on its axis, every month by the moon, every year by the sun, and in the larger and longer cycles of the other planets. The positions of planets in the birth horoscope define predispositions toward particular times in history, genetic characteristics, and cosmic karmic actions that create the individuality of each being. During the 50-year compacted death moment, the soul experiences the whole World Age and will be attracted and attached to those times of most powerful identification. The mechanism is easy to identify. We have affinities with artefacts, books, poetry, knowledge, religion, ideas, and physical locations that are indicators of our formative influences. The California follower of the Krishna cults in the 1960s has a Hindu root in the Cancer time in history, while the Tibetan Buddhist is locked into the late Libra or early Scorpio time in history. The wanderer, the farmer, the religious fanatic, the media freak, the warrior, the magician and the auto mechanic all unconsciously reverberate to their times of origin, recreate such times in their lives, and signal others by assuming the trappings of their past lives, in order to relive the previous times when they were 'home'. A succession of influences and attractions attract us, and we tend to bond to a particular time and place and its attendant influences, while others carry a hodgepodge of historical influences that vie for attention.

In Zen Buddhism, the principle of regaining the purity of the Self through not letting the senses or feelings obscure the primal state is primary. If we understand the Self as a hazed crystal ball, the process of wiping the surface clean is superficial compared to actions that induce the original clean state of the crystal. The true state in astrology is the centre of the horoscope, which is the centre of the Self, which includes the entire periphery as well. The periphery is the residence of the personality, ego, senses, environment, and other qualities; in short, the place from where beingness manifests. Beingness arises at conception, and grows and changes and increases in force until the periphery dominates the centre. Individual nature accepts these qualities as the boundary of the Self, rather than the Self itself. The periphery is the samsara round of birth, sickness and death. Living through and experiencing life, when understood in the context of the Self, leads to the realization that the world and its qualities are the way the world is, but are not the world. Once we die to the world of illusion, if even for a second, our higher Self awakens forever, which brings a recognition that the illusory nature of the universe and life leads to eternal repetition of identification and involvement. Every life is merely a variant of the Buddhic Self. The collective and individual unconsciousness is the source of all human and natural qualities, but every being interprets them from an individual viewpoint. True individuality through individuation is seeing the flow of reality rather than being absorbed in one or the other part of the process. Freedom is absorption in the Self, the centre.

The techniques for determining your previous incarnations in the world age are given in detail in Chapter Eleven – Reincarnation.

Chapter Ten — The Universal Time Scale

The Time Scale of humanity has two phases of development: the World Age of 50,000 years and the Last Judgement of 50 years, the panoramic memory of the historical world age. The ratio of 50,000:50 is the same 1000:1 ratio between the human lifetime of 1,000 lunar months (77 years) and the one lunar month of the ovum. These are only two octaves out of the total of eight, which grade the universe from the subatomic world to the duration of the universe. The logarithmic mathematics governs throughout.

$$\frac{\text{Ovum lifetime}}{\text{Human lifetime}} = \frac{\text{Last Judgement}}{\text{World Age}} = \frac{1}{1000}$$

Darwinians understand humanity as the apex of evolution, but The Divine Plot restores humanity to the centre of the scale of lifetimes in the universe. The short duration of human history is like the narrow spectrum of visible light in the electromagnetic scale. Carl Sagan used the image that if all creation were compacted into one year, the existence of humanity would begin at 22:30pm on 31 December.[169] The true position of humanity defines relative scales shorter and longer than the World Age. The whole range of scales within which humanity exists is the Universal Time Scale.

The ratio of the octaves of 1:10 and the compaction throughout a three-octave world age of 1:1000 are the ratios that govern the

Table 12: The Universal Time Scale (overleaf)
The Universal Time Scale shows all eight scales from the longest, the Big Bang, to the shortest, the Subatomic world – four in the macrocosm and four in the microcosm. Each scale is one thousand times longer than the scale to its left and one thousandth the scale to its right.

The Macrocosm

	Octave IV — Last Judgement	Octave III — The World Age	Octave II — Age of Mammals	Octave I — Era of Creation	
PIS	**Dec 1999 Trial by Fire**	**1950 Atomic Bomb**	**50,000 Multiple pigmentation**	**50,000,000 Saurian Extinction**	**PIS**
	Nov 1999	The Great Wars	75 Primate Stock	70 Primate Stock	
AQU	Nov 1999	1910 Relativity	90,000 90 Protomodern Humans	90,000,000 90 Winged Reptiles	**AQU**
		Age of Nationalism	120 Neanderthals	120 Flowering Planets	
CAP	Sep 1999	1840 Telegraph	160,000 160 Toolmakers	160,000,000 170 Birds	**CAP**
		Industrial Revolution	200 Brain increase	235 Dinosaurs	
SAG		1720 Electricity	280,000 250 Archaic Homo Sapiens	280,000,000 280 Insects	**SAG**
		Renaissance	450 Pithecanthropus	400 Land Vertebrates	
SCO	**Jul 1999 Trial by Pestilence**	**1500 The Black Death**	**500,000 Hominid Transition**	**500,000,000 Swimming Vertebrate**	**SCO**
		The Middle Ages		600 Mollusks	
LIB	Feb 1999	1100 Cathedrals	900,000 900 Peking Man	900,000,000 1B Sexual Repro	**LIB**
		The Dark Ages	1.5 Homo Habilis extinct	1.3 Supercontinents	
VIR	Jun 1998	AD400 Fall of Rome	1,600,000 1.6 Homo Erectus	1,600,000,000 1.6 Protoanimals	**VIR**
		Classical Age	2.5 Stone tools	3.1 Bacterial Algae	
LEO	Mar 1997	800BC Greece and Rome	2,800,000 3.0 Ice Ages begin	2,800,000,000 3.5 Genetic Code	**LEO**
		Kingly civilization	3.7 Homo Habilis	4.55 Earth	
CAN	**Jan 1995 Trial by Water**	**3000 The Great Flood**	**5,000,000 Manlike Apes**	**5,000,000,000 The Solar System**	**CAN**
		Neolithic Age	6 Australopithecus	Tidal Universe	
GEM	Feb 1991	7000 First Cities	9,000,000 10 Ramapithecus	9,000,000,000	**GEM**
		Tribal Societies	14 Hominids		
TAU	Mar 1984 Computer Language	14000 Language+Writing	16,000,000 16 Volcanic activity	16,000,000,000 Symmetry-Duality	**TAU**
	Return to Nature	Earth Mother cults	20 Proconsul		
	Nov 1971 Womens' Liberation	26000 Painting + Sculpture	28,000,000 25 Mountain chains	28,000,000,000 Form-matter	
	Alternative Culture	Celestial Shamans	Mammal upsurge	Existence	
ARI	**Jan 1950 Hydrogen Bomb**	**48000 Consciousness**	**50,000,000 Mammals**	**50,000,000,000 The Big Bang**	**ARI**
	50 years	50,000 years	50 million years	50 billion years	

The Microcosm

	Octave V Cellular World	Octave VI Molecular World	Octave VII Atomic World	Octave VIII Subatomic World	
PIS	.00005y = 26.25 minutes Bacterium fusion	1.575 sec = One Breath	1.6×10^{-4} s = One Millisecond	1.6×10^{-7} s = One Billisecond	PIS
AQU				Low frequency radiation	AQU
CAP					CAP
SAG	.0005y = 4 hours 32 minutes	15.7 sec = Day of Blood Cell	1.6×10^{-3} s = Electron Life	1.6×10^{-6} s = Hadronic Era	SAG
SCO		18 sec = Life of molecule			SCO
LIB					LIB
VIR					VIR
LEO	.005y = 1.82 days	2.625 min	1.6×10^{-2} s = One Perception	1.6×10^{-5} s = Light Photons	LEO
CAN	Small Cells Blood Cells One Week				CAN
GEM					GEM
TAU					TAU
ARI	0.5y = 18.2 days	26.25 min	1.6×10^{-1} s	1.6×10^{-4} s	ARI
	18.2 days	26 minutes	1.6 seconds	1.6×10^{-4} seconds	

Universal Time Scale. The human life represents the enfoldment of the universe in space and time, as a metaphor and mathematically. The same ratios hold true at every level from the shortest unit of time, the lifetime of a subatomic particle, to the longest unit of time, the lifetime of the universe, and there is resonance from level to level. The range of the scale defines humankind's position in the universe, which it in turn reflects.

Every cosmos has natural access to three levels of awareness or temporal dimensions above and below it in the cosmic scheme, and the possibility of extending perception beyond, as in Collin's table of cosmoses. Each being has basic consciousness of its own life, a super-conscious level above it (a shorter temporal dimension) and an unconscious level below it (a longer temporal dimension). Jung perceptively stated, 'Whereas we think in terms of years, the unconscious thinks and behaves in terms of thousands of years'.[170] Our unconscious equates with the World Age as our spiritual dimension equates with the molecular world.

The table shows The Universal Time Scale complete with its eight octaves. The 50,000-year World Age of humanity is adjacent to the 50-year Last Judgement. The 50-million year Age of Mammals is 1,000 times longer than a World Age, graded by the same 12 astrological-developmental stages, in the same proportions.

The Age of Mammals

About the time when the last dinosaurs became extinct, the Age of Mammals, who were to replace them as the primary species, began in the Eocene Era. While the geological and cosmological reasons for the extinction of the dinosaurs is still under dispute, it is usually recognized that a radical change in the earth's climate about 50my (million years) ago is the primary cause, either through a shift in the earth's axis, collisions with comets or asteroids, or the effects of Nemesis. Astronomers are currently studying the 'Nemesis' theory that postulates a twin star to the sun that has eradicated most life on earth on a regular cycle of 25 million years.[171] The modern landmasses formed, and the great mountain chains were pushing up through the damp marshy swamps of the saurian era. The splitting of the continental plates cooled the temperature and lowered sea level. The climate became drier, great plains were created and mammals and birds became dominant, replacing the saurian. The vegetation was tropical and luxurious, and smaller plants had just begun to evolve into trees, providing a habitat for the first proto-primates.

We divide the Age of Mammals into three developmental octaves like the World Age, and the growth of mammals parallels the developmental levels of humanity during a World Age, correlating with the sequence of 12 signs.

In Aries (-50 to -28my) mammals, birds and the proto-primates came into dominance parallel with the attainment of consciousness for humanity. Marsupials and archaic carnivores from the previous era evolved into modern predators. Hoofed mammals became dominant, including sheep, the totem animal of Aries, as large as rhinos. In addition, whales, rodents and hoofed animals, including dog-sized horses, proliferated. The continental plates then separated into continents, threw up the Alps and Rockies, and changed the movement of the sea that progressively lowered the temperature.

In Taurus (-28 to -16my) climatic changes killed the older mammals, which were replaced by giant hoofed animals, dogs and rhinos, as well as pigs and bears. The Aegyptopithecus (-28my), still both monkey and ape, transformed into the more mobile Proconsul and Dryopithecus (-20my). Softer vegetation, flowers and plains grasses fed an inundation of grazing mammals, the bovoid ancestors of modern sheep and cattle (Taurus the Bull).

Throughout Gemini (-16my to -9my) the earth suffered a succession of volcanoes and earthquakes, leading to radical oscillations in temperature. Ramapithecus, apes with man-like teeth, were forerunners of orang-utans and the proliferation of grazing animals, birds and other smaller creatures continued.

In Cancer (-9my to -5my) the forests receded, the plains were criss-crossed by the great rivers and the milk-producing mammals were generated. The anthropologist Richard Leakey identified a 'fossil gap' between -8 and -4my, which is resonant of the Great Flood in the World Age. At both times, extraneous species became extinct by climatic changes. The surviving species contained vestigial qualities of those they superseded, as in the myth of Noah's Ark. In Hebrew Kabala the Ark, understood as the body of Noah, was the vessel that contained pairs (chromosomes) of all known species.

In *Leo* (-5my to 2.8my) great man-like apes such as Australopithecus africanus were disinherited from their three kingdoms by the recession of the huge forest areas that covered central Africa and Asia, creating great plains. The environment-caused individuation created three branches – gorillas, ape men and chimpanzees. These early primates differentiated themselves by attempting to break the bondage of tree-life. Gorillas lived in dense forest, the monkeys in more open forest, and the manlike apes at the forest edge near the plains. The higher primates walked upright, became carnivorous, and learned to use tools to protect themselves as the forest gradually began to vanish before them. Early horses and cats (Leo the Lion?) were beginning to appear, as did very quick and dangerous giant cheetahs. By about -3my a land bridge existed between North and South America, leading to the destruction of many of the species entrenched in South America.

In *Virgo* (-2.8my to -1.6my) ice ages generated noticeable cold and the first small stone tools were made by Australopithecus robustus, and the decrease in rainfall allowed the development of the first true human, Homo habilis the tool-maker. They had large brains and as their diet consisted of a range of scavenged meat and collected plants, their tools were primarily for cutting and cleaning flesh. Homo habilis was the first species to form family groups, exchange food and specialize to increase survival possibilities. They gathered plants and hunted small animals, but had to be very careful of the dangerous cats that prowled the savannah.

In Libra (-1.6my to -900,000 years) a more sophisticated and stronger alternative species appeared. Homo erectus was more hunter than hunter-gatherer at the start of the Pleistocene Era, and a time of rapid proliferation ensued. The two brain halves began to affect the handedness of early humans, and the polarities of hunter-gatherer and of male-female. The more mobile, faster and more intelligent Homo erectus made a quantum jump. They were nomadic, used fire, and moved in groups for a million years.

In Scorpio (900,000 to 500,000 years ago) were many catastrophes, possibly caused by a shift of the earth's axis. Human traces show cannibalism and increased proficiency at killing the many creatures available. Many of the animals that are common features of Chinese astrology, such as the rat, wolf and domestic dog, came into being.

In Sagittarius (-500,000 years to -280,000 years) a change corresponding to the self-realization of AD1500 was the drastic shift from the manlike ape Homo erectus to the more developed Pithecanthropus or Peking Man of 500,000 years ago. This earliest version of Homo sapiens is characterized by the matriarchal transmission of heredity and starts an extensive period of little outward change. They travelled in bands, used a variety of weapons and harnessed the power of fire – stolen from forest fires or places struck by lightning and carried as hot coals while wandering – but they were unable to start the miraculous fire themselves. Fire was particularly useful in the Ice Ages, where warmth and dominion in the caves inhabited by cave lions and bears was necessary for survival. The final mammalian cycle was the development of the Homo sapiens, who were forced to contend with the inclement Ice Ages.

In Capricorn 280,000 years ago, the shift to technical archaic Homo sapiens was accomplished. The final creation of modern man in an elongated 'gestation' coincided with the introduction of ego-consciousness at zero degrees Capricorn in the World Age. Human bone structure became more subtle and human, and although still beetle-browed and very clumsy, the brain capacity increased rapidly to modern size. Humankind domesticated the animals we know today, including the goat, the totem animal of Capricorn.

The primary shift in the Aquarius time beginning 160,000 years ago was the development of more sophisticated flint weapons to attack and eat the woolly mammoths on the plains of Europe and Asia as they migrated yearly to avoid the glacial movements. The Neanderthals inhabited Europe and Asia, had even larger brains than modern humans and developed their own culture. The primary leap in evolution was internal – the development of higher awareness of life, which was absent before.

In Pisces from 90,000 to 50,000 years ago, development led to Tanzanian man with a form similar to modern humanity, who had no apparent evolutionary prototype but just appeared. They were much less efficient or civilized than even the Neanderthal, who remained the most numerous species. The Neanderthals used herbal medicines, painted their bodies, and buried their totem animals and their dead, advancing almost to the fringe of civilization. They worshipped the cave bears and lions with which they competed for caves, survived the harsh climate, and created a culture of sorts.

At the end of the Age of Mammals the Neanderthal had to adapt or perish after the appearance of Cro-Magnon Man, just as the individuals at the end of the world age must transcend consciousness or be imprisoned in the repetition of another world age cycle. Beings of superior consciousness appear at the end of a world age as miraculously as the Cro-Magnons appeared about 50,000 years ago. Cro-Magnons were taller, had a larger brain capacity, and were highly intelligent and very well organized. Over a period of about 15,000 years, they completely wiped out the Neanderthal. Their great weapon was speech, and the rise of our World Age ensued. At the borderline of the Age of Mammals and the beginning of the World Age of humanity, the apes that did not make the transition gradually regressed until they formed the genera of apes that we know today, or hid as the Yeti or Abominable Snowman in Himalayan reaches.

During one cycle of mammals, humanity could go through 1,000 cycles of creation, development and extinction. The World Age of humanity is a death memory for the Age of Mammals that passes by in an instant and carries a dreamlike quality. Human beings have a discrete lifetime and individuality, but in the animal kingdom species reflect each other from generation to generation. The cows or sheep in the fields are virtually the same creatures that existed in vast numbers before humanity.

It is particularly interesting that the Age of Mammals very accurately represents the succession of totem animals and images of the 12 astrological signs, encoded in our memory and genetic code.

The Age of Creation

The *Age of Creation*, one thousand times longer than the Age of Mammals and one million times longer than the World Age, is 50 billion years (by) in duration (Last Judgement 50 years, World Age 50,000 years, Mammals 50,000,000 years and Creation 50,000,000,000 years), which extends back to the origin of the universe (see Table 7). The Big Bang is reciprocal to the creation of mammals after a temperature rise made the dinosaurs extinct, the creation of humanity after the explosion of the first atomic bombs and the greenhouse effect of fossil fuels. All creations involve increases in temperature and relate to the fire sign Aries. Each octave follows the developments of the end of the previous octave, and fits in with the idea that the Big Bang that created our universe was the death of a previous imploded universe.

It is fascinating that the earliest stages in the creation of the universe after the Big Bang closely parallel the first four zodiac signs.

Aries (-50 to -28by) is pure existence and the dissipation of enormous energy spewing outwards at close to the speed of light, which occurs in an instant but is followed by billions of years of steady state.

In *Taurus* (-28 to -16by) the world of form is created from the pure energy and the particulate nature of the universe is determined.

In *Gemini* (-16 to -9by) the universe is symmetrical, galaxies are formed and the intrinsic dualistic nature of the world manifests.

In *Cancer* (-9 to -5by) the universe is tidal as galaxy formation creates a home for what later became planetary systems.

In *Leo* (-5 to -2.8by) the creation of the Sun and Solar System in the Age of Creation coincides with the individuation of manlike apes one octave higher and human individuality and self-consciousness two octaves higher in 3000BC. Beginning with the formation of earth 4.55 billion years ago, and throughout the Leo time of 2.2 billion years, the earth was molten and then liquid, covered by seas. The creation of the genetic code signalled the beginning of life about 3.5 billion years ago and the earliest microfossils of primary life forms date back to this time.

In *Virgo* (-2.8 to -1.6by) the primary life form diversified to produce ocean-breeding blue-green algae (-3.1by), filament algae -2.tby, nuclear cells in -1.7by and then fungi in the Hypozoic era.

In Libra (-1.6by to 900my), a super continent was formed by -1.3by and one billion years ago the Proterozoic Era began, leading to the first multi-celled beings recorded as fossils.

In Scorpio (-900 to -500my), an acceleration in the diversity of the primitive life forms was the advent of sexed life and sexual reproduction, a primary separation and division from the previously unified and undifferentiated life. The continental plates broke apart in the beginning of the Cambrian Era about 600 million years ago, which was also the time of the first molluscs.

The last octave of the Creation Era began 500 million years ago in Sagittarius (-500 to -280my) with a rapid proliferation of life all over earth, coinciding with the settling of the continents, and a shift of life forms from the sea onto dry land. Shellfish (-50my), fish (-450my) and corals (-450my) populated the seas and led to the vascular land plants - 400my ago. Very quickly the land was filled with insects (-395my), seed-producing plants created the forests (-380my) and amphibious creatures (-350my) bridged water and land.

The undisputed kings of Capricorn (-280 to -160my) were the reptiles, which developed from shelled sea creatures and proceeded to dominate the land, ruling the primeval swamp by their number and size. Previously dominant life forms declined in their favour, and a positive outgrowth of the rapid changes was the first primitive mammals, which were very small, herbivorous creatures in about -22my. The super continent Pangea broke apart, providing separate arenas for development all over the earth. It is particularly interesting that the primary coal deposits originated at this time, exactly two octaves before the industrial revolution in the later Capricorn time in the World Age, when they used coal on a massive scale to fuel the industrial revolution.

In the Mesozoic era of Aquarius (-160 to -90my) birds became the bearers of the great evolutionary leap and nature proliferated in the shadow of the dinosaurs, beautifying the landscape with flowering plants (-140 to -120my).

In the final Pisces age (-90my to -50my) was the destruction of the dinosaurs, probably brought about by the decrease in temperature of the earth, caused by collision with asteroids or comets, or the passage of Nemesis, the twin star to earth. The decline of the dinosaurs took place from -65 to -50my, coinciding with the separation of the first primate stock from the mammals proper in about -70my. Then, about 55 million years ago, the cold began and wiped the dinosaurs off the face of the earth, leaving their inheritance in the reptilian creatures and closely related birds, still alive today.

In the context of the Universal Time Scale, each life form developed according to a natural and essential pattern, following one another in evolution to complete the overall earth-organism, just as atoms from which inner electrons have been blasted away first jump inwardly to complete the structure, creating intermediary elements along the way. Life is the organism continuously changing, but always containing the essential unity, whatever the outer form.

Timing the Time Scale

Not only is it impossible for things to be other than they are, it is even impossible that the initial situation of the universe could have been other than what it was. No matter what we are doing at a given moment, it is the only thing that was ever possible for us to be doing at that moment.[172]

Zukav, *The Dancing Wu Li Masters*

Dating developmental stages of a Universal Time Scale is a very contentious undertaking. By necessity, it is a model rather than a statement of fact. The same logarithmic ratios govern in the World Age, the life of the individual human being and in the Age of Mammals and Creation. Among scientists, there is great deviation in the dates attributed to early events in the age of the universe, although scientists believe the age of the solar system and the earth to be between 4.55 and 5 billion years. The creation dates of the various life forms that populate earth are in great question, particularly by specialists. In the 12 years that the author has researched The Divine Plot the accepted age of the universe has increased from seven to almost 15 billion years, an increase of more than 200%. The important factor is therefore not the exact times at which developments occurred, but the ratios inherent in the process. The overall view is more important and illuminating than the details.

Parallels exist across the horizontal file of the Universal Time Scale. Movement from bottom to top in each file is linear development, like Darwinian evolution, punctuated by the shock points from octave to octave and the great leaps at the beginning of each three-octave scale. However, there are other more powerful, if less obvious, organizational mechanisms at work in the creation and maintenance of life in the universe. The universe transmits information by resonance along the horizontal file throughout the development of life on earth. Scientists, with the exception of Sheldrake, ignore inter-scale resonance in favour of linear evolution, but it is a very important organising principle of existence.[173] Similarities of sign manifestations in higher or lower octaves are in the form of the life, in the same way that the many people with the sun-sign Leo have striking inner similarities but appear different. Vertical movement in the Universal Time Scale diagram is

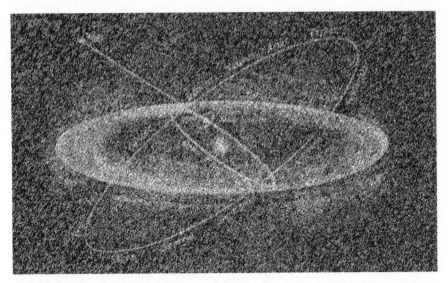

Figure 30: The Solar System in Context
The earth orbits around the sun, which orbits around the centre of the Milky Way galaxy in an estimated 250 million years. The zodiacal constellations are in the ecliptic plane of the solar system, inclined to the plane of the galaxy. The entire mechanism is like a cosmic gyroscope. (After Collin, *Theory of Celestial Influence*)

physical lineage, while horizontal movement is morphogenetic, governed by other than physical transmission.

The complete picture describes all life forms as integral parts of octaves and ages, yet each part is a whole. A being composed of billions of separate molecules is still an individual. Each era in the historical development of the universe is complete, but beings of a much shorter lifespan populate it. This leads to eras of longer duration. Each life form performs an essential role in the whole as a stage in the development of consciousness and spiritual impulse.

The earliest stages of creation remain in the continuous formation and annihilation of galaxies in deep space. Galaxies created at the same time as the Milky Way move away from each other at close to the speed of light. All energy and matter in the universe is expanding at an unimaginable speed, yet since all parts are expanding at similar rates, the relative position of everything remains close to being the same as it must have been just after creation. The length of the spectrum of light reaching us measures distances away from earth. The greater the red shift of the light, the further away, and the older the galaxy. It is clear that we differentiate galaxies primarily by their apparent size and angle of rotation, which could be the only difference between the microcosmic and macrocosmic worlds.

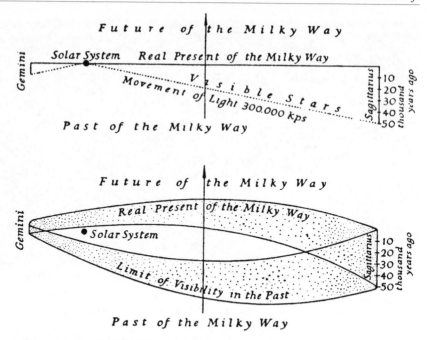

Figure 31: Cross-section of the Milky Way Galaxy
The present of the Milky Way is the plane of its long axis as the galaxy hurtles through space and time. Light received from the direction of Sagittarius takes 50,000 light years to reach earth. When we look towards Sagittarius, we are looking into the past. (After Collin, *Theory of Celestial Influence*)

Rodney Collin investigated the nature of galactic perception in *The Theory of Celestial Influence* (see Figure 30). The zodiac belt of constellations lies in the plane of the ecliptic, at an angle of 231/2° to the plane of the equator, and is a reference circle for measuring the cycles of earth. The plane of the zodiacal ecliptic tilts at an angle of 55° to the Milky Way galaxy. Collin postulated that the sun orbits around its sun, the star Sirius – the planet the Egyptians worshipped as the supreme deity and around which they oriented their yearly calendar. Sirius orbits around the galactic centre, presently at 26° of Sagittarius. The earth therefore orbits around the sun, which orbits around Sirius, which orbits around the galactic centre in a period of 250,000,000 years. All systems, of which earth is a part, relate by their gyroscopic interaction. It is like the multitude of orientations that exist among our various atoms, molecules and cells. The zodiacal belt is the present of earth. To look above the ecliptic, towards the pole star, is looking into the future where earth is going, while looking towards the South Pole is looking towards the past where earth has already been.

The plane of the ecliptic intersects the plane of the Milky Way in the signs Gemini and Sagittarius, which to Collin is the 'cross-section of the ship intersecting the surface of the sea'. Looking towards Sagittarius is looking towards the centre of the galaxy, and looking towards Gemini is looking away from the galactic centre. The nearer Gemini edge is 10,000 light years away and the farther Sagittarius edge is 50,000 light years away. The distance away of these stars reflects the vast period of time it takes light to reach earth from their positions. It takes light 60,000 years to cross the Milky Way. The stars in Gemini are in the positions they occupied 10,000 years ago, while the stars in Sagittarius are where they were 50,000 years ago, at the time when humanity became conscious. Looking into space, we see the past and future of the Milky Way. Perception of the universe is limited by the speed of light, and Collin suggested that there must be energy, with which humanity has not yet become acquainted, which is far faster than light.

As the sun is the source of energy for earth, to face Sagittarius is to align with the centre and source of creative energy of the Milky Way galaxy. In this perspective, the zodiacal signs measure our position relative to the galactic centre at various times of the year.

Collin investigated and catalogued the relations between many cosmoses at levels from that of the Electron to the Absolute, and determined that the relationship between each level of consciousness or development in the universe is exponential, as in the Universal Time Scale. The fact the duration of each age is the cube of its next lower age, as is the case in the UTS, implies the 'introduction of plan, purpose, and possibility'.[174] All levels of organisation – cell, human body, nature, earth, solar system and Milky Way – are complete in themselves, yet part of the whole. All systems contain the pattern and possibilities of the whole. God created humanity in his own image, a divine image of the universe. The Divine Plot of the Universal Time Scale is an image of humanity and its universe, all related mathematically. Humanity occupies a relative position in the middle of the scale of existences in the universe.

The Microcosm

We have described four successively longer phases of the universe in the macrocosm. The mathematical organization of each cycle reflects that of the others, and each cycle is one-thousandth of the previous cycle and one thousand times longer than the following cycle. The ratio 1:1000 describes the Last Judgement or panoramic memory of every cycle in the time scale. The World Age of Humanity is merely an instant within the Age of Mammals, and mammals observe quietly the coming and going of a thousand historical world ages in each developmental stage. Likewise, relative to the Era of Creation, the Age of Mammals represents a recapitulation of the earliest cycle encapsulated within the mammals. It is as though the cells of the body were conscious of the whole.

Table 13: World Cycles

IV	The 50-year cycle of	The Last Judgement
III	The 50,000-year cycle of	The World Age of Humanity
II	The 50,000,000-year cycle of	The Age of Mammals
I	The 50,000,000,000-year cycle of	The Era of Creation

Each successive cycle is shorter by a factor of 1,000, the density increases, and the number of life forms is constant. Cycles become shorter and the apparent fullness of life is greater, but the overall reality of each octave is constant. The number of souls remains the same.

The 50-year cycle of the Last Judgement approximates an average human lifetime throughout an entire world age, and smaller cycles represent realms that within a life. The macrocosm and the microcosm reflect each other, both possessing four developmental cycles. Microcosmic cycles contain as many events as longer cycles, but happen rapidly in what is the realm of particle physics.

Cycle V, *The Cellular World*, extends from 18.26 days (0.05 year) to 26.2975 minutes (0.00005 year). In the first octave is one week, the approximate Life Time of a human blood cell, and three days, the Life Time of small cells in the human body. Towards the end of the cycle is the reproductive cycle of bacterium fission.

Cycle VI, *The Molecular World*, extends from 26.2975 minutes to 1.58 seconds (five ten thousandths of a year), which is one breath. In the midst of the cycle is one minute and molecular cycle of 18 seconds.

Cycle VII, *The Atomic World*, extends from 1.58 seconds to 1.58×10^{-4} seconds, or one millisecond. In the beginning of the cycle is one second, the cycle of the pulsation of a pulsar, and entrance into the realm of subatomic particles. Movement into the infinitely small echoes the infinitely large as the structure of the atomic level of organization reflects the macro scale of solar systems. At the equivalent of the Leo time of the cycle is the duration of one perception of about $1/4$th of a second, and at $1/1500$th of a second is the duration of a quantum of an electron, at the equivalent of the Sagittarius time.

Figure 32: Universal Time Scale Cylinder
The UTS represented as a cylinder, with creation at the bottom and the micro-world at the top. Order decreases and information increases as the spiral ascends. The unit of one day is at the exact centre between microcosm and macrocosm.

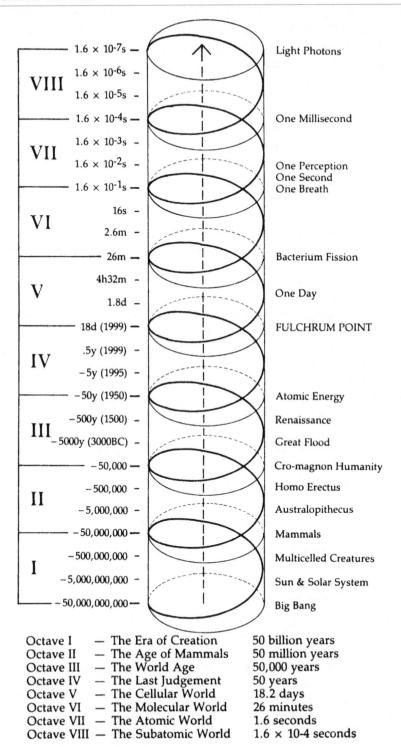

VIII	1.6×10^{-7}s	Light Photons
	1.6×10^{-6}s	
	1.6×10^{-5}s	
VII	1.6×10^{-4}s	One Millisecond
	1.6×10^{-3}s	
	1.6×10^{-2}s	One Perception
	1.6×10^{-1}s	One Second / One Breath
VI	16s	
	2.6m	
V	26m	Bacterium Fission
	4h32m	
	1.8d	One Day
IV	18d (1999)	FULCHRUM POINT
	.5y (1999)	
	−5y (1995)	
III	−50y (1950)	Atomic Energy
	−500y (1500)	Renaissance
	−5000y (3000BC)	Great Flood
II	−50,000	Cro-magnon Humanity
	−500,000	Homo Erectus
	−5,000,000	Australopithecus
I	−50,000,000	Mammals
	−500,000,000	Multicelled Creatures
	−5,000,000,000	Sun & Solar System
	−50,000,000,000	Big Bang

Octave I	— The Era of Creation	50 billion years
Octave II	— The Age of Mammals	50 million years
Octave III	— The World Age	50,000 years
Octave IV	— The Last Judgement	50 years
Octave V	— The Cellular World	18.2 days
Octave VI	— The Molecular World	26 minutes
Octave VII	— The Atomic World	1.6 seconds
Octave VIII	— The Subatomic World	1.6×10-4 seconds

Cycle VIII, *The Subatomic World*, extends from 1.58×10^{-4} seconds to 1.58×10^{-7} seconds (one millionth of a second), which is the fastest perceptual scale, where everything breaks down into pure energy. The creation of the visible universe and shorter lifetimes are in the realm of transitory subatomic particles and high frequency sound, areas in the electro-magnetic spectrum that are beyond human comprehension. In the Hadronic Era, 10^{-7} seconds after the Big Bang, the universe is a seething mass of particles and antiparticles formed from photons, within which proton antiproton pairs annihilate each other. The dissolution into pure energy reflects at microcosmic and macrocosmic levels. After Cycle VIII, the processes of creation overlap into the macrocosmic world.

The Universal Time Scale has eight stages of development from the lifetime of the universe to the lifetime of atoms, the longest and shortest wavelengths that bind the world. Once again, each cycle is one thousandth of its predecessor and one thousand times longer than its successor.

The eight stages of the Universal Time Scale inescapably parallel the Eightfold Path of Buddhism. The intention of Buddhism is to attain 'nirvana' or Buddhahood, which is awakening, but also the disappearance of being from the eternal round of incarnations, an escape into the immeasurable and infinite. There actually is no attainment because there is nothing to acquire. Nirvana can only arise spontaneously when we perceive the impossibility of grasping. The Buddha transcends all such distinctions. The Eightfold Path describes Buddhic 'dharma' – the method by which futility is ended. The first four are thoughts and the second four are actions. The process is the key to liberation from the universe described in the Universal Time Scale.

The Spiral of Time

We can represent the Universal Time Scale in two ways, each clarifying a different mechanism. One is as a spiral cylinder through time and the other is as a series of spirals seen end-on.

The UTS can be shown as a cylinder with the Big Bang at the bottom and the lifetime of the atom at the top (see Figure 32). Within each stage is movement along the cylinder and around the circle, as the whole UTS recurs eternally. Once it manifests, it can only repeat its development in time in infinite permutations, as there is no other way for it to manifest. Each stage repeats and the entire process also repeats.

The UTS describes repetitive creation and the manifestation of form in the world of action and the micro-world where only thoughts exist

– each contains four stages. The organizational structure of the whole is fractal – it repeats at each component level. This reflects the workings of the natural world at every level of perception. Movement from the macrocosmic Era of Creation in the past towards the microcosmic Subatomic World accompanies a decrease in order. Information is stored and recorded in the temporal process by 'entropy', the translation of information into events. The universe continuously exchanges energy, in the form of information, for existence, accompanied by a decrease in order, which is why subatomic events exhibit what appear to be less order and more randomness. Entropic exchange is a universal process that can be perceived from an infinity of possible viewpoints within.

Every being carries every level of the universal process within simultaneously, as well as recapitulating the process through life. Previous stages back to the Big Bang have 'already become' and the cycles of the subatomic world are always in the process of 'becoming', therefore there is always a balance within between being and becoming. The rapid cycles of the subatomic world resonate with those in the macrocosm, and every breath is a recapitulation of the entire universe in time. In recurrence, every level is whole itself, yet is a summation of the larger whole of which it is a part. Each cycle is itself, yet also a spiralling back into the previous cycle and a progression forward into the next cycle. Each world is a judgement of its next longer world, and the seed of the next shorter world.

In the UTS spiral, the centre point is somewhere between a year and a day: the *'eternal present'*. The present moment is always here, and always contains the rest of time – the centre of the universal process from the macrocosm to the microcosm. Humanity is not the ultimate development in the universe, but the central perception from which it is experienced.

The natural way to view the spiral is with the Past at the bottom, which makes the upper half the microcosmic world, the Future. The arrow of time points from bottom to top. The slower cycles of the past and faster cycles of the future reflect our perception of time. Any phenomenon, event or being, from the particles of the microcosm to the galaxies and suns of the macrocosm, has a primary perception within a particular cycle from I-VIII, its past in the next lower cycle and its future in the next highest. The cycle lengths determine how often shock points occur, at which transition to finer and more spiritual cycles becomes possible. For example, it takes hundreds of millions of years for objects in the mineral world to pass through their lifetime; only at the end of the cycle can they be broken down in death and synthesized in a mammalian body. The human body contains traces of all minerals and elements, which date back to the origin of Earth, which in turn is composed of matter split off from the sun. Yet the minerals and elements exist in the finest combined form of which they are capable. In Figure 33, the Universal Time Scale and the Periodic Table of the elements are spirals – the similarity of both to atomic structure is powerful. Larger cycles and entities exist towards Cycle I, while smaller cycles exist towards Cycle VIII, but each being perceives the passage of its lifetime as being the whole of history.

Schopenhauer defined 'Maya' as a dream of the whole knowledge of the world. Humans have two realities: one is the *subject*, the knower and the known, the supporter of the world and all that exists in the world – in short, it is the world; but the body is an *object* among other objects and conditions the laws of objects. The subject is present, entire, and undivided in every being. Schopenhauer states that, 'Any one percipient being, with the object, constitutes the whole world as idea just as fully as the existing millions do; but if this one were to disappear, then the whole world as will and idea would cease to be.'[175] In death, we experience the end of the world and believe it is contingent upon us. As death coincides with the end of the world (as will and idea), so conception coincides with creation. Every being is the entire universe.

The new physics corroborates Schopenhauer. Phenomena only exist relative to an observer. There is no preferential objective frame of reference from which to experience the world: we have to be in it. Every being is the centre of its universe, and the present moment is the eternal present, the fulcrum of the Universal Time Scale. The space-time continuum, which correlates every moment of time with every other moment, is the 'web of Maya' from which the soul wishes to escape. Once we come into the universe, we become entire universe. The object becomes the subject, and the knower the known. The dilemma of existence is the artificial separation of these two principles, where we feel split off from the whole.

Relativity theory is a religious ideology. In relativity, the universe curves and time is circular. The universe begins with a Big Bang,

Figure 33: Spiral Periodic Table of the Elements
The Periodic Table of the Elements may be represented as spiralling out from the central hydrogen. Each layer of the table is defined by the number of electron rings filled out from the centre of hydrogen. An inert gas forms the basis for each layer. (Illustration by author)

Figure 34: Spiral Universal Time Scale
The UTS as a series of circles with creation at the centre, showing unity, and the eight octaves in concentric rings – the diagram looks like both the atomic model and the alchemical/mathematical diagrams of Robert Fludd. (Illustration by author)

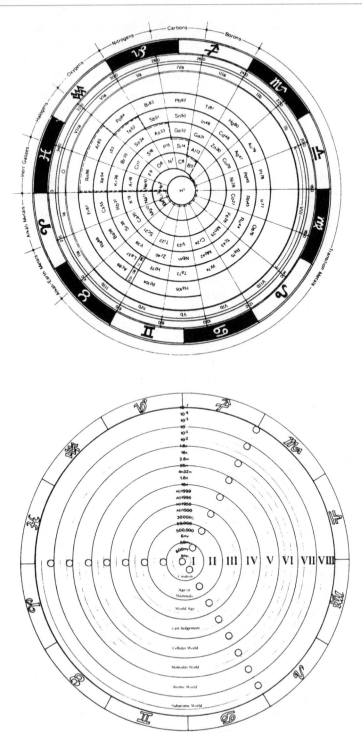

manifests in curving time, then ends when all order is gone and randomness prevails. The compaction of all matter in the universe in a singularity is followed by another Big Bang. The end state creates a new beginning. Understanding the universe is a return to discover how it was created. The word 'religio' means 'to link back' and the function of religion is to regain access to pure Spirit, the Unity, the One.

The End is the Beginning

The process of the universe is circular, as is each component system of the universe. The wholes interlock and are inseparable. And the end is the beginning, just as it is in individual life. In Life Time Astrology, conception coincides with death. At conception, life is all potential, while at death it is all actual. Any stage in life is a phase of the transformation of potential into actual reality. Life transforms reality as the universe transforms information.

Like the ouroburos snake biting its tail, the end and the beginning of the Universal Time Scale join. Figure 35 shows the eight spiral cycles of the UTS joined end to end, making a doughnut shape called a torus. Arrows on the surface of the torus indicate the apparent local flow of time. In physics, the torus furnishes 'different connectivity', where the self can be simultaneously separate and connected with the rest of the universe.[176] Arthur Young discovered that the formula for the volume of the Einstein-Eddington universe, the hypersphere was the same as the volume of a torus with an infinitely small hole. The flow over the surface of a torus is also similar to the pattern of the earth's magnetic field. Once again, microcosm is macrocosm.

When end and beginning are connected, the interaction at their junction is crucial. Subatomic particles called mesons have lifetimes much shorter than Cycle VIII of the UTS, but they 'transitory' particles. Suddenly, below Cycle VIII, subatomic particles have infinite lifetimes. Subatomic particles bridge the gap between the macrocosm and the microcosm. At micro-scale, cause and effect lessen and linear time vanishes. Entropy reaches a maximum and randomness is the result, producing a vortex, like the infinity symbol, at the crossover between the micro- and macro-worlds.

The physicist E H Walker speculates that photons are conscious because they exhibit organic qualities and seem to 'know' how and where to move, process information and act on it. Photons exhibit qualities that belong to both macrocosmic and microcosmic realms. Indeed, subatomic particles like the photon are not particles at all, but rather a 'set of relationships'.[177] Elementary particles are creations of the physicists' theories, mathematics, and observational devices.

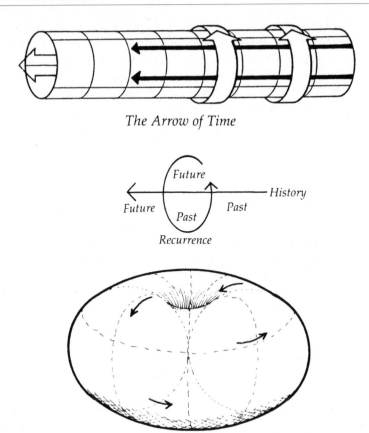

The Arrow of Time

Future

Future — History

Past

Future Past

Past

Recurrence

Figure 35: The Universal Time Scale Torus
When the rectilinear tables of the time scale meet, the beginning and end of each octave join, creating an image of circular history within each octave, shown by the encircling arrows. The length-wise arrows show the illusory processes of evolution and history, from Creation at the right to the Subatomic world at the left. When the cylinder is connected end-to-end, it forms a torus shape. The intersections of each octave at conception and death coincide: the point when all octaves begin and end is always the same eternal moment, outside of time. The simultaneous spiral and circular movements are also those of electrons encircling the nucleus of an atom. The torus shows all these interactions at once. (Illustration by author)

Photons do not exist by themselves as discrete entities — they do not exist apart from the whole. Photons are pure energy, which become manifest as bound electrons enriching the atomic nucleus. Since photons move at the speed of light, their time is infinite according to relativity. They live in the micro-world, but live forever. They only have time when bound in matter. Spirit is subject to time when attached to a body, and liberation is a release of energy and freedom from time.

Another explanation of the linkage between end and beginning concerns black holes. Stars are born, live and die; just like man.[178] When a star reaches the end of its lifetime, its gravitational field becomes so strong that it closes upon itself and compacts not only its mass but also the space in its vicinity, forming a funnel towards the point of disappearance. Within is a spherical egg, a mini-universe, a separate whole whose only one point of contact with the universe is a black hole.

Black holes have their own laws that seem to defy physics. A time traveller approaching a black hole appears from outside to slow down, but due to an anomaly in relativity takes an infinite time to get there. The time traveller would experience great speed and enter an alien world 'crossing the Schwartzchild'. 'Our explorer's time will come back to its start in the same space... the traveller is here the prisoner of a cyclical universe where periodically, with each turn of the black hole, he will live the same event."[179] Black hole time unfolds in reverse order. In our universe, phenomena decrease in order as they develop, while in a black hole negentropy rules and phenomena increase their order as they develop. Information about the universe decreases, but in a black hole, it increases. Charon speculates that black hole space-time is a 'space of thought' or 'space of memory'. He ascribes similar qualities to the constitution of the electron, making it a micro black hole, a 'bearer of the spirit'. An electron has a quasi-eternal lifetime, constitutes a universe on its own, and can exchange information at a distance with other electrons.[180] The electron contains spirit space-time and is a micro-universe with cyclical time that reactivates past states of its own space, increasing entropy (information) in the process.

Charon's attribution of psychic qualities to particles resonates with the Unus Mundus, the unity of all things of the alchemists. The electron is basic to everything in the universe, and through black holes is able to create the transition from matter to spirit and back again. The electron is the shock point crossover between cycles and octaves in the time scale. The electronic realm is an eternal universe within which there is no death, only changes of state.

The Faustian Universe

The structure of the universe is reversible. The events that happen in the macrocosm after creation billions of years ago are the same events that happen in the microcosm in daily life.[181] Scientists consider the 'arrow of time' to be one-directional and irreversible, but it is clearly bi-directional. Nobel Laureate Ilya Prigogine considers the problem of the reversibility of time the primary and most controversial topic in the physical sciences, 'Think of Einstein, Proust, Freud, Teilhard, Pierce or Whitehead.'[182]

In the spiral scheme of the eight worlds, time in the universe runs from creation at the bottom to the electronic realm at the top, but there is another time that acts concurrently with the time of the universe. For every particle in the universe, there is an anti-particle in the anti-universe, the *Faustian Universe* of the physicist Stannard. Like the space-time of the black hole, in the Faustian Universe the arrow of time runs backwards. The present moment is an intersection between universe and anti-universe where the future of the universe is the past of the Faustian Universe, and the past of the universe is the future of the Faustian Universe – they are parallel but mirror-image universes. As our universe moves towards the electronic realm, where there is maximum disorder and minimum information, the Faustian Universe has maximum order and maximum information – a total antithesis. These two mirror universes run in opposite directions in time, and when our universe ends, the Faustian Universe is at its creation, and vice versa. This ensures a continuum and implies a repetitive, eternal world plan. Access to the workings of the universes is through spirit, available to anyone at any time in history.

The Faustian Universe is 'outside of time' and is the realm explored by mystics, yogis, spiritual teachers and everyone who has experienced spiritual or peak experiences, pre-cognitive dreams, déjà vu, or near-death experiences, as well as the realm in which mantic arts such as tarot, I Ching, geomancy, and others operate. It may also be coexistent to the 'unconscious', which contains all information about the future of our universe in its past. The Platonic world of ideas is also correlative to the Faustian Universe. It is accessible to anyone at any time, and contains all information potential to our system. Jean Charon has proposed a 'theory of complex relativity' in which the anti-universe has inverse laws that seem more like those of mind than matter.

Frank Barr has suggested that a universal pigment in all living organisms, the organic superconductor melanin, has properties similar to a black hole and may be the major organizing molecule for living systems.[183] He believes it is a regulating mechanism and the 'key to understanding evolution, embryological development, tissue repair, and regeneration, consciousness and altered states of consciousness, and the trigger-like biasing of mental states'. Others think that melanin may be the matrix for the construction of DNA, RNA and proteins. It also seems to be self-organizing and self-synthesizing, a key in the quest for the answer of the mysteries of life, mind and biological organization.

The correlation of the subatomic realm with higher consciousness does not consider the realms beyond the physical universe. The highest states are unmanifest, unknowable and exist beyond the universe. In Hebrew mysticism such a realm is called Ain Soph, the eternal state of being which results when all qualities are removed – the unconditioned state of all things. The highest state is both the centre of the circle and its territory, the periphery of the universe and its contents; in short, god/dess.

Chapter Eleven — Reincarnation

Gautama Buddha speaks: 'With this heart thus serene, made pure, translucent, cultured, devoid of evil, supple, ready to act, firm and imperturbable, the saint directs and bends down his mind to the knowledge of the memory of his previous temporary states. He recalls to his mind... one birth, or two or three... or a thousand or a hundred thousand births, through many an aeon of dissolution, many an aeon of both dissolution and evolution.'[184]

Reincarnation was an essential philosophy of Vedic India, Egypt, Buddhism, Taoism, Zoroastrianism, Sikhism, Judaism, Christianity, Gnosticism, Islam, shamanism, and many other religions. In its simplest form, it is the periodical reappearance on earth of the same soul. In the Krishna cult, only heroes, leaders and teachers reincarnate – for the masses the process is vague and not automatic.

The *transmigration of souls* is reincarnation through all life forms and introduces an element of morality through reward and punishment. The soul passes through a sequence of increasingly complex animal bodies until it obtains a human body.

The *law of karma* is the universal action of cause and effect governing reincarnation and transmigration. Present life is a product of the qualities of past lives and determines the quality of future lives. Psychic traces of previous lives pass on through the soul without a connecting ego. Every action, thought, emotion, and idea affects karma, which places responsibility upon every being, although the soul itself remains pure. While for most people reincarnation is a matter of faith, yogis and some others do recall past lives in meditation or regression.

The *wheel of samsara* is an image of the cycle of birth, death, and rebirth, liberation from which is enlightenment. Possessing a body impels ceaseless wandering in material existence, while liberation is freedom from compulsion into eternal bliss. Some souls choose to incarnate voluntarily, as do the thousand living Buddhas who renounce nirvana to help others attain enlightenment.

Two fundamental concepts of Buddhism are the concept of Brahman, a metaphysical absolute out of which all things come and to which all things return, and the concept of *atman*, the soul, or universal self, which is identical to Brahman. Atman experiences successive lives, identifying with the body and immersed in the world throughout a succession of incarnations. When the identity of the two is re-established, the quest for salvation is complete. Ken Wilber calls this quest for ultimate unity-consciousness *The Atman-Project*.[185]

The Rosicrucians and the Theosophical Society brought the Eastern approach to reincarnation to the West in the 19th century. In the East, the circular mechanism of time is something from which to escape, while the time-dominated Westerners exist within linear time and wish to live forever. St Augustine (at the midway point in the Time Scale at AD400) formulated the concept of linear time. Previously, there was little conception of time in either East or West. Time is contingent upon consciousness and objectivity, and Libra signals an increased awareness of humanity. The first, lower half of the Time Scale is subjective and unconscious, and transition to the objective and conscious upper half happens at AD400. Individual life contains a subjective childhood, when we receive impressions and behaviour patterns from the family system, and an objective adulthood, when we act on the received principles. Repetitive history is a development of consciousness that brings both subjective and objective attitudes into play. The development of time concepts in history parallels the similar development in individual life. Aries and Taurus periods are timeless, Gemini is an immediacy of present time, Cancer is an extended present, Leo is a primal grasp of temporal sequences, and Virgo is an extended linear time. We tend not to understand the passage of time until our 23rd year, or its equivalent historical time of AD400. Modern concepts of time are very recent, as mechanical clockworks date back only 500 years, to the same time that humankind discovered the laws of perspective. A worldwide time standard only came into being in 1833.

Temporal laws define the soul when incarnate, but the soul can transcend the space-time continuum and its laws. A soul may have its next incarnation thousands of years ago, and its last incarnation hundreds of years in the future. In eternity, there is no time. The soul comes from the boundless and returns to the boundless, tarrying for periods in bodies in the world of time, but always returning to the timeless, like the pure-energy photon. The stream of consciousness is like a river passing through many different lands and natural conditions. In all mystical philosophies, the godhead emerges from the timeless void, and only after this emergence is time created. The return to unity with God is beyond time but through time.

The Tibetan Book of the Dead describes the events between physical death and rebirth into a new womb as the Bardo states. The soul seeks transcendence in the clear light, vouchsafed all sentient beings, but most are attracted to previous reality or illusory states that are mere substitutes or shades of the transcendent purity. The soul passes through the entire universal process between each birth, and in the birth and death of each moment. All levels are eternally present, from God to reptile.

The Four Bodies

Reincarnation happens on many levels and to many bodies. Four bodies of graduating subtlety incarnate – physical, emotional, mental and spiritual – they are analogous to the elements of earth, water, air and fire. Each body metamorphoses in its own way, and indicates emphasis on specific personal and collective developmental stages.

We create our *Physical Body* in gestation and it reincarnates in two ways. First, it constantly interchanges and modifies its material substance and force with the physical world by chemical changes, physical effects, renewal, and exchanges with other organisms, and

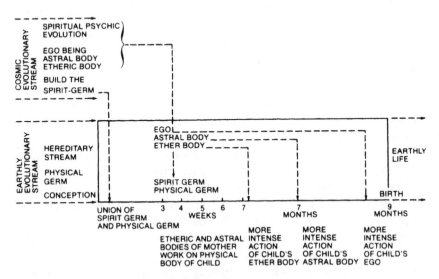

Figure 36: Embryonic Phases of Gestation
The spirit germ activates the physical germ at conception. After seven weeks, or 49 days, the etheric body is formed. The astral body enters at about seven months after conception, and the ego, having entered with the astral, becomes stronger just before birth. (After Wachsmuth, *Reincarnation*)

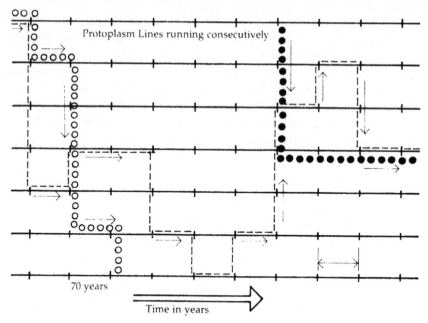

Figure 37: Scientology Reincarnation
The parallel unbroken lines of protoplasm through time form family generations
from grandparents, to parents to children. The dashed line is a Genetic Entity
choosing different protoplasm lines from generation to generation. The circles
of the Theta Being skip from generation to generation without regard to either
proroplasm or GE lines. A human requires the combination of all three, which
accounts for the variety of beings even within the same family. (After Hubbard,
The Ages of Man)

second, it reproduces. The body exchanges its substance with the earth
continuously through life, in a series of bodily incarnations linked by
the same individuality that wears out, passes off, and then attains a new
body. Death occurs when the processes of renewal are not as strong as
the processes of destruction, what Wilber calls the struggle between
Eros and Thanatos.[186] Eros is the drive to perpetuate one's own
existence and Thanatos is everything that carries or threatens
dissolution. These two counter forces are analogous to the Hindu gods
Vishnu and Shiva, or God as Father and Holy Ghost. Reproduction
creates an unbroken line through protoplasmic substance from
generation to generation within the same family. Genealogy traces such
physical connections back into history. The succession of physical
bodies is the most basic form of reincarnation.

The physical body is composed of three components that enter in
sequence during gestation. First, at conception, the *spiritual germ* unites
with the *hereditary stream* in the physical act of conception. Four weeks

after conception, the cellular body begins formation when the fertilized ovum attaches itself to the wall of the uterus, and the *etheric body* links with the spiritual-physical germ. The etheric body is the architect of physical processes, which derives its instructions from the formative forces in the surrounding world and the cosmos. The etheric body is a name for genetic codes that govern and control the formal evolution of the physical body. Scientologists call it the Genetic Entity (GE), which jumps from physical line to physical line in Figure 37. The energetic pattern or morphogenetic field that creates genetic code is the same for all life forms, but utilizes varying combinations of individual components of the code. During gestation, we recapitulate the developmental stages of all life from a one-celled ovum to modern humanity. The process is similar for everyone as a transmission of collective unconscious development. As individual as we feel, we have a common developmental process that is never separate from all other beings. The pure life force of the etheric body carries instinctual urges for survival, sustenance, organ-formation, reproduction and our inner dynamics.[187] Just before birth the astral body, derived from planetary and stellar realms, enters the physical matrix and provides a counterpoint to the biological vital processes of the etheric influence. The astral limits development, makes it concrete and formal, and signals the beginning of consciousness, which is itself a limiting mechanism to pure growth.

We create an *Emotional Body* during childhood, from birth to about seven years old within the context of the home and family system, which contains instinctive and learned responses to the world, behaviour patterns, value systems, emotional expression, and the identification of an individual identity. As the focus in gestation is on the physical and tangible, in childhood the focus is on the relative emotional values to which we are exposed. Personality is the sum total of the various ways in which we see, understand or mask ourselves, and includes the many sub-personalities that we contain. In astrology, the emotional body includes planets in the first four houses and sub-personalities symbolized by planets on or in aspect to the Ascendant. The emotional body surrounds and penetrates the physical body and, being more subtle, senses and perceives a wider range of influences coming from within and the outside world as an instrument of perception. But in turn it is still highly influenced by the atmosphere and nature of the family system.

We create a *Mental Body* during maturity that surrounds and penetrates the physical and emotional bodies, making a trinity of levels of being in the mature human. In the first logarithmic half of its development, from seven to 23 years old, the mental body creates an intellectual perspective formed by family, school, religion and society. It is our ability to create a position in the world and a family, both of which are generators of further karma, and the formation of a 'world view' that will determine our future incarnations.

The *Intuitive or Spirit Body* transcends the triad of personal bodies and is the transition beyond physical, emotional, and mental planes to a realm that activates the others and is in direct connection with the godhead. In Life Time Astrology the spirit body is the higher octave of gestation, including impulses and energies transformed beyond the 'real' life into transpersonal or transcendent life, utilized through creativity and higher purpose. The spirit body symbolizes and identifies with Christ-consciousness or Buddha-nature.

The distribution of planets in the horoscope by octave and element shows the proportional emphasis upon each of the bodies. Gestation (9th, 10th, 11th and 12th house) planets function both on the physical and transcendent levels. Horoscopes with a majority of planets in childhood (1st, 2nd, 3rd and 4th houses) focus in the emotional body and in maturity (5th, 6th, 7th and 8th houses) in the mental body. The element earth is physical, water is emotional, air is mental, and fire is intuitional or spiritual. Everyone is a combination of both systems and contains most if not all four elements and all three octaves. The overall aspect pattern connecting planets and octaves shows the degree of possible integration between components of the self and historical ages. Aspects that contact the centre of the horoscope also provide 'windows to the soul', and access to higher levels of consciousness.

Higher Levels of Being

The scheme of the four bodies is a basic model of the development of consciousness, but there are more elaborate models that utilize seven levels or planes of consciousness through which the soul progresses to reunite itself with the Divinity. Alice Bailey describes a typical model of seven planes in *A Treatise on Cosmic Fire*, which relates to the progress of the soul, the chakras (centres in the energetic body) and the states of enlightenment of Buddhism (see Figure 39). Each of the seven planes of existence has seven sub-planes within, making 49 levels of awareness. The first three planes are personal. The thousand-petal lotus symbolizes our entrance onto the Intuitional plane through initiation, which reminds us of the mathematical scheme of The Divine Plot. The first four planes correspond to the four bodies of Plato.

The *Atmic-Nirvanic Plane* is the fifth plane, the first spiritual plane of

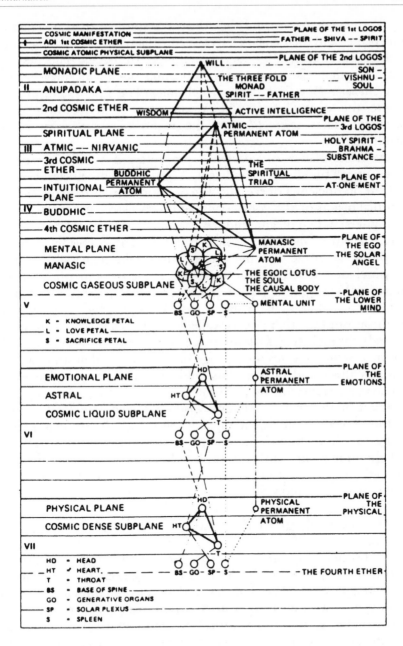

Figure 39: Alice Bailey Esoteric Bodies
The lower half contains the physical, emotional, and lower mental planes. The
higher mental plane is a synthesis of these and a transitional state to higher
intuitional, atmic, nirvanic, monadic, and logoic planes of manifestation. The
complexity of this diagram attests to the many higher levels of being experienced by
certain individuals. (After Bailey, *The Treatise on Cosmic Fire*)

the Permanent Atom, and the apex of a spiritual triad of energies. The planes and their chakra energy centres are lotuses floating on the surface of eternity with varying numbers of petals. The first five lotuses contain 50 petals, again reflecting our divine mathematics. The *Monadic Plane* is a higher level unity. The Logos, the word, is where the qualities of Will, Wisdom, and Active Intelligence originate. The *Logoic Plane* is the realm of pure spirit before manifestation.

Sevenfold planes of existence are referred to in Christianity, Theosophy, Buddhism, Hinduism, Yoga, Judaism, Rosicrucianism, Sufism, in ancient Greece and Egypt, Zoroastrian religion and the spiritual beliefs of the Polynesians, and such a structure is essential to the understanding of any study of the subtle anatomy of humanity.[188]

The sevenfold model is naturally transposed onto a planetary model of the seven planets of the ancient world (although called planets, they include the Sun and Moon as well as the five innermost planets Mercury, Venus, Mars, Jupiter and Saturn). The passage through the planetary spheres is central to Kabala, and in Steiner's Anthroposophy, where it is called *Etheric Astronomy*. Humanity ascends through stages of the planetary spheres in uniting with the cosmos. Steiner locates the passage between life and death as a living through the world of the stars, and identifies humanity in earlier epochs as a transition through the spheres. Mundane astrology is a remnant of the ancient primeval wisdom, which contained an exact methodology describing the metamorphosis of the spiritual-psychic being of humanity. The complex and important process of enlightenment in Anthroposophy describes by transformation through the planetary spheres of the evolution of humanity reflected in the process of individual life.

Astrological Reincarnation Time Scale

The *Astrological Reincarnation Time Scale* (ARTS) is a matrix of information shown on the page tops throughout the sequence of signs in The World Age. The ARTS describes the influences of The World Age as times in history when primary and secondary incarnations register, the historical events to which they are related, and the gods, goddesses and historical individuals who symbolize the incarnations.

The scheme conforms to the structure of the 12 zodiacal signs divided into seven planetary categories. The ARTS uses the scale of dates from 48,000BC until AD1950. The scale of dates tabulates the time in history for each degree of each zodiacal sign. For example,

19° Taurus is equivalent to 17,527BC, 27° Libra is AD1058, and 4° Aquarius is August 1853. The scale compacts logarithmically so that one degree in early Aries is about 1,000 years, in early Leo about 100 years, while a degree in the end of Pisces is one year. It takes a thousand times longer for humanity to experience or perceive developments at the beginning of the Time Scale than at the end. Time passed a thousand times slower, and the world was a thousand times less dense than now. Degrees in the first four signs, from Aries through Cancer, are longer than a lifetime, and therefore describe many generations or lineages of people, like the biblical records of Genesis. From Leo through Scorpio, each degree is a lifetime or less, while from Sagittarius through Pisces, a degree is a quite short period, until they represent singular events rather than lives.

Dates before the historical era of 3000BC encompass long periods of time when no tangible historical events may be dated, but reading across each line shows the harmonics of the original primordial event, bringing it into the recent past.

Table 14: Astrological Reincarnation Time Scale (pages 290-5)

The ARTS shows the gods and individuals that animate the historical World Age from 50,000 years ago to AD1950. To find your previous planetary incarnations, locate the exact date of each planet in your horoscope in the Table of ARTS Dates. Locate the nearest historical prototypes in the appropriate planet's column in the ARTS tables in this section. As the Ascendant and MC are independent of a particular column, read across the entire width of the appropriate sign to find the correct date.

48000BC   Aries to Cancer

	Sun	Moon	Mercury

7000BC — Cancer

City Religion

Feeling and Emotion
Matriarchal
Tigress-Euphrates
Nuclear Family Homes — N
Neolithic Societies — E
Cities and Nations — H
Mythological Religions
Buildings

Sun	Moon	Mercury
Apollo	Artemis	Hermes
Dionysius	Diana	Mercury
Bacchus	Hera	Iris
Hercules	Hestia	Keryx
Talos	Demeter	
Mithras	Kore	
	Sati	
Vil — N	Idunn — N	
HorusOsiris		
Manu — E	Isis — E	Thoth

14000BC — Gemini

Tribal Language

Verbal
Patriarchal
Mediterranean
Instinctive Movement
Communication
Diversification — B
Music and Dance — E
Multi-god Cults — H

Sun	Moon	Mercury
Helios	Selene	Metis
Eos	Skylla	Mnenosyne
Hyperion	Io	Coeus
	Cybelle	Kaius
		Charybdis
		Muses
		Sirens
		Kabiri
Tammuz — B	Sin — B	Bel
Amun/Amon — E	Nut	
Prajapati — H	Soma	

26000BC — Taurus

Earth Mother Cults

Physicality
Matriarchal
Fertility
Domestication of — B
Animals — E
Possessions — H
Bull and Skull Cults — H
Tools

Sun	Moon	Mercury
Ouranos	Gaia	Sky
Nature	Earth/Da	Psyche
Pan	Chthon	Monos
	Io\Fates	Idyia
	Moirae	Telesta
	Nemesis	Tyche
Anu — B	Ishtar/Ea	
Ra/Aten — E	Hathoor — E	Nut
Varuna		
Aditya		

48000BC — Aries

Celestial Nomads

Self-consciousness
Patriarchal
African
Primitive — N
Self-assertion — B
Hunting Bands — E
Celestial Cults — J
Weapons — H

Sun	Moon	Mercury
Heaven	Earth	Aither (Air)
Wind	Eurynome	Boreas
Sky	Tethys	Aeolus
Ophion	Nya(Night)	
	Auka	
	Neith	
— N	Ymir — N	Odin/Wotan
Apsu — B	Tiamat	
Nun — E	Maat — E	Ptah
Jehovah/Adonai		
Brahma/Vishun — H	Maya/Kali — H	Vayu

N=Norse B=Babylonian E=Egyptian H=Hindu J=Jewish

3000BC

	Venus		Mars		Jupiter		Saturn
	Venus		Mars		Jupiter		Saturn
	Europa		Ares		Zeus		Athena
	Daedalus		Adonis		Philos		Proserpina
	Phaethon		Atlas		Balleus		Asklepios
			Priapus		Ktesius		Pan
			Pluto		Prometheus		Minerva
N	Bragi	N	Tur				
E	Nepthys					E	Set
H	Parvati	H	Shiva				
	Nemesis		Hades		Themis		Kronos
	Narkissos		Crius/Krios		Eurymedon		Rhea
	The Graces		The Gorgons				Nepthys
	Lamia		3 Eryines				Hydra
			3 Graiae				Echnida
			Nergal				Sabazius
B	Beltis			B	Marduk	B	Ninurta
		E	Typhon			E	Geb
	Sea		Cyclopes		Poseidon		Mala/Era
	Leda		Neith		Achetos		Persephone
	Ceres		Adonis		Dike		Styx
	Aphrodite		Priapus		Python		Cybelle
			Haephestos				Delphyne
							Moros
B	Astarte	B	Baal				
				H	Brahaspati	H	Bhuta
	Phanes				Okeanos		Chronos
	Protogonos				Metis		Erebos
	Iao/Iahu				Eileithya		Tartaros
	Hemera						Ais
N	Frigga	N	Baldur	N	Thor		
H	Kama	H	Agni	H	Indra	H	Yama

3000BC   Leo to Scorpio

	Sun	Moon	Mercury

AD1100
Scorpio

	Sun	Moon	Mercury
The Middle Ages	1491-1527 **Henry VIII**	1488-1561 Mother Shipton	1486-1535 Agrippa
The Black Death Plagues	1466-1520 Montezuma	**1485-1536 Cath Aragon**	1463-1494 Mirandola
Medieval Societies	1452-1485 **Richard III**	1480-1519 L Borgia	1433-1499 Ficino
Matriarchal	1449-1497 Lorenzo Great	1451-1504 Isabella	1378-1484 Rosencreutz
Medieval Europe	1389-1464 **Cosimo Medici**	1474-1539 **Isabelle Este**	1330-1410 Flamel
Inquisition and Crusades	1348-1413 Henry IV	**1412-1431 Jeanne d'Arc**	**1265-1321 Dante**
Separation	1350-1405 Timurlane	1363-1431 De Pisan	1260-1327 Eckhardt
Feudal and Monastic	1284-1327 Edward III	**1347-1380 Cath Sienna**	1235-1316 Lull
The Cathedrals	1274-1329 Robert Bruce	1303-1380 St Birgitta	**1306-1280 Albert Magnus**
	1216-1294 Kubla Khan	1272-1307 Matilda	1150-1185 ChretienTroyes
	1212-1250 Frederick II	1271-1309 Jean Navarre	1145-1202 Joachim Floris
	1137-1193 Saladin	1256-1301 Gertrude	1126-1198 Maimonides
	1162-1227 Genghiz Khan	**1122-1204 Eleanor Acq**	1128-1198 Averroes

AD400
Libra

	Sun	Moon	Mercury
The Dark Ages	1167-1216 John I	1098-1179 Hildegard Bingen	1039-1105 Rashid
East-West Balance	**1157-1199 Richard I**	c -1097 Trotula Salerno	1020-1078 Psellus
Patriarchal	1068-1135 Henry I	978-1015 Lady Murasaki	1000-1070 Avicebron
China and Islam	1027-1087 William I	935-1002 Hrosvitha	**980-1037 Avicenna**
Sublimation	**848-900 Alfred Great**	901-964 Theodora	772-846 Po Chu-I
Law and Justice	790-823 Mamun Great	752-803 Empress Irene	750- Cybewulf
State-Religion Schism	**742-814 Charlemagne**	**625-705 Empress Wu**	735-804 Albinus
Zen	720-768 Pepin	644-723 Bertha	721-775 Geber
Troubadours	688-741 Chas Martel	c520- Iseult	610-650 Hsuan-Tsung
	c590-628 Li Yuan	c510- Guinevere	c490- Procopius
	c500-550 King Arthur	508-548 **Theodora**	**c480- Merlin**
	400-453 Attila	472-512 Empress Julia	c450- PseudoDionysus
	400-461 Leo I	430-500 St Genevieve	450-540 Eudoxus

AD800
Virgo

	Sun	Moon	Mercury
Classical Civilization	331-363 Julian	325-410 Marcella	340-420 St Jerome
Discrimination	**272-337 Constantine**	**370-415 Hypatia**	293-373 Athanasius
Matriarchal	245-313 Diocletian	307-367 Catherine	185-254 Origen
Greek and Roman	121-180 Aurelius	-230 St Cecilia	150-220 Clement Alex
Classical Learning	76-138 Hadrian	210-254 St Agnes	100- Vitrivius
Culture	37-68 Nero	170-230 Julia Domina	c75- Apollonius
Christianity/Buddhism	**63-14 AD Augustus**	130-212 Irenaeus	**23-79 Pliny**
Classical Architecture	**102-44 Julius Caesar**	20-50AD **Mary**	106- Metrodorus
Rationalism	300-230 Asoka	**69-31 Cleopatra**	372-29 Mencius
	356-323 Alexander	372-318 Philista	500-428 Anaxagoras
	597-562 Nebuchanezar	470-410 Aspasia	**582-507 Pythagoras**
	668-626 Assurbanipal	612- **Sappho**	**551-479 Confucius**
	c820- RomulusRemus	6th- Judith	**606-563 Ezekiel**

3000BC
Leo

	Sun	Moon	Mercury
First Great Civilizations	c970- **Solomon**	c850- Jezebel	
Self-consciousness	1090- **King Wen**	**1194- Helen of Troy**	
Patriarchal	c1150- David	1200- Medea	1122- **Duke Chou**
Babylonian and Egyptian	c1300- **Moses**	c1320- Miriam	
Individuality	1360-1340 Tutankhamen	1360- Meritaton	
Organizations	1375-1350 Amenhotep	1370- Ankhsenamon	
Civilizations	1377- **Rameses**	c1400- **Nefertiti**	1760- **Joseph**
Monotheism	c1900- **Abraham**	1503-1480 **Hatshepsut**	
Temple Monuments	2181-2123 **Hammurabi**	1580-1536 Bathsheba	
Divine Kings	c2300- Sargon	1750- Amat-Namu	
	c2400- **Gilgamesh**	2489-2460 Neter	
	2750- Zozer	2500- Shub Ad	
	2852- Tai Ho	2600- Hetep	

AD1500

Venus	Mars	Jupiter	Saturn
1483-1570 Raphael	1485-1546 Cortez	1491-1556 Loyola	1490-1541 Paracelsus
1465-1560 Michaelangelo	1485-1557 S Cabot	**1483-1546 Luther**	1473-1543 Copernicus
1471-1528 Durer	1480-1521 Magellan	1478-1538 Thomas More	1466-1536 Erasmus
1452-1519 Leonardo Vinci	1460-1524 Da Gama	1469-1539 Guru Nanak	1436-1476 Regiomontanus
1444-1514 Bramante	1469-1527 Machiaveli	1486-1538 Chaitanya	1401-1464 Nicholas Cusa
1404-1472 Alberti	1451-1506 Columbus	1452-1498 Savonarola	1397-1468 Gutenberg
1394-1481 Ikkyu Sogun	1454-1512 Vespucci	1370-1415 Huss	1340-1400 Cresca
1377-1446 Brunelleschi	1450-1498 John Cabot	1304-1374 Petrarch	1220-1296 Campanus
1340-1400 Chaucer	1250-1300 Marco Polo	1265-1308 Duns Scotus	-1288 de Voraigne
1320-1399 Hafiz	1232- Marburg	**1225-1275 St Th Aquinas**	1257-1327 Cecco
1313-1375 Bocaccio	1220-1263 Nevsky	1214-1249 Roger Bacon	1170-1250 Fibonacci
1267-1337 Giotto	1122-1190 Barbarossa	1207-1273 Rumi	1114-1202 Lille
1165-1240 Ibn Arabi	1117-1170 Becket	1081-1170 St Francis	1100-1150 Thierry
1120-1200 Chu Hsi	1070- De St Omer	1090-1153 Gampopa	1033-1109 St Amselm
c -1123 Khayyam	1070- De Payens	1057-1135 Milarepa	973-1040 Al-Biruni
995-1050 D'Arezzo	1042-1099 Urban II	1011-1100 Naropa	965- Alhazen
940-1020 Firdusi	1040-1099 El Cid	968-1069 Tilopa	865-925 Rhazes
c 900- Beiruni	994-1035 Eriksson	c -747 Padmasambhava	786-886 Albumasar
768-824 Han Yin	994-1035 Canute	c -800 Shankarcharya	740-814 Alcuin
c -762 Li Po	956-1015 Vladimir	638-713 Hui Neng	680-741 Leo III
670- Caedmon	764-809 al-Rachid\	c502- Isadorus	673-735 Bede
500- Anthemius	541-604 Sui Wen Ti	570-632 Mohammed	687 Ibn Nafis
c550- Taliesin	c510- Parzifal	c534- St Columba	c598- Brahmagupta
540-604 Gregory	c500- Launcelot	433-468 St Patrick	560-630 Isidore
400-480 Kalidasa	454-526 Theodoric	410-485 Proclus	483-565 Justinian
c450- Musaeus	440-500 Clovis	480-544 St Benedict	c450- Capella
c350- Macrobius	370-410 Alaric	**354-430 St Augustine**	233-303 Porphyry
c250- Ossian	330-380 Sallustus	**216-277 Mani**	280-330 Iambliicus
204-270 Plotinus	160-205 Chang Chou	**c200- Patanjali**	129-182 Ho Hsiu
123-170 Apuleius	53-117 Trajan	4-64 St Paul	**129-199 Galen**
46-120 Plutarch	9-79 AD Vespatian	**0-33 AD Jesus Christ**	**100-178 Ptolemy**
99-55 Lucretius	74-4 Herod	300- Chuang Tsu	287-212 Archimedes
100-29 Virgil	247-183 Hannibal	**284-322 Aristotle**	**c300- Euclid**
106-45 Cicero	**490-449 Pericles**	429-347 Plato	469-379 Hippocrates
496-406 Sophocles	514-449 Themistocles	484-424 Herodatus	c500- Empedocles
495-406 Euripides	521-486 Darius	**479-399 Socrates**	**c540- Democritus**
c500-432 Phidias	c500- Nehemiah	**563-483 Buddha**	c520- Hesiod
525-463 Aesculus	c570- Solon	**c600- Lao Tse**	640-546 Thates
620-560 Aesop	590-529 Cyrus	**620-551 Zoroaster**	c600- Miletus
850- Homer	1190- Menelaeus		
Demodocus			
	1170- Ulysses	**1000- Zoroaster**	
1350- Orpheus	**Aeneas**		**1376- Asklepius**
	1250- Jason	1500- Seheb	
	1300- Cadmus		
		2000- Melchizedek	
2600- Imhotep	**2716- Theseus**		Ur-engur
	Perseus		
	Odysseus	Fu Hsi	

AD1500   Sagittarius to Pisces

	Sun	Moon	Mercury

AD1910 — Pisces

The Great Wars
Disintegration
Germany, USSR and USA
Matriarchal
Karmic Isolationism
Illusion
Abstraction
Nihilism
War Devices

Sun	Moon	Mercury
1948- Prince Charles	1941- Joan Baez	1943- Fisher
1937- Aga Khan IV	1934- Sophia Loren	1935-1996 Carl Sagan
1931- Gorbachev	1932- Eliz Taylor	1929- J Osborne
1935-2000 King Hussein	1929-1994 J Onassis	1927- G Grass
1927- Castro	1929-1983 Kelly-Rainier	1921-1989 Sakharov
1921- Edinburgh	1926-1962 M Monroe	1918- Solzhenitsyn
1918-1981 Sadat	1926- Elizabeth II	1915-1985 Welles
1918-1963 J F Kennedy	1925- M Thatcher	1915- Arthur Miller
1916-1995 Wilson	1921- Friedan	1913-1960 Camus
1913-1994 Nixon	1918-1990 Bailey	1913-1976 Benj Britten
1911-1974 Pompidou	1917-1984 Indira Gandhi	1911-1983 Williams
1911- Reagan	1911-1937 Harlow	1912-1968 Ionesco
1902-1989 Khomeini	1910-1997 Mother Teresa	1911-1982 M McLuhan

AD1840 — Aquarius

Idealistic Nationalism
Humanitarianism
The United States
Patriarchal
Romantic Utopians
Idealism
Bureaucracies and Unions
Victorian Age
Socialism-Communism
Modern Government

Sun	Moon	Mercury
1897-1978 Paul VI	1907-1964 Rach Carson	1901-1988 Ebertin
1893-1976 Mao Tse-Tung	1901-1978 Marg Mead	1901-1978 Walt Disney
1890-1970 De Gaulle	1898-1937 Earhardt	1899-1982 Al Hitchcock
1889-1945 Hitler	1895-1964 Langer	1891-1946 Dion Fortune
1886-1973 Ben Gurion	1890-1960 Th Neumann	1887-1950 Carter
1884-1962 Truman	1884-1962 E Roosevelt	1890-1943 H Zimmer
1883-1945 Mussolini	1879-1966 Marg Sanger	1878-1965 Evans-Wentz
1882-1945 F D Roosevelt	1878-1927 Duncan	1875-1947 Crowley
1879-1953 Stalin	1874-1946 Stein	1861-1925 Steiner
1876-1958 Pius XII	1861-1937 Salome	1857-1942 A E Waite
1868-1918 Nicholas II	1859-1924 Duse	1859-1930 Conan Doyle
1858-1914 T Roosevelt	1858-1928 E Pankhurst	1854-1918 Mathers
1859-1941 Wilhelm II	1844-1923 Bernhardt	1842-1933 Annie Besant

AD1720 — Capricorn

Industrial Revolution
Physical Perfection
England
Matriarchal
Revolutionary Materialism
Nationalism
The Reformation
Capitalist Machine Age
Ascendancy over Nature

Sun	Moon	Mercury
1835-1867 Maximilian	1821-1910 Mary Baker Eddy	1831-1891 M Blavatsky
1830-1916 Franz Joseph	1820-1912 Mary Barton	1821-1880 F Dostoevsky
1818-1881 Alexander II	1820-1910 F Nightingale	1823-1880 Max-Muller
1809-1865 Lincoln	1820-1906 M B Anthony	1812-1870 Chas Dickens
1796-1855 Nicholas I	1819-1901 Queen Victoria	1810-1875 Eliphas Levi
1773-1850 Louis Phillipe	1804-1876 G Sand	1809-1849 E A Poe
1769-1821 Napoleon	1804-1861 E B Browning	1802-1870 A Dumas
1767-1845 Jackson	1759-1797 Mary Shelley	1802-1885 V Hugo
1757-1828 Karl August	1763-1814 Josephine	1799-1850 H Balzac
1754-1793 Louis XVI	1755-1793 M Antoinette	1785-1859 De Quincey
1740-1786 FrederickGreat	1746-1793 Du Barry	1775-1817 Jane Austen
1738-1820 George III	1750-1848 Herschel	1743-1795 Cagliostro
1732-1799 G Washington	1729-1796 Cath Great	1743-1803 St Martin

AD1500 — Sagittarius

The Renaissance
Self-realization
Artistic Perfection
Patriarchal
New Colonial Worlds
Reconstitution
Philosophical Humanism
Wholistic World View
Rebirth to Higher Mind

Sun	Moon	Mercury
1712-1786 Fred Prussia	1717-1780 Maria Theresa	1602-1681 Wm Lilly
1710-1774 Louis XV	1709-1762 Eliz Russia	1586-1654 Andraeae
1672-1725 Peter Great	**1684-1727 Catherine I**	1575-1624 Jacob Boehme
1638-1715 Louis XIV	1665-1727 Anne	1574-1637 Robert Fludd
1630-1685 Charles II	1607-1678 Schurman	1568-1639 Campanella
1600-1649 Charles I	1623-1701 Jane Leade	1565-1622 Meier
1566-1625 James I	1596-1662 Eliz Palal	**1561-1626 Francis Bacon**
1556-1605 Akhbar Great	1591-1643 Hutchinson	1554-1586 Philip Sidney
1552-1612 Rudolf II	1542-1587 Mary Stuart	1548-1600 Giordano Bruno
1532-1592 Wilhelm IV	**1533-1603 Elizabeth I**	**1547-1616 Cervantes**
1530-1584 Ivan Terrible	**1519-1589 Cath Medici**	1534-1577 Isaac Luria
1520-1566 Suleimann	1516-1558 Mary I	**1527-1608 Dr John Dee**
1500-1558 Charles V	1515-1582 Theresa Avila	**1503-1588 Nostradamus**

AD1500

Venus	Mars	Jupiter	Saturn
1941- BobDylan	1943- Lech Walesa	1935- Erhard	1944- Rich Leakey
1940-1980 John Lennon	1942- Muhammed Ali	1933- Dalai Lama XIV	1942- Sheldrake
1935-1977 Elvis Presley	1931-1955 Jas Dean	1931- Rajneesh	1934- Yuri Gargarin
1928-1987 Andy Warhol	1929-1968 M L King	1927- R D Laing	1930- Neil Armstrong
1928- K Stockhausen	1928-1967 Che Guevarra	1925- C Casteneda	1928-1991 M Gauquelin
1928- Ed Albee	1925-1968 R Kennedy	1923-1982 Karmapa Xl	1922-2001 Chr Bernard
1925- Rauschenberg	1919-1949 Ed Hillary	1920- Tim Leary	1921- John Glenn
1925- Pierre Boulez	1919-1972 J robinson	1918- Billy Graham	1916- Crick
1924- M Brando	1918- Schmidt	1915-1982 Watts	1914-1995 Jonas Salk
1924-1987 Jas Baldwin	1916- Mandela	1913-1969 Pike	1913- Lovell
1918-1990 L Bernstein	1914- Heyerdahl	1913- Makarios	1912-1954 Alan Turing
1912-1992 John Cage	1914-1993 Thos Watson	1911- Hubbard	1912-1977 Von Braun
1910-1987 Jean Anouilh	1911-1969 Ho Chi Minh	1910-1955 Rodney Collin	1910- Rich Shockley
1882-1941 Jas Joyce	1906-1975 Onassis	1905-1980 Sartre	1901-1976 Heisenberg
1882-1971 Stravinsky	1908-1976 Hughes	1889-1951 Wittgenstein	1897-1957 Reich
1881-1973 Picasso	1900-1945 Himmler	1888-1974 Assagioli	1896-1980 Piaget
1875-1955 Thos Mann	1900-1976 Mountbatten	1881-1955 de Chardin	1900-1958 Pauli
1875-1926 Rilke	1897-1945 Goebbels	1879-1950 Maharshi	**1885-1962 Bohr**
1874-1951 Schoenberg	**1890-1970 Eisenhower**	**1877-1945 Gurdjieff**	1880-1926 Spengler
1871-1922 Yeats	1885-1945 Patton	1875-1968 Suzuki	**1879-1950 Einstein**
1866-1946 H G Wells	1879-1940 Trotsky	1875-1965 Schweitzer	1874-1937 Marconi
1862-1918 Debussy	**1874-1965 Churchill**	**1875-1961 Jung**	1867-1934 Mme Curie
1860-1911 Mahler	1871-1916 Rasputin	1872-1970 Russell	1863-1947 Ford
1856-1950 Bern Shaw	**1870-1924 Lenin**	**1869-1948 Gandhi**	1854-1932 Eastman
1854-1897 Rimbaud	1853-1902 Rhodes	**1856-1939 Freud**	1847-1922 Bell
1844-1896 Verlaine	1847-1934 Hindenburg	**1844-1900 Nietzsche**	**1847-1931 Edison**
1833-1897 Brahms	1822-1890 Schliemann	1836-1886 Ramakrishna	1837-1915 J P Morgan
1820-1910 Tolstoy	1822-1885 Grant	1820-1903 Spencer	1834-1907 Mendeleev
1813-1883 Wagner	1818-1883 Marx	1817-1862 Thoreau	1831-1879 Maxwell
1810-1849 Chopin	1815-1898 Bismarck	1801-1877 Brigham Young	1822-1865 Mendel
1801-1886 Liszt	1807-1882 Garibaldi	1796-1859 H Mann	1822-1895 Pasteur
1797-1827 Schubert	1804-1881 Disraeli	1788-1860 Schopenhauer	1809-1882 Darwin
1795-1821 Keats	1783-1830 Bolivar	1786-1856 Webster	1766-1844 Dalton
1792-1824 Shelley	1769-1852 Wellington	1776-1822 Hoffman	1738-1822 Herschel
1788-1824 Byron	1771-1858 Owen	1770-1831 Hegel	1744-1829 Lamarck
1770-1827 Beethoven	1768-1818 Tecumseh	1759-1803 Schiller	1743-1794 Lavoisier
1757-1827 Blake	1761-1806 Pitt	1749-1832 Goethe	1733-1815 Mesmer
1750-1791 Mozart	1757-1834 Lafayette	1737-1787 Gibbon	1731-1810 Cavendish
1732-1790 Haydn	1740-1794 Robespierre	1724-1804 Kant	1723-1790 Adam Smith
1685-1759 Handel	1708-1796 Pitt	1717-1778 Rousseau	1706-1790 Franklin
1685-1750 Bach	1700-1750 Walpole	1711-1771 Hume	1701-1783 Euler
1632-1723 Wren	1689-1775 Montesquieu	1709-1784 Sam Jonson	1646-1716 Leibniz
1632-1675 Vermeer	1643-1687 La Salle	**1694-1778 Voltaire**	**1642-1727 Newton**
1608-1674 Milton	1604-1660 Mazarin	1688-1772 Swedenborg	1632-1723 Leuwenhoek
1606-1669 Rembrandt	1600-1658 Shah Jahan	1686-1761 Law	1627-1691 Boyle
1573-1631 Donne	1599-1658 Cromwell	1632-1704 Locke	1578-1657 Harvey
1567-1633 Monteverdi	**1585-1642 Richelieu**	1632-1677 Spinoza	1577-1644 Van Helmont
1564-1616 Shakespeare	1583-1634 Wallenstein	1623-1662 Pascal	**1571-1630 Kepler**
1564-1593 Marlowe	**1552-1618 Raleigh**	**1596-1650 Descartes**	**1564-1642 Galileo**
1552-1597 Spenser	1540-1596 Drake	1585-1642 Richelieu	1550-1614 Napier
1508-1580 Palladio	1536-1598 Hideoyoshi	1542-1591 St John Cross	1546-1601 Brahe
1511-1574 Vasari	1526-1630 Babar	1509-1564 Calvin	1512-1594 Mercator

LOGARITHMIC TIME SCALE

Deg	Pisces	Aquarius	Capricorn	Sagittarius	Scorpio	Libra
00	Jan 1911	Nov 1843	Oct 1719	Jan 1500	AD1309	AD419
01	Oct 1912	Nov 1844	Mar 1724	Jul 1509	1128	449
02	Jun 1914	Nov 1847	May 1729	Oct 3518	1143	478
03	Jan 1916	Sep 1850	Jul 1734	Dec 1527	1161	507
04	Aug 1917	Aug 1853	Aug 1739	Dec 1536	1177	536
05	Mar 1919	May 1856	Jul 1744	Sep 1545	1192	564
06	Oct 1920	Jan 1859	May 1749	May 1554	1208	591
07	Apr 1922	Oct 1861	Mar 1754	Nov 1562	1223	618
08	Sep 1923	May 1864	Nov 1758	Feb 1571	1237	644
09	Mar 1925	Dec 1866	Jun 1763	Jan 1579	1252	670
10	Aug 1926	Jun 1869	Dec 1767	Apr 1587	1266	695
11	Jan 1928	Dec 1871	Apr 1772	Feb 1595	1280	720
12	May 1929	May 1874	Aug 1776	Nov 1602	1294	744
13	Sep 1930	Oct 1876	Nov 1780	May 1610	1307	768
14	Jan 1932	Feb 1879	Jan 1785	Oct 1617	1320	791
15	Apr 1933	Jun 1881	Feb 1789	Jan 1625	1333	814
16	Aug 1934	Sep 1883	Feb 1793	Mar 1632	1346	837
17	Oct 1935	Nov 1885	Feb 1797	Mar 1639	1358	859
18	Jan 1937	Jan 1887	Dec 1800	Jan 1646	1371	881
19	Apr 1938	Mar 1890	Sep 1804	Oct 1652	1383	902
20	Jun 1939	Apr 1892	Jun 1808	May 1659	1394	923
21	Jul 1940	Apr 1894	Jan 1812	Oct 1665	1406	943
22	Sep 1941	May 1896	Aug 1815	Mar 1672	1417	964
23	Oct 1942	Apr 1898	Feb 1819	Jul 1678	1428	984
24	Nov 1943	Mar 1900	Aug 1822	Jul 1684	1439	1002
25	Dec 1944	Feb 1902	Dec 1825	Jul 1690	1450	1021
26	Jan 1946	Dec 1903	Apr 1829	May 1969	1460	1040
27	Jan 1947	Oct 1905	Jul 1832	Mar 1702	1470	1058
28	Jan 1948	Aug 1907	Sep 1835	Oct 1707	1480	1076
29	Jan 1949	May 1909	Oct 1838	May 1713	1490	1094
30	Jan 1950	Jan 1911	Nov 1841	Oct 1719	1500 AD	1109 AD

NB. 0° and 30° of the next sign are synchronous.

Table 15: ARTS Dates 1950 to 1999 – The World Age

The table shows when in history each planetary incarnation registers. Just find the horizontal file for the correct sign – such as Aries or Sagittarius. Then read down the column for the correct degree – 7° or 26°. By reading across the degree file you can find the Harmonic Incarnations before and after the Primary Incarnation.

DATES FROM 48000BC TO AD1950

Virgo	Leo	Cancer	Gemini	Taurus	Aries	Deg
811BC	3000BC	6891BC	13811BC	26117BC	48000BC	00
758	2905	6722	13511	25583	47050	01
705	2818	6557	13216	25059	46118	02
654	2720	6394	12927	24544	45203	03
604	2630	6234	12643	24040	44306	04
554	2543	6078	12365	23545	43426	05
506	2456	5924	12092	23059	42563	06
458	2371	5774	11824	22583	41716	07
412	2288	5626	11561	22116	40885	08
366	2206	5481	11304	21658	40070	09
321	2127	5339	11050	21208	39270	10
277	2048	5200	10803	20767	38486	11
233	1971	5063	10559	20334	37716	12
191	1896	4928	10321	19910	36962	13
149	1822	4597	10087	19493	36221	14
108	1749	4668	9857	19085	35494	15
68	1678	4501	9632	18684	34782	16
29BC	1608	4417	9411	18291	34083	17
AD10	1540	4295	9194	17905	33397	18
48	1472	4175	8981	17527	32725	19
84	1406	4058	8772	17156	32065	20
121	1341	3943	8567	16792	31417	21
157	1278	3830	8366	16435	30782	22
192	1216	3719	8170	16084	30159	23
223	1155	3610	7976	15741	29548	24
260	1095	3503	7787	15404	28948	25
293	1036	3399	7601	15073	28360	26
325	978	3296	7418	14748	27783	27
357	921	3196	7239	14430	27217	28
388	966	3096	7064	14118	28662	29
AD419	811BC	3000BC	6891BC	13811BC	26117BC	30

LOGARITHMIC TIME SCALE (Second Octave)

Deg	Pisces	Aquarius	Capricorn	Sagittarius	Scorpio	Libra
00	28 Nov 1999	3 Nov 1999	19 Sep 1999	1 Jul 1999	9 Feb 1999	2 Jun 1998
01		4 Nov 1999				
02		5 Nov 1999				
03		6 Nov 1999				
04		7 Nov 1999				
05	1 Dec 1999	8 Nov 1999	29 Sep 1999	18 Jul 1999	11 Mar 1999	25 Jul 1998
06	(11.94 hr)	9 Nov 1999				
07		10 Nov 1999				
08		11 Nov 1999				
09		12 Nov 1999				
10	4 Dec 1999	13 Nov 1999	7 Oct 1999	2 Aug 1999	8 Apr 1999	11 Sep 1998
11	(19.28 hr)	14 Nov 1999				
12		15 Nov 1999				
13		16 Nov 1999				
14		17 Nov 1999				
15	6 Dec 1999	18 Nov 1999	15 Oct 1999	16 Aug 1999	2 May 1999	24 Oct 1998
16	(8.43 hr)	19 Nov 1999				
17		20 Nov 1999				
18		20 Nov 1999				
19		21 Nov 1999				
20	8 Dec 1999	22 Nov 1999	22 Oct 1999	29 Aug 1999	24 May 1999	2 Dec 1998
21	(2.97 hr)					
22						
23						
24						1 Jan 1999
25	10 Dec 1999	25 Nov 1999	28 Oct 1999	9 Sep 1999	13 Jun 1999	8 Jan 1999
26	(2.39 hr)					
27						
28						
29						
30	12 Dec 1999	28 Nov 1999	3 Nov 1999	19 Sep 1999	1 Jul 1999	9 Feb 1999

NB. 0° and 30° of the next sign are synchronous.

Table 16: ARTS Dates 1950 to 1999 – The Last Judgement

The table shows the dates when the entire zodiacal sequence compacts in the last 50 years of the 20th century.

FROM JANUARY 1950 TO DECEMBER 1999

Virgo	Leo	Cancer	Gemini	Taurus	Aries	Deg
10 Mar 1997	1 Jan 1995	9 Feb 1991	9 Mar 1984	18 Nov 1971	1 Jan 1950	00
30 Mar 1997	3 Feb 1995	11 Apr 1991	28 Jun 1984	1 Jun 1972	12 Dec 1950	01
17 Apr 1997	9 Mar 1995	11 Jun 1991	13 Oct 1984	10 Dec 1972	18 Nov 1951	02
6 May 1997	12 Apr 1995	9 Aug 1991	27 Jan 1985	15 Jun 1973	18 Oct 1952	03
23 May 1997	15 May 1995	6 Oct 1991	10 May 1985	17 Dec 1973	10 Sep 1953	04
11 Jun 1997	16 Jun 1995	3 Dec 1991	20 Aug 1985	15 Jun 1974	29 Jul 1954	05
29 Jun 1997	17 Jul 1995	28 Jan 1992	28 Dec 1985	9 Dec 1974	9 Jun 1955	06
1 Jul 1997	17 Aug 1995	24 Mar 1992	5 Mar 1986	1 Jun 1975	14 Apr 1956	07
3 Aug 1997	17 Sep 1995	16 May 1992	9 Jun 1986	19 Nov 1975	11 Feb 1957	08
19 Aug 1997	16 Oct 1995	8 Jul 1992	11 Sep 1986	26 Jul 1976	6 Dec 1957	09
5 Sep 1997	15 Nov 1995	29 Aug 1992	12 Dec 1986	16 Oct 1976	23 Sep 1958	10
21 Sep 1997	13 Dec 1995	19 Oct 1992	2 Jan 1987	26 Mar 1977	7 Jul 1959	11
7 Oct 1997	11 Jan 1996	8 Dec 1992	13 Mar 1987	31 Aug 1977	15 Apr 1960	12
22 Oct 1997	7 Feb 1996	26 Jan 1993	29 Aug 1987	2 Feb 1978	14 Jan 1961	13
7 Nov 1997	6 Mar 1996	15 Mar 1993	29 Nov 1987	4 Jul 1978	21 Sep 1961	14
21 Nov 1997	1 Apr 1996	1 May 1993	21 Feb 1988	30 Nov 1978	3 Jul 1962	15
6 Dec 1997	27 Apr 1996	17 Jun 1993	14 May 1988	2 Apr 1979	21 Mar 1963	16
20 Dec 1997	23 May 1996	1 Aug 1993	3 Aug 1988	15 Sep 1979	1 Dec 1963	17
4 Jan 1998	17 Jun 1996	14 Sep 1993	21 Oct 1988	4 Feb 1980	8 Aug 1964	18
17 Jan 1998	11 Jul 1996	28 Oct 1993	7 Jan 1989	22 Jun 1980	11 Apr 1965	19
31 Jan 1998	5 Aug 1996	10 Dec 1993	24 Mar 1989	4 Nov 1980	7 Dec 1965	20
13 Feb 1998	29 Aug 1996	21 Jan 1994	27 Feb 1989	17 Mar 1981	23 Jul 1966	21
26 Feb 1998	20 Sep 1996	3 Mar 1994	19 Aug 1989	25 Jul 1981	21 Mar 1967	22
11 Mar 1998	11 Oct 1996	13 Apr 1994	30 Oct 1989	30 Dec 1981	3 Nov 1967	23
24 Mar 1998	4 Nov 1996	22 May 1994	9 Jan 1990	26 Mar 1982	14 Jun 1968	24
5 Apr 1998	26 Nov 1996	20 Jun 1994	19 Mar 1990	6 Aug 1982	19 Jan 1969	25
17 Apr 1998	18 Dec 1996	7 Aug 1994	26 May 1990	4 Dec 1982	22 Aug 1969	26
29 Apr 1998	15 Jan 1997	14 sep 1994	31 Jul 1990	2 Apr 1983	20 Mar 1970	27
10 May 1998	28 Jan 1997	21 Oct 1994	5 Oct 1990	27 Jul 1983	13 Oct 1970	28
22 May 1998	18 Feb 1997	26 Nov 1994	8 Dec 1990	18 Nov 1983	3 May 1971	29
22 May 1998	18 Feb 1997	26 Nov 1994	8 Dec 1990	18 Nov 1983	3 May 1971	30

Personal Inner Planets

Sun	Creators, fathers, sun gods, heroes, kings, patriarchs, popes, emperors, presidents, lords and the masculine, conscious and objective archetypes.
Moon	Creatrix, earth mothers, chthonic goddesses; queens, empresses, heroines, significant women, matriarchs, unconscious and subjective archetypes.
Mercury	Titans, twin gods, Dioscuri; Intellectuals, orators, authors, critics, mystics, alchemists, magicians, mental and communicative archetypes.
Venus	Fertility and grain goddesses, deities of rhythm, harmony and integration, artists, musicians, architects, poets, playwrights, dramatists, aesthetic and creative archetypes.
Mars	Heroic, deities of war, energy, and destruction; heroes, conquerors, generals, politicians, explorers, tyrants, martyrs, athletes, masculine aggressive archetypes.
Jupiter	Wise, procreative, expansive deities; Prophets, religious leaders, philosophers, psychologists, sages, saints, expansive and wise old man archetypes.
Saturn	Paternal, orderly, material deities; Scientists, doctors, mathematicians, inventors, bankers, and the repressive father archetypes.

Collective Outer Planets

Uranus	Magicians, inventors, eccentrics, intuitive scientists.
Neptune	Psychics, mediums, sensitives, drug addicts, dreamers.
Pluto	Warriors, political leaders, politicians, transformers, revolutionaries.

Personal Points

Ascendant	Personality, personal characteristics, environmental qualities, ways of acting, physical appearance, milieu.
Midheaven	Spiritual awareness, ego-consciousness, objectives, sense of purpose.

The *Sun* is the primary masculine incarnation and describes fatherly qualities, consciousness, self-awareness, and sense of objectivity. The Sun in one of the first four signs creates a paternal sense that is mythical and often omnipotent, in the sign Leo kingly, in Scorpio inquisitorial, or in Aquarius Victorian.

The *Moon* is the primary feminine incarnation and shows motherly feelings, emotions, the ability to nurture, protect and the valuing mechanisms. The Moon in the first four signs is the mythical divine mother in her protective and devouring form as Kali. In Aries the Moon evokes the emotional reality of a cavewoman, in Virgo it represents an early Christian virgin, in Scorpio a Joan of Arc, and in Aquarius a Victorian matron.

Mercury is the intellect, the quality of intelligence, communicative abilities, mental set and ideas about the self and the world. Mercury in Gemini is a continual invention of language or means of communication, in Virgo is the classical scholar, while in Pisces is illusory media and cinema.

Venus is the aesthetic sense, creativity, cultural affinities, and the quality of relationships, as well as sexual mores, attractions and taste in people. Venus in Taurus is raw sensuality, in Libra by chivalric idealism, in Sagittarius Shakespearean bawdiness.

Mars is the warrior, aggressive, changing by force, and exploratory, and the urge to destroy and revel. Mars in Aries is celestial assertion, in Virgo the Homeric hero, in Scorpio the Crusader and in Capricorn the robber baron.

Jupiter is the religious belief system or philosophical stance that creates a world view. Jupiter in Taurus worships the earth mother, in Cancer the home and family, in Aquarius worships the machine. Religions change from sign to sign. Jupiter in mid-Virgo would be early Christians contemporary with Jesus Christ or Gnostics, in Scorpio crusaders, in Sagittarius reformation Protestants, in Pisces atheists or existentialists.

Saturn describes the incarnation that determines the attitude to reality and the degree of scientific understanding and the material attitude. Saturn in Aries accepts only what it can see and touch. Saturn in Leo is the divine right of the Caesar in Libra Roman law, and in Aquarius it is the rule of the capitalist factory owner.

The *Outer Planets* move slowly and in birth horoscopes describe collective influences shared by entire generations. In to respect reincarnation, they do not have their own column of influence, but are a band across all seven planets with a strong focus on the planet of which it is a higher octave. *Uranus* is the higher octave of Mercury; it is an incarnation representing eccentricity, individuality, independence and inventiveness. *Neptune* is the higher octave of Venus; it is an incarnation representing psychic influences, mediumship, sensitivity, weakness and contact with disease. Often Neptune registers when psychic regression is the keynote, and is times in history that contain mystical and magical connections. *Pluto* is the higher octave of Mars and indicates the incarnation that was most revolutionary, transformative and had the greatest contact and influence upon the masses.

The *Personal Points* are more general influences, shown as a band across the entire ARTS. The *Ascendant* is very important as it describes the time in history of the personality, physical appearance, and environmental characteristics. The *Midheaven* is ego-consciousness, spiritual realization, and objectives in life related to an incarnative time in history. The personal points are often a combination of many influences, rather than one in particular.

Constellations of more than one planet signify powerful times of influence, where multiple influences are in operation. If the Sun and Venus are conjunct in 10° of Sagittarius in the birth chart, indicating artistic or aesthetic aspirations and awareness, the reincarnation influence could be a man who was artistic in 1587, or a young woman who exhibited a very strong consciousness, and the influence combines the two categories. Planets such as Mercury (intellect), Jupiter (religion), and Saturn (practical influences) in the sign Virgo, the time of classical civilization, would be appropriate for a classicist who specialized in language and religions.

Aspects in the horoscope indicate planets that are in relationship with each other, and the same logic transposes into the reincarnation scheme. Aspects in the ARTS show connections between historical periods and their equivalent incarnations. For example, planets in opposition between the signs Leo and Aquarius are in opposing eras in history. The Leo time (3000 to 800BC) is the age of kings when the individual was highly valued, while the Aquarius time (1840 to AD1910) is the antagonistic Victorian era when social causes and the collective national attitudes totally dominated society and signalled the effective end of monarchy. Supportive aspects such as trifles show octave developments of a similar theme. In Leo time, the individuality originated and self-consciousness developed, and in the next fire sign, Sagittarius the humanistic Renaissance man was valued. The aspects are harmonics, and we read them along each horizontal file.

Reincarnation Case Histories

The positions of the planets and personal points in the horoscope indicate twelve primary incarnations and their historical times. The mechanism may be symbolic historical characters that influence future generations with their ideas or personalities. It also shows influence from previous generations. Although the mathematics of The Divine Plot is quite specific, you should allow a certain leeway, in keeping with the acceptable margin of error in astrology of one degree each way, a deviation of 00.27%.

A well-known case of reincarnation is *Napoleon Bonaparte*, who believed himself to be a reincarnation of Alexander the Great (356-323BC is 9° to 10° Virgo) and Charlemagne (AD742-812 is 12° to 15° Libra). Napoleon has Neptune (psychic connection) at 9° Virgo, which

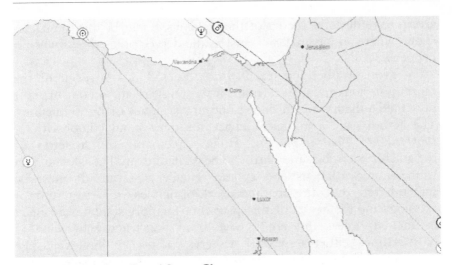

Figure 40: Napoleon Local Space Chart
Napoleon's local space chart shows his Leo sun corresponding to the height of
Egyptian culture passing near Cairo. *(Local Space Chart by Matrix Software)*

registers in 377BC; Mars (warlike influence) at 12° Virgo, which
registers in 233BC; and a square from Uranus (individuality and
inventiveness) at 11° Virgo retrograde (moving backwards), which
registers in 254BC. The Ascendant in Napoleon's horoscope is 16°
Libra, showing that his personality is within one degree of the time of
Charlemagne. What is even more amazing, in a speculative chart for
Alexander, he has planets registering in the time of Napoleon!

Using a new technique pioneered by Michael Erlewine, called Local
Space, the lines of planetary force are mapped onto the globe.
Napoleon has a Sun Leo line passing through Egypt, where he sent his

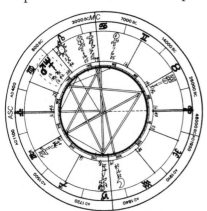

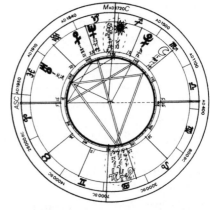

Figure 41: Napoleon Buonaparte
Born 15 August 1769 at Ajaccio, Corsica.

Figure 42: Michele de Nostradamus
Born 14 Dec 1503 at St Remy, France.

armies to retrieve the secrets of the pharaohs. It may be that these lines shows where an incarnation is just as the degree point shows when it happens.

The great prophet and seer *Nostradamus* (1503-1566) is one of the most mysterious and magical individuals in history, and no one has ever presented a theory to explain the uncanny accuracy of his predictions. The author gave astrological advice for the second edition of *The Prophecies of Nostradamus* by Erika Cheetham, and a series of remarkable facts became clear.[189] The structure of The Divine Plot from a time after its end is intellectually satisfying. It must be remembered that the mathematical principles, the structure of astrology and the nature of the space-time memory system were intact in ancient times, and could have been constructed by such as Nostradamus, either as part of a secret tradition or intuitively. The horoscope of Nostradamus is interesting because one planet, Pluto, registers during his lifetime and a number of planets register after his lifetime in the ARTS, coincidentally at the times of his most accurate future prophecies. The implication must be that Nostradamus had experienced and remembered his future as well as past incarnations. Pluto registers at 6° Sagittarius 12°, equivalent to a date of 1556, when Nostradamus was 53 years old. The year is highly significant because of the story of Nostradamus' most famous prediction. In the first edition of his *Centuries* in 1555, Nostradamus predicted the death of King Henri II in Century I, 35, in a duel. The quatrain reads: 'He will pierce his eyes in their golden cage; two wounds in one, then he dies a cruel death.' Because of the prediction, Queen Catherine de Medici summoned him to the French court on 14 July 1556 to explain the prophecy. Henri II fulfilled the prediction in 1559, when he died in a joust when an opponent's spear shattered, piercing his golden helmet and wounding him in the neck. He lived in agony for 10 days before he died. Nostradamus also predicted that four of Catherine and Henri's children would be kings, which was true. The registration of Pluto (the masses and powerful people, magical influence over others) in the 8th house of death and the sign Sagittarius of sporting events, merged in the most critical time of his life.

The planets that register in the ARTS after the lifetime of Nostradamus are highly significant. Coincident with the Sun at 1° Capricorn, Nostradamus predicted the Accession of George I in 1714. In Century III,77 he predicted the exact date of a treaty between the Persians and Turks in October 1727, within a degree of his Midheaven at 2° Capricorn. The registration of Neptune in 22° Capricorn, dated in 1815, fits with his numerous and very precise predictions concerning Napoleon's 100 days, his escape from Elba and the Battle of Waterloo

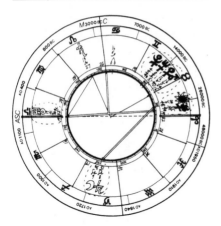

Figure 43: Adolf Hitler
Born 20 April 1889, Branau, Austria.

Figure 44: Thomas Mann
Born 6 June 1875, Lubeck, Germany.

in 1815 in Centuries I,23, II,70, IV,75 and X,24. At the registration of Venus at 2° Aquarius in 1848, he accurately predicted the creation of the National Assembly of 1848 (IX,5), very descriptive of the integration (Venus) of a group (Aquarius), the involvement of Napoleon III in French revolutionary activity, and the Marriage of the Count de Chambard. One of the more notorious quatrains, describing the Munich Putsch started by Adolf Hitler in 1923, coincides exactly with Uranus at 8° Pisces. The opposite point to his Saturn at 15° Cancer coincides with the French Revolution of 1789 to the year. The correlations are truly astonishing.

Another example is the horoscope of *Adolf Hitler*, the Austrian maniac who professed strong belief in a mystical inheritance of the Aryan racial memory and was obsessed with the Grail legend. The strong and unconscious influence he had upon the German nation can be understood in six planets and the Midheaven that register in the first four signs, Aries, Taurus, Gemini and Cancer. The conjunction of Neptune and Pluto describes 'the supernatural, clairvoyant visions, a magical influence over the masses, as well as manias, self-torment, peculiar states of soul experience and possession',[190] and its location in Gemini indicates a magical power from the use of language and communication alone – a fact in Hitler's rise to power.

A most fascinating example of reincarnation theory is the great German novelist *Thomas Mann* (1875-1955) and his masterwork *Joseph and His Brothers*, started in 1927 and not finished until 1944. In the first of the four volumes, *Tales of Jacob*, Mann frequently refers to the astrological heritage of Joseph's time and specifically describes the positions of the planets and personal points in the horoscope of Joseph using Persian terminology. When translated, Joseph and

Thomas Mann have the same horoscope! In both horoscopes, the Gemini Sun is conjunct the Midheaven, indicating a noon birth, the sign Virgo is rising on the Ascendant and the Moon is in Cancer:

As there is no knowledge that Thomas Mann knew astrology, it would be natural for him to use his own horoscope as that of Joseph, but the agreement between the two lives is striking. It would seem obvious that Mann felt a sympathy and strong connection to Joseph, but the life parallels are beyond chance because the Bible records the plot of the Joseph story. What is amazing is that the life of Joseph is prophetic of Thomas Mann's life during the years when he wrote the novel. Many of the events in Mann's life happened after he had written about them in Joseph's story. The parallels are below:

Joseph	Thomas Mann
– The youngest son in large family	– The youngest son in large family
– Competitive with older brothers	– Competitive with brother Heinrich
– Mocked his brothers	– Buddenbrooks exposed the bourgeois
– Given coat of many colours	– Awarded the Nobel Prize
– Abandoned by brothers in a well	– Rejected by Heinrich and the Nazis
– Lived in exile in north Egypt	– Lived in exile in Switzerland
– Moved again to southern Egypt	– Moved again to Princeton, USA
– Supported by Potiphar	– Supported by publisher in New York
– Rejected advances from P's wife	– Rejected advances from P's wife
– Moved again to acclaim	– Moved to California with acclaim
– Interpreted the Pharaoh's dream	– Convinced Roosevelt about WW2 coming
– Was honoured for patriotism	– Honoured for support
– Reunited with his brothers	– Sponsored Heinrich in the USA

It is tempting to speculate that Thomas Mann *was* formerly Joseph in the biblical story. This very powerful novel occupied 17 years of his most creative time.

Another interesting aspect of Thomas Mann's horoscope is its connection to the ARTS times when his novels were set. Mann's primary concern was with language, reflecting the Sun (spiritual centre and vitality) and the Midheaven (ego-consciousness and spiritual awareness) both in Gemini, the time when language was developed. The mythical Moon in Cancer corresponds to an ancient Indian legend about the true love of a woman in *The Transposed Heads*. Uranus in Leo registers at the time of the patriarch Abraham, very much contemporary to the Joseph story, and very near the time of the short story *The Tables of the Law*. Jupiter in AD964 falls near the time of Pope Gregory, the central character in *The Holy Sinner*. Mars in Capricorn occurs at about the time of his short novel *Royal Highness*. The most significant correlation, however, is the registration of Saturn (hereditary influences) at the time when his first great novel, *Buddenbrooks*, about a family dynasty based on his own family, took place. The principle that creative people work out reincarnation influences that derive from the times in history when their planets register is a very helpful and intriguing way to use the mechanism of the ARTS.

Varieties of Reincarnation

The history of reincarnation ideas is very wide and vague. Two wonderful books describe people and groups in history who have supported some form of reincarnation. *Reincarnation: An East-West Anthology* by Head and Cranston includes quotations from over 400 Western thinkers, including those already mentioned, as well as Thomas Huxley, Albert Schweitzer, Thomas Edison, Walt Whitman, Emerson, Thoreau, Tom Paine, William James, Carl Jung, Hesse, J B Rhine, Darwin, Einstein, Planck, Schrodinger, Fromm, Henri Bergson, Flaubert, Kierkegaard, Ibsen and many others. A sequel, *Reincarnation: The Phoenix Fire Mystery*, is a comprehensive look at reincarnation with a focus on scientists and various national cultural contexts. Terms used include palingenesis, pre-existence, transmigration, and rebirth, as the word 'reincarnation' did not come into vogue until the French introduced the term in the middle of the last century.

While the actual mechanism of reincarnation is unknowable except on a psychic level, the most thorough understanding of it is Eastern:

> *The ancient Indian thinkers believed that the happenings in an individual's present life are to be understood against the background of the previous life, which itself is to be looked upon as the nearest link in a beginning less series of rebirths. 'Avidya' itself is something that does not have a beginning in time: it is beginningless. Thus it is supposed that the mind of a newborn infant is, at birth, full of traces (samskaras) of those actions that were made over countless past lives, for the embryo in the mother's womb is itself supposed to be equipped with these samskaras, for they form a part of the subtle body luga sharira, which leaves one gross body at the time of death, entering into an embryo as guided by the samskaras.*[191]

The discovery of genetic code has allowed the concept of reincarnation to be seen in a different light. Reincarnation is a collective phenomenon because all life is the cumulative effect of many former lives, parallel to the action of genetics. Every being carries, via genetics, a history back to the first life, and before that to the creation of the world. The qualities that differentiate one individual from another are the result of the dominance of certain genetic impulses over others, in turn formed by the karma of the incarnating soul. Everyone has the same fund of possibilities, but the drive to manifestation varies in strength and qualities. That we derive certain qualities from father or mother, or grandparents is verifiable, but to go further back is impossible due to the lack of information – such as photographs, birth records, biographical information, and so on. When one's genetic line is taken back one hundred years, the qualities inherited from any one ancestor is 1:4000, while back one thousand years, a brief time in the total span of history, all family lines converge, and 15,000 years ago even racial differences disappear. The similarities between all present humans are more than 95% of the total pattern. Reincarnation is the forerunner of genetics, and is a superior knowledge because it is concerned with more than only the protoplasmic line, and addresses the differential requirements of the other, higher bodies in the process of cosmic manifestation. The Divine Life is the integration of traditional reincarnation technology and modern genetics, and an attempt to quantify and qualify the individual inheritance.

Individuals 'remember' past lives when they feel the resonance of historically based genetic and spiritual impulses activated by contact with artefacts, places, other individuals, or information. Instead of valuing only those inherited qualities which are quantifiable – like hair and eye colour, facial structure, weight and height – the qualities derived from historical ways of behaving, holding a world view or instinctively acting can be correlated with astrological qualities that may be checked against a birth horoscope. Although in the early stages, a new science of reincarnation is beginning.

The concept of planetary bodies implies multiple ways of reincarnation. The physical incarnation process is tangible and follows the protoplasmic family trees without the freedom to deviate, and is carried strictly through the protoplasmic line. The physical line carries all impulses derived from the family descent, but focuses on those that correspond to the Ascendant position in the horoscope. The emotional incarnation is a finer process, not limited by the direct substance of which the body is composed but changes, jumping from family to family within a general racial and hereditary pattern, and which the Moon activates in the horoscope. The Moon characteristics may lie dormant for generations, and may activate qualities that originate from outside of the direct protoplasmic line. The Moon is equivalent to the Genetic Entity. Each planetary body reincarnates at certain times in history, has an effect upon the individual life, and passes on to other lives.

Planetary positions in the birth horoscope determine the relative importance of our historical periods or incarnations. Planets near the

Ascendant are sub-personalities. Planets near the MC, at the apex of the horoscope, are the most conscious. Planets in the 7th house would affect the nature of partners and relationships.

This group of space-time beings symbolize the potential for integration of our birth chart in various historical manifestations, as we attempt to discover a higher purpose. Afflicted planets are difficult individuals or indicate an imperfect understanding of a particular lifetime. As in personal psychology, each planetary sub-personality attempts to dominate the whole by recreating its natural time and mode of consciousness and behaviour, as sub-personalities can dominate an individual. Present-time reality is a collage of historical beings and their times joining, conflicting or integrating. Everyone is a multi-temporal being, eternally shifting from one identity to another. The only ordering possible is to encompass all time and determine how to express all natural instincts and modes of consciousness. Each individual component is unique and potentially dominant, but the whole serves to integrate experiences of all components. We must identify our historical parts before we can liberate ourselves from them.

According to the *pattern* of the birth chart, there is either a representative selection of times (splay shape), a concentrated focus (bundle shape), an awareness of half of reality (a bowl shape) or a seesaw from one constellation of attitudes to others opposite (sling shape). Closer groupings weight the whole towards one particular attitude and its time, and show an attempt to revive the spirit of the time irrespective of the other times. The process works two ways. Each person has certain interests and a worldview derived from the times in history that struck a familiar chord, and seeks confirmation of this approach to life. Some people allow their love of historical games or attitudes to dominate them, at the expense of the whole.

The aware individual has primary consciousness only of the stage in which they live in the present time, with partial access to the octave immediately before or after. In gestation, previous lives are simultaneously lived, and in childhood, the gestation octaves of previous lives are manifest, although most societies invalidate such memories. There have been many cases of young children remembering past lives so vividly that they recognize immediately objects, words, and ideas very alien to their new life. Such a process is in action in the selection of Tibetan Buddhist Lamas' incarnations, in fact a young Westerner who is the incarnation of a high Tibetan Buddhist lama. He discovered this at the age of seven years old in Kathmandu. Usually, once the 5th house cusp has been passed at about seven years old and the octave of maturity entered, the memories of previous incarnative influences begins to fade, if not disappear totally.

Taste, fashion, faddism, revivalism, romanticism, historicism, and pragmatism are all snares to entrap the unwary in history. We can absorb ourselves into the past, drawn into attitudes that mirror illusory parts and take away from the whole, just as in life the trap of family or individual psychological patterns are often total and binding. The mechanism of former realities can dominate, cycle after cycle. It is necessary to disidentify from such historical patterns in order to transcend their bondage. Attraction influences future incarnations, as similar periods are returned to, time after time. Multiple personalities result when the identities have no knowledge of each other and create inner collisions. The creative process of collating spatio-temporal existences is part of the individuation and transpersonal processes in psychology. It is necessary for us to grasp the connection between our various identities as related to each other, no matter how unlikely, and to combine them to generate a true whole.

Plato believed that our current lives bind most of us. When given the opportunity at death to transcend their limitations, to move to a higher state, they choose to live their previous life again, regardless of the pain or entrapment implied by that life. The fear of the unknown is stronger than the desire for liberation. This principle permeates not only the individual in the incarnation process, but also our world age. In order to transform our world, everyone must be willing to give up their past patterns of which they are enamoured. We must know the nature of life and the world before we can liberate ourselves.

Chapter Twelve — The Divine Life

The world itself is the judgement of the world.[192]

Schopenhauer

The end of a World Age of humanity is a terrifying prospect that many would think a very negative speculation. Not only is it a possible projection of the immediate future, but it is also a story that forms the nucleus of all mythical representations of the nature of the world. Myths are the essence of religious, political and social systems. Investigating the mechanism of the End of the World allows speculation on the elusive key to what is happening in the world now, where the evolution of consciousness is leading, and presents a way to come to terms with The Divine Life.

There are many ways to interpret The Divine Life: as history, as a metaphysical speculation, as a key to the nature of the world, as a programme for the human bio-computer, as a religious stance, or as a description of the physical world. The scientist might criticize the free use of science, where some principles are accepted and used as evidence, while we openly negate others, but that is common scientific practice. The search for physical laws is fruitless because we must modify laws as understanding increases. The psychiatrist might resist combining behavioural principles with the workings of the mundane world. The astrologer might resent their sacred science dragged down into physical manifestation. The transpersonal psychologist might feel that a circular view of time is too fated and closed, and would not allow freedom for self-expression. The historian might find the history described inaccurate and incomplete, dealing as it does with both inner and outer history. The optimist might resist what seems like a negative picture of the world – after all, the Aquarian Age is just around the corner. It is difficult to satisfy everyone, but everyone is a part of time and history. We must create and then work with models, even if they

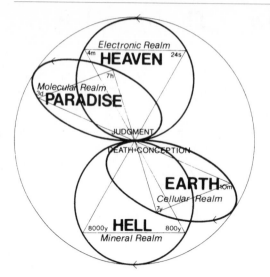

Figure 45: Four Worlds
The four circles at right angles to each other symbolize the relationship between the four dimensions of human existence. The horizontal circles are the Cellular world of our visible body and the Molecular world of our invisible body. They intersect at the moment of conception and death. The lower circle is the Hellish mineral domain and the upper circle is the Heavenly Electronic Realm of pure spirit. Collin considered the Four Worlds a philosophical machine. (After Collin)

prove to be inaccurate, if they further understanding and compassion for life on earth.

In the West we focus upon extending the duration of life, thereby conquering time, while the traditional Eastern goal is liberation from the wheel of time and karma, an end to the series of incarnations. In this sense, history is a programming from which we must escape. Rodney Collin's 'Four Worlds' from his book *The Theory of Eternal Life* shows two horizontal circles that are the 1,000 lunar month lifetime of the cellular body, and the one lunar month lifetime of the ovum. They intersect like the symbol for infinity at the point of conception and death. An individual experiences an entire lifetime in essence during the lunar month of the ovum, and the cellular life then unfolds in its own time. By using the familiar factor of 1,000, Collin states that the next longer phase of 80,000 years would be equivalent to life in the mineral realm, where change is excruciatingly slow, pressure is great and heat intense – like what we call hell. At death, at the intersection of the cellular and molecular circles, it is possible, if the identification with material goods or precious metals is dominant enough, to descend to the hellish mineral realm. Instead of experiencing a lifetime of about 80 years until the next opportunity for liberation, the wait is 1000 times longer. Every body is composed of mineral elements and has access to their equivalent time perspective. The importance of precious metals like gold and silver, or gems like diamonds and rubies, stems from the sense of immense time that they encapsulate. If descent into the mineral realm is hell, Collin postulates that ascent into the higher electronic realm is heaven. The heavenly realm is always available, and we can compare it to transpersonal or transcendent energies ready to merge with the self. The sphere in which all four circles of existence spin around their axes is a fifth dimension of eternal recurrence, or the revolution of things in their own place. A sixth dimension where all four circles spin around their meeting point is the world in which everything is everywhere and 'all possibilities are realized'.[193] Beings who live in a higher state than the four sensible worlds have gone beyond the sphere of earthly beings and are free of the sun, the galaxy and the universe. Physical existence requires obedience to the cyclic laws of the various circles of being. In the context of the Universal Time Scale, we cannot escape, even though it seems that movement from one octave level to another, finer level constitutes heaven. Whatever the octave, the same laws are in operation relative to that dimension. The only liberation is beyond the world of such laws, into the timelessness associated with God. Liberation is unity with God.

Now the world is in a state of chaos that is beyond comprehension. The world is in great peril through:

1. Population explosion
2. Food crisis
3. Resource scarcity
4. Environmental degradation, ecological imbalance due to burning fossil fuels, deforestation due to acid rain or pollution
5. Nuclear abuse by design or accident from weapons and power plants
6. Science and technology unleashed
7. Political anarchy on a worldwide scale
8. Freak climatic catastrophes

The world is in danger of self-destruction. Everyone alive now is responsible for the state of affairs, and for any potential change of that state. Whatever the means by which a world age ends, it brings with it an inevitable necessity for deep revaluation. Whether the end of the World Age is a necessary step in the creation of an enlightened world, or an actual cataclysm, we must face the reality of it. We assume that this is the first time such a crisis of preservation has occurred, yet persuasive evidence shows that it may not be the first time.

An age of darkness follows the end of a World Age, just as an age of darkness preceded the present cycle of civilizations. Whatever the cause of the End of the World, there are survivors. The enormity of the conflict that creates the End is too much to comprehend, and those who survive wander through the world reverting to primitive reality. Those prepared to understand and confront the End of the World must develop rituals to carry on the meaning of the End from generation to generation. The purpose is multifold. On the mundane level, it is to ensure survival on the principle that to know the problem is the first step to preventing its recurrence, but on a higher level it is to carry over into the next world knowledge of the sacred. The ritual of the end of a world is a unique heritage of all humans, and the death and burial rituals are a re-enactment of the ultimate event.

Can it be possible that the world as we know it will end? All it takes is a look at the daily news to see that the entire world is in violent chaos right now. People are killing each other in ever-increasing numbers. The quantity of information available increases every day, and most individuals are submerging themselves in meaningless media. Large computers go down, planes crash and whole industries stop. People are unhappy amid the greatest opulence ever imagined. We travel more each year on holiday than the greatest travellers the world knew 500 years ago in a lifetime. Our annual income is more than a lifetime of wages 50 years ago. The world is already very different from the world we were prepared to grow up in as children. Many people wish it all to end.

There are many different theories to account for what is happening in our world today. Five of the more prominent theories follow. Much of the material they present is included within the wide range of The Divine Life.

Contemporary Theories of Universal History

The Divine Life combines mechanisms from mythology, science, psychology, history, anthropology, and many others, organized by the cosmic art and science astrology. Other ways of organizing the universal process are useful as comparison and show that the UTS integrates many of their ideas. These are: *The Reflexive Universe* by Arthur M Young, the inventor of the Bell helicopter; the Holographic Theory of Mind from *The Invisible Landscape* by Dennis and Terence McKenna, botanists, anthropologists, and philosophers; *Up From Eden* by the transpersonal psychologist Ken Wilber; *Earth Ascending* by Jose Arguelles; and *Exo-Psychology* by Timothy Leary, the prophet of psychedelics. Although written from various viewpoints, the conclusions are very similar and consistent.

1. The Reflexive Universe: Evolution of Consciousness[194]

Arthur Young proposes a 'theory of process' of seven stages in the sequence Light, Particles, Atoms, Molecules, Plants, Animals, (Man), which has a distinctive pattern including a 'fall' or descent into matter. Although he starts with the mechanics of the torus form, the seven

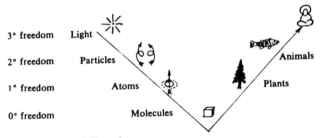

Figure 46: Kingdoms of Freedom
The relative kingdoms of the natural world represented as a symmetrical fall from
the uncertainty of photons to the total bond of molecules, followed by an ascent
from animals to humanity. (After Young)

stages follow a V-shape with four Kingdoms of Freedom of action,
with molecules as the fulcrum at the depth of the descent with no
freedom at all. Atoms and plants reflect each other with 1° of freedom,
followed by particles and animals with 2°, and light and man with three
degrees. Young ingeniously correlates the model to quantum
mechanics, the structure of the Periodic Table of the Elements,
mechanisms in chemistry, physics, psychology, and the natural world.
He subdivides each Kingdom of organization into seven stages of
potential, binding, identity, combination, growth, mobility and
dominion. The grid theory compares with the mythologies that
describe sevenfold processes of creation, including Iranian, Greek,
Mayan, and Egyptian myths and Genesis. He presents a Teleology of
seven stages of human evolution of consciousness from Spirit-1 down
to Soul-1 down to Mind-i down to Body, and then as ascent from
Mind-2 to Soul-2 to Spirit-2. His conclusion is that the photon of light
falls into matter, there to undergo its transformations until in the
process of the creation of the light, it recognizes itself.

2. 'The Invisible Landscape: Mind, Hallucinogens and the I Ching'[195]

The McKennas' theory is derived from shamanism via the effects of
psychoactive drugs upon the psyche, and is a computer-generated time
scale based on the Chinese I Ching. They understand that the interaction
of two hyper-universes as a hologram created by the interaction of two
lasers create the world. Every part contains the information of the whole
– every atom is the brain of the whole universe. Certain hallucinogens
create transmitters that allow the mind to tap into the cyclic processes of
DNA and RNA, possibly by activating melatonin and pineal serotonin. A
cyclic recurrent universe on many different scales grows directly from the
idea. Hallucinogens alter metabolism by affecting the electron spin

resonance (ESR) of genetic molecules, and encourage the nervous system to resonate with the waveform hologram of the universe. ESR molecules are superconductors of the holographic information storage system containing all genetic and experientially coded information within its wave pattern.

They base their mathematics on the hexagrams of the I Ching, creating 64 exponential time-scales that exist in the universe – all are collective and will all peak together in the year AD2012. The concept is similar to The Divine Plot, particularly in the use of lunar months as the units for the time-scale. The following scales all peak together:

— A 4,300-year cycle from urbanization to modern science
— A 384-year cycle in which science has dominated humanity
— A 67-year cycle from the 1940s when DNA and nuclear energy were discovered, when there is more acceleration than from the Renaissance to the present
— A 384-day cycle in 2011-2012 when there will be more transformations than in all previous cycles
— A six-day cycle at the end; leading to

In the last 135 minutes, 18 barriers, comparable to the appearance of life, the invention of language or the achievement of immortality, will be crossed, 13 of them in the last 75×10^{-4} seconds.

Access to the quantum information system is movement into the Faustian universe, and psychedelics are one way to make the transition. The McKennas believe that humanity is in a unique position to accomplish a Resurrection into the Light, of which the Gnostics and alchemists dreamed.

3. 'Up From Eden: A Transpersonal View of Human Evolution'[196]

Ken Wilber describes the path of transcendence according to the perennial philosophy: the Great Chain of Being is a universal sequence of hierarchic levels of increasing consciousness from matter to body to mind to soul to spirit. Transpersonal history is the unfolding of successively higher-order structures. A circular map is divided into three sections of Subconscious (pre-personal), Self-conscious (personal) and Superconscious (trans-personal), a structure similar to the Universal Time Scale. The sequence of stages in the great chain parallels the 12 developmental stages of The Divine Life, but without dates, and uses inward and outward arcs, as in the 'descent into matter' of Young. The message is the same: the universe is a whole and every individual possesses the entire psychological evolutionary reality of history.

4. 'Earth Ascending: An Illustrated Treatise on the Law Governing Whole Systems'[197]

Jose Arguelles has created a series of holonomic maps presenting a theory of history and man based on a 'psi bank', a repository of all information parallel to the spiritual electron of Charon, the ESR molecule of the McKennas and the torus of Young. The maps combine principles from the binary DNA triplets, Chinese geomancy, I Ching hexagrams, Benjamin Franklin's magic square of 16, movements of tectonic plates and the Mayan calendar with its pulse of 260 days, integrated with the yearly cycle of nature. Arguelles makes many references to myth, shamanism, and the mantic arts in a spherical and rectilinear model of a 'planet art network' manifest through the global psi bank.

5. 'Exo-Psychology'[198]

Timothy Leary's book is subtitled, *A Manual on the Use of the Human Nervous System According to the Instructions of the Manufacturers*, and describes the purpose of life as S.M.I.L.E., which is 'Space Migration Intelligence increase Life Extension'. Leary uses an eightfold process and an astrological model of 2 × 12 phases to describe from a galactic perspective the biological development of the human neurological system, its evolution on earth, and the direction of its future in space. Leary also uses the quantum mechanical model and the mechanism of genetic code, neurogenetics, to explain how extraordinary mutations arise. Leary recognizes that evolution is accelerating but does not attempt to attribute dates to the process, although he insists, 'the key to evolution beyond the larval forms is the understanding and control of time'.

Leary believes in immanent space migration, the indefinite extension of life, and the necessity to reimprint the genetic template in order to make the next leap in understanding, which he calls 'Neuro-Atomic Contelligence'. The newly discovered freedom of quantum physics at the subatomic level is symbolic of a newly acquired freedom of will, and he implies, with Young and Charon, that 'any system dominated by quantum mechanical fluctuations is conscious'. The ultimate linkage is the black hole, the final vortex, 'the linkage of the universe of everything with the void of everything'.

* * * * * * *

The common goal of these five books is the discovery of a unified theory of the universe that includes humanity, presented from the viewpoints of the scientist, hallucinogenic anthropologist, transpersonal psychologist, artist, and space-oriented philosopher. It is necessary to combine and synthesize many varied and even contradictory viewpoints in order to redeem the world.

We often use reincarnation to rationalize difficulties in the world. It is easy to attribute the cause of disease to 'karmic debts' inherited from previous lives. We can blame our lack of wholeness of life on parents, social milieu, a time in history, government, religious education, and many others, but the ultimate life lies within each of us as individuals. Each of us must take on the entire history of the world in our lives and redeem it, in order to liberate the world and ourselves. Freedom is in living in the present and incorporating all past and future in the moment.

UFOs and Space Fertilization

Whence this creation originated;
Whether He caused it to be or not,
He who in the highest empyrean surveys
He alone knows, or else, even He knows not.[199]

Since 1950, two related controversies have raged, both of which can be understood in the context of The Divine Life.

The first was the barrage of reports of *UFOs* (Unidentified Flying Objects) seen by people all over the world. Sightings were usually of circular, disk or cigar-shaped objects moving through the sky at terrific speeds and performing impossible aerial antics. Commercial or military pilots saw many of them to move in ways that defied the laws of time and space. There have also been people who insisted they were taken into the saucers and examined by spacemen.[200] There have been many cases of sightings. It is therefore reasonable to consider the possibility, but there has been no proof of their existence.

The psychologist Carl Jung felt that flying saucers were collective projections onto the sky of feelings related to either the salvation or destruction of the planet, as well as being images of the totality of the self.[201] The circular mandala plays an experiential role in uniting apparently irreconcilable opposites and split-mindedness. Simultaneous sightings imply that different people are receiving similar ideas. Such images were also prevalent just before the year AD1000, when there were many predictions of the end of the world. Jung states that when our conscious minds resist unconscious contents, we project them onto objects that reflect hidden meaning. The saucer symbolizes the circular nature of time itself as a totality.

Esoteric healer David Tansley presents a more intriguing explanation. Humans are manifestations in a multi-dimensional universe comprised of many levels of reality. Underlying physical reality are etheric forces, a scaffolding of energies upon which physical forms are built. Beyond the etheric lies the astral plane, and higher intuitive and spiritual levels of awareness. Theosophists posit two higher monadic planes, making a total of seven. They subdivide each plane into seven parts, related to planetary spheres, yielding 49 planes of manifestation, which recalls the numerological and mythological significance of the numbers 49 and 50 in the structure of The Divine Life.

In esoteric teachings the symbols of the third and first etheric levels are half-moon and lenticular in shape, similar to that of the UFO sightings, and a similar form to red blood corpuscles. The UFO sightings are, in Tansley's conception, a manifestation of forces that exist in the etheric level of reality attempting to communicate with or break through to our reality. Tansley suggests that the UFOs are a form of organic life:

> *If we recognise that the solar system we live in is the body of a vast entity, one in whom we live and move and have our being, it is only a short step to consider the possibility that some of the UFO forms we see, particularly those that are spheroidal lights, may be some form of cosmic corpuscles that flow into the body of the earth which is an organ of the solar man (system)... if the consciousness of an atom in our body perceives a blood cell as a spheroidal travelling light winging its way across galaxies of cells, it is just possible to see in the UFO phenomena that occur around our planet, a similar pattern.*[202]

UFO sightings are contact with finer and more subtle levels or reality, which interpenetrate the gross physical plane, and in the framework of The Divine Life are access to other levels of the Universal Time Scale through the circular mandala shape characteristic of each level of manifestation. A popular explanation for mysterious origin is that of a visitation of earth by spacemen. Popularized by Erich van Daniken[203] and followed by hundreds of similar works, the theory attributes the origin of language, myths of sky battles and gods, and even consciousness itself to the influence of errant spacemen in prehistory. While most information advanced is allusive rather than concrete, many of the questions raised are relevant and perplexing. Van Daniken explores – megalithic monuments; earth markings and ley lines; primitive art of beings in what look like space helmets; Indian legends of white gods descending from the sky; prophetic protestations from

Ezekiel and the Book of Revelations; and the unresolved enigma of the origin of life – in such a way that the entire issue is simultaneously absurd and profoundly stimulating. Until now, there are no answers to the questions he asks.

Rene Noorbergen finds traces of extra-terrestrial migration in Hindu accounts of the detonation of an atom bomb in 2400BC, the use of X-rays in China in 206BC, model aircraft found in pre-Incan sites, Egyptian drawings depicting a vacuum tube, and a planetarium computer found in ancient Greece.[204]

The co-discoverer of the structure of the genetic code double helix, Nobel Laureate Francis Crick, hypothesized that life may have come to earth billions of years ago from an advanced civilization in another galactic system via an unmanned rocket, an interstellar Noah's Ark, carrying microbial spores.[205] Crick is a highly respected scientist and it was a shock to the establishment that he rejected the Oparin-Haldane mechanism that life arose by random accidents in the primeval bouillon. The question of the origin of life is the greatest scientific mystery and, as Louis Pasteur proved, life does not originate from non-living matter. Crick proposed that the doomed galactic civilization sent spaceships to many galaxies, knowing that the required chemical soup would exist on many planets in many solar systems. Bacteria can be frozen for the tens of thousands of years it takes for such an immense journey. Crick's theory is similar to that of the British astronomer Sir Fred Hoyle, who also believes that life has an extraterrestrial origin, and that bacteria may have come to earth through space itself. The unanswered question is: if this is the case, how did life originate on the parent planet?

A fascinating idea emerges through the integration of the hypotheses of UFOs and Space Fertilization. A model derived from electron microscope photographs of a virus looks strikingly like the NASA lunar landing module (LEM). The virus lands on a human cell and lowers its legs like the LEM lands on the surface of the moon. What if UFOs have already landed, but are the product of a microscopic galaxy (an atom?) and are so small that they cannot be perceived by our eyes but only by our perceptions tuned to the much faster and finer reality of such beings? The logarithmic relativity of such beings would mean that an entire world age for them would be the duration of a minor virus infection for us.

Just imagine it. The microscopic module has travelled from its galaxy from within the same human body and has landed upon the surface of a cell. The few bacteria (we are ourselves are composed of very complex bacteria) land and colonize the cell system. Gradually they evolve, civilize the system, and even populate neighbouring cells, until they have an advanced civilization. In the final stages of the evolution

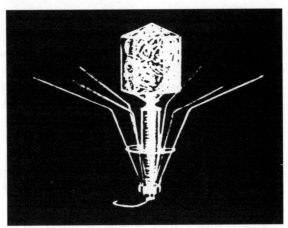

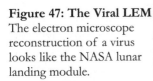

Figure 47: The Viral LEM
The electron microscope
reconstruction of a virus
looks like the NASA lunar
landing module.

of the civilization, they overpopulate, grow out of control like a cancer, discover atomic weapons, and finally overheat their environment, leading to a cataclysm – a trial by fire. The high temperature that accompanies brief illness would be the final conflagration of the bacterial society. They would send, just before their demise, scout rockets with colonists on long journeys to survive somewhere else in the universe. The situation is a familiar one. It is possible that identical processes are happening in the microcosm, in the miniature world, as happen in the outer world.

There is no reason to assume that other galaxies and their inhabitants would be the same size as earthlings. On the contrary, it is possible that in other galaxies beings are so much larger than us that the solar system exists as an atom within their bodies, or that they are so much smaller that they would exist within us. The relativity of dimensions of being is important in understanding our place within the universe.

We must understand the powerful impact of UFOs and fertilizing spacemen in the context of a recurrent universe. During the last decades of the 20th century, television was so widespread in the world that almost every individual alive either saw man landing on the moon – the most widely viewed event in human history or one of the many science fiction movies along the lines of *Star Wars*. The capability of travelling into outer space exists, but the extent to which we can utilize it constructively remains to be seen. Many people fantasize the escape into deep space and other solar systems or galaxies are the only solution to world problems. The fantasy has become the primary myth of our age. The brilliant science fiction work of Ray Bradbury, called *The Martian Chronicles*, shows that humans from earth colonizing Mars and then stranded there become the Martians that they are seeking. With the concept of recurrent world ages, it is entirely possible that the collective myth of space fertilization is a matter of thinking that we are fertilizing ourselves. It is open to question whether there is even one other solar system in the universe that has planets. We may be alone.

Modern nations believe that they can dominate outer space, which gives the misleading notion that humanity can survive self-created ecological catastrophes simply by sending enough beings off earth to inhabit other planets. While possible, it remains a rationalization. When each last world age terminates in a cataclysm, space fantasies are rife. The first conscious beings evolving thousands of years after the end of a world age would naturally utilize the powerful images of the spaceman-god with the universe at his command, yet having no remote idea of the derivation of the image. Maybe we fertilized ourselves in prehistory, and attributed it to other beings. Early humanity after a cataclysm retains fragments of technological information, interbred domesticated animals and garbled languages – only these fragments of the previous world age. Humanity itself could be a self-perpetuating myth.

The structure or programme that determines the form of not only galaxies and solar systems but also life is inherent in the mechanism of time. Life has not evolved: it is eternal – we have always been here in the same niche in the universal matrix. We can identify with higher or lower worlds, but all worlds are Maya – illusions of reality.

Megaliths and Pyramids

The Divine Life clarifies questions about the origin of monuments such as Stonehenge, Macchu Picchu, or the Great Pyramid. Megalithic Stonehenge contains stones transported over hundreds of miles, across the Irish Sea. How can this be? Stonehenge is one of the few monuments that exist through multiple world ages. In every world age, humankind rediscovers Stonehenge, moves it to a more propitious site, restores it by adding extra rings of stones, and makes a sacred remainder of the previous world age. Over many world ages it moves hundreds of miles and contains energies from many world ages, many purposes, and provides magical clues to The Divine Life.

The same process operates for the Great Pyramid, rediscovered in ruins, refaced with new alabaster, revered, used as the basis for many other crude imitations, allowed to fall into ruin again, and so on. The smoothness of the impermeable megalithic monuments is a testimony to multiple world ages. The theory of Schwaller de Lubicz, that such monuments were continuously disassembled and rebuilt on new sites, would support our contention. Archaeologists often mistakenly identified such objects as tombs, but they contain no proof of their identity because they are transmitters capable of spanning the vast ages of multiple world ages. The orientation of the ascending and descending passages of the Great Pyramid show that it was built when the pole star was Alpha Draconis. This makes its date about 2170BC. However, since equinoctial cycles of about 25,000 years are repetitive, the date of its last rebuilding could equally be 29,000 years ago or 54,000 years ago. Modern humankind is often confused by such astronomically sited monuments.

A parallel type of evidence for repetitive history is the phenomenon of prophets. If an individual has the capacity to remember lives in earlier times or even during previous world ages through cycles of death and conception, a profound but challenging process confronts them. The prophet must learn prevailing languages and customs in which to express the ideas that time is circular. A prophet 2,000 years ago trying to describe modern cities and transport would probably be considered very mad. The dangers of civilization would be difficult if not impossible to express, except through the medium of parables or myths, which is why all prophets must couch their message in such forms. The ability to make predictions or to present teachings that retain relevance through many generations is the primary quality that defines such beings. A similar profound memory of past lives and worlds is integral to prodigies. Mozart would remember his compositions earlier and earlier each lifetime, until he was writing symphonies at five years old, before the age or reason. The understanding of the cyclic nature of time is the most profound mystery.

The End of Time

Strong is the system of the Pleroma; small is that which broke loose and became the world. But the All is what is encompassed. It has not come into being; it was existing.
'Treatise on Resurrection', *Nag Hammadi Gospels*[206]

The paradox of The Divine Life is that life cannot have originated without life. Similarly, the universe cannot have created itself. We cannot be here without having been here before. Creation, life and death are, as the Hindu religion correctly surmised, illusions we invest with reality to make the world. We are composed of electrons that were present at the birth of the universe, and these pure energies will remain until the universe explodes in a Big Crunch and reforms into another universe. Once the divine nature of the plot of which we are the perpetuators, actors, set designers, producers, directors and audience becomes clear, the play may be experienced, loved and worshipped as it should be.

When we eat, a primary message is encoded in the time in history of the origin of our food. The closer to the origin of things something originated, the purer and more spiritual the message. Water evokes the time when the planet was composed of vast seas. Seaweed is a very primitive vegetable created in the earliest Virgo period in the Age of Creation and seafood evokes a later Scorpio period, while the meat of cattle is in the later Age of Mammals. Information from each period communicates directly through the very substances we eat and breathe to sustain ourselves. We are what we eat. The entire past is omnipresent within, if only we can experience it directly. Humanity is divine, and divinity is inherent in our nature and in the mechanism of our world.

In early history, humanity measured time by the sun or the moon. Some cultures developed lunar calendars, such as the builders of the megaliths in Europe, the Chinese, the Indians, the Jews, Islamic people, or generally agricultural peoples. Others developed solar calendars, such as Egypt, Greece, Rome, and Western civilization. According to astrological symbolism, lunar cultures are primarily instinctive and unconscious, while solar cultures place importance on rationality and consciousness. On the mathematical level, the two numbers are incommensurable, as the number of days in the lunar month (27.3) does not divide evenly into the number of days in the solar year (365.24). Life Time Astrology is unique because it combines, for the first time, a temporal view of individual life and history that integrates the two required halves of the whole: solar and lunar, masculine and feminine, conscious and unconscious, left and right brain halves, and both rays of the holographic image. The fraction created when we place the moon over the sun is the mathematical constant of Life Time Astrology and at the core of the mathematics of The Divine Life.

$$\text{Life Time Constant} = \frac{27.3 \text{ days in the lunar month}}{365.24 \text{ days in the solar year}} = .07474$$

The most powerful and central alchemical image concerned the coniunctio of the King (Sol) and the Queen (Luna). While Jung has analyzed the psychological implications in particular,[207] the symbolism is extremely rich and relevant. The alchemists, in making the gold that they symbolized by the spiritual body, transmitted not only a metaphor but also a mathematical equation that integrates masculine and feminine qualities. The basis of history, both individual and collective, is the mystery of procreation.

The processes of history and the evolution of consciousness are circular, spiralling and labyrinthine.

Figure 48: The Coniunctio
The conjunction of the queen surmounting her king is a central image of integration in alchemy. Beyond its symbolic union of male and female, the Divine Life is based on the mathematical formula of the days in the lunar month divided by the days in the solar year, making the ratio of .07474.

Then it seemed like falling into a labyrinth; we thought we were at the finish, but our way bent a around and we found ourselves as it were back at the beginning, and just as far from that which we were seeking at first.[208]

The mysteries of time and being lead back to the sovereign Self, from where they started. After the descent from Unity into the eternal turmoil of multiplicity, the ever-pressing goal becomes the Return. The Return is the perpetually central theme of atoms, molecules, compounds, elementary life, complex life, humanity, moons, planets, solar systems and galaxies. In every pursuit of reality the motif of return is present, ever subtle and hidden, ever obvious, and always indescribable. It has given sanity and civilization to the world, but at the price of madness and chaos. It confuses and clarifies, expands and contracts, gives and takes, loves and hates. The path of being throughout time is variously called Jacob's Ladder in the Kabbala, the chain of causation Alaya, the movement of the planets through time, and the double heliacal genetic code. Every being, mundane or mythical, rich or poor, ecstatic or depressive, must confront the process of life and death. Whether we see, experience, hear, feel, divine, ignore, worship, or condemn it, our life is The Divine Life.

For time is just a delusion of creatures
who cannot cope with eternity.
            The Supreme Law by Maurice Maeterlinck

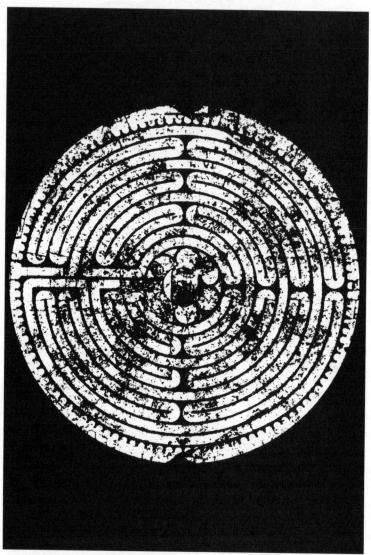

Figure 49: The Chartres Maze
The maze on the floor at Chartres Cathedral is based on planetary
rings, the procession through which constitutes a rebirth into a higher
state of being. Here architecture, mathematics, art, cosmos and
astrology join in creating a cosmic initiation.

Appendix A – Planetary Aspects

Sun Aspects

SU/SU   The will to live; power; the physical body; health and energy; bodily and spiritual harmony. Lack of incentive; illness; weakness; changes in direction; being without focus. The body; father and son; grandfather to son; colleagues; man to man.

SU/MO   Conscious and unconscious; relationship; inner balance; public life; success. Inner discontent; conflict; unrelated; inner tension; struggle. Man and wife; father and mother; marriage partners; friends.

SU/ME   Common sense; understanding; thoughts; practical mind; businesslike; organizational. Unclear; confusion; aimlessness; nervousness. Youngsters; intellectuals; business people.

SU/VE   Physical love; beauty; popularity; social life; aesthetics; romantic. Frigidity; ugliness; unpopular; antisocial; tasteless; cold; indulgence. Artist; beloved man or woman.

SU/MA   Vitality; vigour; advancement; vocational success; endurance; impulsiveness. Dissidence; violence; headstrong; contentious; daring. Fighter; soldier; doctor; husband; quarreller.

SU/JU   Health; recognition; religious; expansive; happy; successful; creative. Materialistic; indulgent; arrogant; illegal, lazy. Wealthy; prominent; socialites.

SU/SA   Separate; concentrated; absorbed; serious; hard worker; ambitious; dedicated. Selfish; inhibited; suppressive; pessimistic; inferior; anxious; weak; negative. Serious people; elderly; sick; inhibited; cruel father; weak father; missing father.

SU/UR   Progressive; eccentric; technological; original; free; changeable; dynamic; individual. Obstinate; self-destructive; rebellious; tense; irritable. Innovator; reformer; rebel; technician; trouble-maker.

SU/NE   Sensitive; delicate; imaginative; uncertain; refined; inspired; visionary; psychic. Insecure; weak; sick; deceptive; seducible; tasteless. Medium; romantic; dreamer; psychic; sensitive; drug addict; seducer; weak father.

SU/PL   Power; attainment; conscious objectives; leading; growing; autocratic; ruthless. Ruthless; arrogant; forced; brutal; fanatical; destructive. Leader; fighter; revolutionary; transformer; martyr; strong father.

SU/NO   Physical associations; public; adaptive; sociable; popular; educational. Anti-social; disharmonious; unadaptable; unrelated; isolated. Associate; fellow; colleague; witness; relative; dignitary; police.

SU/AS   Personal relations; physical relations; confidence; advancement; esteem; recognizable. Pushy; disharmonious; disliked; self-seeking; shy; quarrelsome; dependent. Men in the environment; contact; husband.

SU/MC   Individual; objective; self-knowledge; success; missionary; authority; famous. Egocentric; unclear; arrogant; conceited; uninteresting; misguided. Body and Soul; 'I'; one's own ego.

Moon Aspects

MO/MO   Emotional life; feminine relations; changeable things; pleasant moods; motherliness. Emotional suppression; moodiness; separation from mother; unemotional; tension. The feelings; the soul; mother and daughter.

MO/ME   Emotional thoughts; perception; judgement; valuation; feminine ideas; discretion. Changeable; lying; gossip; criticism; calumny; ingenuous; highly strung. Intellectual women; girls; authoress; psychologist; traveller.

MO/VE   Love; devotion; art; conception; romantic; cultured; marriage; graceful. Moody; shy; tasteless; sterile; irritable; loveless. Lover; expectant mother; mother; artist; woman; actor.

MO/MA   Excitement; intense emotion; frankness; candid; sincere; feeling will; industrious. Impulsiveness; rash; fighting; intolerant; rebellious; irritable. Wife; woman colleague; hard worker; housewife; businesswoman.

MO/JU   Happy; religious; social conscience; travel; faithful; recognition; positive feeling. Indifferent; negligent; rebellious; unpopular; illegal; marital problems; sloppy. Successful; generous; happy woman; females; bride; expectant mother; official women.

MO/SA   Self-control; duty; care; attentive; circumspect; lonely; ascetic; critical; ambitious. Depressive; separated; widowed; inferior; melancholy; anxious; estranged. Inhibited people; sad; widow; single parent; female grandparent.

MO/UR   Subconscious forces; instinct; sudden events; occult; intellectual specialization.

Schizophrenia; emotional tension; overstrain; abrupt; exaggeration; anxiety. Restless woman; ambitious; reformists; schizophrenic.

MO/NE   Refined; inner vision; imagination; inspiration; relaxation; romantic; idealistic. Frail; self-deception; unreality; weakness; addicted; seductive; supernatural. Sensitive; medium; impressionable people; card-readers; psychic; indolent; weak.

MO/PL   Extreme emotion; one-sided; fanaticism; overzealous; devouring; dynamic; insatiable. Fanatic; sadistic; obsessed; shocking; jealous; demanding; insane demands; upheavals. Emotional people; public relations people; publicists; schizophrenic; revolutionary.

MO/NO   Spiritual union; inner relationships; alliances (between women); family ties; devoted. Estrangement; multiple relationships; unadaptable; frustrated; unfamilial; insular. Woman alliances; blood union; associates.

MO/AS   Emotional relations; obliging; feminine; adaptable; personal ties; subjective ties. Hypersensitivity; disagreements; moody; changeable; over-reactive; annoyed. Feminine environment; mother; alcoholics; drug addicts; lovers; personalities.

MO/MC   Emotional objectives; sentiment; home; family; soul-ties; intuitive understanding. Difficult women; unprofessional; vacillation; unreliable; sentimental; wavering. Women; feeling and emotional people; governesses; mother; soul people.

Mercury Aspects

ME/ME   Movement; thinking; mind; news; opinions; perception; good comprehension; understanding; easy. Static states; subjectivity; dullness; lacking objectivity; lying; no communication. Active people; friends; confidants; mediators; intellects; teachers; siblings; the young.

ME/VE   Love thoughts; beauty sense; design; feeling intellect; hilarity; art success; writing. Vanity; conceit; hypersensitive; irresolute; squandering; luxury. Lovers; author; writer; beauty sales person; art dealer; aesthete; artist; female friends.

ME/MA   Thought power; realized plans; resolution; repartee; enterprise; debate; settling affair. Criticism; nagging; malice; hasty action; speech difficulty; obstinate; cynical. Critic; quarreller; debater; writer.

ME/JU   Constructive mind; erudition; literature; business sense; common sense; science; fluent. Negligence; fraud; unreliable; exaggerating; conflict; indiscreet. Speaker; authority; negotiator; businessperson; publisher; traveller; philanthropist.

ME/SA   Mental work; concentration; deep thought; logic; organization; experience; industry. Dullness; reserve; shyness; estrangement; difficulty; hard infancy; distrust. Philosopher; intellectual; scientist; crook; logician.

ME/UR   Intuition; astuteness; flexibility; independence; influence; mathematics; original mind. Scattered; madness; nerves; erratic; eccentric; contradictory. Mathematician; scientist; technician; musician; astrologer; lively people.

ME/NE   Imagination; fantasy; deep perception; vision; presentiments; poetic; idealistic; clear. Faulty judgement; paralysis; deception; fraud; dissipated; foolish. Actor; fantasizer; dreamer; saint; liar; faith healer; psychic.

ME/PL   Persuasion; understanding; cunning; diplomacy; influence; wit; slyness. Breakdown; hasty expression; excessive opposition; overeager; impatience; crudeness. Speaker; politician; fascist; critic; tyrant; propagandist.

ME/NO   Joint plans; exchanging ideas; social-business meeting; correspondence; relationship. Unsociable; unpopularity; closed; blocked; disloyalty. Joiners; groupy; writer; organizer; negotiator; networker.

ME/AS   Personal ideas; definition; verbal communication; meetings; intelligence; talkative. Gossip; misjudgement; anxiety; superficial; flighty. Thinker; gossip; organizer; friend; administrator; diplomat.

ME/MC   Intellectual objectives; observation; self-knowledge; meditation; own aims; clarity. Aimlessness; unselfconscious; changeable; vacillation; dishonest. Expressive people; talkers; media people; MCs; job counsellors.

Venus Aspects

VE/VE   Peace; goodwill; love; desire; feeling love; humour; beauty sense; art. Unrelated; listless; tasteless; aberration; carelessness. Lover; aesthete; beauty; model; girl; actor; artist; musician; clothier; nurse.

VE/MA	Sexual love; artistry; passion; creativity; lively expression; intimacy; prolific. Asexuality; seduction; unsatisfied; infidelity; irritable; sexual disease. Lover; sexist; seducer; polygamist; active lover.
VE/JU	Joyous love; happiness; popularity; form sense; marriage; bliss; comfort; gay; hedonism. Laziness; lacking feeling; indolence; arrogance; legal conflict; indulgence. Artist; filmstar; model; socialite; expansive lover.
VE/SA	Dutiful emotion; soberness; loyalty; inhibition; sacrifice; fidelity; economy; reserve. Jealousy; torment; deprivation; lonely; depressed; mother separation. Lonely people; widow(er); illegitimate children; older lover.
VE/UR	Arousal; eccentricity; impulse; talent; music; sentimentality; refinement. Repressed sexuality; inconstancy; estrangement; unconventional; loose. Musician; artist; eccentric lover.
VE/NE	Rapture; eroticism; mysticism; idealism; platonic affairs; travel; refinement. Seducible; tasteless; infatuation; dreaming; illusion; escapist. Artist; musician; dreamer; visionary; romantic; drug dealer; addict; weak lover.
VE/PL	Fanatic love; sensuality; gifted; attractive; compulsive; devoted; talented; magnetic. Lusty; stressed love; sado masochism; vulgarity; excessive desire. Lover; pornographer; menstruating woman; artist.
VE/NO	Love union; adaptation; universal love; ties; obliging; artistic communities. Isolation; separation; unhappy affair; flighty. Lover; marrieds; singles; art groupies; gallery owner.
VE/AS	Harmonious love; beauty; attractive personality; adornment; art; taste; gentility. Bad taste; desertion; unsociable; wasteful; indulgent. Woman; mother; wife; lover; artist.
VE/MC	Objective love; affection; benevolence; artistic; attached; attractive individual. Vanity; conceit; jealousy; dissipated. Lover; artist; admirer.

Mars Aspects

MA/MA	Energy; activity; work; aggression; impulse; resolve; will; decision; accomplishment. Wasting energy; violence; injury; destruction. Fighter; soldier; athlete; craftsman; surgeon; police.
MA/JU	Successful creativity; joy; activity; organization; prowess; rebellion; practicality. Conflict; estrangement; precipitancy; haste; restlessness; dispute. Manager; organizer; jurist; judge; official; athlete.
MA/SA	Inhibition; endurance; danger; fanaticism; spartan life; ascetic; tough. Destruction; danger; death; impotence; obstinacy; separation; tests; dispute; illness. Labourer; miner; fighter; killer.
MA/UR	Applied effort; intervention; courage; independence; operation; revolutionary; birth. Argument; obstinacy; emotional tension; stress; nerves; operation; injury; accident. Surgeon; violent people; revolutionary; reactionary; driver; fireman.
MA/NE	Inspiration; desire sensitivity; escapism; romanticism; fantasy; denial. Destruction; infection; misdirection; drugs; inferiority; smoking; paralysis; narrowness. Sick people; addict; sailor; pathologist; dealer.
MA/PL	Superhuman force; violence; vigour; great ambition; success; obsession; research. Cruelty; assault; aggression; injury; sadism; homicide; ruthlessness. Dictator; disabled; nuclear scientist; politician; general.
MA/NO	Physical collaboration; team spirit; union; shared success; progeny; betrothal. Quarrels; lack fellowship; disrupted meetings; eunuchism; dissolution; dissociation. Collectives; communists; socialists; eunuchs.
MA/AS	Fighting spirit; forced will; teamwork; attainment; resolution; creative work; surgery. Caesarean; forceps birth; operation; fighting; aggression; conflict; dispute; quarrel. Surgeon; soldier; colleagues; boxer.
MA/MC	Ego-conscious action; order; decision; success; resolution; occupation change; prudence. Excitable; stress; prematurity; purposeless; fever; fraud; agitation; murder. Organizer; leader; politician; leading personality.

Jupiter Aspects

JU/JU	Contentment; optimism; luck; financial gain; religion; philosophy; social life. Unlucky; losses; pessimism; illegal; extravagant; materialistic; greedy; corpulence. Lawyer; judge; banker; insurer; physician; uncle; grandparent; publisher.
JU/SA	Patience; perseverance; industry; diplomacy; seclusion; duty; philosophy; calm; real estate.

Vacillation; discontent; upset; failure; illness. Professor; teacher; lawyer; official; politician; relatives; tenant.

JU/UR   Optimism: fortunate ideas; perception; sudden recognition; bliss; invention; change. Independence; opposition; magnifying matters; arguments; tension; stress. Organizers; inventors; adventurer; optimist; religious zealots.

JU/NE   Speculation; imagination; metaphysics; idealism; luck; ethics; generosity; profit. Susceptible; dreaming; unreality; enmity; insult; losses; swindlers. Speculator; dreamer; mystic; visionary.

JU/PL   Plutocracy; spiritual-mental power; leadership; regeneration; organization; transfusion. Fanaticism; losses; guilt; failure; legal liability; bankruptcy; exploitation. Organizer; professor; teacher; speculator; dictator; propagandist.

JU/NO   Good contact; adaptability; tact; common interest; fortunate union; life force. Lack fellowship; anti-social; selfish; conflict; lifeless. Philosophical communities; fellows; partners; associates.

JU/AS   Agreeable; favourable influence; generosity; wealth; cure; success; easy birth; teamwork. Waste; friction; rebellion; hypocrisy; conceit; bragging. Generous people; wealthy people; uncles; grandparents; aunts.

JU/MC   Philosophical objectives; conscious aims; contentment; bliss; success; purpose. Risks; unclear aims; changes in lifestyle; desire for importance. Successes; philosopher; psychologist; priest.

Saturn Aspects

SA/SA   Restriction; patience; concentration; industry; crystallisation; earnestness. Hindrance; illness; developmental crisis; depression; inefficiency; sorrow; paralysis. Inhibited people; scientist; father; paternalism; the elderly; farmer; miner; businessperson; doctor.

SA/UR   Tension; determination; collected thinking; calmness; technical affairs; travel; endure. Emotional tension; provocation; force; backlash from past; limitation of freedom. Violent people; the dying; amputees; chronically ill.

SA/NE   Renunciation; suffering; sacrifice; caution; method; duality; asceticism; patience. Insecurity; illness; pestilence; habit; neuroses; emotional inhibitions; insecure. Ascetics; chronically ill; elderly; druggists.

SA/PL   Cruelty; hard labour; tenacity; self-discipline; adepts; martyrdom; struggling; silence. Egotism; violence; divorce; slow separation; murder; self-destruction; loss of money. Scientists; murderers; reactionaries; martyrs.

SA/NO   Isolation; inhibited union; maturity; sponsorship; mystery. Unadaptable; difficulty co-operating; death of relatives; depression; inhibition. Elderly persons; mourners.

SA/AS   Inhibited personality; difficult birth; early maturity; lonely; isolated; inmates. Depression; wrong outlook; poor family; disadvantages through others; segregation. Inmates; patients; lonely people; doctors; hospital staff; grandparents.

SA/MC   Serious objectives; slow development; separation; self-preoccupation; experience. Emotional inhibition; dejection; illness; insanity; loss of consciousness; despondent. Inhibited people; patients; burden.

Uranus Aspects

UR/UR   Suddenness; ambitions; enterprise; creativity; crisis change; reform; many plans. Hard conditions; change; catastrophe; nervous crises; suicidal thoughts; danger. Reformers; inventors; technicians; revolutionaries; astrologer; healer; physicist.

UR/NE   Unconsciousness; inner vision; inspiration; mysticism; art; research; journeys; spirit. Instability; confusion; death; revolution; crisis; incapacity; confusion psychically. Mystics; mediums; psychics; revolutionaries.

UR/PL   Transformation; revolution; innovation; mobility; reform; mutation; explosion; changes. Impatience; mania; destruction; upsets; subversive activities; enforcement; explosion. Pioneers; reformers; geniuses; explorers; gunmen.

UR/NO   Shared experience; sudden attraction; unstable relations; variety; innovation; activity. Disturbance; quarrels; separation; restlessness; flighty; irritable; incidents; dreamy. Politicians; labour unions; excited family; nervous people.

UR/AS   Environmental response; invention; new contacts; original; nervousness; rearrangement. Excitable; inconstancy; disquiet; accidents; quick changes; compulsion; rudeness. Excitable people; originals; eccentrics; technicians; neurotics.

UR/MC   Original objectives; assertion; fortunate changes; organising; successful; stress. Tension; prematurity; unreliability; temper; upsets; sudden turns of destiny. Yogis; gurus; inventors; physicists; musicians.

Neptune Aspects

NE/NE   Spiritual development; intellectual perception; travel; empathy; mysticism; drugs. Hypersensitivity; nervousness; confusion; health crisis; deception; addiction; deceit. Mediums; frauds; channels; sensitives; perceptive people; spiritual people; addicts; dreamers.

NE/PL   Supernatural; intensification; active imagination; psychics; parapsychology; evolution. Confusion; torment; obsession; craving drugs or alcohol; loss; possession; falsehood. Mystics; astrologers; psychics; occultists; mediums; addicts; gamblers.

NE/NO   Idealistic associations; sensitive groups; mysticism; Utopian associations; spiritual. Antisocial; deceptive; cheating others; deception; sleeplessness; disturbed dreams. Groupies; psychic groups; mystical organizations; magic circles; covens.

NE/AS   Impressionability; sensitivity; sympathy; strangeness; refinement; idealism; water birth. Betrayal; weakness; confusion; disappointment; escapism; fraud; illusion; drugs. Anaesthetists; sensitives; mediums; addicts; psychics; mystics; the weak.

NE/MC   Uncertain objectives; vagueness; peculiar ideas; Utopian; supernatural; artistic. Feigning; falsehood; acting; numbness; strange ideas; depression; deception. Spiritual people; idealists; propagandists; gurus; Utopians; parapsychologists; weaklings; actors; the mentally disturbed; psychotics.

Pluto Aspects

PL/PL   Inner change; metamorphosis; transformation; propaganda; mass influence; powerlust. Ruthlessness; fanaticism; agitating efforts; weakness; coercion; indoctrination. Dictators; hypnotists; politicians; magicians; public speakers; actors.

PL/NO   Collective destiny; public figures; influencing others; group associations; movements. Tragic destiny; karma; being cramped by others; antisocial; suffering; suffocation. Crowds; mass meetings; armies; political parties; unions; multinational corporations; sports teams; tournaments; clubs.

PL/AS   Fascinating personality; ambition; magic; unusual influence; control; transformation. Changing environment; dictatorship; ruling others; repulsion; readjustment; injury. Specialists; fascinating personalities; stars; politicians; public figures.

PL/MC   Transformed objectives; individuality; strength; growth; authority; expert knowledge. Misused power; resistance; vindictiveness; anti-social conduct; recuperation; destiny. Transformers; authorities; specialists; magicians; surgeons.

Node Aspects

NO/NO   Unions; connections; junctures; communication; approach; groups; clubs; fellowship. Limitations; antisocial; incompatibility; unsocial; unadaptive. Contacts; mediators; relatives; family; associations; colleagues.

NO/AS   Fellowship; personal relationships; family contacts; social conscience; charm; loves. Short relations; estrangements; disturbed domestic relations; antisocial; difficult. Family; associates; workmates; fellows; friends.

NO/MC   Group objectives; individual relationships; astral relationships; mutual understanding. Inconstancy; differing; individual over collective; difficult collectives; Marxists. Associations; political parties; unions; friends.

Ascendant

AS/AS   Acquaintance; location; surroundings; the place; body; social relations; personal relations. Maladjustment; feeling lost; misplaced; difficult birth. People in the environment; doctors; midwives.

AS/MC   Individual synthesis; higher self and lower self; personality and ego; integration. Impossible synthesis; irreconcilable goals; lack of direction. Synthesizers; strong personalities with direction.

Midheaven

MC/MC   The Ego; spiritual, intellectual and social impressions; goals; objectives. Egoless; materialistic; goal-less; insane. Egotists; people who live in the moment; goal-oriented people.

Appendix B – Life Time Astrology Timescale Table

Deg from ASC	Week	Deg from ASC	Week	Deg from ASC	Yr	Mth	Deg from ASC	Yr	Mth
240°	0 4	300°	0 12	00°	00	00	60°	1	8
241		301		01			61		
242		302		02			62		
243		303		03			63		
244		304		04			64		
245	0 4	305	0 13	05	0	1	65	1	11
246		306		06			66		
247		307		07			67		
248		308		08			68		
249		309		09			69		
250	0 4	310	0 15	10	0	2	70	2	2
251		311		11			71		
252		312		12			72		
253		313		13			73		
254		314		14			74		
255 9th	0 5	315 11th	0 16	15 1st	0	3	75 3rd	2	5
256		316		16			76		
257		317		17			77		
258		318		18			78		
259		319		19			79		
260	0 5	320	0 18	20	0	4	80	2	9
261		321		21			81		
262		322		22			82		
263		323		23			83		
264		324		24			84		
265	0 6	325	0 20	25	0	6	85	3	2
266		326		26			86		
267		327		27			87		
268		328		28			88		
269		329		29			89		
270	0 7	330	0 22	30	0	7	90	3	6
271		331		31			91		
272		332		32			92		
273		333		33			93		
274		334		34			94		
275	7	335	0 24	35	0	9	95	4	0
276		336		36			96		
277		337		37			97		
278		338		38			98		
279		339		39			99		
280	0 8	340	0 26	40	0	11	100	4	5
281		341		41			101		
282		342		42			102		
283		343		43			103		
284		344		44			104		
285 10th	0 9	345 12th	0 29	45 2nd	1	0	105 4th	5	0
286		346		46			106		
287		347		47			107		
288		348		48			108		
289		349		49			109		
290	0 10	350	0 32	50	1	3	110	5	6
291		351		51			111		
292		352		52			112		
293		353		53			113		
294		354		54			114		
295	0 11	355	0 35	55	1	5	115	6	2
296		356		56			116		
297		357		57			117		
298		358		58			118		
299		359		59			119		
300	0 12	360	0 40	60	1	8	120	6	10

Deg from ASC		Yr	Mth	Deg from ASC		Yr	Mth	Deg from ASC	Yr	Mth
120°		6	10	180°		23	5	240°	75	11
121		7	1	181		23	11	241	77	5
122		7	2	182		24	4	242	78	11
123		7	4	183		24	10	243	80	6
124		7	6	184		25	4	244	82	0
125		7	8	185		25	10	245	83	6
126		7	10	186		26	4	246	85	4
127		8	0	187		26	11	247	86	11
128		8	2	188		27	5	248	88	8
129		8	4	189		28	0	249	90	5
130		8	6	190		28	6	250	92	2
131		8	8	191		29	1	251	94	0
132		8	10	192		29	8	252	95	10
133		9	0	193		30	3	253	97	8
134		9	3	194		30	11	254	99	7
135	5th	9	5	195	7th	31	6	255	101	7
136		9	7	196		32	2			
137		9	10	197		32	9			
138		10	0	198		33	5			
139		10	3	199		34	1			
140		10	5	200		34	9			
141		10	8	201		35	5			
142		10	10	202		36	2			
143		11	1	203		36	10			
144		11	4	204		37	7			
145		11	7	205		38	4			
146		11	10	206		39	1			
147		12	1	207		39	11			
148		12	4	208		40	8			
149		12	7	209		41	6			
150		12	10	210		42	3			
151		13	1	211		43	2			
152		13	4	212		44	0			
153		13	8	213		44	10			
154		13	11	214		45	9			
155		14	2	215		46	8			
156		14	6	216		47	7			
157		14	9	217		48	6			
158		15	1	218		49	5			
159		15	4	219		50	5			
160		15	8	220		51	5			
161		16	0	221		52	5			
162		16	4	222		53	6			
163		16	8	223		54	6			
164		17	0	224		55	7			
165	6th	17	4	225	8th	56	8			
166		17	8	226		57	10			
167		18	1	227		58	11			
168		18	5	228		60	1			
169		18	10	229		61	3			
170		19	2	230		62	6			
171		19	7	231		63	9			
172		20	0	232		65	0			
173		20	4	233		66	3			
174		20	9	234		67	7			
175		21	2	235		68	11			
176		21	7	236		70	3			
177		22	1	237		71	7			
178		22	6	238		73	0			
179		22	11	239		74	5			
180		23	5	240		75	11			

Life Time Scale Dating

We date planets, sign cusps and house cusps according to their distance in degrees from the ASC. Determine the number of degrees of a planet or other point from the ASC, enter the table and opposite is weeks after conception during gestation based on a 40 month period. Events in childhood and maturity are measured in years and months of age. For example, a planet registering 200° from the ASC, correlates with the age of 34 years and nine months. Read across columns to see aspect resonant times in life.

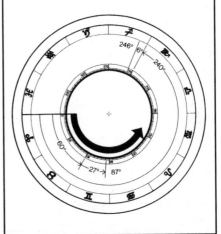

Dating Using the Time Scale Disk

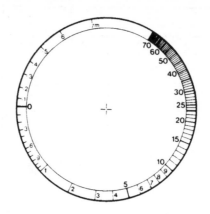

Dating House and Sign Cusps

Align 0 on the left of the dating disk with the ASC and read off the ages of the house and sign cusps to the nearest year. In childhood, simply estimate the ages when a cusp falls between even years. In gestation, the time is measured in months before birth and it is necessary to round off to the nearest month.

When a cusp is more than 240° from the Ascendant, the age must be in the table for Old Age on the previous page. To date the house cusps during gestation, the results are in weeks before birth:

Table: Dating House Cusps

Cusp	Zod Position	Abs	-ASC	=	Deg	Age (Yrs and Mths)
Ascendant	20° Aries	020°	-020°	=	000°	Birth
2nd House	00° Gemini	060°	-020°	=	040°	00yrs 1imths
3rd House	20° Gemini	080°	-020°	=	060°	01yrs 08mths
4th House	07° Cancer	097°	-020°	=	077°	02yrs 07mths
5th House	25° Cancer	115°	-020°	=	095°	04yrs 00mths
6th House	22° Leo	142°	-020°	=	122°	07yrs 02mths
7th House	20° Libra	200°	-020°	=	180°	23yrs 05mths
8th House	00° Sagittarius	240°	-020°	=	220°	51yrs 05mths
9th House	20° Sagittarius	260°	-020°	=	240°	75yrs 11mths
9th House	20° Sagittarius	260°	-020°	=	240°	-40 weeks
10th House	07° Capricorn	277°	-020°	=	257°	-35 weeks
11th House	25° Capricorn	295°	-020°	=	275°	-33 weeks
12th House	22° Aquarius	322°	-020°	=	302°	-27 weeks

Dating Signs, Houses and Planets
The house and sign cusps can be dated
by superimposing the dating disk on
the horoscope, synchronizing the 0
point with the ASC. Then simply read
off the dates.

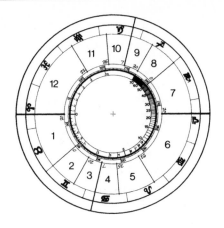

Since the ninth cusp/conception point is the end of the first lunar
month lifetime of the ovum, four weeks must be added to the figure in
the table to arrive at the approximate conception time.

This completes the dating of the twelve 12 cusps in the horoscope.

This completes the dating of the 12 signs in a horoscope and shows
the ages at which the individual passes from sign to sign, and house to
house in his life. We follow the same process in dating the position of
planets.

Life Time Astrology Computer Program

A T Mann and John Astrop created a computer programme that calculates a list of
dates in life from conception to 99 years old that runs on personal computers. The
program is available through the author. Contact him through his website:
http://www.atmann.net or through his e-mail address: **atmann@atmann.net**
From December 2002 see **http://www.newvisionastrology.com** for updates.

A sample of the printout shows all house and sign cusps, planets and sensitive points
with their zodiacal degrees and minutes and their dates by month and year.

SQQ	ASCENDANT	AUG 1942	23.30	AQU
SQQ	MC	OCT 1942	24.24	AQU
★★★ 0	SUN	OCT 1943	29.22	AQU
★★★ 0	0 PISCES	DEC 1943	00.00	PIS
SSQ	URANUS	MAR 1945	05.32	PIS
SQQ	PLUTO	JUL 1945	06.37	PIS
★★★ 0	MERCURY	NOV 1945	07.53	PIS
★★★ 0	N NODE	DEC 1945	08.19	PIS
QNX	ASCENDANT	DEC 1945	08.03	PIS

* References *

Chapter One – The Divine Plot

1. *Oxford English Dictionary* (unabridged)
2. Eliade,*Myths, Dreams and Mysteries* (London, 1968), p. 235.
3. Oswald Spengler, *The Decline of the West* (London, 1961), p. 425.
4. Mann, *The Round Art: The Astrology of Time and Space* (London, 1979), *Life Time Astrology* (London, 1984) and *Astrology and the Art of Healing* (London, 1989).

Chapter Two – Life History

5. Fraser, ed., *The Voices of Time* (London, 1968), p. 91, quote by Sadogoshi.
6. Friedenthal, *Goethe: His Life and Times*, p. 418.
7. Eliade, *Myths, Dreams*, p. 54.
8. Marcus, *Freud and the Culture of Psychoanalysis* (London, 1983), p. 166.
9. Eliade, *Myths, Dreams*, p. 54.
10. Spengler, *Decline*, p. 3.
11. Mann, *Joseph and His Brothers* (London, 1950), p.81.
12. Eliade, *Myth and Reality* (London, 1964), p. 85.
13. Ibid, p. 91.
14. Eliade, *Myths, Dreams*, p. 235.
15. Mann, *Joseph*, p. 6.
16. Collin, *The Theory of Eternal Life* (London, 1950).
17. Eliade, *The Myth of the Eternal Return* (New York, 1954), p. 144.
18. Blacker and Loewe, ed., *Ancient Cosmologies*, (London, 1975), p. 132.
19. Ibid, p. 123, from the Mahabharata.
20. *Rig Veda*, X, 29.
21. Blacker, *Cosmologies*, p. 128.
22. Thorndike, *The History of Magic and Experimental Science*, Vol. I (New York, 1941), p. 384.
23. According to the numerology of the Hebrew gematria, ShMITAH = 365 and ShMITA is 360, the number of days in the year and degrees in the circle, respectively.
24. Spengler, *Decline*, p. 346.
25. Fraser, *Voices*, p. 111.
26. Thorndike, *History*, Vol. 1, p. 384.
27. *Malachi* IV:1.
28. Jung, *Letters I 1906–1950* (London, 1973), p. 138.
29. Jung, *Aion*, *CW 9*, Part II (London, 1951), p. 81.
30. Blacker, *Cosmologies*, p. 162.
31. Corbin, 'Cyclical Time in Mazdaism and Ismailism', *Man and Time*, Eranos Yearbook 3, edited by Joseph Campbell (New York, 1957, p. 157–60.

32. Wolben, *After Nostradamus* (London, 1973), p. 43.
33. Jung, *Symbols of Transformation*, CW 5 (London, 1952), p. 81.
34. Turville-Petre, *Myth and Religion of the North* (London, 1964), p. 276.
35. Donnelly, *Atlantis: The Antediluvian World* (London, 1950), p. 7.
36. Ibid, p. 7.
37. Robinson, *Is It True What They Say About Edgar Cayce?* (London, 1979), p. 119.
38. Donnelly, *Atlantis*, p. 316.
39. See Galanopoulos and Bacon, *Atlantis* (London, 1969).

Chapter Three – Eternal Recurrence

40. See Stephen Hawking, *The Universe in a Nutshell*.
41. Russell, 'Time in Christian Thought', Fraser, *Voices*, p. 68.
42. John 6:62, *RSV*.
43. John 14:3, *RSV*.
44. Pagels, *The Nag Hammadi Gospels* (London, 1979), p. 42.
45. Ibid, p. 46.
46. Nietzsche, Ms. 1066, March–June 1888.
47. Nietzsche, Ms. 1067, 1885.
48. Kollerstrom, *The Actual and the Real: A Way of Thinking About Eternity* (London, 1974), p. 149.
49. Nicoll, *Living Time* (London, 1952), p. 138.
50. Zukav, *The Dancing Wu Li Masters* (London, 1979), p. 318–19.
51. Plato, *The Republic*, 620.
52. Collin, *Celestial Influence*, p. 20.
53. Ibid, p. 21.
54. Ibid, p. 24.
55. *The Living Thoughts of Schopenhauer*, trans. by Haldane and Kemp, presented by Thomas Mann (London, 1939), p. 99.
56. Wendt, *Before the Deluge: The Story of Paleontology*, trans. Richard and Clara Winston (London, 1968), p. 119.
57. Ibid, p. 90–1.
58. Ibid, p. 105.
59. Knight, Charles Fort, *Prophet of the Unexplained*.
60. See my book *The Genetic Book of the Living: The Spiritual Potential of Junk DNA*, to be published 2003.
61. Worshofsky, *Doomsday: The Science of Catastrophe* (London, 1979), p. 131.
62. Velikovsky, *Earth in Upheaval* (London, 1956), p. 128.

63. Jonas and Klein, *Manchild: A Study of the Infantilization of Man* (New York, 1970), p. 5.

64. Woodcock and Davis, *Catastrophe Theory* (London, 1980), p. 131.

65. Ibid, p. 15.

66. Ibid, p. 32.

67. Ibid, p. 81.

68. Ibid, p. 162.

69. Nicoll, *Living*, p. 149.

70. Esdras Gospel, *The Nag Hammadi Library* (Leiden, 1977).

71. Bohm, *Wholeness and the Implicate Order* (London, 1980), p. 9.

72. Ibid, p. 15.

73. Ibid, p. 25.

74. Dethlefsen, *The Challenge of Fate* (London, 1984), p. 75.

75. Spengler, *Decline*, p. 6.

76. Ibid, p. 7.

77. Sheldrake, *A New Science of Life* (London, 1981), p. 27.

78. Ibid, p. 95.

79. Ibid, p. 96.

80. Jung, 'The Rediscovery of the Soul', *The Red Book* (unpublished).

Chapter Four – Life Time Astrology

81. Landscheit, *Cosmic Cybernetics* (Aalen, 1973), p. 56–7.

82. Du Nouy, *Biological Time* (London, 1936), p. 121; Collin, Celestial, p. 156; and Mann, *The Round Art*, p. 109.

83. Fischer, 'Biological Time', Fraser, *Voices*, p. 362.

84. Eliot, T S, from *Four Quartets*, Little Gidding, *The Complete Poems and Plays 1909–1950*, p.145.

85. John 3:4–5, RSV.

86. Jung, *Psychology and Alchemy, CW 12* (London, 1966), p. 23.

87. Ferguson, Marilyn, ed., *Brain/Mind Bulletin*, March, 1984.

88. Collin, *Eternal Life*, p. 66.

89. Fischer, 'Biological Time', Fraser, *Voices*, p. 325.

Chapter Eight – Divine Time & History

90. See Greene: Saturn; *Relating*; and *The Astrology of Fate*.

91. 'Noisy Nucleotides', *Scientific American*, September 1992.

92. See *The Spiritual Potential of Junk DNA*, by A T Mann, to be published in 2003.

93. Needham, 'Time and Knowledge in China and the West', Fraser, *Voices*, p. 112–3.

94. Piel, *The Acceleration of History* (New York, 1972), p. 21.

95. Ibid, p. 22.

96. Ibid, quote by H G Wells, p. 24–5.

97. Bennett, *The Dramatic Universe, Volume Four: History* (London, 1966), p. 166.

98. Ibid, p. 168.

99. Ibid, p. 169.

100. Huntley, *The Divine Proportion* (New York, 1970), p. 164–8.

101. Fischer, *Voices*, p. 372.

102. Ibid, Kalmus, 'Organic Evolution and Time', p. 338.

103. Calder, *Timescale* (London, 1984), p. 75.

104. Plato, *The Republic*, 144.

105. Von Franz, *Number and Time* (Wisconsin, 1974), p. 80.

106. Ibid, p. 82.

107. Schwaller de Lubicz, *Sacred Science* (New York, 1982), p. 207.

108. *Plotinus*, trans. MacKenna (London, 1962), p. 443.

109. Levi, *The Key to the Mysteries* (London, 1959).

Chapter Nine – The World Age

110. *Esdras Gospel*, Nag Hammadi Gospels.

111. Piel, *The Acceleration of History* (New York, 1972), p. 29; and Calder, *Timescale*, p. 157.

112. Leakey and Lewin, *Origins* (London, 1977), p. 254.

113. Toynbee, *A Study of History* (London, 1946), p. 48.

114. Piel, *Acceleration*, p. 29.

115. Laidler, the *Observer*, 19 April 1984.

116. The Book of Revelations, XX, 12–15, RSV.

117. Russell, *The Awakening Earth* (London, 1982).

118. Lenormant, *La Magie chez les Chaldeens*, trans. George Andrews.

119. Piel, *Acceleration*, p. 29–30.

120. West, *Serpent in the Sky* (New York, 1979), p. 105.

121. Ibid, p. 106.

122. Temple, *The Sirius Mystery* (London, 1976).

123. Ibid, p. 130.

124. Ibid, p. 85.

125. Ibid, p. 154.

126. Ibid, p. 155.

127. Ibid, p. 117.

128. Ibid, p. 113.

129. Ibid, p. 154.

130. Ibid, p. 89.

131. Graves, *The Greek Myths I* (London, 1955), p. 138.

132. Ibid, II, p. 85.

133. Ibid, p. 74.
134. Ibid, p. 156.
135. Leviticus, 25: 8–10, *RSV*.
136. Tansley, *Subtle Body* (London, p. 84–5).
137. Von Franz, *Jung: His Myth in Our Time* (London, 1975), p. 276.
138. Mann, *Joseph*, p. 124.
139. Landscheit, *Cosmic*, p. 26–7.
140. Auel, *The Clan of the Cave Bear, The River of Horses*, et al.
141. Eliade, *The Forge and the Crucible* (London, 1978), p. 39.
142. Wilber, *Atman*, p. 7–8.
143. Jung, *Symbols of Transformation* (London, 1952), p. 151.
144. Wilber, *Atman*, p. 8–11.
145. Graves, *The White Goddess* (London, 1961), p. 128–30.
146. Wilber, *Atman*, p. 12–21.
147. Beard, *An Outline of Piaget's Developmental Psychology* (London, 1969), p. 17.
148. See Mann and others, *The Phenomenon Book of Calendars* 1979–1980 (New York, 1979).
149. Wilber, *Atman*, p. 22–29 and Beard, *Piaget*, p. 17.
150. Calder, *Timescale* (London, 1984), p. 107.
151. Wilber, *Eye to Eye* (New York, 1983), p. 132 and Beard, *Piaget*, p. 57.
152. Plutarch, *Moralia*, p. 38.
153. See the works of Schwaller de Lubicz and West.
154. Davidson and Aldersmith, *The Great Pyramid* (London, 1925).
155. Wilber, *Atman*, p. 30–35 and Beard, *Piaget*, 45.
156. Ibid, p. 35–7 and Beard, Piaget, p. 98.
157. Ibid, p. 4–5.
158. Ibid, p. 45.
159. Cowen, *Rose Windows* (London, 1979).
160. Wilber, *Atman*, p. 56–7.
161. Ibid, p. 59–62.
162. Ibid, p. 66-7.
163. Eliade, *Eternal Return*, p. 148–56.
164. Wilber, *Atman*, p. 67–9.
165. Ibid, p. 71–3.
166. Matthew XIX, 28–30, RSV.
167. John I, 10, RSV.
168. Jung, 'Psychological Commentary', Evans-Wentz, *The Tibetan Book of the Dead* (London, 1960), p. xxxix.

Chapter Ten – The Universal Time Scale

169. Sagan, *The Dragons of Eden* (New York, 1977), p. 16.
170. Jung, *The Structure and Dynamics of the Psyche,*
 CW 8 (London, 1960), p. 40.
171. *International Herald Tribune*, 27 December 1984 and *Time Magazine*, 6 May 1985.
172. Zukav, *Dancing*, p. 94.
173. See Sheldrake, *New Science*.
174. Collin, *Celestial Influence*, p. 17.
175. Schopenhauer, op. cit., p. 30.
176. Young, *The Reflexive Universe* (San Fransisco, 1976). p. 262.
177. Zukav, *Dancing*, p. 94.
178. Charon, *The Unknown Spirit* (London, 1983), p. 50.
179. Ibid, p. 54.
180. Ibid, p. 64.
181. *Scientific American*, April 1980, p. 107.
182. Prigogine and Stengers, *Order Out of Chaos*, p. 17.
183. Ferguson, *Brain/Mind Bulletin*, Vol. 8, No. 12/13, Jul/Aug 1983.

Chapter Eleven – Reincarnation

184. *Samannaphala Sutra*, trans. T W Rhys-Davids.
185. Wilber, *Atman*, p. ix–x.
186. Ibid, p. 104.
187. Wachsmuth, *Reincarnation*, p. 40.
188. Tansley, Subtle Body, p. 80.
189. See Erika Cheetham, *Prophecies of Nostradamus*, p. 38, and Mann, *Millennium Prophecies*.
190. Ebertin, *Combination of Stellar Influences*, p. 206.
191. Joshi, 'Avidya: A Psychological Interpretation', *Chakra*, Vol. 4, p. 170.

Chapter Twelve – The Divine Life

192. Schopenhauer, op. cit.
193. Collin, *Eternal Life*, p. 121.
194. Young, Arthur M., *The Reflexive Universe*.
195. McKenna, *The Invisible Landscape*.
196. Wilber, *Up From Eden*.
197. Arguelles, *Earth Ascending*.
198. Leary, *Exo-Psychology*.
199. Wilber, ed., *The Holograph Paradigm*.
200. Feuerstein and Mitter, *Yoga and Beyond*.
201. Jung, *Flying Saucers*.
202. Tansley, *Omens of Awareness*, p. 24.
203. van Daniken, *Chariots of the Gods*.
204. Noorbergen, *Secrets of the Lost Races*.
205. Crick, *Life Itself: Its Origin and Nature*.
206. Jung, *Mysterium Coniunctionis*.
207. *Nag Hammadi Gospels*, p. 52.
208. Plato, *Euthydemus*.

Bibliography

Arquelles, Jose, *Earth Ascending: An Illustrated Treatise on the Law Governing Whole Systems* (Boulder, Shambhala, 1984)

Bateson, Gregory, *Mind and Nature* (London, Wildwood House, 1979)

Beard, Ruth M., *An Outline of Piaget's Developmental Psychology* (London, RKP, 1969)

Bellamy, H S, *The Atlantis Myth* (London, Faber and Faber, 1948)

Bennett, J G, *The Dramatic Universe, Volume Four: History* (London, Hodder and Stoughton, 1966)

Bergier, Jacques, *Mysteries of the Earth* (London, Sidgwick and Jackson, 1974)

Bergson, Henri, *Creative Evolution*, trans. Arthur Mitchell (London, Macmillan, 1913)

Berlitz, Charles, *Without a Trace: More Evidence from the Bermuda Triangle* (London, Souvenir, 1977)

Blacker, Carmen and Loewe, Michael, eds., *Ancient Cosmologies* (London, Allen & Unwin, 1975)

Blavatsky, Madame Helena, *The Secret Doctrine* (Los Angeles, Theosophical, 1947)

Bohm, David, *Wholeness and the Implicate Order* (London, RKP, 1980)

Brennan, J P, *An Occult History of the World* (London, Futura, 1976)

Calder, Nigel, *The Key to the Universe* (London, BBC, 1977)
Timescale: An Atlas of the Fourth Dimension (London, Chatto & Windus/The Hogarth Press, 1984)

Campbell, Joseph, ed., Papers from the Eranos Yearbooks: *Man and Time* (Princeton, Bollingen, 1957)

Capra, Fritjof, *The Tao of Physics* (London, Wildwood House, 1975)

Charon, Jean, *The Unknown Spirit* (London, Coventure, 1984)

Cheetham, Erika, *The Prophecies of Nostradamus* (London, Spearman, 1973)

Cles-Reden, Sibylle von, *The Realm of the Great Goddess* (London, Thames & Hudson, 1961)

Collin, Rodney, *The Theory of Celestial Influence* (London, Robinson and Watkins, 1954).
The Theory of Eternal Life (London, Robinson and Watkins, 1950)

Cornell, Dr. H. L., *Encyclopedia of Medical Astrology* (Revised Edition, New York, Llewellyn Publications and Samuel Weiser, 1972)

Cowen, Painton, *Rose Windows* (London, Thames and Hudson, 1979)

Darwin, Charles, *The Descent of Man* (London, John Murray, 1901)
The Origin of Species (London, John Murray, 1892)

Davidson and Aldersmith, *The Great Pyramid* (London, Williams and Norgate, 1925)

Davison, Ron, *Astrology*, New York (Arco Publishing Company, 1963)

Dethlefson, Thorwald, *The Challenge of Fate* (London, Coventure, 1984)

Divine, David, *The Opening of the World* (London, Collins, 1973)

Donnelly, Ignatius, *Atlantis: The Antediluvian World* (London, Sidgwick and Jackson, 1950)
Ragnarok: The Age of Fire and Gravel (New York, Steiner, 1971)

Dossey, Dr. Larry, *Space, Time & Medicine* (Boulder, Shambala, 1982)

Dunne, J W, *An Experiment With Time* (London, A & C Black, 1927)
The Serial Universe (London, Faber and Faber, 1934)

Du Noüy, Pierre Lecomte, *Biological Time* (London, Methuen, 1936)

Ebertin, Reinhold, *The Combination of Stellar Influences* (Tempe, The American Federation of Astrologers, 1981)

Eisler, Robert, *The Royal Art of Astrology* (London, Herbert Joseph, 1946)

Eliade, Mircea, *The Forge and the Crucible* (Chicago, University of Chicago, 1978)
Images and Symbols (London, Harvill Press, 1961)

Myth and Reality (London, Allen & Unwin, 1964)

Myths, Dreams and Reality (London, Collins, 1968)

The Myth of the Eternal Return (Princeton, Bollingen, 1954)

Shamanism: Archaic Techniques of Ecstacy (Princeton, Bollingen, 1946)

Erlewine, Michael, *Manual of Computer Programming for Astrologers* (Big Rapids, Matrix, 1980)

Evans-Wentz, W Y, *The Tibetan Book of the Dead* (London, Oxford, 1960)

Flanagan, Geraldine Lux, *The First Nine Months* (London, Heinemann, 1970)

Fraser, J T, ed., *The Voices of Time* (London, Allen Lane/Penguin, 1968)

Frazer, Sir James, *The Golden Bough: A Study in Magic and Religion* (London, Macmillan, 1950)

Freud, Sigmund, *The Letters of Sigmund Freud 1873-1939*, ed. Ernest Freud, trans. Tania and James Stein (London, The Hogarth Press, 1961)

Galanopoulos, A C and Bacon, Edward, *Atlantis* (London, Nelson, 1969)

The Epic of Gilgamesh, trans. N K Saunders (London, Penguin, 1960)

Graves, Robert, *The Greek Myths*, Volumes I and II (London, Penguin, 1955)

The White Goddess (London, Faber and Faber, 1961)

Hall, Manley Palmer, *Secret Teachings of All Ages* (Los Angeles, Philosophical Research Society, 1968 (1928))

Hawkes, Jacquetta, *The Atlas of Early Man* (London, Macmillan, 1976)

Hawking, Stephen, *The Universe in a Nutshell* (New York, Bantam, 2001)

Head, Joseph and Cranston, S L, *Reincarnation: An East-West Anthology* (New York, Julian Press, 1961)

Reincarnation: The Phoenix Fire Mystery (New York, Julian Press/Crown, 1977)

Hick, John, *Death and Eternal Life* (London, Collins, 1976)

Homer, *The Iliad*, trans. E V Rieu (London, Penguin, 1950)

The Odyssey, trans. E V Rieu (London, Penguin, 1946)

Hone, Margaret, *The Modern Textbook of Astrology* (London, L. N. Fowler, 1951)

Huber, Bruno & Louise, *Man and His World* (New York, Weiser, 1978)

Huntley, H E, *The Divine Proportion* (New York, Dover, 1970)

Jacob, Francois, *The Logic of Living Systems*, trans. Betty Spillman (London, Allen Lane, 1974)

Jonas, David and Klein, Doris, *Man-child: A Study of the Infantilization of Man* (New York, McGraw-Hill, 1970)

Jung, Emma and von Franz, Marie Louise, *The Grail Legend*, trans. Andrea Dykes (New York, Jung Foundation, 1970)

Jung, Carl G, *Aion, CW 9*, (London, RKP, 1951) (Collected Works translated by R F C Hull)

Alchemical Studies, CW 13 (London, RKP, 1966)

The Archetypes and the Collective Unconscious, CW 9, Part I (London, RKP, 1959)

C G Jung Letters, Volume One 1906-1950 (London, RKP, 1973)

C G Jung Letters, Volume Two 1906-1961 (London, RKP, 1977)

C G Jung: Psychological Reflections, ed. Jolande Jacobi (London, RKP, 1953)

Memories, Dreams and Reflections (New York, Random House, 1961)

Mysterium Coniunctionis, CW 14 (London, RKP, 1963)

Psychological Types (London, RKP, 1923)

Psychology and Alchemy, CW 12 (London, RKP, 1966)

Symbols of Transformation, CW 5 (London, RKP, 1952)

and Pauli, Wolfgang, *The Interpretation of Nature and the Psyche* (London, RKP, 1955)

Kahn, Herman, Wiener, Anthony and The Hudson Institute, *The Year 2000* (London, Macmillan, 1967)

Kerenyi, Carl, *Dionysios: Archetypal Image of Indestructible Life*, trans. Ralph Manheim (London, RKP, 1976)

The Gods of the Greeks, trans. Ralph Manheim (London, Thames and Hudson, 1951)

Prometheus: Archetypal Image of Human Existence, trans. Ralph Manheim (London, Thames and Hudson, 1962)

The Religion of the Greeks and Romans, trans. Christopher Holme (London, Thames and Hudson, 1962)

Kollerstrom, Oscar, *The Actual and the Real: A Way of Thinking About Eternity* (London, Turnstone, 1974)

Laing, R. D., *The Facts of Life* (London, Allen Lane, 1976)

Landscheit, Dr Theodore, *Cosmic Cybernetics*, trans. Linda Kratsch (Aalen, Ebertin-Verlag, 1973)

Leakey, Richard and Lewin, Roger, *Origins* (London, Macdonald and lanes, 1977)

Leary, Timothy, *Exo-Psychology* (Los Angles, Starseed, 1977)

Levi, Eliphas, *The Key of the Mysteries* (London, Rider, 1959)

Lockyer, Sir Norman, *The Dawn of Astronomy* (Cambridge, MIT Press, 1964)

Luce, Cay Gaer, *Body Time* (London, Temple Smith, 1972)

Mann, A T, *A New Vision of Astrology* (New York, Simon & Schuster, 2002)

  Astrology and the Art of Healing (London, Unwin Hyman, 1988)

  Elements of Reincarnation (Shaftesbury, Element, 1995)

  Life Time Astrology (London, Allen & Unwin, 1984)

  Millennium Prophecies (Shaftesbury, Element, 1992)
  The Divine Plot (London, Allen & Unwin, 1986)

  The Round Art: The Astrology of Time and Space (London, Dragon's World, 1979)

  ed., *The Future of Astrology* (London, Allen & Unwin, 1988)

  with Sesti, Giuseppe, Cowen, Painton and Flanagan, Mary, *The Phenomenon Book of Calendars 1979-1980* (New York, Simon & Schuster, 1979)

Mann, Thomas, *Joseph and His Brothers*, trans, H T Lowe-Porter (London, Secker & Warburg, 1950)

  Lotte in Weimar, trans. H T Lowe-Porter (London, Secker & Warburg, 1964)

Marcus, Steven, *Freud and the Culture of Psychoanalysis* (London, Allen & Unwin, 1983)

Marwick, Arthur, *The Nature of History* (London, Macmillan, 1970)

Mayo, Jeff, *Astrology* (London, Hodder and Stoughton, 1964)

McKenna, Dennis and Terence, *The Invisible Landscape: Mind, Hallucinogens and the I Ching* (New York, Seaburg Press, 1975)

McNeill, William, J, *Plagues and People* (Oxford, Basil Blackford, 1977)

Muck, Otto, *The Secret of Atlantis*, trans. Fred Bradley (London, Collins, 1978)

Neumann, Erich, *The Great Mother*, trans. R F C Hull, (London, RKP, 1955)

  The Origin and History of Consciousness, trans. R F C Hull (Princeton, Bollingen, 1954)

Nicoll, Maurice, *Living Time* (London, Stuart and Watkins, 1952)

Noorbergen, Rene, *Secrets of the Lost Races* (London, New English Library, 1978)

O'Flahery, W O, *Hindu Myths* (London, Penguin, 1975)

Pagels, Elaine, *The Gnotic Gospels* (London, Penguin, 1979)

Pauwels, Louis and Bergier, Jacques, *The Dawn of Magic*, trans. Rollo Myers (London, Pantheon, 1964)

Pfeiffer, John E, *The Emergence of Man* (London, Nelson, 1970)

Piazzi-Smyth, C, *The Great Pyramid* (London, Isbister, 1880)

Piel, Gerard, *The Acceleration of History* (New York, Knopf, 1972)

Plato, *Timaeus and Critias*, trans. Desmond Lee (London, Penguin, 1965)

Plotinus, *The Enneads*, trans. Stephen MacKenna (London, Faber and Faber, 1962)

Prigogine, Ilya and Stengers, Isabelle, *Order Out of Chaos* (Boulder, Shambhala, 1984)

Ptolemy, *Tetrabiblos*, trans. and ed. by F E Robbins (Cambridge, Harvard University Press, 1971)

Renfrew, Colin, *Before Civilisation: The Radiocarbon Revolution and Prehistoric Europe* (London, Jonathan Cape, 1973)

Robinson, James M, ed., *The Nag Hammadi Library in English* (Leiden, Brill, 1977)

Robinson, Lytle, *Edgar Cayce's Story of the Origin and Destruction of Man* (London, Spearman, 1972)

    Is It True What They Say About Edgar Cayce? (London, Spearman, 1979)

Russell, Bertrand, *History of Western Philosophy* (London, Allen & Unwin, 1946)

Sagan, Carl, *The Dragons of Eden* (New York, Random House, 1977)

Santillana, Giorgio de and Dechand, Herta von, *Hamlet's Mill: An Essay Investigating the Origins of Human Knowledge and its Transmission Through Myth* (Boston, Codine, 1969)

Schopenhauer, Arthur, *The Living Thoughts of Schopenhauer*, trans. R B Haldane and J Kemp, presented by Thomas Mann (London, Cassell, 1939)

Schwaller de Lubicz, R A, *Sacred Science*, trans. Andre and Goldian Vanden Broeck (New York, Inner Traditions, 1982)

    Symbol and Symbolic: Egypt, Science and the Evolution of Consciousness, trans. Robert and Deborah Lawlor (Brookline, Autumn Press, 1978)

    The Temple in Man: The Secrets of Ancient Egypt, trans. Robert and Deborah Lawlor (Brookline, Autumn Press, 1977)

Scott-Elliot, W, *The Story of Atlantis* (London, 1909)

Sheldrake, Rupert, *A New Science of Life* (London, Blond and Briggs, 1981)

Scholem, Gershom, *Major Trends in Jewish Mysticism* (London, Thames and Hudson, 1955)

Spence, Lewis, *Will Europe Follow Atlantis?* (London, Rider, 1942)

Spengler, Oswald, *The Decline of the West* (London, George Allen & Unwin, 1961)

Talbot, Michael, *Mysticism and the New Physics* (London, RKP, 1981)

Tansley, David, *Omens of Awareness* (London, Spearman, 1977)

    Subtle Body (London, Spearman, 1977)

Tarling, D H and M P, *Continental Drift* (London, Bell and Sons, 1971)

Taylor, Gordon Rattray, *The Doomsday Book* (London, Thames and Hudson, 1970)

Temple, Robert K C, *The Sirius Mystery* (London, Sidgwick and Jackson, 1976)

Thorndike, Lynn, *The History of Magic and Experimental Science*, Nine Volumes (New York, Columbia University, 1941)

Toynbee, Arnold, *A Study of History*, abridged by D C Somervell (London, Oxford University, 1946)

    Change and Habit (London, Oxford University, 1966;)

    Mankind and Mother Earth (London, Oxford University, 1976)

Trinkus, Erik and Howells, William, *The Neanderthals* (New York, Scientific American, December 1979)

Turville-Petre, E O G, *Myth and Religion of the North* (London, Weidenfeld and Nicholson, 1964)

van Daniken, Erik, *Chariots of the Gods* (London, Souvenir Press, 1969)

Velikovsky, Immanuel, *Earth in Upheaval* (London, Gollanz, 1956)

    Worlds in Collision (London, Gollanz, 1950)

    and the Editors of Pensee, *Velikovsky Reconsidered* (London, Sidgwick and Jackson, 1976)

Watson, James, *The Double Helix* (London, Weidenfeld and Nicolson, 1968)

Yates, Frances, *The Art of Memory* (London, Routledge & Kegan Paul, 1966)

Zukav, Gary, *The Dancing Wu Li Masters* (London, Rider and Hutchinson, 1979)

A T Mann

A T Mann is an architect and astrologer, and the author of 14 books on astrology, reincarnation, healing, sacred architecture, sacred sexuality, the tarot and other subjects. He is a graduate of the Cornell University College of Architecture and lived in England and Denmark for 25 years. He now lives in Hudson, NY. His website is www.atmann.net and his e-mail is atmann@atmann.net.

Photograph by Anne Fuller

INDEX